Aspects of Anglo-Scandinavi. ⌐ork

By R.A. Hall, D.W. Rollason, M. Blackburn, D.N. Parsons,
G. Fellows-Jensen, A.R. Hall, H.K. Kenward, T.P. O'Connor,
D. Tweddle, A.J. Mainman and N.S.H. Rogers

Published for York Archaeological Trust by the
Council for British Archaeology

2004

Contents

List of Figures

Figures 71–128 are included in the text and Fig.129 is presented on an unbound sheet in a pocket on the inside back cover. This figure is distinguished in the text by **s** in bold type.

List of Tables

Foreword

In 1976, at the very beginning of 'The Viking Dig', a five-year campaign of excavation at 16–22 Coppergate, York, a conference entitled 'Viking York and the North' was organised by York Archaeological Trust and the University of Leeds. Recent discoveries and new interpretations were described by a series of expert commentators, and subsequently these papers were published by the Council for British Archaeology as their *Research Report* **27**, entitled *Viking Age York and the North* (Hall (ed) 1978). Such was the interest that the book was soon reprinted, but the range and scale of new information coming from the four Viking-Age tenement plots revealed by 'The Viking Dig' meant that the chapters relating to archaeological discoveries in York rapidly became outdated.

Since excavation at 'The Viking Dig' came to an end in 1981 there has been a major research programme to investigate the full significance of what had been revealed, undertaken with considerable financial assistance from English Heritage. York Archaeological Trust has processed, ordered, evaluated and analysed the huge quantity of data recovered there, including over 36,000 archaeological contexts ('layers' and 'features'), over 40,000 individually recorded objects, an estimated five tons of animal bones, 250,000 sherds of pottery and the residues from sieving over eight tons of soil. The results of these studies have been published in sixteen thematic and chronologically based reports in *The Archaeology of York* series. Now, with that research programme virtually complete, this volume provides an opportunity to assess these discoveries within the context of a wider view of Jorvík.

As in 1976, a panel of experts has been asked to contribute overviews of their specialist fields. In terms of topics, although not of contributors, there is a noticeable degree of overlap between this book and its predecessor. While the hinterlands of York and the city's more distant contacts are not represented here by a discussion of any specific site, as they were previously, issues of external relationships pervade many of the chapters. Other themes common to both are dealt with more extensively here — a study of sculpture, for example, is replaced by one which em-

braces many media. What had been a single short chapter on environmental evidence has now swollen to two substantial contributions, mirroring both the increasing amounts of evidence and the recognition of their value in reconstructing past societies. Innovations include a detailed discussion of the origins of York's street names, and a consideration of the inscriptions found in the city.

In all of this there has been no editorial compulsion to impose upon authors a single uniform spelling for personal names which were written in a variety of ways by contemporaries or near contemporaries, depending upon the language of transmission and a series of other factors.

The chapters here demonstrate how far the study of Anglo-Scandinavian York has progressed in the last quarter century. Many of the contributions, overtly or by implication, also indicate the extent to which the results from 16–22 Coppergate dominate current knowledge and interpretations of life in Jorvík. Yet great swathes of the Viking-Age city remain unexplored — a situation which needs to change if comprehension is to be expanded. Presently, it must be remembered, both local and national planning policies are geared principally to the preservation of archaeological deposits in situ, notwithstanding that their state of preservation may be deteriorating (p.424). Indeed, it is salutary to speculate that 'The Viking Dig' might never have been undertaken had the present policy framework been in place in the mid 1970s. Under this regime the last decade or more has seen few opportunities for anything but small-scale excavations in York, and of all these excavations many did not penetrate to the depth at which Viking-Age remains might be found. In these circumstances, archaeologists face many challenges in responding to the research issues flagged up in the pages that follow. Not least among them is the need to recognise and seize opportunities, so that the obviously formative influence of this Anglo-Scandinavian era upon the city of York can be explored and explained more fully to the advantage of residents, visitors and scholars alike.

866 – 'captured' by Danish 'great army'

60 yrs – 'Viking kings' resident in Jorvik.

927
12 yrs   } King of Wessex 'in control directly/indirectly
939

15 yrs   political turmoil as various factions vied for
         supremacy; Wessex, Hiberno-Norse (Dublin)
952/954. and exiled Eric Bloodaxe

Volume 8 Fascicule 4

Aspects of Anglo-Scandinavian York

By R.A. Hall, D.W. Rollason, M. Blackburn, D.N. Parsons, G. Fellows-Jensen, A.R. Hall, H.K. Kenward, T.P. O'Connor, D. Tweddle, A.J. Mainman and N.S.H. Rogers

Key words: Anglo-Scandinavian, animal bones, archaeology, art, coinage, crafts, economy, environment, historiography, history, inscriptions, street-names, topography, Viking, York

A Historiographical Introduction to Anglo-Scandinavian York

By R.A. Hall

Introduction

In the two centuries before the Norman conquest York was a prize coveted and contested by external forces. A place of first rank ecclesiastical and economic importance for the Anglo-Saxon kingdom of Northumbria, it was captured by the Viking 'great army' in 866, and Vikings or their descendants were recognised as kings of York and its region more often than not in the six decades thereafter. From 927 to 939 the king of Wessex controlled York directly or indirectly, and then for fifteen years there was political turmoil as Wessex, Hiberno-Viking rulers from Dublin and the exiled Norwegian prince Erik Bloodaxe vied for supremacy. Only with the expulsion of Erik Bloodaxe in 952 x 954 was Wessex left in longterm, albeit sometimes contested, control of York and thus of a united kingdom of England. An influential Scandinavianised element remained among York's population until the Norman conquest and beyond, identifiable through their own names and through the names that they gave to the city's streets. It was, presumably, the presence of these potential supporters which ensured that York survived unscathed through the invasions of the Danish King Svein Forkbeard and his son Cnut in the late 10th–early 11th century.

Modern commentators have reflected this historical pedigree in the varied terms they have coined to designate this era in York's evolution. Today it is known as the city's Anglo-Scandinavian or Viking-Age period. This introduction charts the principal stages of investigation that have contributed to current knowledge of what contemporaries called *Jorvík*. Subsequent chapters examine in detail particular aspects of the evidence for what York was and how it functioned about one thousand years ago.

Viking-Age York after the Viking Age

Contemporary records of the Viking invasion, conquest and settlement of England, and of subsequent events in York and Northumbria, were copied or abridged from the *Anglo-Saxon Chronicle* and other documents into the works of Anglo-Norman writers, whence they were transmitted and transmuted, ultimately to form the basis of local York historiography and legend. So, from the 17th century onwards, as the penchant for local and regional history and topography developed, York writers regularly alluded to the 'Danish' epoch of the city's history (Hall 2000, 311–14).

Until the 19th century, documents of one sort or another were virtually the sole source of information about this era. The first record of uncovering any buried remains of Viking-Age York refers to 1696, when traces of a timber building and an associated hoard of coins of William the Conqueror were found in High Ousegate. The coins suggest that the building remains were from the end of the Viking Age or the early years of Norman rule. This discovery of apparently closely dated structures was not to be equalled for another 200 years but, at the time, it was not recognised just how remarkable it was to retrieve such ancient and well-preserved timbers. Indeed, there are few references to the finding of Viking-Age objects in York during the 18th and early 19th century, despite many opportunities to uncover buried remains. As new, Georgian-style houses were erected along many of the city's main streets, cellars were dug out in what was often the first major disturbance of archaeological stratification. Yet although easily recognised stone-built Roman structures and common Roman objects such as coins or pots were uncovered, identified, illustrated and published, the less eye-catching debris of later centuries was apparently shovelled away unnoticed. Nevertheless, in 1736 Francis Drake's massive historical tome *Eboracum*, its very name exhibiting the classical bias of the age, secured a niche in Viking-Age York's historiography by being the first publication to include drawings of Viking-Age objects from York (Drake 1736). The items in question were coins minted at York during the Anglo-Scandinavian period; their prominence in Drake's work reflects the facts that they were clearly recognisable and identifiable through their inscriptions, and had an obvious intrinsic value (Fig.71).

In the mid- and late-19th century, collectors' interests widened to include everyday items of non-precious materials. As areas such as that within the medieval wall south-west of the River Ouse were infilled with buildings, and as the railway, with its substantial earth-moving consequences, came to York, a lively and competitive market arose for the artefacts discovered by labourers (Moulden in *AY* 8/1, 14–23). Wealthy private collectors from the bourgeoisie vied, through their agents, with the newly created Museum of the Yorkshire Philosophical Society (now The Yorkshire Museum), which had been established in York in 1823. While some objects must have passed unrecorded into private ownership, a considerable number were amassed by a handful of serious collectors. Some of these collections are now housed outside York, such as that of Thomas Bateman which is in Sheffield City Museum, but many of them eventually reached the Yorkshire Philosophical Society's Museum (Fig.72).

There the objects were ably catalogued, firstly by Rev. Charles Wellbeloved (1769–1858), Honorary Curator of Antiquities and Numismatics, and then by his successor, James Raine (1830–96).

It was as a result of these 19th-century activities that the importance of the Museum's Viking-Age collection was gradually established. The earliest *Handbook* to the collection, written by Wellbeloved in mid century, made no mention of Viking objects from York, but the 6th edition of 1875 included *'A fine series of Saxon or Danish combs and buckles, all found in York, several with the interlacing ornament on them, and one with the beginning of a Runic inscription'*. Despite this, in the 7th edition of 1881 Raine lamented that, although there were comparatively few remains of Anglo-Saxon York, *'there is still greater paucity of memorials of the Danish occupation of York'*. It was in the 8th edition of the *Handbook* in 1891 that the fruits of collecting Viking-Age objects really began to show. For the first time there was a considerable array of 'Scandinavian curiosities', many found during the building of the Quaker Meeting House in Clifford Street in 1884. Doubts about their origin and pedigree had been banished when they were identified as Scandinavian by the noted Danish expert Dr Sophus Müller (1846–1934). Among them was a wide range of everyday objects made from a great variety of raw materials, including amber, bone, pottery and wood.

The early years of the 20th century brought more serious and dedicated attempts to study Viking-Age York systematically, and among the means employed was the recovery of data through archaeological investigations. The very first of these investigations, carried out by the York architect George Benson (1856–1935), were what today would be termed 'watching briefs' — simply visiting building sites to record what the labourers had uncovered during their work. Over a period of five months in the winter of 1902–3 Benson salvaged what information he could from a large site in High Ousegate, close to where the Norman coin hoard had been found over two centuries before. Being an architect, he was accustomed to drawing plans of buildings, and so he made a drawn record of what he interpreted as the foundation beams of a massive structure, 27·1m (89ft) long, running between High Ousegate and Coppergate at a depth of about 2·2m (7ft) below present street level. Below the beams, in turn, were large rectangular plank-lined cuts arranged one behind another across

Saxon *and* Danish *Coins struck at* York.

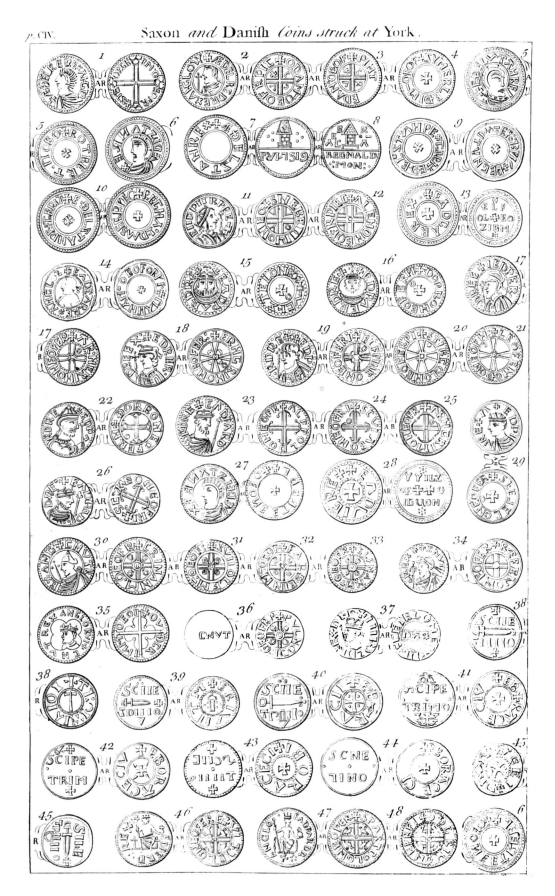

Fig.71 *'Saxon and Danish coins struck at York' as published in Drake's* Eboracum, *1736*

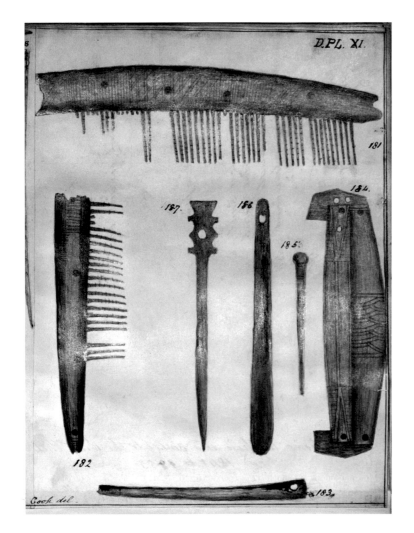

Fig.72 *Detail of combs, a comb case and pins from a page of James Cook's illustrated manuscript catalogue of artefacts, reproduced by courtesy of The Yorkshire Museum*

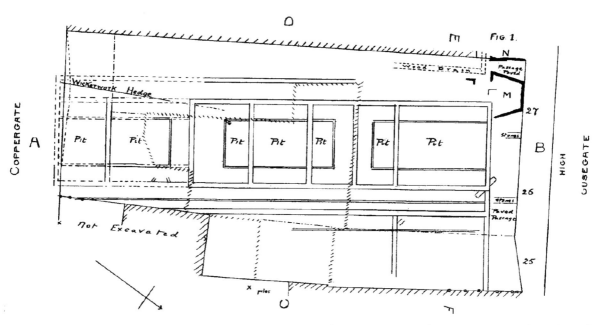

Fig.73 *Benson 's plan of the features recorded during the digging out of cellars at 25–7 High Ousegate in 1902 (reproduced from Benson 1902, pl.III)*

the site. Benson thought they were tan-pits, and dated them to the 'Danish' period on the basis of accompanying objects (Benson 1902). This watching brief, and another one nearby (Benson 1906), indicated that this part of York has benign soil conditions which preserve a wide range of objects and materials in nearly pristine condition (Fig.73). Although some local commentators remained oblivious to the new perspectives which these discoveries presented (Platnauer 1906), the York doctor George Auden drew them to the attention of a national and international audience in several short illustrated reports to *The Saga Book of the Viking Club* (Auden 1907; 1908; 1910).

Unfortunately, no immediate successor chose to follow up Benson's discoveries and further elucidate Viking-Age York. Although carefully planned and executed archaeological excavations took place in York in the 1920s, their instigators single-mindedly pursued remains of the Roman era. Other lines of scholarly enquiry were not so neglected, however, and the first half of the 20th century saw the publication of a diverse range of studies which laid the foundations for lines of enquiry that remain relevant today — as the chapters in this book demonstrate. W.G. Collingwood's catalogue of pre-Norman sculpture from the city (Collingwood 1908), part of his overview of Yorkshire's monuments (Fig.74), put this material into a typological, stylistic and iconographic framework that has inspired a succession of subsequent expert analyses, including the up-to-date *Corpus* compiled by Lang (see p.303). The significance of York's street- and place-names, many of which incorporate Old Norse elements, was first investigated in academic fashion by Lindkvist (1926) and then by Smith (1937); here, Gillian Fellows-Jensen builds upon and refines their work, placing it in the broader national and international context (pp.357–71). Historical overviews drawing variously upon documentary, numismatic and place-name evidence were presented by many scholars, notably F.M. Stenton, whose survey of 11th-century York (Stenton 1927) was a preliminary to his overview in *Anglo-Saxon England*, first published in 1947. A similarly wide-ranging approach is taken by David Rollason in his contribution to this book (pp.305–24).

York escaped World War II almost unscathed in comparison to other blitzed historic cities, and so there were not the opportunities for archaeology among the ruins that occurred, for example, in post-war London. There were, however, requirements for new buildings in the late 1940s, and one of these schemes, for a new telephone exchange by the banks of the River Foss in Hungate, prompted the first archaeological excavation in York that uncovered and recorded substantial Viking-Age features. It brought to light what the excavator, Katherine Richardson (d.1993), interpreted as a Viking-Age river embankment, together with an array of associated objects. Their publication (Richardson 1959) was a timely reminder of the unusual information which lay buried in York;

Fig.74 *Illustration of an Anglo-Scandinavian cross-slab formerly in the porch of St Mary Bishophill Senior (reproduced from Collingwood 1908)*

the report was also notable for ground-breaking scientific appendices on 'Soil Conditions Conducive to the Preservation of the Ironwork' by Leo Biek (1922–2002), and on 'Plant Materials' by H. Godwin and K. Bachem, which provided species identifications for samples of fruits, seeds and wooden stakes. The artefactual wealth of pre-conquest York was re-emphasised that same year when Dudley Waterman (1918–79), who had briefly (1947–8) been Archaeologist at the Yorkshire Philosophical Society's Museum, published his masterly catalogue entitled *Late Saxon, Viking and Early Medieval Finds from York* (Waterman 1959). At a time when assemblages of this date were largely unknown in England, this demonstrated beyond question the significance of York as a source of archaeological information about the Viking Age. He identified, recorded and illustrated a large and varied collection of Viking-Age objects, and also compiled distribution plots showing the incidence of this material. Both these lines of enquiry have subsequently been enlarged upon by a succession of scholars. Here, Mainman and Rogers synthesise the series of artefact studies, both thematic and materials-based, that have emanated from more recent excavations; they provide an overview of craft activity around the city as well as offering an integrated view of the microcosm of manufacturing uncovered in excavations at 16–22 Coppergate (pp.459–87).

The 1950s and 1960s brought first a trickle and then a stream of redevelopment proposals. Even as late as 1966 some very important sites including, ironically, the Viking Hotel (now the Moathouse), a site of enormous potential) on the riverside in North Street, were developed without any form of archaeological record but with the inevitable destruction of buried remains. Increasingly, however, some small-scale archaeological observation or excavation was negotiated with site owners, and sometimes paid for by the national government, through the Ancient Monument Inspectorate of the Ministry of Public Buildings and Works, forerunner of English Heritage. Peter Wenham (1911–90), from the Department of History, St John's College, York, directed groups of students and local volunteers at a number of research excavations, particularly upon and within the defences of the former Roman legionary fortress (Wenham 1961; 1962; 1968; 1972). Among his discoveries was a small group of burials with accompanying grave goods adjacent to the church of St Mary Bishophill Junior; these are firmly dated to the early–mid 10th century and represent most clearly the period of Scandinavian immigration and assimilation (*AY* 8/2). Ian Stead, formerly a pupil at York's Nunthorpe Grammar School, also excavated sites on the Roman fortress defences in 1956 and 1957 (Stead 1958; 1968) (Fig.75). In 1964 Herman Ramm (1922–91), from the York office of the Royal Commission on Historical Monuments for England, excavated within the demolished church of St Mary Bishophill Senior, which had retained structural traces of a late Viking-Age building phase (Ramm 1976).

Meanwhile, works of synthesis were starting to appear. After Dickens (1961, 9–17, 332–6) discussed first the documentary evidence and the 'Anglo-Scandinavian Antiquities' in the Victoria County History's volume on York, Rosemary Cramp brought the published material into a wider historical and cultural context in her essay *Anglian and Viking York* (Cramp 1967). Jeffrey Radley (1935–70), seizing the opportunities for observation and recording that a quickening pace of redevelopment was presenting, combined new investigations with tracking down old reports of previous discoveries. On these twin foundations he wrote an influential and innovative summary of Anglo-Scandinavian York's economy, mainly addressing such questions as the extent of *Jorvík*, the nature of its buildings and defences, and the economic importance of the industrial and commercial area off the northern end of Ouse Bridge. It was published posthumously (Radley 1971).

One other major archaeological project of this era was the investigation below and around York Minster during 1966–73. Its first, small-scale phase was initiated, under the archaeological direction of Brian Hope-Taylor (1923–2001), as a subterfuge to allow an appraisal of the structural condition of the cathedral's foundations. As the necessary large-scale remedial civil engineering progressed, archaeological investigations continued under the auspices of the York Minster Excavation Committee, chaired by Sir Mortimer Wheeler, and with Hope-Taylor's oversight. In 1967–8 Herman Ramm, working virtually single-handedly, could do little more than observe the contractors' large-scale earth-moving; from July 1968 until 1973 Derek Phillips and his small team were able to accomplish more detailed excavation and recording. These operations showed that the Viking-Age cathedral does not lie below its Norman and medieval successor; instead, parts of a Viking-Age graveyard were recovered (Fig.76; see below).

Fig.75 *Squared upright posts with horizontal planks behind them define parts of two walls of a timber building excavated at King's Square in 1957 (Stead 1968). The foundation trench for the south-west wall cuts through the lighter coloured clay of the Roman fortress rampart; the rear face of the fortress wall lay 1.22m (4 feet) beyond the south-east wall. Photograph by R.A. Hill, looking from north-west to south-east, taken at a later stage of excavation than Plate IV in Stead 1968. Scale unit 1 foot*

Other avenues of research into Anglo-Scandinavian York were also expertly pursued. For example, numismatists, notably Michael Dolley (1925–83), Christopher Blunt (1904–87) and Ian Stewart, have teased out the historical secrets of the prolific York mint, clarifying the sequence of minting and identifying the kings for whom the coins were struck. They thus paved the way for Mark Blackburn's analysis of York's coinage (pp.325–49), in which he demonstrates the important advances made over the last decade or so, advances that significantly assist an understanding of the history, economy and organisation of the York kingdom. A series of introductory essays on the city's topographical development compiled by The Royal Commission on Historical Monuments for England (RCHMY **2**, 7–9; RCHMY **3**, xxxviii–xlii; RCHMY **4**, xxiv–xxxvi) drew together the evidence for the physical evolution of the city; they, together with other important summaries of this evidence (Ramm 1972), are precursors of the study here by Hall (pp.488–97).

The archaeological study of Viking-Age York entered a new era in 1972, thanks to Peter Addyman's vision for how York Archaeological Trust could contribute to unravelling the city's history. An excavation undertaken below Lloyds Bank at 6–8 Pavement was the first to be mounted in York with the specific research objective of elucidating the Anglo-Scandinavian period. It demonstrated the quantity and quality of archaeological deposits of the 9th–11th centuries in this part of York (Fig.77), highlighted yet again the remarkable preservation of organic and inorganic objects in the oxygen-free soils, and showed the great potential for palaeoenvironmental studies (Buckland, Grieg and Kenward 1974; *AY* 14/4; *AY* 8/3). From it sprang a more widespread public appreciation of York's Viking Age, a process that received a further stimulus in *The Viking Kingdom of York* exhibition, held at The Yorkshire Museum to celebrate the eleven hundredth anniversary of the Viking settlement of Yorkshire (Hall 1976). It also inspired 'The Viking Dig' at

Fig.76 *Part of the Viking-Age graveyard at York Minster. © Crown copyright. NMR*

nearby 16–22 Coppergate, where approximately 1000m² were examined during more than five years of continuous excavation in 1976–81 (Fig.78). It was apparent within a few weeks of its commencement that this excavation would yield an entirely new set of perspectives on the Anglo-Scandinavian city, and to set the scene for these advances a conference, *Viking-Age York and the North,* was held in 1976 (Hall 1978a). To showcase some of the exciting discoveries and place them in a wider context, an exhibition was held in Denmark and in The Yorkshire Museum in 1981–2, accompanied by a book *The Vikings in England*

(Roesdahl et al. 1981). Shortly after the excavation finished a popular summary account of its major findings was published under the title *The Viking Dig* (Hall 1984).

Throughout the 1980s York Archaeological Trust continued its research into Anglo-Scandinavian York. Earlier discoveries were re-assessed and the results published (e.g. *Anglo-Scandinavian Settlement South-West of the Ouse* (AY 8/1); 'Structures at 5–7 Coppergate with a Re-assessment of Benson's Observations of 1902' (Hall in AY 8/3, 238–50). There was structural analy-

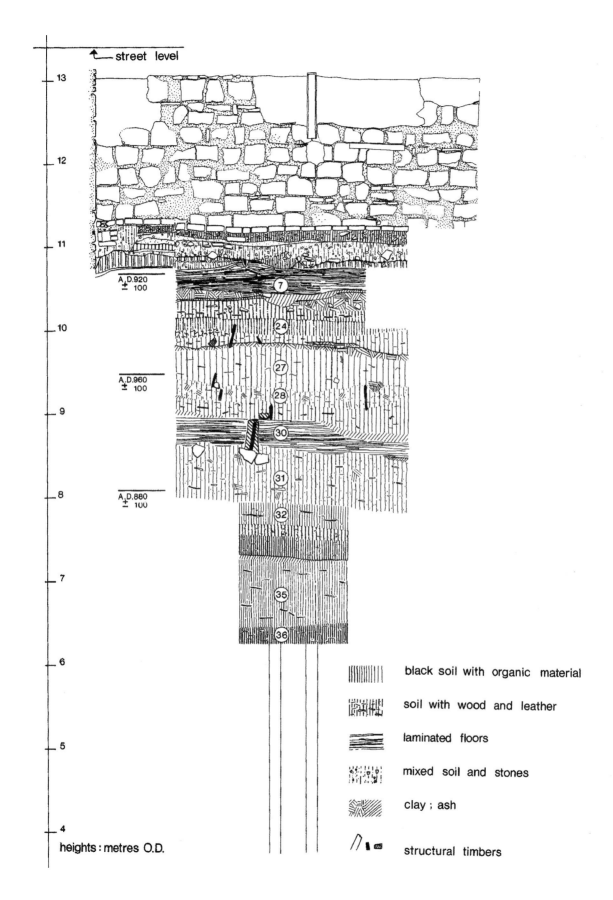

street level

13

12

11

A.D.920 ± 100

7

10

24

27

A.D.960 ± 100

28

30

9

31

A.D.880 ± 100

32

8

7

35

6

36

black soil with organic material

soil with wood and leather

5

laminated floors

mixed soil and stones

clay ; ash

4

heights : metres O.D.

structural timbers

Fig.77 *Section showing the great depth of archaeological deposits below Lloyds Bank, 6–8 Pavement. The bottoms of the bore holes indicate the base of archaeological strata*

301

Fig.78   *General view of the excavations at 16–22 Coppergate, showing Viking-Age levels*

sis and excavation of ecclesiastical sites, and the discussion of sculptured stonework from them (*AY* 8/2). Artefacts from 6–8 Pavement (*AY* 17/3) and other small sites (*AY* 17/4) were published, as was a catalogue and comment on Viking-Age coins from excavations 1972–81 (*AY* 18/1). Rollason's edition and study of the documentary sources for York up to AD 1100 (*AY* 1), an invaluable aid to scholarship, underpins his discussion here (pp.305–24).

Reports on material from the 16–22 Coppergate excavations also began to appear in *The Archaeology of York* in the 1980s, and some of them informed an introductory summary entitled *Viking Age York* (Hall 1994). This series of reports is now virtually complete, with the last volume being prepared for press. They confirm, *inter alia*, that York has some of the best-preserved and most assiduously sampled deposits of the 9th–11th centuries in north-west Europe. This, combined with the methodological advances of the last twenty years, has made a consideration of bio-archaeological data central to any discussion of Anglo-Scandinavian York. Analyses of vertebrate remains from 16–22 Coppergate (*AY* 15/3) and of plant and invertebrate remains from 6–8 Pavement and 16–22 Coppergate (*AY* 14/4; *AY* 14/7) have demonstrated how this material can inform a wide range of issues, including some which were previously obscure or invisible. In their respective contributions to this volume the key proponents in this study, O'Connor (pp.427–45), and Hall and Kenward (pp.372–426), provide an updated commentary on the significance of these remains, emphasising in the process what a considerable, if vulnerable, asset these deposits are to historical enquiry.

Other major contributions to understanding Anglo-Scandinavian York made since the 1980s include the publication of the 1966–73 York Minster excavations (Phillips and Heywood 1995). An important facet of the pre-Norman discoveries there was the notable diversity in rites of interment and commemoration apparent within the cemetery below and beyond the medieval south transept. The precise social context of this cemetery is not clear, particularly as that might be defined in terms of its spatial relationships to the pre-Norman Minster church and to any other surrounding burial grounds. While Norton's (1998) analysis of the documentary evidence for the Minster precinct has suggested a topographical context for the Viking-Age cathedral, questions

related to its burial grounds require further elucidation. Interpreting their significance is also bedevilled by the rarity of comparable assemblages from York. A series of graves associated with a timber-built 11th-century church in Fishergate represents the only other reasonably well-dated analogy (*AY* 12/2), but does not exhibit the same variety of funeral rites. This uniformity is presumably a function of both date and status, but it, in turn, needs to be assessed against other contemporary cemeteries in the city.

Related arenas of study, the demography, pathology and biometry of York's Anglo-Scandinavian population, likewise rest at present on a very restricted corpus of material. The York Minster excavations recovered only 67 burials dated before c.1100 that could be examined (see Fig.76), and many of these were incomplete (Lee 1995). Sixty human skeletons predating or just post-dating the Norman conquest were recovered from a cemetery in Fishergate believed to be that of the church of St Andrew mentioned in *Domesday Book* (*AY* 12/2, 127, 131). Additionally, there is the group of burials from Wenham's excavation at St Mary Bishophill Junior that was mentioned above, and other modest numbers of skeletons found in pre-Norman contexts at Swinegate and adjacent to the former Female Prison at York Castle. Together, these add up to perhaps 0·0001 per cent of the total population of York in the Anglo-Scandinavian period. Demographic and related studies may not make significant advances until further data are recovered.

The important collection of carved stone grave markers from the Minster excavations, recovered either in situ or from where they had been re-used later in the medieval period as building materials, has been fundamental to the study of York's pre-Norman sculpture. This has culminated, for the time being, in a study by James Lang (1935–97) which catalogued and analysed the pre-Norman sculpture from York (Lang et al. 1991). The York Minster monuments were crucial to the definition there of a York metropolitan school of sculpture (cf. Lang 1995). An overview of artistry and style in other media, a topic hitherto published only in a piecemeal fashion, is provided here by Dominic Tweddle (pp.446–58), and David Parsons places in an international context the few inscriptions carved on some of them (pp.350–6).

Lang's *Corpus*, seen in tandem with the comparable study of Lincolnshire sculpture (Everson and

Stocker 1999), inspired a more recent observation by Stocker (2000), that the church of St Mary Bishophill Senior has an unusual quantity of grave stones. His explanation of this is that the church was patronised by a new, 10th-century mercantile elite. This hypothesis might be linked to observations by Palliser (1984, 105–8), who has drawn attention to the importance of the city south-west of the River Ouse, and mooted the possibility of deliberate town planning there linked to commercial exploitation of the area under the auspices of the archbishops from about the late 9th century onwards.

Building on the earlier works mentioned above, the chapters that follow present current views on a number of the key aspects of the evidence for Anglo-Scandinavian York. In addition to summarising usefully the present state of information, they demonstrate some of the approaches taken to the evidence, and illustrate some of the themes that demand further attention. Also, in proposing some alternative interpretations of the evidence, they demonstrate that Viking-Age York remains a place of some contention.

Anglo-Scandinavian York: The Evidence of Historical Sources

By David Rollason

Introduction

The relationship between historical (in the sense of written) and non-written (archaeological, numismatic and art historical) evidence is a complex one. First, there is a constant risk that interpretation of the one will be influenced by data derived from the other in ways which go beyond what either type of evidence is capable of sustaining; secondly, it is frequently the case that the two types of evidence do not illuminate the same aspects of the past, so that wide-ranging and subtle approaches are required to achieve cross-fertilisation between them. The aim of this chapter is, therefore, to set out what the historical evidence for Anglo-Scandinavian York is capable of establishing about the character and history of the city in that period, so far as possible without reference to non-written evidence. The intention is that this should facilitate cross-references between the types of evidence precisely because the import of the historical evidence will have been established without preconceptions derived from the non-written.

The Anglo-Scandinavian period, that is from the capture of York by the Viking 'great army' in 866–7 to the definitive imposition of the rule of William the Conqueror over York in 1069–70, was one of considerable political and military instability (AY 1, 63–83; Stenton 1971, 247–52, 334–63, 601–5; Kapelle 1979, 3–26; Rollason forthcoming). The capture of the city was followed by a period when a series of Viking kings held some sort of power in Northumbria, perhaps in York itself; but this series was, as we shall see, a broken one, with periods when there appear to have been no kings at all, and periods when kings had been expelled, sometimes to be replaced by other Viking kings, sometimes with the result that York fell for a time under the rule of the West Saxon kings, claiming now to be kings of England. Following the expulsion and killing of the last Viking king, Eric Bloodaxe, in 954 (or possibly 952), York was nominally under the rule of the kings of England, but in practice it was ruled by a series of earls, whose position was often ill defined and unstable. A revolt in 1065 expelled the then earl Tostig, who launched a temporarily successful attack on York in alliance with King Harold Hardrada of Norway in 1066. The first

Norman earl to be sent to Northumbria, Robert Cumin, was killed by Northumbrian insurgents in Durham in 1069, leading to a revolt in which York was deeply implicated and as a result of which it was plundered by the Normans. Such an unstable history is unlikely to have encouraged systematic record-keeping or the patronage of historical writing. This is certainly one of the reasons why this period of York's history is notably badly documented even by the standards of some other early medieval cities such as Canterbury and Winchester, or even in comparison with the 8th century in York, for which we have relatively rich information in the apparently contemporary annals known as the Northern Annals (AY 1, S.37), and in the writings of Alcuin, both of which come to an end in the early years of the 9th century, in 806 in the case of the Northern Annals (AY 1, S.37, S.28–9). From then until the Viking capture of the city, we are almost wholly in the dark, apart from some annals and chronological notes of very uncertain reliability preserved in 12th- and 13th-century sources such as *The First Coming of the Saxons* (AY 1, S.57) and Roger of Wendover's *Flowers of History* (AY 1, S.72).

For the Anglo-Scandinavian period, what annals we possess are much less satisfactory. The only such which may have originated in Northumbria in the 10th century are preserved in the 12th-century compilation known as the *History of the Kings* (AY 1, S.59) and refer to events in the British Isles from 888 to 957 (Arnold 1882 **1**, 92–5). They show considerable interest in the Viking kings of York, and may have been written in the north, although their lack of interest in the archbishops of York (there are only two references, in 892 and 900) makes it unlikely that they were produced at York itself. They may have been composed contemporaneously, for their entries are sometimes so laconic ('901: Osberht was expelled'; '902: Brihtsige was killed', for example) as to suggest that they were written when the events concerned were fresh in mind and no more extensive explanation was considered necessary. If so, they were modified later, for the last annal mentions Edward the Confessor who became king in 1042. Their value for the study of

Anglo-Scandinavian York is very difficult to assess. Some annals provide information not known in other sources, some of it of value, for example, the occupation of York in 919 by Ragnall (*Inguald*). The series also contains errors, however, which undermine confidence in its reliability (referring to the East Anglian Viking leader Guthrum as 'king of the Northumbrians' in 890, for example; Blair 1963, 104–6).

Aside from this series, we have odd annals, which may or may not be founded on contemporary records, preserved in the work of later writers, such as in Symeon of Durham's *On the Origins and Progress of this the Church of Durham*, written between 1104 and 1107 (*AY* 1, S.55), and in Roger of Wendover's *Flowers of History* (13th-century; *AY* 1, S.72). We also have the relevant sections of the *Anglo-Saxon Chronicle* which provide the essential framework for York history in the 10th century. The earliest version of this last text, however, is a West Saxon composition, albeit begun in the late 9th century, so its information about York is necessarily fragmentary, and its approach possibly prejudiced by its close association with the West Saxon kings. Only in the so-called 'northern' version, represented now by the D and E manuscripts, do we find authentically northern annals, especially for the period of Archbishop Ealdred (1061–9) who may have patronised its composition (*AY* 1, S.38). The information it provides, however, is very restricted. Other writers, such as Asser in his *Life of Alfred* (*AY* 1, S.39) and Æthelweard in his Latin translation and modification of the *Anglo-Saxon Chronicle* (*AY* 1, S.41), and the 12th-century writers John of Worcester (*AY* 1, S.61) and William of Malmesbury (*AY* 1, S.64–5), provide scraps of information, but, given the late date of the last two and the West-Saxon-influenced approach of the first two, confident assessment of their validity is impossible. Even more problematic is the information provided by the Irish annals, especially the *Annals of Ulster* (*AY* 1, S.40), which may have originated in the 10th century and were concerned with those Viking kings who were active in Ireland, especially Dublin, as well as in York. Their perspective was naturally an Irish rather than a Northumbrian or indeed a Viking one, and it is very difficult to achieve certainty in collating the information they give with that given by English sources about the Viking kings of York.

If historical and annalistic writing pertaining to York is so fragmentary, documentary records are almost non-existent. There are memoranda about the estates of York Minster in the 10th and 11th centuries (Robertson 1956, no.54; Barker 1986, 81–99) and charters relating to the same, for example, a probably authentic charter granting Amounderness in Lancashire (Sawyer 1968, no.407); but there are no charters whatsoever relating to the city itself or its churches in the period in question. Nor are there any documents of any other type, aside from two legal compilations, one called the *Northumbrian Priests' Law*, produced in York, probably by Archbishop Wulfstan II in 1020–1 (Liebermann 1903 **1**, 380–5; Whitelock 1979, no.53), which does potentially have a bearing on the organisation of the clergy of York in the 10th century (see p.320), and another known as the *Law of the Northumbrian People* (Liebermann 1903 **1**, 456–69; Whitelock 1979, no.52), which may cast light on the society in which York functioned. We should not of course expect to find in this period the sort of documentation — rentals, deeds and so forth — that exists for later periods (Rees Jones 1987); nonetheless, that for Anglo-Scandinavian York is notably meagre by comparison, for example, with Canterbury where a rich series of charters preserved by the cathedral casts light on the historical framework and character of the city (Sawyer 1968, index, *s.n.*; Brooks 1984, 15–36), and Winchester, where we find similarly rich archives thanks to the Old and New Minsters in the city (Sawyer 1968, index, *s.n.*).

The absence of such material from York — as from the rest of Northumbria — may result from lack of record-keeping, as suggested above, or from destruction of archives, perhaps in the plundering following the revolt of 1069 (*AY* 1, N.1.7). It is certainly the case that the library of York Minster, which was rich in the 8th century (*AY* 1, A.4.24–5), seems scarcely to have survived and only two or three extant manuscripts can be tentatively argued to have been at York. The Durham *Cassiodorus* of the 8th century (Durham, Dean and Chapter Library, B.II.30) may have been produced in York, although this is controversial, and it may have remained there in the Anglo-Scandinavian period, unlike a leaf of the same work at Werden (Germany) which may have been produced at York but was taken to Germany by Alcuin's pupil Liudger (Bullough 1983, 172–5). The York Gospels (York, Minster Library, Add.1; Ker 1969 **4**, 784–6) were certainly at York from 1020–3, where additions were made to them in the course of the 11th century and later, although the book was in fact made in the south, possibly at Canterbury (Barker 1986, 41–2, 81–99, 101–6). A copy of Alcuin's letters of 9th- or 10th-century date (BL, Harley 208) may only have come to York in the later medieval period (D.A. Bullough, pers. comm.; cf. Ker 1964, 216). Otherwise, only some manuscripts associated with Archbishop Wulfstan II can be argued to have been at York: BL, Harley 55, fos.1–4v and BL, Cotton Nero A.i (D.A. Bullough, pers. comm.). As all that is left of a great library of the early medieval period, this is a meagre harvest.

In the late 11th and early 12th century we begin at last to find written evidence specifically about York as a city, in the shape of the *Domesday Book* entry for York (1086; *AY* 1, S.50), a survey of the land and privileges of the archbishop of York in the city (*The Rights and Laws which Archbishop T. has throughout York*; 1070 x 1086/8; *AY* 1, S.51) and a record of an inquest held in 1106 into the rights in York of the chapter of the Minster (*AY* 1, S.66). Valuable as these surveys are, however, it is important to emphasise that they contain nothing of the detailed information about tenements and properties which is found, for example, in two 12th-century Winchester surveys (Barlow et al. 1976, 9–28), in the rentals available for Canterbury in the Angevin period (Urry 1967), or indeed in the later property deeds for York, on the basis of which Rees Jones has been able to make such detailed reconstructions of the later medieval city (Rees Jones 1987; *AY* 10/2, 51–62; *AY* 12/3, 301–13; *AY* 10/5, 380–91; *AY* 10/6, 684–98).

This account of the historical sources is not intended to engender despondency, but rather to underline the limitations and uncertainties of what can be derived from the historical evidence. We need to be very precise about what it is that we are expecting this evidence to yield, and how we envisage that it might inter-relate with the non-written evidence. We need also to ask questions of it which are appropriate to its character, and these will not always be questions closely related to the immediate concerns of archaeological research, which might, for example, be preoccupied with the topography of the Anglo-Scandinavian city (e.g. Hall 1978). Rather, the questions to be addressed in the light of the historical sources are of a more general character, and can be grouped under three broad headings: York as a centre of government; York as a religious and cultural centre; society and economy in York.

The insights which the historical sources can offer into the character of Anglo-Scandinavian York under these headings may nonetheless provide an essential background and context for research into non-written sources, and may guide interpretations of it in ways which will be explored below.

York as a centre of government

York and Viking kings

It is often assumed that York was the capital of the Viking Kingdom of York, in the sense that it was the centre of government, the permanent seat of the king and an attendant bureaucracy (Hall 1988, 238; Hall 1994, 16). How far do the written sources support this assumption and allow it to be extended into the period of the English kings who supplanted their Viking predecessors?

Let us consider first the Viking capture of York in 866–7. The Viking 'great army' (in Old English *micel hæðen here*, so called by the *Anglo-Saxon Chronicle*; e.g. Plummer 1892 **1**, 69) made two attacks on York, the first on 1 November 866, the second on 21 March 867 (*AY* 1, 71, V.1.1). After the first, it departed to plunder the area around the River Tyne, leaving the two Northumbrian kings, Osberht and Ælle, to recapture the city. In the second, it again captured York and the Northumbrian kings were taken and killed. These attacks appear to have been high on its list of priorities, for, once its leaders had made peace with the East Angles (in whose kingdom the 'great army' had landed) and had obtained horses, York was its first goal despite the city's distance from East Anglia. It is possible to argue from the text of the *Anglo-Saxon Chronicle* that the 'great army' landed in East Anglia in 866 (*AY* 1, 71), and that, having arranged winter quarters and made peace with the East Angles, it proceeded almost immediately to York to make its November attack. Attractive as this interpretation is in the present context, however, it is not the most natural reading of the *Anglo-Saxon Chronicle* (Simon Keynes, pers. comm.), which is that the 'great army' landed in East Anglia in the autumn of 865, over-wintered there, and attacked York in November of the following year (e.g. Stenton 1971, 246). That is also the reading placed on the text of the *Anglo-Saxon Chronicle* by John of Worcester (*AY* 1, S.61), who refers directly to the 'great army' overwintering in East Anglia (Darlington, McGurk and Bray 1995, 280–1) as distinct from the *Anglo-Saxon Chronicle*'s 'took winter quarters'; and by Æthelweard (*AY* 1, S. 41) who notes that the 'great army' went north to York 'after a year' (Campbell 1962, 35). Nevertheless, the fact that the first attack was made at such an unpropitious time of year as November (*AY* 1, 71) underlines the purposefulness of it.

Certain 13th-century and later sources, including the *Saga of Ragnar Loðbrok*, suggest that the 'great army' was in fact directing its attack against the king of Northumbria personally as the fulfilment of a vendetta. According to this tradition, the leaders of the 'great army', Ivar and Halfdan, were sons of a Dane called Ragnar Loðbrok, who had been cruelly executed by King Ælle of the Northumbrians by being put in a snake-pit and left to die. Ivar and Halfdan's goal was therefore vengeance on Ælle rather than the capture of York for its own sake. Alfred P. Smyth has argued that this tradition arose in Northumbria and should be taken seriously as a key to the motivation of the leaders of the 'great army'; but, although it cannot be proved that the tradition has no reliable foundation, the lateness in date of the sources which have transmitted it and their romanticised character make such a conclusion very difficult to accept (Smyth 1977, 36–67). Moreover, the fullest accounts of the attack, those in the *Anglo-Saxon Chronicle* (Plummer 1892 **1,** 68–9) and in Symeon of Durham's *On the Origins and Progress of this the Church of Durham* (Rollason 2000, 96–9), are not altogether consistent with such a position. They imply that the Northumbrian kings were not in fact in York at the time of the first attack, so that we might argue that it was the city rather than the kings which was the goal, and that this underlines its political importance at the end of the Anglian period.

York may have suffered less from the disruption of royal government in Northumbria on the eve of the Viking capture than is sometimes supposed. It is true that the *Anglo-Saxon Chronicle* states in connection with the arrival of the 'great army':

And there was great civil strife going on in that people, and they had deposed their king Osberht and taken a king with no hereditary right, Ælle (Plummer 1892 **1,** 69; Whitelock 1979, no.1, *s.a.* 867).

The compiler, however, had reason to emphasise the dire consequences of civil discord in order to discourage it in his native Wessex, and he may for that reason have exaggerated the political instability of Northumbria at the time of the Viking attack. An early 11th-century Durham source, the *History of St Cuthbert* (*AY* 1, S.47; Arnold 1882 **1,** 202), represents Ælle as Osberht's brother rather than a 'king with no hereditary right'. Moreover, numismatic evidence has been interpreted as suggesting that Ælle's reign was limited to a very short period in 866–7, with Osberht reigning from c.852–67 (*AY* 1, 54–7; Pagan 1969), although there remains considerable uncertainty regarding this chronology (see p.325). Nevertheless, it is possible that political disturbance in Northumbria was of very recent origin, and may indeed have been precipitated by the first Viking capture of York on 1 November 866, rather than being a cause of it.

The reference in the *Anglo-Saxon Chronicle* to the Vikings breaking into the city suggests that York was fortified (Plummer 1892 **1,** 69), and this accords with earlier texts (for example, Alcuin's *On the Bishops, Kings and Saints of York; AY* 1, S.29) which refer to walls, although significantly the walls in question (presumably re-used Roman walls) seem to have been those around the ecclesiastical quarter of the city which may have lain in the Roman fortress (*AY* 1, A.1.1–3). It is true that Asser in his *Life of King Alfred* (893), although drawing on the *Anglo-Saxon Chronicle* in describing the capture of York, states additionally that the city at that time 'did not yet have firm and secure walls' (*AY* 1, V.1.1; Stevenson 1959, 22–3; Keynes and Lapidge 1983, 76–7); but he is unlikely to have had reliable information since he had no Northumbrian sources, and his observation is best discounted.

York then was an important political and military centre on the eve of the Viking capture. To what extent did the Vikings make it their capital? We must emphasise first the disrupted character of the power of the Vikings in Northumbria, which must have had an effect on York's role in relation to them. It is possible to piece together from 12th- and 13th-century sources that a series of English kings, possibly puppets of the Vikings, were ruling north of the Tyne between 867 and 895: Egbert, perhaps from 867 to 872, Ricsige from 873 to 876, then another king called Egbert, who is said to have been ruling the 'Northumbrians' (i.e. presumably those north of the Tyne) contemporaneously with Guthfrith, who was ruling, presumably south of the Tyne, from 880/5 to 895 (*AY* 1, 63). As for York itself, all we know is that in 869 the 'great army' returned to stay there for one year (Plummer 1892 **1**, 70–1); in 872 Archbishop Wulfhere was expelled to be reinstated by the Viking army in 873 (see p.313). In 874 the 'great army' conquered Mercia, expelling its king, Burgred, and, according to the *Anglo-Saxon Chronicle*, installing a 'foolish king's thegn' called Ceowulf as a puppet king (Stenton 1971, 252; Plummer 1892 **1**, 72–3). It then split up, with one of its original leaders, Halfdan, bringing a contingent to the Tyne on what was evidently a raiding expedition aimed, according to the *Anglo-Saxon Chronicle*, not only at Northumbria itself but also at the lands of the Picts and the Strathclyde Britons (Plummer 1892 **1**, 72–4 (*s.a.* 875)). It would seem that the raiding plan was changed to one of settlement, for at the end of the annal for 876, which is mainly devoted to events in Wessex, the *Chronicle* has the single sentence: 'And that year Halfdan shared out the lands of the Northumbrians and they proceeded to plough and to support themselves' (Whitelock 1979, *s.a.*; 'Healfdene Norþan hymbra lond ge dælde, and ergende wæron and hiera tilgende' (Plummer 1892 **1**, 74–5). This sentence is all we have, apart from a statement in the 11th-century *History of St Cuthbert* which may not be reliable (*AY* 1, S.47) but which states that the Viking army 're-built the city of York, cultivated the land around it, and remained there' (Arnold 1882 **1**, 204). It is therefore by no means clear that the historical sources are sufficient to show that Halfdan was a king in any sense. If he established a kingdom, his reign was transitory, for Symeon of Durham describes how he fled from the River Tyne never to return (Rollason 2000, 120–3) possibly in late 876, if he is identical with the *Albann*, 'king of the dark heathens', mentioned by the *Annals of Ulster* as having been killed in Ireland in 877 (Mac Airt and Mac Niocaill 1983, 332–3; Smyth 1977, 263–4). The annal in the *History of the Kings* which mentions Halfdan as having been killed by King Alfred's forces in Devon in 877 is clearly corrupt; its source evidently assigned this incident to a brother of Halfdan and Ivar, as Asser and the *Anglo-Saxon Chronicle* (*s.a.* 878) do (Arnold 1882 **1**, 111; Stevenson 1959, 43 (paragraph 54); Plummer 1892 **1**, 74–5).

Our information about Halfdan's successors is extremely unsatisfactory, to the extent of creating a strong presumption that there was no settled kingship of York with a definite and continuous line of succession. It is reasonably certain, because attested by the 10th-century chronicler Æthelweard, that a king with the Viking name Guthfrith was buried in York Minster in 895 (*AY* 1, V.4.1; Campbell 1962, 51), suggesting that this person had been a king of York. This is corroborated by the evidence of a single surviving coin naming him (see p.327). There is a strong possibility that he is to be identified with the Guthred who was, according to the *History of St Cuthbert*, made a king by the religious community of St Cuthbert not later than 885 and not earlier than 880 (*AY* 1, 64; Arnold 1882 **1**, 203).

For the association between York and two succeeding Viking kings, Siefred and Cnut, we are solely dependent on the evidence of coins bearing their name (in some cases both their names) and apparently minted in York (see p.329) (*AY* 1, 65; North 1994, 110–12). The identity and length of reign of these kings are impossible to establish satisfactorily, and the occurrence of both names on certain of the coins may suggest that we are dealing with a joint reign. A Viking leader called *Sigeferð* besieged the north coast of Devon in 893, and a jarl called *Sichfrith* caused a dissension in Dublin in the same year (Campbell 1962, 50; Mac Airt and Mac Niocaill 1983, 346–7). If these persons were one and the same and are to be identified with the Siefred of the York coins, the evidence is not inconsistent with a reign beginning after Guthfrith's death in 895; but the identification is no more than a suggestion. Similarly, later sagas describe the arrival at Scarborough in c.900 of a Viking leader called Cnut (Smyth 1975 **1**, 47–8), but whether the tradition is reliable, whether, if so, this was the Cnut of the York coins, and whether he was in any sense a king of York are all uncertain.

We are on slightly firmer ground with the D version of the *Anglo-Saxon Chronicle*'s account of the first West Saxon intervention in the kingship of Northumbria, that is the arrival in 899 of a cousin of King Edward the Elder, Æthelwold, who 'went to the Danish army in Northumbria, and they accepted him as king and gave allegiance to him' (Whitelock 1979, no.1, *s.a.* 900; Cubbin 1996, 36). This reference to the 'Danish army' may itself be significant, suggesting that Viking organisation in Northumbria was still based on that of raiding armies. The only evidence that York was the centre of Æthelwold's power is provided by coins from York with his name (see p.329) (North 1994, 111). His reign, however, was very short and he was evidently concerned with using

Northumbria as a base from which to gain dominance of the south, for in 901 he was accepted as king by the Vikings of Essex, and in 902 he was killed fighting against King Edward the Elder (Plummer 1892 **1**, 92–3).

From then until the accession of Ragnall (914 x 919–920/1), the only hint we have as to Viking kings in Northumbria is provided by the account in the *Anglo-Saxon Chronicle* of the Battle of Tettenhall (910), at which the 'army of Northumbria' was defeated and the kings, Halfdan, Eowils and Ivar, were killed (Plummer 1892 **1**, 96–7). It is quite unknown whether these persons were ruling from York, whether they were ruling different parts of Northumbria, or whether indeed they were kings in any real sense of the word rather than just leaders of the Viking army. The date of the accession of Ragnall is uncertain: it may have followed either from his victory at Corbridge in 914 or from his seizure of York in 919 (*AY* 1, 66). That his accession was violent is suggested by the annals in the *History of the Kings,* which give under 919: 'King Ragnall (*Inguald*) broke into (*irrupit*) York' (Arnold 1882 **2**, 93). The latter event, and the evidence of his coins, which have the name of York on the reverse, associate him with the city (North 1994, 113 (Regnald I); see also pp.333–5). Following Ragnall's death, we find a somewhat more consistent succession of kings, for he was succeeded by his brother Sihtric Caoch (920/1–7), who is described in the *Anglo-Saxon Chronicle*, D version, as 'king of the Northumbrians' (Cubbin 1996, 41), and in whose name coins were also produced although possibly in Lincoln rather than in York itself (North 1994, 113 (Sihtric I), Stewart 1982a). His successor was apparently a certain Guthfrith, who may possibly have been another brother (*AY* 1, 67), and who was, according to the *Anglo-Saxon Chronicle*, driven out by Athelstan, king of England, in 927, when the latter established his power over Northumbria (Plummer 1892 **1**, 107). Although no coins of Guthfrith survive (see p.335), William of Malmesbury's account of how, following his expulsion, Athelstan razed a Viking fortress at York suggests that York was his base also (*AY* 1, S.65, V.1.3; Mynors, Thomson and Winterbottom 1998, 214–15).

Athelstan died in 939, and in 941, according to the D version of the *Anglo-Saxon Chronicle,* the Northumbrians chose 'Olaf from Ireland as their king' (Cubbin 1996, 43). This was Olaf Guthfrithson (939–

41), who, the *History of the Kings* states, 'came first to York' on assuming power (Arnold 1882 **2**, 93). He was succeeded by Olaf Sihtricson (Cuaran, 941–3, 944/5), whose reign appears very confused in the historical evidence, for he seems twice to have been expelled by Edmund, king of England, and to have been expelled alongside another king, apparently of York, Ragnall Guthfrithson (943–4/5; *AY* 1, 68). We seem here to have another case of joint rule. Edmund then 'obtained the kingdom of the Northumbrians' (Arnold 1882 **2**, 94) and ruled until his death in 946, being succeeded in York for a short period (946–8) by his brother Eadred, who also became king of England. The situation shortly afterwards becomes confused once more. According to the *Anglo-Saxon Chronicle* (D version), 'the councillors of the Northumbrians' accepted as king Eric Bloodaxe (948), but expelled him in response to threats of ravaging by Eadred (*AY* 1, 69; Cubbin 1996, 44). According to the *Anglo-Saxon Chronicle* (E version), Olaf Sihtricson returned to Northumbria and re-established his position (949), but was expelled in 952 by 'the Northumbrians', who again received Eric Bloodaxe as king until his expulsion and death in 954 (Plummer 1892–9, 113; *AY* 1, 69). Other interpretations of the evidence, however, have been advanced. Simon Keynes has placed Eric's first reign in 947–8, and has assigned the years 948–50 to Eadred (partly on the basis of newly discovered charter evidence; Simon Keynes, pers. comm.), thus reducing the reign of Olaf Sihtricson to the years 950–2/3 (Lapidge et al. 1998, 492, 505). A different approach was suggested by P.H. Sawyer, who argued that dislocations in the annals could be interpreted to mean that Olaf Sihtricson's reign should be dated 947–50, and that Eric Bloodaxe had only one reign, from 952 to 954 (Sawyer 1995, 39–44). If weight is given to the later Icelandic sources and to the *Life of Catroe* (*AY* 1, S.46) yet another interpretation is possible: that Eric Bloodaxe did have a first reign but in c.937–40 (Woolf 1999, 189–93). Neither of these last two interpretations has found much favour.

It may be that the confusions in the sources which make these varying interpretations possible result from the fact that the sequence of kings was a very broken and complex one, marked by violence and political instability, such that it seems unlikely that the kings' presence in York (in so far as that can be established) would have had a major influence on the development of the city, aside from a negative one arising from the instability it must have induced, and a positive one in the wealth from accumulated plunder which it may have brought (see p.322). Given the growth of York in the 10th century, the kings are very likely to have had an interest in it (Hall 1994), but was it in any real sense their capital? The strongest evidence in favour is provided by surviving coins in their names which can be assigned to a mint in York (Pirie 1975, xliv–lv). But how far do these coins prove that the kings were really in control of the mint, however much for financial reasons they may have wished to be? The occurrence of pagan symbols on coins whose predecessors had been purely Christian in imagery (the sword on the coins of Sihtric Caoch, and the raven on those of Olaf Guthfrithson; Dolley 1965, pls.30–2) was certainly due directly to the power of the kings. Many coins, however, particularly those of Siefred and Cnut, show Christian and Frankish-influenced ideas, notably the use of the cross and the inscriptions 'Lord God the King' and 'He has worked miracles' (AY 1, V.4.8). Mark Blackburn has speculated that the Viking kings of York were recent and ardent converts to Christianity and that these coins reflected their need to proselytise (see pp.331–2). Of the Viking kings, however, only Guthfrith (883–95) is known to have undergone a lasting conversion to Christianity, while Sihtric Caoch underwent a transient conversion for political reasons, and there is only the faintest of possibilities that Eric Bloodaxe was Christian (see p.318). It is therefore a more economical interpretation to assume that all these kings were, with the possible exception of Guthfrith, pagan and were therefore unlikely in any real sense to have had a defining role in the inclusion of Christian inscriptions on the St Peter coinage. Blackburn is unwilling to accept that the church played a major, at times a dominant, role in the minting of coins in Viking York, perhaps even controlling the mint in partnership with the Viking kings (see p.332). Unusual as this would have been, however, it nevertheless seems a more plausible interpretation than his own (see pp.313–14).

The existence of a royal palace in York would be another indication of its status as a capital. The only text which mentions such an edifice is the 13th-century *Saga of Egil Skallagrimsson* (AY 1, S.73), which describes a visit by the hero to Eric Bloodaxe in York, but this text's late date, inaccuracy in other details, and literary style make it extremely unreliable as a source for the Anglo-Scandinavian period (AY 1,

V.2.2; Nordal 1933, 176, 183, 195; Pálsson and Edwards 1976, 151, 153, 155–7, 163). Otherwise, we have only the place-name King's Square which is of Scandinavian origin and may refer to the site of a royal residence, although such an interpretation is far from certain (Palliser 1978, 8). It is nevertheless likely that the Viking kings did have a residence in York, as is suggested by a passage in the *Chronicle of Æthelweard* describing how in 894 an envoy of King Alfred 'contacted the enemy' in the city of York, where their leader was presumably resident (Campbell 1962, 51). If, as seems likely, this was Guthfrith, we have already seen that he was buried in the following year in York Minster. Another source, admittedly of very doubtful reliability, is the *Life of Catroe* which describes a visit of the saint to Eric Bloodaxe in York (AY 1, V.2.3; Anderson 1922 **1**, 441).

Were there still fortifications in York which the kings could use? Basing ourselves solely on historical sources, the 12th-century *Chapters on the Miracles and translations of St Cuthbert* (AY 1, S.52) state that part of the 'great army' (presumably that led by Halfdan) 'restored the defences of the city of York' (AY 1, V.1.2). This detail is suspect, however, for the passage appears to be an elaboration of the *Historia de sancto Cuthberto* (AY 1, S.47), which simply states that part of the army 'rebuilt the city of York' (Arnold 1882 **1**, 204). William of Malmesbury's *Deeds of the Kings of England* (12th-century; AY 1, S.65, V.1.3; Mynors, Thomson and Winterbottom 1998, 214–15) does refer to King Guthfrith besieging York in 927, after which King Athelstan razed to the ground a Viking fortress (*castrum*) there. This latter reference, however, seems to be to something more restricted in area than the walls of the city themselves, but, if so, it is unknown whether it was subsequently rebuilt, where it was, and what its precise character was.

Did the kings possess a bureaucratic machinery such as would have required royal officers and space for them to work? This too is unknown, but the presumption must be that kings whose reigns were so disrupted and transitory did not possess anything of this kind; it is much more likely that they were basically leaders of a Viking army based in York. It should be emphasised in this connection that the geographical scope of whatever kingdom the Viking kings ruled is very uncertain. The rule of English kings north of the Tyne (see p.308) suggests that the remit of York's Viking kings did not extend north of that river. As far as the southern and western boundaries go, we can only guess at them on the basis of hints in the *Anglo-Saxon Chronicle*: that Dore near Sheffield was the boundary of Mercia and thus presumably also of Northumbria; that Manchester was 'in Northumbria' and that Edward the Elder built a *burh* there and at nearby Thelwall as if he were fortifying a frontier; that Edward the Elder built a *burh* and received the homage of various northern rulers, including Ragnall, at Bakewell (Derbyshire) in 924, suggesting that this may have been a frontier location (Plummer 1892 **1,** 110 (942A), 104 (923, 924A)). Although the Viking Five Boroughs (Nottingham, Lincoln, Derby, Stamford, Leicester) were under different control from York at the beginning of the Anglo-Scandinavian period and therefore constituted a frontier to the south, it appears from the *Anglo-Saxon Chronicle* that they were for a time, even if only a short time, under the control of the Viking kings of York, for a piece of alliterative verse preserved as the annal for 942 in the A version describes the liberation of the Danes of these boroughs by Edmund, king of England, from forced subjection to the heathen 'Norsemen', presumably the Viking kings of York (Plummer 1892 **1,** 110; Mawer 1923).

In any case, the ambitions and interests of these kings were by no means always focused on York. Several of them were as concerned with events in Ireland and with the kingdom of Dublin as they were with York, and it is unclear that they thought of York as a settled kingdom rather than as another base from which to conduct raids (Smyth 1975; 1977). It is barely possible to assert any more than this about the intervals of rule of the West Saxon kings. Athelstan's presence in York in a peaceful context is attested by the account of the late 10th-century writer Richer of Rheims of how a Frankish embassy came to the king, apparently in 936, 'in the city of York, where he was deliberating on the affairs of the kingdom' (*AY* 1, S.44, 73; Latouche 1930, 200–1), and by a passage in William of Malmesbury's *Deeds of the Kings of England*, which describes how envoys of King Harold Fairhair of Norway were 'royally entertained' in York (*AY* 1, S.65, V.2.1; Mynors, Thomson and Winterbottom 1998, 216–17). His charter granting Amounderness to York Minster was given not at York itself but at Nottingham (Sawyer 1968, no.407). The tradition that King Athelstan granted thraves of corn to the Minster is found only in the late cartulary of St Leonard's Hospital and is very unlikely to be reliable (see p.319).

In general, we find the West Saxon kings before 954 governing, when they were in a position to do so, by means of direct military intervention or by ravaging of the land of Northumbrians, as Edward the Elder did in 909: his army 'ravaged very severely the territory of the northern army, both men and all kinds of cattle, and they killed many men of those Danes, and were five weeks there' (Plummer 1892 **1,** 94–7). The actions of King Eadred in 948 are especially instructive and the account of the D version of the *Anglo-Saxon Chronicle* is worth citing in full:

In this year King Eadred ravaged all Northumbria, because they had accepted Eric [Bloodaxe] as their king … and when the king was on his way home, the army [which] was in York overtook the king's army at Castleford, and they made a great slaughter there. Then the king became so angry that he wished to march back into the land and utterly destroy it. When the councillors of the Northumbrians understood that, they deserted Eric and paid to King Eadred compensation for their act (Cubbin 1996, 44; Whitelock 1979, no.1, *s.a.*).

This was indeed what W.E. Kapelle called for a later period 'government by punitive expedition' (Kapelle 1979, ch.5).

Although there is no certainty, we may be seeing in this passage the importance of a group which appears here and elsewhere in the *Anglo-Saxon Chronicle* as the 'councillors of the Northumbrians' or simply as 'the Northumbrians', which was in a position to accept and expel kings (Cubbin 1996, 37 (909), 43 (941), 44 (947–8), 45 (954); Plummer 1892 **1,** 113 (952E)). If so, we must reckon with a powerful aristocracy capable of acting in concert in a political way. It is impossible, of course, to establish the make-up of this aristocracy, let alone to discover whether its members were resident in York. It seems reasonable to suppose, however, that it consisted of an amalgam of the native Northumbrian aristocracy (hence the use of the term Northumbrians) and the incoming Viking aristocracy, men whom Halfdan had settled on the land in 876, such as Scula and Onlafball, or to whom, according to the *History of St Cuthbert*, Ragnall had given church lands as their endowment in County Durham (Arnold 1882 **1,** 209). Certainly the existence of a powerful aristocracy, using both Old English and Old Norse terms for its status, is discernible in the *Law of the Northumbrian People* (Liebermann 1903 **1,** 456–69; Whitelock 1979, no.52).

Farther than that we cannot go, other than to note that the Northumbrian aristocracy was also prominent in the pre-Viking period, expelling kings according to the Northern Annals in much the same way as we see it expelling Eric Bloodaxe in 948 (Bund 1979, 625–61).

Real power in York, however, may have been in the hands of the archbishops, as (it has been argued elsewhere; *AY* 7/2, 131–4) it was in the Anglian period. In 872 the Northumbrians expelled Archbishop Wulfhere of York (*AY* 1, 63; Arnold 1882 **1**, 56, 225; Coxe 1841 **1**, 325), and — significantly — he was re-instated in 873, presumably by the return of the Viking army recorded in that year (Arnold 1882 **2**, 110). These events are consistent with York as a city ruled by its archbishop rather than directly by a king, so that Wulfhere's expulsion would have been the result of a Northumbrian revolt against Viking power which the archbishop was seen as representing in York, his re-instatement testimony to the existence of an alliance between the archbishop and the Viking invaders. This finds some corroboration in the archiepiscopate of Wulfstan I, who was archbishop of York from 930/1, apparently until his deprivation in the early 950s, dying in 955/6 (Lapidge et al. 1998, 492–3). We find him acting in concert with the certainly pagan King Olaf Guthfrithson when, sometime between 940 and 943, that king, after sacking the English royal centre of Tamworth, was with Wulfstan when he was besieged by Edmund, king of England, in Leicester (*Anglo-Saxon Chronicle*, D version; Cubbin 1996, 43, *s.a.* 943). It is impossible to escape the conclusion that Wulfstan was collaborating with Olaf at this time in a military raid on territory controlled by the king of England. Again in 947, we find the *Anglo-Saxon Chronicle*, D version, specifically naming Wulfstan alongside 'the councillors (*witan*) of the Northumbrians' in pledging loyalty to King Eadred, a pledge to which, the *Chronicle* tells us, they were afterwards false (Cubbin 1996, 44) — that is, by subsequently accepting Eric Bloodaxe as their king. That Wulfstan had played a role in bringing Eric to power is corroborated by the fact that he was arrested in 952 and imprisoned by King Eadred, because 'accusations had often been made to the king about him' (Cubbin 1996, 44–5). Two years later, Eric Bloodaxe was once more expelled and this time killed, and it is tempting to conjecture that his fall was hastened by the fact that Wulfstan was no longer in York to support him. It may have been unease about the polit-

ical role of the archbishops of York which prompted the kings of England after Eric's expulsion often to combine the see of York with that of Worcester so that the archbishops of York would have a vested interest in maintaining their loyalty to the south, although it is possible that this was also an attempt to make good the loss of York's lands catalogued in Archbishop Oswald's memoranda (Whitelock 1959, 73–4; Robertson 1956, no.54).

Nothing is known of the political activities of the archbishops between Wulfhere and Wulfstan I, but the St Peter coinage may fit with the scenario of a city dominated by the archbishops in alliance with the Viking kings. This coinage consists of two series of coins, both inscribed with some version of 'money of St Peter'. As far as can be discerned from numismatic evidence, the first series begins around 905, following on from the coinage of Siefred and Cnut. This series is succeeded by the rare series of coins assigned to King Ragnall of York (c.919–21), which is in its turn replaced by the second series of St Peter's coins (c.921–7), characterised by the appearance on them of a sword (North 1994, 31). It has been argued that both series of St Peter coins were 'secular', on the grounds that they were in their time the only coins produced in York, and because the first and second series were interrupted by the explicitly royal coinage of Ragnall. Blunt and Stewart, for example, conjectured that the first series represented 'the coinage of the leaders of the Danish community of York between the royal coinages of Cnut and Ragnall, issued under whatever military, municipal or other form of lay authority was in being at the time', and that the second series (with sword) was the "'civic" coinage of York during the 920s, in the time of Sihtric' (Blunt and Stewart 1983, 156). Blackburn has supported the conjecture to the extent that 'it would be without precedent in Europe for control of all minting to be granted away by a state' (see p.333). The conjecture, however, is based on the perceived implausibility of the principal York coinage, which is what the St Peter series must have been when it was minted, being regarded as that of the archbishop. This is only implausible if the hypothesis that the archbishops were in fact the dominant authority in York is rejected. Once we accept that York was in the Viking period a city dominated politically by the church and by the archbishop in particular, nothing would be more natural than that the archbishop should control the mint, using ecclesiastical inscriptions on the coins when he could or when perhaps there was no king in York, ceding to royal demands for recognition on the coins when he could not. This may have been unusual, but it is hardly impossible. The first series of St Peter coins would correspond with a period during which it is possible that York had no king at all, so that the archbishops would have minted in the name of St Peter with no royal name (Grierson and Blackburn 1986, 322–3, 626; *AY* 18/1, 34–7). The coins of Ragnall would then be evidence that that king had taken control of the mint. The second series of St Peter coins, following his reign, would have marked the reassertion of archiepiscopal control. It is striking in this context that the coins of Sihtric Caoch (920/1–7), which were contemporary with the second series of St Peter coins, may have been minted in Mercia, possibly in Lincoln, so that the York mint in his reign would have produced only St Peter coins (see p.333) (Stewart 1982a). Sihtric Caoch's power in York was clearly not equal to that of Ragnall.

York under the earls

Following the expulsion of Eric Bloodaxe, the kings of England assumed at least nominal rule of Northumbria. Their visits to the north were extremely rare (Hill 1981, maps 158, 160–3, 167–9), and they appointed earls to govern on their behalf. There is, however, some uncertainty in the historical evidence as to which of these earls were in a real sense earls of York (*AY* 1, 74–6). The first of them, Oswulf I (954–66), appears earlier as high reeve of Bamburgh and was, according to Roger of Wendover, responsible for the expulsion of Eric Bloodaxe, after which the *History of the Kings* and the *First Coming of the Saxons* state that Northumbria (presumably north and south of the Tyne) was entrusted to him. It is likely that his base continued to be Bamburgh, and in 966, according to the *History of the Kings*, he renounced control of York and its area to Oslac (966–75). He was succeeded by two rather obscure earls, Thored (975 x 979–92/3) and Ælfhelm (992/3–1006). The first of these seems to have been ineffective or corrupt, since Archbishop Oswald considered the lands of York Minster to have been despoiled in his time (Robertson 1956, no.54). After Ælfhelm, we again find the whole of Northumbria in the hands of the house of Bamburgh, represented now by Uhtred, whose father Waltheof had probably only controlled northern Northumbria. Uhtred sided with the English prince Edmund Ironside in his struggle against the invasion of Cnut the Great, but he was compelled to submit to the latter and was murdered by his enemy Thurbrand, probably for political reasons, in 1016 (Kapelle 1979, 15–22). Cnut then gave the earldom of Northumbria, possibly but not certainly excluding northern Northumbria, to one of his generals, Eric of Hlathir (1016–23 x 1033), who was in turn succeeded by Siward (1023 x 1033–55). After Siward's death, King Edward the Confessor appointed Tostig (1055–65), brother of Harold Godwinson. After a Northumbrian revolt expelled him, King Edward appointed in his place the Mercian Morcar (1065–7), who was deposed as a result of the Northumbrian revolt against William I.

This sequence of earls, while not as disjointed as that of the Viking kings who preceded them, is nevertheless not notably stable, and it consequently raises the same questions about the real character of their rule. There are only two texts suggesting that they had a residence and centre of government in York. First, a passage in the *Anglo-Saxon Chronicle*, D version, describes how Earl Siward was buried in the church of St Olave, which he had founded (*AY* 1, V.4.4; Cubbin 1996, 74). The fact that this was in the area known to the 18th-century antiquary Francis Drake as *Earlsburgh* has led to the suggestion that the earl's residence was in that area, close to St Olave's (Hall 1988, 235; Smith 1937, lx, 288). Secondly, the *History of the Kings*, in describing the revolt which expelled Earl Tostig in 1065, focuses its account on York, where Tostig had in the previous year treacherously arranged killings of nobles in his 'chamber' (*camera*). The insurgents entered the city, had Tostig's housecarls executed 'without the walls of the city' and 'broke into his treasury' (*AY* 1, V.2.4; Arnold 1882 **2**, 178). This shows, first, that the earls by that date possessed at the least a chamber and a treasury in the city; secondly, that the city was walled in 1065, a circumstance which is confirmed by a reference in *Domesday Book* to a house which had been built in the town ditch (*AY* 1, N.1.6, N.5.2, paragraphs 8, 16), and which may have been a reflection of the political status of the city. Certainly, *Domesday Book* shows the inhabitants of the 84 outlying carucates of York (the future Ainsty area) performing to the city the king's three works — presumably the *trinoda necessitas* — of army-service, bridge-building and, relevant to the question of the city's defences, work on the defences (*AY* 1, N.5.2, paragraph 24). The location of the defences is nowhere made clear, and the fact that the

Life of St Oswald mentions them as 'left to the ravages of age' (*AY* 1, V.3.1; Raine 1879 **1,** 454) in the 970s should make us cautious in assigning significance to them (*AY* 1, V.3.1).

There are in addition more general indications of York's status at the end of the Anglo-Scandinavian period, which point to a city of major importance. It was one of the 32 English towns and cities for which *Domesday Book* made a separate entry at the beginning of the return for the county in which it stood (Martin 1985, 154–5). It features in the *Domesday Book* account of Exeter, where it is classed with London in the statement that Exeter was only required to pay geld when York and London paid geld (Tait 1936, 127). The reference to shires (below) may also be an indication of importance, for the only comparable references in *Domesday Book* are in respect of Stamford, Huntingdon and Cambridge (Palliser 1990, 2). The reason for this in the case of these three towns is not clear, but in the case of York there can be little doubt that it was a sign of the sophistication and status of the city. *Domesday Book* refers to it as a *ciuitas* more often than an *urbs*, terminology which may indicate that York was one of the 'grander or more important towns' (Palliser 1990, 8; cf. Reynolds 1987, 299–300). In the early 12th century, at any rate, it was, according to William of Malmesbury, 'second only in dignity to Canterbury . . . a large town and an archbishopric, still displaying signs of its Roman elegance' (*AY* 1, N.3.4; Hamilton 1870, 208).

We need, however, to keep in perspective the likely level of sophistication of the government of the earls on behalf of the king in York. Certainly the earls could exact fines and dues of which they presumably took a share, as *Domesday Book* and *Rights and Laws* show (*AY* 1, N.5.1, paragraphs 2, 4; N.5.2, paragraphs 38, 43). At the time of these surveys, and probably much earlier, the city was divided into six shires which probably corresponded with the later governmental subdivisions known as wards (there had been seven but one had been destroyed when the Norman castles were built; *AY* 1, N.2.2, N.1.4). Moreover, there was a royal mint in the city, the only one in northern England (Hill 1981, map 217), with perhaps as many as twelve moneyers active in it at any one time (although we are dependent on numismatic evidence for our knowledge of this) (*AY* 1, N.3.10; Pirie 1975, xliv–lv; Palliser 1990, 14; Metcalf 1987c, 290–1), and the earls were presumably respon-

sible for it and took profits from it. In *Domesday Book,* York had four 'lawmen' (*iudices*) who may have constituted a borough court as distinct from a county court (*AY* 1, N.2.3), although this is not certain (cf. Reynolds 1987, 307–8).

Beyond the city it is very unlikely that the earls deployed anything sophisticated in the way of administrative machinery, so that York's role as a governmental centre is unlikely to have been well developed. It is clear, for example, that the basic mechanisms of the government of the kings of England in the 10th and 11th centuries simply did not extend into Northumbria. The system of counties with county towns and subdivision into hundreds was not present there in any real sense (Hill 1981, maps 83–98, 174–7) although by 1067 x 1069 Yorkshire does seem to have had a sheriff, Gamel son of Osbern, who received a writ from William I (Bates 1998, no.32). Moreover, it is just possible that the two reeves of Earl Harold referred to in *Domesday Book* (*AY* 1, N.5.2, paragraph 11) were government officials, although they could equally well have had responsibility for his private estates. The intensive distribution of mints found in southern and midland England was quite lacking, York being (as noted above) the only one. The area north of the Tees, which was omitted from *Domesday Book,* was probably not subject to geld (taxation); and York was only subject intermittently as is indicated by the statement in *Domesday Book* that York only paid geld when Exeter, Winchester and London did (Tait 1936, 127), although this is of course also an indication of its superior status. It is clear that the sophistication of royal government to be found in southern and midland England was not present in the north, even in the Norman period, and this must have a bearing on our view of the extent to which York was really a capital.

Nevertheless, by the late 11th century York's importance in the political life of the north was not in doubt. It was York which was the focus of a rebellion which expelled Earl Tostig in 1065 (*AY* 1, V.2.4), and it was York which King Harold Hardrada of Norway and Tostig first captured after invading northern England via the Humber in 1066 (*AY* 1, 81, N.1.1). Most eloquent of all of York's importance was William the Conqueror's placing of one of his first northern castles at York, and the subsequent role of the city as a focus for the Northumbrian revolt of 1069–70 (*AY* 1, 82, N.1.2). Likewise it was York that William hastened to recapture and where he symbolically spent Christmas, and where he built a second castle the more effectively to control the city (*AY* 1, 82, N.1.4).

It may be, however, that, as in the period of the Viking kings (see pp.313–14), York's importance owed as much or more to the archbishops as to royal government. The political role of the archbishops in the period of the earls is admittedly less apparent, but York Minster nevertheless had a dominant position in the city. By the end of the 11th century, two of the shires of York were under the full or partial jurisdiction of the archbishop. The first, the archbishop's shire, included Minster Close and took in also the whole north-east part of the Roman fortress (the area north-east of Petergate) and properties in other parts of the city (Palliser 1990, 11–12; Rees Jones 1987 **1**, 87–109). The second, in which the archbishop had the 'third penny' (i.e. one-third of the revenues due to the king), can be located from the evidence of *Rights and Laws* (*AY* 1, N.5.1, paragraph 2) in Walmgate, Fishergate and the area called *Gildgarth*, probably land near Lower Priory Street in the parish of St Mary Bishophill Junior (Rees Jones 1987 **1**, 87–107), although Palliser reads the text to include in this Monkgate, Layerthorpe and Clementhorpe, which Rees Jones would place in the archbishop's shire (Palliser 1990, 12). Aside from its dominant situation, the latter was also a very important shire in commercial terms.

The archbishops also held judicial rights. An inquest of 1106 established that York Minster possessed extensive sanctuary rights in the city, and also rights of holding a court for the affairs of the canons (*AY* 1, N.4.5). The antiquity of these arrangements cannot be demonstrated, but they are unlikely to have been new. The archbishop also possessed a court (*curia*) in York (*AY* 1, N.5.2, paragraph 23), and he had control of two moneyers recorded in *Domesday Book* (*AY* 1, N.3.10). Moreover, later documentation demonstrates the extent to which the ecclesiastical complex around the Minster monopolised the area of the former Roman fortress and thus formed a very significant element indeed in the city's topography (Rees Jones 1987 **1**, 101–4, 111–13).

York as a religious and cultural centre

After the middle of the 9th century, we find none of the evidence for York's status which is so apparent in the time of Alcuin (d. 804). No requests for books such as that sent by the Frankish abbot Lupus of Ferrières in 852 have survived for subsequent years (Whitelock 1979, no.216; Levillain 1964 **2**, 78–81), no evidence of scholars such as Liudger visiting York (*AY* 1, A.3.2), no correspondence between the archbishops of York and churchmen elsewhere on scholarly matters, or indeed on any other. It is true that a large proportion of our evidence for York's reputation in the 8th century is derived from the writings of Alcuin, without which, for example, we would have no inkling of the scholarly aspirations of the 8th-century archbishops. So it is not impossible that York continued its scholarly activities through the 9th century and beyond but that no information about it has survived. There is, however, not even any indirect evidence to support such a possibility, and it seems much more likely that the plundering of the city by the 'great army' in 866 put an end to its pre-eminent position. In fact, we have no information whatsoever about any scholarly or cultural activity associated with the archbishops or church of York between the time of Alcuin and that of Archbishop Oswald (970/1–92), and it is hard to envisage that, given the military and political instability of their times, the archbishops from Wulfhere until Oswald were really in a position to promote ecclesiastical learning and art as their 8th-century predecessors had done. Indeed, one of the great glories of 8th-century York, the church of the *Alma Sophia*, either disappeared physically, or disappeared to such an extent from the historical evidence that its very location — perhaps the church of Holy Trinity Micklegate (*AY* 1, A.4.27), perhaps even the chapter house of the Minster (Norton 1998) — is now a matter of debate.

With Oswald, we find on the archiepiscopal throne of York a churchman who was, if not a patron of learning like his 8th-century predecessors, one of the most important figures in the English church of the late 10th century. He was one of the leaders of the 10th-century reformation of English monasteries and some cathedral churches which made them conform to the Rule of St Benedict (Brooks and Cubitt 1996). Oswald's career, however, had been formed in the south and on the continent, for he was educated in Canterbury where his uncle Oda was archbishop, given a monastery in Winchester, trained at the monastery of Fleury on the Loire, and in 961 appointed bishop of Worcester, a see which he held in plurality with York as did other archbishops of York in this period (Lapidge et al. 1998, 348; see p.313). It was Worcester and not York, however, which he reformed in line with the policy of the 10th century by committing it to a community of monks following the Rule of St Benedict (Robinson 1919), and it was in the south that he established Benedictine monasteries, notably Westbury-on-Trym, Ramsey and Pershore. At York Minster, the cathedral community was not converted into one of Benedictine monks, nor were reformed Benedictine monasteries established in its diocese before the refoundation of Monkwearmouth and Jarrow (Co. Durham) in the early 1070s (Knowles 1963, 165–9). Oswald could have made York Minster the base for a 10th-century reformation in the north; that he did not speaks volumes for the low status and resources of the church in York. Indeed, the only surviving document relating to York Minster in his time is his memorandum on that church's lands, in which the archbishop specifies lands which have been stolen, especially estates which had been acquired 'with his own money' by Archbishop Osketel (954 x 956–70/1) (Robertson 1956, no.54).

Even where cathedral clergy did not live as monks, it was still possible for them to be reformed to the extent of living a communal life as canons, following a rule such as that of St Chrodegang as many cathedral chapters on the continent did (Barrow 1994, 32). In the case of York, however, it seems clear that the Minster clergy did not live communally, for it was not until the time of Archbishop Ealdred (1061–9) that a refectory was established for them to eat in common (*AY* 1, V.4.5). *Domesday Book* and a charter of Henry I (issued between 1102 and 1106) show the canons living in individual houses (*AY* 1, N.4.5, N.5.2, paragraph 23, N.5.3, paragraph 7; *EYC* **1**, 118, no.128). Moreover, an inquest of 1246 remembered that they were called Culdees (*AY* 1, N.4.10), a term which was invariably applied to canons who were uninfluenced by reforming ideas and lived separate lives (Reeves 1864).

Oswald's successor Archbishop Ealdwulf (992–1002) seems to have lacked distinction, but his successor, Wulfstan II (1002–23), was a very distinguished homilist and statesmen, who wrote a series of homilies in Old English, including the famous *Sermon of the Wolf to the English* (Whitelock 1976), contributed significantly to the law-codes of Æthelred the Unready and Cnut, was responsible for the *Northumbrian Priests' Law* (see p.306) and may have composed sections of the D version of the *Anglo-Saxon Chronicle*.

Although he was responsible for additions made to the York Gospels, and may have been concerned with the Minster's possessions at Otley, Ripon and Sherburn-in-Elmet, surveys of which are amongst those additions (Barker 1986, 85, 104–5), his career, like Oswald's, was formed in the south. In 996 he had become bishop of London where he was already using his pen-name Lupus ('wolf'), and in the year of his appointment to York (1002) he was like Oswald made bishop of Worcester, a see he held in plurality with York until 1016 (Lapidge et al. 1998, 494–5; Whitelock 1965; Whitelock 1968). His successor, Ælfric Puttoc (1023–51), is known to have endowed Beverley and possibly to have concerned himself with regaining some of York's lands, but nothing is known of any other distinction on his part, although he seems to have been involved in national politics (Cooper 1970, 14–18). The next bishop, Cynesige (1051–60), has left little trace (although he too is said to have endowed Beverley; ibid., 22). The next incumbent, Ealdred (1061–9), was concerned with reform (we have already seen him building a refectory for the canons of York, and he built one also for the canons of Southwell; *AY* 1, V.4.5) and patronage of literature, for to him was dedicated the *Life of John of Beverley* by Folcard, a Flemish hagiographer working in England (Cooper 1970, 23–9; Lapidge et al. 1998, 153). As in the case of Oswald and Wulfstan II, however, his career was a product of the south, for he was by origin a monk of Winchester, becoming abbot of Tavistock (c.1027–c.1043) and bishop of Worcester in 1046. It was probably following an embassy to Cologne in 1054 that he brought back to England a copy of a pontifical (a liturgical book containing the offices proper to a bishop) known as the Romano-German Pontifical (Lapidge 1983) which was to be influential on the liturgy in southern England — but not, so far as we can judge, at York.

There is nothing in the above to suggest that York Minster in the Anglo-Scandinavian period aspired to the glories of its 8th-century past, and much to convince us that its resources in that period were poor as a result of loss of lands, and its standards at best mediocre. Its restoration and rebuilding by Archbishop Thomas of Bayeux (1070–1100; *AY* 1, N. 4.2) was necessitated either by the fire damage suffered by the church in 1069 or by the Viking sack of 1075 (*AY* 1, N.4.1, N.4.3), but there is no reason to suppose that he would not in any case have needed to improve greatly the standards of the church to bring it into line with those of continental churchmen like himself, even if it had not been damaged in the ways mentioned (Barlow 1979, 54–103).

Partly as a result of the Viking invasions, York was at the end of the Anglo-Scandinavian period an archbishopric with only one bishopric subject to it. This was Durham, which was notionally within its archdiocese, but seems to have owed little real obedience — there is no evidence, for example, that York influenced the appointment of bishops (Cooper 1968). Only in the early 12th century did York become the archbishopric for the refounded sees of Whithorn and Carlisle (Brentano 1953; Summerson 1993 **1**, 30–8).

This is not to say that York Minster and the church in general in York in the Anglo-Scandinavian period were not functioning in an adequate way, and had not been able rapidly to assimilate Viking incomers to Christianity as in the rest of eastern England. The only historical evidence we have for the persistence of paganism in Northumbria is provided by two clauses in the *Northumbrian Priests' Law*: one specifies a penalty for anyone who 'carries on any heathen practice, either by sacrifice or divination, or practises witchcraft by any means, or worship of idols' (paragraph 48); the other forbids keeping 'on anyone's land a sanctuary round a stone or a tree or a well or any such nonsense' (paragraph 54) (Liebermann 1903 **1**, 383; Whitelock 1979, no.53). It is not clear, however, how far these practices were actually being followed, and not clear anyway that the clauses relate specifically to York (cf. Whitelock 1965, 225–6). It is assumed, of course, that the Viking kings of York were mostly pagans, although we have seen that the King Guthfrith who died in 895 was probably a Christian, possibly owing his position to the community of St Cuthbert, and certainly having been buried in York Minster in 895. Sihtric Caoch, on the other hand, was certainly a pagan since in 926 he made an agreement with King Athelstan, which he subsequently repudiated, involving his conversion to Christianity (*AY* 1, 67). There is, however, a faint possibility that Eric Bloodaxe was in some sense Christian, since the *Life of Catroe* refers to him as being married to a relative of the saint (*AY* 1, V.2.3). There is an entry for 'King Eric' in the *Liber Vitae* of Durham, but this probably does not refer to Eric Bloodaxe and is therefore not relevant to this question, for the entry is 12th-century and is associated

with one for Botilda, possibly the queen of a later and entirely Christian King Eric Ejegod of Denmark (1095–1103), to whom this entry presumably refers (Insley forthcoming; Thompson 1923, fo.55v.)

Below the level of the kings, there is every reason to suppose that Anglo-Scandinavian York was a Christian city, although the historical evidence is very slight. Ulf, son of Thorold, must have been a wealthy inhabitant of Viking extraction (to judge from his name), who used his wealth to endow the Minster with lands in the city, allegedly donating the early 11th-century Horn of Ulf, now in the Minster Treasury, as a symbol of his gift (Hill and Brooke 1977, 39, pl.2 and n.; Rees Jones 1987 **1**, 110) (see p.458 and Fig.117). His son was Styr, who (according to the *Siege of Durham*; *AY* 1, S.53) married his daughter to Earl Uhtred of Northumbria and who was (according to the *History of St Cuthbert*; *AY* 1, S.47) responsible for granting Darlington to the community of St Cuthbert (Arnold 1882 **1**, 212, 216, cf. 83) . Within York itself, Grim and Æse, named on the dedication stone in the church, were responsible for the foundation of St Mary Castlegate, and were, to judge from their names, men of Viking origin, although evidently thoroughly Christianised (*AY* 1, V.4.6) (see p.353).

The provision of churches in Anglo-Scandinavian York is potentially a clue to the level of Christianity in the city. In comparison with other cities, we might expect to find, for example, great abbeys such as that of St Augustine at Canterbury (Brooks 1977) or the New Minster and Nunnaminster at Winchester (Biddle 1975, 127–30). We might also expect to find collegiate churches, that is churches served by communities of secular priests or canons like the Minster itself. As noted above, the 10th-century monastic reformation had no effect on Northumbria in general before the 1070s, and we consequently find no Benedictine monasteries in York. St Olave's, which Earl Siward founded and where he was buried in 1055, is described as a monastery (*mynstre*) (*AY* 1, V.4.4; Cubbin 1996, 74), but is more likely to have been a college of canons or secular priests. Holy Trinity Micklegate was apparently also a college of canons, for the charter establishing it as a monastery in 1086 referred to it as 'built in former times by canons' (*AY* 1, N.4.15; *EYC* **6**, 67–8). Fragments of 10th-century sculpture from the church (Lang et al. 1991, 80–1), and the survival of a complex of lands which may represent the residual lands of a large pre-conquest estate, suggest that its origins lay in the Anglo-Scandinavian period or even before (Burton 1999, 45–51; Morris 1986, 84–6; Solloway 1910, 41; *AY* 1, 157). It has been argued that it was in origin the church of the *Alma Sophia*, built by Archbishop Æthelberht, but this is uncertain (see p.316).

It is equally uncertain whether the Hospital of St Peter (St Leonard) was a pre-conquest foundation. The tradition that King Athelstan founded it, granting thraves of corn to the Minster to establish it, is found only in the hospital's late medieval cartulary and is unlikely to be reliable, especially as it is inconsistent with the earlier record of an inquest held in 1246 which attributes the foundation to King William I (*AY* 1, N.4.10; Raine 1879 **3**, 162–3). It was not uncommon for churches in the later medieval period to name Athelstan as a donor without, apparently, any real basis for the claim, as was the case with Beverley (Cambridge and Morris 1989, 11). While it is possible that the allusion to a grant of thraves, also part of the Beverley tradition, points to a genuine origin in the 10th century (Palliser 1996, 211), this is very doubtful, and it is best to regard the hospital as a foundation of the Anglo-Norman period, which is how its 11th-century foundation charter presents it (*AY* 1, N.4.9).

Only one parish church can be definitely proved on the basis of historical evidence to have been in existence in the pre-conquest period: St Mary Castlegate which has a dedication inscription of the Anglo-Scandinavian period (see p.318). The existence in that period of a second church, All Saints Pavement, may also be demonstrable if it is indeed referred to in the corrupt inscription on the Anglian helmet from Coppergate (*AY* 1, A.4.32). It was certainly in existence in the late 11th century, since it is referred to in *Domesday Book* (*AY* 1, N.4.17, N.5.2, paragraph 3). Otherwise, we have only sources of the late 11th and early 12th centuries, *Domesday Book* and charters, which create a presumption but not a certainty that the churches they refer to were founded before the Norman conquest. Even so, these sources allow us to document only the following thirteen parish churches (see Fig.129**s**):

A church of St Saviour (possibly that in St Saviourgate) (*AY* 1, N.4.13)

All Saints Fishergate (*AY* 1, N.4.16)

All Saints Pavement (*AY* 1, N.4.17)

Holy Trinity (possibly Goodramgate) (*AY* 1, N.4.18)

St Andrew Fishergate (*AY* 1, N.4.19)

St Crux (Holy Cross) (*AY* 1, N.4.20)

St Cuthbert (*AY* 1, N.4.21)

St Helen Fishergate (*AY* 1, N.4.22)

St Martin Micklegate (later St Martin-cum-Gregory) (*AY* 1, N.4.23)

St Mary Bishophill Junior (*AY* 1, N.4.24; cf. *AY* 8/2, 85–9)

St Mary Castlegate (*AY* 1, N.4.25)

St Michael Spurriergate (*AY* 1, N.4.13)

An unnamed church belonging to a certain Odo the Crossbowman (*AY* 1, N.5.2, paragraph 18).

It seems very unlikely, however, that the thirteen churches for which we have historical evidence were anything like the sum total, and it is probable that a considerable number of York's 40 or so later medieval parish churches (Wilson and Mee 1998, 11–13; Raine 1955, *passim*) were in fact in existence in the pre-conquest period. The reasons for thinking this are as follows. First, comparisons made with other towns, since thirteen seems a very small number when compared with Norwich, for which *Domesday Book* records between 49 and 54 churches and chapels in 1086 (Campbell 1975, 3), or London, for which in the medieval period there were over 100 churches (Brooke and Keir 1975, 122–3). Secondly, the fact that *Domesday Book* is notoriously uneven in its recording of churches — in the case of York, it seems only to mention a church in cases of change of ownership (Palliser 1990, 15), and it rarely specifies that a church existed in 1066 as opposed to 1086 when the survey was made. Thirdly, the fact that studies of the non-written evidence have already expanded the number of churches certain or likely to have existed in the Anglo-Scandinavian period and have the potential to expand this still further in the future (see pp.496–7). Already the evidence of surviving pre-conquest sculpture from York churches establishes a presumption that an additional two churches were in existence in the Anglo-Scandinavian period even though we have no historical evidence for this (St Denys and St Mary Bishophill Senior; Lang et al. 1991, 81–2, 88–95), while archaeological excavation has done the same for St Helen-on-the Walls (*AY* 10/1).

Some of the parish churches of York may have come into existence as the type of loosely organised collegiate church which modern historians have called a 'minster' (Cambridge and Rollason 1995; Blair 1995), although this is not provable. Many, however, were probably founded as *Eigenkirche* or proprietary churches (that is churches founded by individuals or groups on a quasi-private basis), since the period in which such proprietary churches were founded most frequently was precisely the Anglo-Scandinavian period (Brooke and Keir 1975, 131–43). It may be that the dedication stone in St Mary Castlegate is in fact proof of the existence of a church of this type, founded by the donors named on the stone as a proprietary church (see p.318). Another indication may be the reference in *Domesday Book* to the church which belonged to Odo the Crossbowman (*AY* 1, N.4.29), who was himself a substantial land-owner (Keats-Rohan and Thornton 1997, 141) and presumably acquired the church from an Anglo-Scandinavian owner or owners. Here too there is potential for further elucidation by archaeological work as it has been possible to show that, at Winchester, the church of St Mary Tanner Street went through a stage of development in which the church door opened only into a private dwelling, presumably that belonging to the person or persons who had founded it as a proprietary church (Biddle 1972, 104–7).

In the 11th century, proprietary churches were a source of anxiety to church reformers, who feared excessive domination of the church by the laity, which might bring about a decline in the standards of religious observance (Tellenbach 1993). The *Northumbrian Priests' Law* shows just this concern in a clause (paragraph 52) which forbids anyone from wrongfully driving a priest from a church (Liebermann 1903 **1**, 380–5; Whitelock 1979, no.53). It was, of course, a powerful defence against lay domination if a priest could not be removed by a layman, even if the church accepted that he could be installed by one. More explicit in this respect are the clauses which forbid trafficking in churches (paragraph 20) and bringing a church under subjection (paragraph 21). Priests too are forbidden from deserting their churches (paragraph 28) and buying or selling another's church 'unless anyone becomes guilty of a capital crime so that he is henceforth unworthy to minister at the altar' (paragraph 2). It is of course impossible to evaluate how effective a set of regulations was, but it is striking that in the *Northumbrian Priests' Law* the compiler is legislating in some detail not only to mitigate the potentially deleterious effects of proprietary churches,

but also to regulate the collective life and discipline of the clergy in general. 'If anyone offer wrong to any priest,' reads one clause, 'all his colleagues are to be zealous about obtaining compensation with the help of the bishop' (paragraph 1). Priests must not neglect the summons of the bishop or the archbishop; they must not refuse anyone baptism or confession; they must fetch chrism 'at the proper time'; they must baptise children within nine days of birth; they must direct the people about festivals and fasts; they must celebrate mass under proper circumstances, and so on (paragraphs 4–18). References to the bishop show, what is in any case clear, that this code was not exclusively directed at the church of York. Of course, there are indications that the clergy were more secularised than an archbishop like Wulfstan II would have wished. They are forbidden, for example, from bringing weapons into a church (paragraph 37), and from becoming 'a gleeman or tavern minstrel' (paragraph 41). But such criticisms of the clergy were common in later ages too, and the general impression of the *Northumbrian Priests' Law* is that we are dealing, in the early 11th century at any rate, with a well-regulated and well-organised clergy.

Society and economy of York

It is on York's society and economy that the historical sources cast least light, until *Rights and Laws* and *Domesday Book* (*AY* 1, S.50–1). The interpretation of these is, of course, problematic because they relate to the period after 1069–70, although *Domesday Book* does in part refer back to the time of Edward of the Confessor. *Domesday Book*, however, is little concerned with economic and social matters as such, and about the former in particular it has relatively little to tell us (Darby 1987, 117–18; Reynolds 1987, 308). Nonetheless, something can be made of the historical evidence, even if in a negative way. What has been established about the city's character from the preceding sections may have a bearing on how we evaluate its development from a commercial and industrial viewpoint.

For all its limitations, *Domesday Book* makes clear that York at the end of the Anglo-Scandinavian period was a city of considerable size. It was the largest town for which a description exists in that survey, admittedly because *Domesday Book* omits Winchester and London (Barlow et al. 1976, 5; Tait 1936, 118). Nevertheless, *Domesday Book* assigns to York in 1066 a total of 1,607 dwellings (*mansiones*) in the six of its seven shires (administrative subdivisions) which were still occupied in 1086 (*AY* 1, N.5.2, paragraphs 1–2). Had the seventh not been destroyed by the Normans for the construction of the castles, the total might have been of the order of 1,875, giving (depending on how we calculate the relationship between dwellings and the number of their inhabitants) a population of 9,000 or considerably more (Palliser 1990, 12–13). Even at the figure of 9,000, York was (by James Tait's calculations) well ahead of the next largest towns surveyed in *Domesday Book*, Norwich with a population of perhaps 6,600, Lincoln with a populaton of upwards of 5,500, and Thetford with 4,750 (Tait 1936, 76). That York was a very large city a century earlier is suggested by a passage in the *Life of St Oswald*, archbishop of York (970/1–92), which forms a prelude to a story about the archbishop's time in York and which emphasises the populousness of the city:

*The city rejoices in the multitude of its population, which, counting men and women but not infants and children, is numbered at not less than 30,000 (AY 1, V.3.1; Raine 1879 **1**, 454).*

The population figure can be questioned, especially as it is so much higher than the figures deducible from *Domesday Book*, but the author of the *Life*, who was almost certainly the scholar Byrhtferth of Ramsey (*AY* 1, S.45), was a contemporary and, even if we cannot have confidence in his statistical precision, we must accept that he regarded York as a very substantial city.

Another indication of the relative importance of York is provided by the figure for the 'farm', that is, the consolidated payment for the city's various monetary renders which the sheriff made to the royal government. In the absence of a *Domesday Book* description of London, that city's is not known, but later sources give it as £300 in the time of William I (Tait 1936, 154). In 1066, York's was £53 (*AY* 1, N.5.2, paragraph 22), the highest of any English town for which we have a figure. In 1086, it was £100, equal to Lincoln's but more than any other city (although Norwich's figure of £90 may need to be as much as doubled since it does not include separate payments made to the sheriff) (Tait 1936, 154, 184). The farm is admittedly not a good indicator of status, since its amount could have been influenced by other factors, such as royal hostility to the town in question, but

the scale of York's payment must in part have reflected its resources.

There is enough evidence in *Domesday Book* and *Rights and Laws* (*AY* 1, N.2.2) to suggest that the shires of York recorded by *Domesday Book* corresponded broadly to the area of the later medieval city, thus giving an indication of its size in the late 11th century. Moreover, the implication of *Domesday Book* is that they were actually settled, for the account of York mentions the laying waste of the original seventh shire for the destruction of the castles, a process which swallowed up at least one important tenement, the house of the Northumbrian rebel Merleswein (*AY* 1, N.1.4). Tenements could be densely packed, as indicated by *Domesday Book*'s reference to William de Percy having seven dwellings (messuages) in a frontage of 50ft. Moreover, it may be significant that where *Domesday Book* speaks of the men of York cultivating land, it is a reference to the extramural area attached to the city (*AY* 1, N.5.2, paragraph 24). Even the area taken in for the King's Pool, presumed to be part of the Norman defences of the city, was being used previously for two mills which were destroyed in the process of making the pool (*AY* 1, N.1.5, N.5.2, paragraph 24).

Is it possible to discern from the historical sources the reasons for York's prominence as a city? Unsatisfactory as they are for answering this question, some lines of thought can nevertheless be suggested. First, the prominence of the church in York may have been a factor in its growth. It seems likely that the church in York was concerned with financial affairs, if it was indeed responsible for the St Peter coinage, and we know in any case that the church played an important role in many parts of England in fostering urban development (Reynolds 1977, 40–1; Beresford 1967, 326–7). At a later date, the development of the boroughs of St Alban's and Bury St Edmund's under the auspices of their respective churches are classic examples (Reynolds 1977, 41–2; Lobel 1935, 1–15). It is unfortunately impossible from the historical sources to corroborate the hypothesis suggested by archaeological and topographical analysis that the church played a leading role in the planning and laying out of the quarter around Coppergate and the reorientation of the river crossing to the line of the present Ouse Bridge (Hall 1978).

Secondly, York's role as a political centre must have affected its urban growth. As noted above, the extent of York's position as a capital may have been more limited than is often asserted, but the fact remains that the Viking kings were closely associated with it, and that their wealth, whether acquired by trade or by plunder, must have enriched it considerably. An influx of Viking silver by this means is surely the best explanation for the sudden increase in silver content from the almost wholly base coins (stycas) of the 9th-century Northumbrian kings (see p.325) to the silver-rich pennies of the period after the Viking capture of the city (Grierson and Blackburn 1986, 295–303, 320–5). Moreover, the presence of mints in York, both royal and archiepiscopal, was itself a source of enrichment for the city, since minting was a profitable activity with the moneyers taking a proportion of the proceeds (Brooke 1950, 79–80). Under the Viking kings, moneyers seem mostly to have come from abroad (see p.342). They were in fact men of high status, and it is no accident that of the twelve names who witnessed *Rights and Laws* (*AY* 1, N.5.1, paragraph 6), no fewer than five (Oudergrim, Oudolf, Ulfkil, Ouderbern and Hardolf) can be identified with moneyers of York whose names appear on York coins of William I's reign (*AY* 1, N.3.10; Martin Allen, pers. comm.). The residence of moneyers in York would therefore also have been a source of enrichment, as would the presence in York of earls and of aristocrats such as Merleswein (see p.321) who were no doubt in part drawn to the city by its political importance (cf. Worcester; Baker and Holt 1996, 140). Aside from Merleswein, we have a clue to aristocratic presence in York in Ulf and his son Styr (see p.318), possibly the latter's enemy Thurbrand if it is his house referred to in *Rights and Laws* (Morris 1992; *AY* 1, N.5.1, paragraph 2), and the founders of St Mary Castlegate (see p.318), assuming them to have been of comparable status. Other inhabitants included, intermittently, the bishop of Durham who had a house in York in the time of *Domesday Book* (*AY* 1, N.2.6, N.5.2, paragraph 3) and very likely in the Anglo-Scandinavian period also.

Thirdly, the historical sources reflect to some extent York's role as a commercial centre. As we have seen, it is in this respect that *Domesday Book* has least information to offer, but there are some hints in *Rights and Laws* and in earlier sources. The first, and most important of these latter, is the passage in the *Life of St Oswald*, which, in addition to the city's populousness, refers to its commercial activities:

The city is crammed beyond expression, and enriched with the treasures of merchants, who come from all parts, but above all from the Danish people (*AY* 1, V.3.1; Raine 1879 **1**, 454).

We have no reason not to accept this comment on the mercantile wealth of the city, which finds confirmation in the archaeological record (Hall 1994), and on the importance of merchants from all parts, especially Danish merchants, although it should be emphasised that the merchants in question may have come from elsewhere in England (the Danelaw perhaps), rather than directly from Denmark.

The second passage, which refers to the year 974 and is much less reliable and specific, being derived from the 13th-century *Flowers of History* by Roger of Wendover, corroborates the *Life of St Oswald* to the extent of referring to York merchants who landed on the Isle of Thanet and were taken captive by the islanders and robbed of their goods (*AY* 1, V.3.2; Coxe 1841 **1**, 414–15). Still less reliable, because not only 13th-century in date but also literary in character, is the third passage, comprising the end of the story in *The Saga of Egil* of how the Icelander Egil was shipwrecked and found himself in the York of Eric Bloodaxe. After the king had spared Egil, who was an enemy, the saga relates that Egil's companions and shipmates were 'able to sell their cargo', presumably in York, before travelling to the south (*AY* 1, V.2.2, 169).

Fourthly, *Rights and Laws* illuminates in some detail the commercial activity of the city. We find mention of what may have been a guild-hall (*lei Gildegard*) in the Old French version (*AY* 1, N.2.7, N.5.1, paragraph 2), although this need not of course have been the hall of a commercial guild. The survey also refers to merchants coming to York with horses or waggons to pay toll, to sales of fish and grain in Walmgate and Fishergate, and to a fishery which paid tax to the archbishop (*AY* 1, N.3.5–7, N.5.1, paragraphs 2–3).

Fifthly, although *Domesday Book* contributes little to this subject, it does refer to a meat-market (probably in the Shambles) (*AY* 1, N.3.9, N.5.2, paragraph 4), which may have been involved in trade at least with York's hinterland. Further indication of commercial vigour may be found in William of Malmesbury's statement, that York 'enfolds in its bosom, with buildings on both banks of the River

Ouse, ships coming from Germany and Ireland' (*AY* 1, N.3.4; Hamilton 1870, 208). We must of course be aware that development may have occurred between 1066 and William's time, but it is hard to believe that what he describes did not in large measure exist in the Anglo-Scandinavian period.

Is it possible to take the enquiry a stage further and explore, in the light of the historical sources, the reasons for York's success as a commercial centre? *Domesday Book* casts a little light on the city's communications, referring to the routeways in Yorkshire by land and water, and specifically to royal protection for traffic on the road to York, and to the duty of the burgesses of York to escort the king's messengers 'with their boats and other means of navigation' from Torksey to York (*AY* 1, N.3.5). The city's access to these routes must have facilitated its commercial development, as also must the fact that it had no rivals in the north. Whereas southern England was characterised from the time of King Alfred onwards by a large number of towns which each came to have its own mint, urban development in northern England was restricted to only a few centres. Aside from Pocklington, Tanshelf and Dadsley, which were towns on a much smaller scale, York had no rivals in the whole of Yorkshire. Its nearest rival to the south was Lincoln, and it had none to the north, just as it was the only mint north of the Humber (Hill 1981, maps 234, 217).

Other lines of thought can only be of the most general type. York's role as a political and ecclesiastical focus is very likely to have stimulated its commercial activity, if only because men of status and wealth were resident there (see p.322). Its hinterland in the Vale of York, as seen in *Domesday Book,* was relatively rich and populous, at least in the west (Darby and Maxwell 1962, 17, 81–2, 161, 231), and this may have fed its commercial growth. The passage from the *Life of St Oswald* cited above implies that foreign and particularly Danish merchants were an important element in the city's growth, but beyond this it is not possible to go. That the Scandinavian element in the population was very considerable is shown by the moneyers' names (see p.322), the street names (Palliser 1978), and by the Scandinavian names listed in *Domesday Book* (*AY* 1, N.5.2; cf. Feilitzen 1937). It is not possible, however, to prove that York's commercial development was stimulated by Danish presence in itself. Although towns within Danish-settled areas (Lincoln, Thetford, Norwich, for example) experienced considerable growth, similar growth occurred in towns unaffected by Scandinavian activity, for example, London, Canterbury and Exeter (Reynolds 1977, 37–42).

Conclusion

This chapter has aimed to define the extent of what the historical sources can contribute to the understanding of Anglo-Scandinavian York, and to raise the problems and difficulties of interpretation of York which those sources pose. The conclusions it has offered have been only partial ones, based wherever possible solely on those historical sources. Just as we have underlined the uncertainty in the historical sources as to the role of York as a political centre and as a residence for the Viking kings and the earls who were their successors, archaeological investigation as to the existence and location of a royal or comital palace would offer the potential of a major breakthrough with respect to this problem, although even the discovery of structures would not necessarily mean (as seen in the cases of Cheddar and Northampton; Blair 1996) that these were readily distinguishable as royal or comital, as distinct from ecclesiastical, complexes. As to York's role as a minting centre, remarkable discoveries have already been made in the case of the Coppergate dies (admittedly the lead strips formerly regarded as 'trial pieces' are now more plausibly interpreted as customs tags; Archibald 1991, 335–6), although it would be very desirable for archaeological work to clarify the relationship between the places where coins were minted and the foci of political power in the city. Does, for example, the lack of proximity between the Coppergate finds (which include a St Peter's coin die) and the centre of ecclesiastical power in Minster Close lead us to doubt the connection between the ecclesiastical authorities and those coins postulated above? Or were the dies found at Coppergate related to the production of customs tags rather than to minting?

Archaeology and related art historical studies have potentially a major contribution to make to the understanding of the development of parish churches, both their chronology (how many had been established in the Anglo-Scandinavian period) and the nature of their development, particularly the question of how far they were proprietary churches. Archaeological investigation of cemeteries in York has also considerable potential for understanding of the level of Christianisation and culture of the population, as is evidenced most clearly by the Anglo-Scandinavian cemetery under the Minster (Phillips and Heywood 1995, 433 67, 489–521). Finally, and perhaps most importantly, archaeology appears of crucial importance in comparison with the historical sources in understanding the social and economic development of the city. The data derivable from the historical sources gives a wholly inadequate impression of the nature, early date and scale of York's commercial and industrial development and, although it does cast light on the population at the end of the Anglo-Scandinavian period, it is on archaeology that the onus rests to provide a more detailed picture of the state and status of that population.

The Coinage of Scandinavian York

By Mark Blackburn

For more than two hundred years before the Scandinavian conquest of the city, York had been producing its own independent coinage. It was among the first Anglo-Saxon mints to be established, striking a distinctive series of gold shillings in the mid-7th century and an overtly royal Northumbrian coinage in silver from the time of King Aldfrith (685–704) (Metcalf 1993–4 **1**, 49–51, 117–19; **3**, 576–600). In the later 8th century, however, Northumbria became increasingly isolated, politically and economically, and it did not adopt the model of the reformed Carolingian silver penny that was current in most of Europe. Its small dumpy coins, known today as stycas, became increasingly debased, until latterly they were made of pure brass (Metcalf and Northover 1987).

The numismatic evidence calls into question the traditional chronology of the 9th-century Northumbrian kings and archbishops of York, suggesting that some transposition had occurred in the regnal dates as recorded in the later documentary sources. However, there is no consensus on the degree of dislocation (Pagan 1969; Lyon 1987; Dumville 1987), and in consequence it remains an open question whether the large, idiosyncratic coinage of stycas came to an end as a result of some unrecorded crisis in the 850s or with the Viking conquest of York in 866/7. The last coins are in the name of King Osberht and Archbishop Wulfhere, and there is none of Ælla or the nominal English kings that the Vikings established after 867. What is important for our purposes is that by the time of the Scandinavian settlement of Northumbria in 875/6 there had been no minting at York for a decade or more, and local expertise had been lost. Even the circulation of stycas in York is unlikely to have continued beyond the 870s. Thus, there was no continuity between the Northumbrian mint and the Anglo-Scandinavian mint at York, so that the new Viking rulers had to establish a system of coinage from scratch.

There was a dramatic change in the pattern of minting in England between the middle and the end of the 9th century to which the Scandinavian rulers of the Danelaw contributed in no small measure. No longer was virtually all the silver coined in the south-east, for the Danes had established a series of mints in the southern Danelaw, as well as that in York, which had shifted the balance northwards. In the same period Alfred (871–99) had started to create a network of inland mints to support the fortified burghs in Wessex and Mercia, which was further extended in the 10th century as the Danelaw mints passed under English control (Blackburn 1996, 162–5). The output of the Scandinavian mints in the Danelaw was formidable at times, and in the later 10th and 11th centuries Lincoln and York would be the most productive mints in England after London (Metcalf 1998, 18–21).

The Anglo-Scandinavian coinages struck at York between c.895 and 954 are rich and varied, and their sequence and chronology have been progressively refined over the years. Our understanding of these coinages was quite simply chaotic until Dolley (1958) applied to it a study of the hoard evidence. This demonstrated that all the St Peter coins and the coinage of Ragnald I belonged to the period before 927, rather than after 939 as had generally been thought, while conversely the *Triquetra* coins in the name of a Sihtric belonged to the later rather than the earlier of these periods. Further significant changes have been made since then, in particular through the recognition that some coins of the kings of York were actually struck in the Five Boroughs, which was at times a dependent territory of the York kingdom.

The sequence of coin types produced at York spanning the various changes of control between Danish, Norse and English kings is summarised in Table 4, which also shows the situation in the Five Boroughs. This chapter will not describe the coinages in detail, for they are admirably surveyed in Blunt, Stewart and Lyon (1989, chs. 4 and 14) or more succinctly by Grierson and Blackburn (1986, 316–25), partly superseding Dolley's very readable survey (1965). It will focus instead on particular aspects that may assist our understanding of the history, economy and organisation of the York kingdom.

Information about the currency of Scandinavian York comes entirely from the coins themselves and the contexts in which they have been found. The York

Table 4 Coinages at York and in the Five Boroughs, c.885–954

York	Five Boroughs

Danish settlement from 876
Imitative 'Alfred' coinage, possibly struck at York before c.895
	Danish settlement from 877
	Anonymous imitations, from mid-880s
	   'Alfred', *London monogram* type
	   'Alfred', *Two-Line* (*Horizontal*) type
	   Guthfrith (883–95)
	   Halfdan (mid-880s?)

York regal coinage, c.895–905 Sigeferth (*c*.895–900) Æthelwold (900–2) Cnut (c.900–5)	*From mint(s) in the Five Boroughs or northern Danelaw* 'Alfred', 'Oxford' (ORSNAFORDA) type 'Alfred', 'Canterbury' types 'Alfred', *Two-Line* types 'Cnut'/'Quentovic'
Anonymous coinage, c.905–19 Swordless St Peter type	'Edward the Elder', *Two-Line* type

Hiberno-Norse control, 919–27
Ragnald I (919–20/1): St Peter with monogram? and three
   regal issues
Sword St Peter, c.921–7:
   Cross type
   Mallet type
   Hammer type
	Hiberno-Norse control of parts, 919–27
	Sihtric II Caech (920/1–7)
	   Cross type
	   Mallet type
	   Hammer type
	St Martin (Lincoln)
	Anonymous *Sword* type

English control 927–39
Athelstan (924–39), from 927
   Church type
   Circumscription type
	English control 927–40
	Athelstan (924–39), from 927
	Edmund (939–46), until 940

Hiberno-Norse control 939–944/5
Olaf Guthfrithsson (939–41)
   Raven type
Olaf Sihtricsson (1st reign, 941–944/5)
   Triquetra/Banner type
   Circumscription Cross and *Cross Moline* types
Sihtric (c.943–4)
   Triquetra/Banner type
   Circumscription Cross type
Ragnald II Guthfrithsson (943–944/5)
   Triquetra/Banner type
   Cross Moline type
	Hiberno-Norse control 940–2
	Olaf Guthfrithsson or
	Olaf Sihtricsson
	   Raven type (?Lincoln)
	   Horizontal type (?Lincoln and Stamford)
	   Circumscription type (Derby)
	
	English control from 942

English control, 944/5–7 Edmund (939–46), *Horizontal* type, from 944/5 Eadred (946–55), *Horizontal* type, until 947	
Norse control, 947–8 Eric Bloodaxe (1st reign, 947–8) *Horizontal* type 'Eltangerht', *Horizontal* type (here or later)	
English control, 948–50? Eadred, *Horizontal* type	

Norse control, 950?–54
Olaf Sihtricsson (2nd reign, 950?–52)
   Circumscription type
   Flower type
Eric Bloodaxe (2nd reign, 952–4)
   Sword type	

excavations have yielded impressive material from this period, including fourteen coins, two dies and three lead pieces with the impression of dies (*AY* 18/1, 53–7). If we include stray finds from York and from the county of Yorkshire, the number of single-finds known from the northern Danelaw amounts to 40 coins (see Appendix, pp.347–9). This is precious evidence for coin circulation, but to study the coinages themselves we must rely on the much larger number of coins found in hoards. Their coverage is very uneven, depending on chance and on the economic and political circumstances which led to the formation and non-recovery of hoards. Thus for the earliest phase down to c.905 we are well informed by the massive hoard found in 1840 at Cuerdale in Lancashire, one of the largest Viking-Age treasures unearthed in the British Isles or Scandinavia. For other periods, notably the 940s, we are very short of material and long for new finds to enhance our knowledge.

Imitative coinages in the northern Danelaw

The earliest coinages in the Danelaw followed the designs of the contemporary issues of Wessex and Mercia, often even copying the names of King Alfred and his moneyers. It is not unusual for newly formed states to establish their first monetary system by emulating the coinage of a successful neighbour. In due course they would normally replace this with a new coinage of distinctive design that would provide both a symbol of independence and a means of excluding the foreign coin from circulation, enabling the state to exploit a closed currency. This is the pattern we find in the Danelaw, where the initial imitative phase was succeeded in the mid-890s by strong distinctive coinages (Blackburn 2001a): the St Edmund issue in the south and the York regal coinage in the north.

Although the northern Danelaw was the first region of England to be settled by the Danish army, the rulers of the southern Danelaw appear to have taken the lead in establishing mints to produce coins. The recent redating of Alfred's *London Monogram* and *Two-Line* issues to c.880 rather than after 886 (Blackburn 1998, 120–1) has allowed us to move back the beginning of the coinages in the southern Danelaw to the mid-880s or earlier. Further north there is considerable uncertainty about the beginning of Scandinavian coinage at York — whether it commenced with the

York regal coinage of c.895 or with an earlier anonymous issue. The difficulty stems from the fact that only a small proportion of the imitative coins carries the name of a Scandinavian ruler, and a tiny handful that of the mint where they were struck. This makes their attribution difficult. There are some forty coins of Guthrum (880–90), the leader of the southern Danelaw, but only one names Guthfrith (c.883–95), his contemporary as king of York (Fig.79, 1), and this coin was probably struck in the Five Boroughs since in style it is close to coins of that region (Blackburn 1989a, 19). This need not come as a surprise, for during Guthfrith's reign the *Chronicle of Æthelweard, s.a.* 894, records some activity of the York Danes in an area west of Stamford, although it may have been no more than raiding. At other times kings of York exercised authority south of the Humber, and Sihtric Caech (921–7), Olaf (or Anlaf) Guthfrithsson (939–41) and Olaf Sihtricsson (941–4) all had coins struck there.

Among the earliest coins from this imitative phase are those that copy Alfred's *London Monogram* type. They were present in the Stamford hoard, deposited c.890, and on some specimens the monogram was adapted from reading *Londonia* to *Lincolla,* for Lincoln (Mossop 1970, pl.1, 1–6). Production of these imitations seems to have been centred on the Five Boroughs. They did circulate in East Anglia, as shown by five specimens found in excavations at Ipswich, but their absence from the Ashton (Essex) hoard, deposited c.895, implies that the type was superseded in that region by the *Two-Line* (or *Horizontal*) type. The only *London Monogram* imitation found in Yorkshire is from near Doncaster (Appendix, no.9), close to the border with the Five Boroughs.

One coin from this group, which erroneously combines a *London Monogram* reverse with the reverse of the earlier *Two Emperors* type, bears the name of a King Halfdan (VLFDENE RX). For long this coin was attributed to Halfdan, the first Scandinavian king of York (875/6–7), and specifically to his wintering in London with the 'great army' in 871/2 (Haigh 1876, 48–9). Since this coin, and also a unique halfpenny of the *Two-Line* type with the name of +ALFDENE RX, can have been struck no earlier than the early–mid-880s, they clearly belong after Halfdan's expulsion from Northumbria in 876/7. If he died shortly afterwards in Ireland (Smyth 1977, ch.20), the coins provide evidence of an otherwise unrecorded King

Halfdan ruling perhaps in the Five Boroughs during the 880s.

The *Two-Line* design was commonly used in the southern Danelaw in the 880s and early 890s. It dominated, for example, the Ashton hoard (Blackburn 1989a), and single-finds have occurred in East Anglia and the east midlands. The only specimen from north of the Humber, found 'near York' in 1988 (Appendix, no.10), is typical of the southern issues that were superseded by the St Edmund type c.895. Some *Two-Line* imitations continued to be produced after this, for they occasionally combine the *Two-Line* design on one side with a design taken from the York regal coinage (e.g. *BMC* Alfred 454, copying the Cnut cruciform type, or *MEC* 1:1386, a halfpenny of the moneyer Everat with the long-cross-on steps motif; Fig.79, 2). These must emanate from a mint either in the Five Boroughs or the northern Danelaw.

Two other substantial groups of anonymous imitations appear to belong to the later 890s or early 900s, that is, after the St Edmund and York regal coinages had commenced. One copies the rare Oxford issue, but the mint name OHSNAFORDA has been corrupted to ORSNAFORDA (Lyon 1970, 196–7) (Fig.79, 4). Although the prototypes were produced c.880 (Blackburn 1998, 120), the imitations date from c.900, for some specimens copy the long-cross-on-steps design from coins of King Sigeferth of York (c.895–900) (Fig.80, 2). Some fifty specimens were present in the Cuerdale hoard and at least one in the Harkirk hoard,

while the only other recorded find is from mud dredged from the River Ouse in York (Metcalf 1958, 94). The group is likely to originate from a mint in the Five Boroughs or the northern Danelaw, but not from York itself, for die-linking within the contemporary York regal coinage is so strong that there is no place for this issue with its very different character.

The last group (Fig.79, 3) copies a range of Canterbury coins, in the names of Alfred and Archbishop Plegmund, and includes the variety with the Canterbury mint-signature (DORO) struck c.895–99. They are known almost exclusively from the Cuerdale hoard, the only other recorded provenances being one from the Morley St Peter, Norfolk, hoard and a stray find from Forncett St Peter, Norfolk. It is tempting to attribute the group to East Anglia, a near neighbour of Kent, the home of the prototypes, but the St Edmund issue so dominated the East Anglian currency that there seems little place for these coins. An attribution to the Five Boroughs or to a second mint in the northern Danelaw is therefore more probable at this date.

The search for a Scandinavian coinage at York before c.895 has not proved fruitful. The two early groups (*London Monogram* and *Two-Line*) that can be identified in this imitative phase are associated with the southern Danelaw, and, while it is possible that some specimens within them could be from York, there is no firm evidence of this. It is clear, however, that after the introduction of distinctive 'state' coin-

Fig.79 *Anglo-Scandinavian imitations from the Five Boroughs or Northern Danelaw:*
(1) Guthfrith, Two-Line; (2) Anon. halfpenny, Two-Line, Everat; (3) 'Alfred', 'Canterbury', halfpenny; (4) 'Alfred', 'Oxford', Bernwald;
(5) 'Cnut', 'Quentovic'

ages, viz. the York regal and St Edmund issues, there continued to be a quite substantial output of anonymous imitative coinages, influenced by the York regal series. To those mentioned above (further *Two-Line* imitations, *Orsnaforda* imitations, and possibly the Canterbury imitations), we should add a series combining the York 'Cnut' design with the reverse of Frankish coins of Quentovic (*BMC* 1005–17; *MEC* 1:1447; Fig.79, 5). Together these issues represent a substantial output, albeit spread over several years. Whether more than one mint was involved is unclear, as is its location, for there have been few finds of any of these groups outside the Cuerdale hoard. The most likely region for this production must be the Five Boroughs, where we know there had been mints at Lincoln and Leicester, but a second mint in the northern Danelaw operating in parallel with York is also a distinct possibility.

Establishing a state identity: the York regal coinage, c.895–905

The first identifiable Anglo-Scandinavian coinage from York is an exceptional and truly distinctive series of issues (Fig.80, 1–10). More than 3,000 specimens were present in the 1840 Cuerdale hoard, and its high survival rate has ensured that our knowledge of this coinage is better than almost any other from the Anglo-Saxon period. It was the subject of an exemplary die-study and analysis (Lyon and Stewart 1961), which has to be the basis for any further interpretation.

Two kings are named on the coinage — Sigeferth (SIEFREDVS or SIEVERT REX) and Cnut (CNUT REX) — and one other person, ALVVALDVS, who is given no title, perhaps because the name is a long one. From the pattern of die-linking one can see that Sigeferth was the earlier ruler, but there may have been some overlap since a number of coins have his name on the obverse combined with Cnut's on the reverse in what appears to be a deliberate combination. Sigeferth was probably the Sigeferth *piraticus de Northymbriorum* who according to the chronicler Æthelweard harried the English coast in 893/4, and he was presumably a successor of Guthfrith at York after 895 (see p.309) (Haigh 1876, 30–1; Smyth 1975–9 **1**, 33–7). Cnut, who on the coin evidence appears to have ruled in York for a few years c.900–5, is even more shadowy, but he may be the Cnut later Scandinavian sagas mention as invading Northumbria and being initially re-

pelled by an English king of York, whom he later defeated at Scarborough (Smyth 1975–9 **1**, 47–52). The association is plausible, for a West Saxon prince, Æthelwold, having failed in a challenge to Edward the Elder's succession, moved to Northumbria where he was accepted by the Danes as their king (*Anglo-Saxon Chronicle, s.a.* 900). How long he remained there is unclear, for two years later he died leading an East Anglian army against Edward. The coins reading ALVVALDVS (Fig.80, 10) can reasonably be attributed to Æthelwold (Blunt 1985), but they may have spanned only a few months since only six specimens are known, albeit each struck from different pairs of dies.

The York regal coinage is remarkable not merely for supplying the names of rulers who would otherwise barely be known, but also for its size, complexity and sophistication. In many aspects it differs significantly from the earlier Anglian coinage of York and from the contemporary issues of Wessex and Mercia. Rather than striving for a uniform design, in the York coinage there are some forty different combinations of obverse and reverse designs; far from being haphazard, the pairings seem to have been selected with great care. Breaking with Anglo-Saxon tradition, no moneyers' names appear on this coinage, but the mint-name (EBRAICE CIVITAS) frequently does. Also exceptional is the use of phrases from the Liturgy such as DNS DS REX (*Dominus Deus Rex* 'The Lord God (is) King'; Fig.80, 10), DNS DS O REX (*Dominus Deus Omnipotens Rex*, 'The Lord God Almighty (is) King'; Fig.80, 9), and MIRABILIA FECIT ('He has done marvellous things' from *Psalm* 98, v.1; Fig.80, 8–9), implying the presence of a highly literate and innovative person or group of people behind the designs, even if the die-cutter who executed them introduced errors on repeated copying.

The most novel feature of the coinage is its designs. These owe surprisingly little to either Anglo-Saxon or Carolingian precedents, but they display remarkable imagination and intellectual vigour. On most of the coins the reverse motif is some form of cross, displayed without an inner circle (in itself quite unusual) and of such a size as to dominate the design. This cross takes many different forms, none of which was specifically inspired by other coin types. They include a simple Greek cross (Fig.80, 3), a cross-crosslet (either within the inscription or breaking the inscription into four parts; Fig.80, 4–5), a cross with two arms crosslet, a patriarchal cross (Fig.80, 6–8)

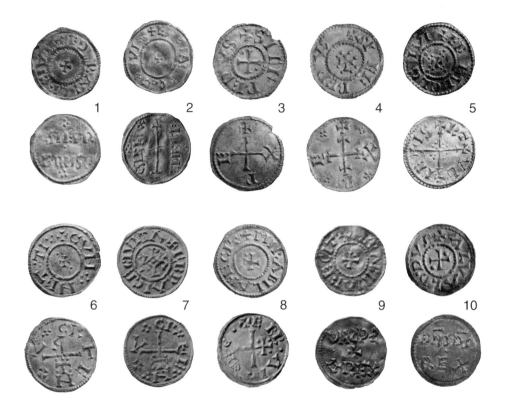

Fig.80 *York regal coinage, c.895–905:*
(1) Edraice Civi/C Siefredus E *(two-line);* *(2)* Ebiaice Civi/C Siefredus Rex *(cross-on-steps);* *(3)* Siefredus/Rex *(Greek cross);*
(4) Siefredus/Rex *(cross-crosslet);* *(5)* Ebiaice Civi/Sievert I *(anti-clockwise;* long *cross-crosslet);* *(6)* Cunnetti/Cnut Rex (Chi-Ro); *(7)* Ebraice Civita (Karolus *monogram*)/Cnut Rex *(patriarchal cross);* *(8)* Mirabila Fecit/Ebraice C *(patriarchal cross);*
(9) Mirabila Fecit/Dns Ds O Rex *(two-line);* *(10)* Alvalddus/Dns Ds Rex *(two-line)*

(occasionally with an R on the upper limb to form a *Chi-Ro* monogram; Fig.80, 6) or a long-cross-on-steps (Fig.80, 2). The latter, a representation of the Golgotha Cross erected in Jerusalem in the 4th or 5th century to mark the place of Christ's crucifixion, is commonly found on Byzantine coins, but these were not the model for the York coins for the cross has quite different proportions and does not have three arms potent as the Byzantine ones do. Small crosses or groups of pellets forming crosses also often appear in the field or in the inscriptions (Fig.80, 1–2, 4, 6–7). The cruciform design is occasionally reinforced by the arrangement of letters of the legends +REX or CNVT REX at the end of the arms to be read (top, bottom, left, right) in the order of a blessing (Fig.80, 3–4 and 6–7). Such an arrangement is also found on the 8th-century Ruthwell Cross where one is forced to make the sign of the cross in reading the inscriptions, and there are earlier continental parallels in the Cross of Justin II in the Vatican Treasury and the Icon of Santa Maria in Trastevere (C.E. Karkov and E. O'Carragain, pers. comm.). Such devices may have been part of the general stock of Christian symbolism and widely used, but they had never been employed as coin types in such a concentrated and systematic way.

It is clear that the designs and the inscriptions in this coinage were chosen with the utmost care. It is all the more frustrating, then, that two elements of the inscriptions have eluded satisfactory interpretation (Lyon and Stewart 1961, 113–18): the initial c in C SIEFREDUS REX (Fig.80, 1–2) and the word CUNNETTI (Fig.80, 6) which is always combined with dies reading CNUT REX. The position of the unexplained 'c' suggests that it stands for a title or epithet, but it could alternatively be an abbreviation for the enigmatic *cunnetti*, in the same way that that normally qualifies *Cnut rex* (Lyon and Stewart 1961, 114–15). Stewart (1987, 348) has revived an old interpretation by Haigh (1876, 58–60) of *cunnetti* as the name Hun(e)deus, the

Viking *dux* who raided up the Seine valley in 896 and in following year accepted baptism from Charles the Simple (Keynes and Lapidge 1983, 284, 288). While it is theoretically possible that *Hun(e)deus* is a Frankish Latinisation of the word *cunnetti*, there are more plausible personal names which it could represent (e.g. Old Norse *Hundi*, *Hundr*, 'dog'; Fellows Jensen 1968, 144), and the problem remains that *cunnetti* does not look like an Old Norse personal name; nor does its context on the coins make a personal name the most likely interpretation. Mention of Hundeus, however, does suggest a possible explanation for a third unresolved question, namely why a *Karolus* monogram was used as the design for two types of Cnut (Fig.80, 7). Had Cnut, like Hundeus and other Viking leaders of the period (Coupland 1998), been baptised with Charles the Simple standing sponsor, and was Cnut acknowledging his godfather on these coins? Indeed, might Charles have been his baptismal name, just as Guthrum had used his own baptismal name, Athelstan, on his coins? Such a message would be entirely consistent with the strong Christian theme this coinage conveys. What better way to show that the York Vikings were members of the community of Christian nations than to advertise an association with the Carolingian king of West Francia?

That the York regal coinage draws so little on Anglo-Saxon coin prototypes is surprising, considering that they were dominant in the context in which the York coinage was created. Indeed there must have been a positive decision to differentiate the York coinage, for example, by not putting the name of the moneyers on the coins. Some Anglo-Saxon influence can be seen among the earlier issues, ones of Sigeferth, with the occasional use of a *Two-Line* design or the division of the circular inscription into four parts (Fig.80, 1–5), as found on many coins of Alfred. Even the influence of Carolingian coinage, which has often been emphasised (Keary 1887, 204; Archibald 1980, 106), is very limited. The use of the *Karolus* monogram, already referred to, occurs on only twelve of the 250 recorded obverse dies and it is a relatively late feature of the coinage. The lozenge-shaped o with four wedges at the corners, found on dies reading DNS DS O REX (Fig.80, 9), could have been copied from Carolingian coins such as those of Le Mans, Chartres and Limoges, or from Alfred's Canterbury *Two-Line* coins, but this form of the letter o is occasionally found in other media as well and its cruciform shape

was no doubt seen as a further opportunity to introduce a cross into the design. The innovations most clearly inspired by Carolingian coinage are in the use of the mint's name and description, *Ebraice civitas*, the concept of including liturgical phrases on the coinage, and perhaps the occasional use of the Latin nominative, SIEFREDVS REX. There is no question that those designing the York coinage were familiar with contemporary Anglo-Saxon and Frankish coins, and hence aware of the features required for a functional coinage. But their work was highly original, drawing upon a wider artistic and theological culture to create a distinctive new coinage with powerful political and spiritual messages, yet within the bounds of what was practical.

What messages were these coins intended to convey? First and foremost, independence — independence not only from Wessex and Mercia but from the southern Danelaw as well. Secondly, royal power, for more than 90% of the coins prominently display the name of the Scandinavian king of York, and this is in contrast to the earlier Danelaw coinages, which only occasionally named the ruler, and to the contemporary St Edmund issue from the south, which was quite anonymous. The third and perhaps most surprising message promulgated by this Scandinavian coinage is Christianity. It is not simply that crosses dominate the designs and phrases from the liturgy are included in the inscriptions, but their variety and originality show how important this aspect was to those responsible for the coinage. We can speculate on the reason for this. Were the York Vikings such ardent converts to the Christian faith that they needed to proselytise more than others? Alternatively, were they so weak or so indifferent to the coinage that they allowed the church to move in and seize the initiative? Or was it part of a deliberate political policy, encouraged by the church, for the Scandinavian rulers to be seen to have embraced Christianity?

It is evident that some Viking leaders in both England and Francia were willing to accept conversion to Christianity, although the speed and depth of Christianisation of the people is questionable (Abrams 2001). York was one of the few sees in the Danelaw to have survived through the Scandinavian period. Archbishop Wulfhere remained in office from 854 until 892 x 900, and seemingly was able to establish a working relationship with the York kings, especially Guthfrith who endowed with land the monastery at Chester le Street and was buried in York Minster in 895 (Smyth 1975–9 **1**, 43–6). There is little, apart from this and the coinage, to suggest that the late 9th and early 10th century was a flourishing period for the church, although Rollason has argued that it was in fact a significant power in York during the Scandinavian period (see p.313). Seven per cent of the coins in this series omit the name of a ruler because a phrase such as MIRABELIA FECIT is combined with the mint name, and it has been argued that these were ecclesiastical issues (Rashleigh 1869, 75–6). This is possible, though as they are heavily die-linked with regal coins and evidently come from the same mint, they may simply reflect the rich and innovative variety within the regal series (Stewart 1982b, 249). It is clear from the coins themselves that authority for minting stemmed from the kings, Sigeferth and Cnut. Had this been a purely archiepiscopal coinage, one would have expected the archbishop's name to appear on the coins, as can be found in pre-Viking York or at Canterbury, though only on a minority of the coins.

The whole nature of the York regal coinage — its size, organisation and economic success — points to strong, rather than weak, political control, so the notion that the designs were of little significance, having been influenced by the clergy merely by stealth, is surely misplaced. One cannot avoid the conclusion that the Scandinavian rulers authorised the use of the coinage as a means of publicising their adoption of Christianity to demonstrate to other kingdoms (Anglo-Saxon, Frankish and British) as well as to their own people that the York kingdom had the credentials to be a respected member of the western Christian states. It can be argued that the rulers of the southern Danelaw were pursuing a similar policy, evidenced by Guthrum's use of his baptismal name on his coins and the adoption of the St Edmund legend for the coinage after c.895 (Blackburn 2001a). No doubt the York kings had advice from the church, probably from the archbishop himself, and perhaps from foreign delegations, but the policy must have received sanction from the highest level, or else it would not have been implemented so effectively or been sustained over so many years. Thus, the picture presented here is one of Scandinavian rulers who were not only militarily powerful, but also politically and diplomatically astute, and who came to recognise the political benefits the church could offer to a newly established kingdom. Wulfhere would have played a key role in fostering such an un-

derstanding, and he evidently developed a successful relationship with the Scandinavian rulers, as did Archbishop Wulfstan I (931–56) two generations later (see p.313). The church, then, may well have played a significant role in the York kingdom, but that does not mean that it was *the* dominant power in York, as Rollason argues. Indeed, the evidence of Sigeferth and Cnut's coinage would suggest otherwise.

A fourth, if unintentional, aspect was to show the administrative ability and intellectual vitality of the people organising the coinage. Having decided to initiate an independent regal coinage with a strong Christian element to its design, someone had to implement it — not only to set about finding people with the necessary artistic and technical expertise to plan and engrave the dies, but to organise moneyers and exchangers, and to set and regulate standards of weight and fineness. Frankish moneyers may well have been brought in to assist, as they were in the southern Danelaw, and the die-cutter may have been continental too, though if so one might have expected a higher standard of literacy (see below). The designs appear to have been drawn up with advice from a cleric, perhaps from the archbishop himself, and this relationship was maintained over some ten years as new types were introduced gradually during the life of the coinage. Within the mint administration there remained sufficient interest in promoting the messages of state independence and Christianity for new innovative designs to continue to be introduced. Rollason questions whether the kings of York possessed a bureaucratic machinery of government (see p.311), but the coinage provides ample evidence of this and speaks highly of the calibre of the administrators and advisors available to them in York at the end of the 9th century. Among these there may well have numbered native Northumbrians, including churchmen, though, as we shall see, the poor literacy that is characteristic of Anglo-Scandinavian, but not Anglo-Saxon, coinages suggests their overall management probably remained with Scandinavians.

The coinages of St Peter and Ragnald I, c.905–27: iconography and status

This regal coinage was replaced c.905 by an issue that was very different. All reference to the king was dropped, and the name of the city (initially EBRAICE, later EBORACE CIVITAS) on one side was accompanied by a two-line inscription, SCI PETRI MO, on the other (Fig.81, 1). In contrast to the variety of designs in the previous phase, this one basic type lasted for almost fifteen years. That in itself is not a weakness, since from a monetary point of view standardisation in design can be desirable, creating a uniform currency in which foreign coins can readily be recognised and removed. This coinage is, however, notable for its progressive and dramatic decline in literacy and weight (Stewart and Lyon 1992, 53–9, with a review of the issue, though a full study has yet to be undertaken).

The design is derived from the *Two-Line* type of Alfred and Edward the Elder, and a few coins have symbols inserted on the reverse — a key (of St Peter), branched symbol (tree of life?; Fig.81, 1), star and letter S — while one very late variety revives the *Karolus* monogram design that had been used fifteen years earlier on coins of Cnut. The introduction of a coinage without the name of a ruler but invoking St Peter, to whom York Minster was dedicated, was no doubt primarily inspired by the St Edmund coinage of the southern Danelaw, which for ten years had been the principal coinage of that region. While its inscription was in the vocative, SCE EADMUNDE REX ('O Saint Eadmund the King'), the form on the York coinage, SCI PETRI MO ('St Peter's mint' or 'money'), followed 9th-century Carolingian precedents, e.g. under Charles the Bald (840–69) *Sci Gavgerici mo* (Cambrai), *Sci Martini moneta* (Tours), *Sci Medadi mont* (Soissons), *Sci Petri moneta* (Corbie), *Sci Quintini monet* (St Quentin), *Sci Sebastini m* (Soissons), *Sci Stephani mone* (Dijon), etc. These are generally thought to represent ecclesiastical or abbatial mints, a view reinforced in some cases by the existence of contemporary coins in the name of the city: *Camaracus civis* (Cambrai), *Turones civitas* (Tours), *Suessio civitas* (Soissons).

The York St Peter coins could, then, be seen as having a double or complex mint name ('the mint of St Peter, in the city of York'), and previously some numismatists had regarded the St Peter coinage as an ecclesiastical issue that ran in parallel with regal issues from York (e.g. Blunt 1974, 57, 90–1). It is now clear, however, that this was the sole coinage of the Kingdom of York for some 20 years, c.905–19 and c.921–7, briefly interrupted by the coinage in the name of King Ragnald (c.919–21). Coinage was a major source of revenue for early medieval kings and, while there are many examples of rulers granting local minting rights to a church by way of endow-

ment, it would be without precedent in Europe for control of all minting to be granted away by a state. It is now generally accepted by numismatists that the St Peter coins are secular issues (Archibald 1980, 108; Stewart 1982b, 249–50; *CTCE*, 98–9), though whether their characterisation as a 'civic coinage of the Viking community generally' (Stewart and Lyon 1992, 59–60) is justified might be doubted. The fact that the coinages of both the northern and the southern Danelaw were anonymous at this period must reflect the political policies of the rulers, but it would be wrong to imply from this that the structure of government was more akin to that of an Italian commune than a hierarchical kingdom. In the 920s, when we know York was ruled by Sihtric Caech, the St Peter coinage was restored and coins bearing his own name were only issued in the Five Boroughs.

Developing his theme of the dominant position of the church in York affairs, Rollason sees the St Peter issues as ecclesiastical coinages — indeed this is one of the mainstays of his theory (see pp.313–14). Yet, while the St Peter issues undoubtedly show that the church had a significant influence on secular policy and affairs at this time, they do not demonstrate that it controlled them. As we have seen, other explanations are possible. One would need firm evidence from elsewhere that ecclesiastical control was likely before overturning the normal presumption that a state's coinage was issued by the ruling secular authority. One should perhaps remember that in the southern Danelaw the St Edmund coinage had analogous inscriptions, but it would be hard to identify an ecclesiastical authority there that could have been responsible for the coinage. Moreover, if the church had taken control of the York coinage in c.905, one might expect to have seen an improvement rather than a decline in the literacy of the inscriptions.

The dating of these coinages has been much debated, with some wishing to date Ragnald's coinage to c.915 or earlier and spread the Sword St Peter issues over the remaining twelve years, c.915–27 (Smyth 1975–9 **1**, 104–7; Dolley 1978). However, the hoard evidence points to a later date, fitting in with Ragnald's only well-attested period in York, c.919–20/1 (Dolley 1982; Stewart and Lyon 1992). The restoration of the Dublin kingdom in 918 and the conquest of York in 919 marked the culmination of a five-year campaign by Ragnald and his brothers(?), Sihtric Caech and Guthfrith, to regain the territories

Fig.81 *York issues c.905–27:*
(1) St Peter without sword (early, with branched ornament); (2) Ragnald I, Karolus *monogram/ Bust type; (3) Ragnald I,* Bow/hammer *type; (4) Sword St Peter,* Sword/cross *type; (5) Sword St Peter,* Sword/mallet *type*

of their famous grandfather Ivar, who had led the 'great army' in its conquest of York in 867 (Smyth 1975–9 **1**, 107–13; Higham 1992). For the Danes of York and the Five Boroughs, Ragnald's arrival offered the prospect of resisting the progressive advance of Edward the Elder across the Danelaw. In this context, it is not surprising to find a change of emphasis in the coinage, with Ragnald using it to promote himself and the Scandinavian heritage of the ruling elite. The designs seem to have been selected as carefully as those of the earlier regal coinage, many of the motifs being capable of bearing a Christian message as well as a Nordic one. The distinctive blend of Anglo-Saxon and Scandinavian culture, evident in sculpture, metalwork and other media from the Danelaw, was now also emerging in the coinage.

The coinage in Ragnald's name (RAIENALT, RAC-NOLDT, in the most literate forms) employed three successive types (Blunt and Stewart 1983, with an illustrated corpus of his coins). The first has a bust of the king, on one die deliberately bearded, presenting the only contemporary image of a Scandinavian ruler before the late 10th century (Fig.81, 2). The other side has a *Karolus* monogram and the mint-name EIARICE CT. The second type has a degraded form of the same monogram, paired with an open hand. The hand was probably inspired by Edward the Elder's *Manus Dei* issue from the west midlands, but the rounded palm on earlier dies is lost as a crude linear style develops, giving the appearance of a glove rather than a hand. It has been suggested that this was a deliberate attempt to represent the iron glove

of Thor (Haigh 1876, 69), and the double meaning, reinforced by one die having a cross in the cuff, may have been intentional. The third type is completely novel, having a Thor's hammer (doubling as a Christian *Tau* cross?) combined with a bow loaded with a feathered arrow (Fig.81, 3).

In its iconography Ragnald's coinage was radically different from that which had gone before, and it seems likely that he was also responsible for the late variant of the Swordless St Peter coins with the *Karolus* monogram obverse. Only four specimens are known, and they seem to mark some restoration of the weight standard (Stewart and Lyon 1992, 58–9). This was the most marked development of the coinage during the fifteen years of the Swordless St Peter issue, and the fact that it came so near to the end and that the same type and inscription was continued in Ragnald's first two issues suggests that he had been responsible for choosing it. The monogram design surely had significance. As well as being one of the designs used on Cnut's coinage, it would have been well known as the emblem of the by now long-ruling king of the West Franks, Charles the Simple (897–922). Ragnald's activities in the British Isles are recorded from 914 onwards, but as a young man he could have been campaigning in France and have participated in a peace accord with Charles, perhaps accepting baptism as many other Vikings did (most notably Rollo, the founder of Normandy, in 911), even if Ragnald's later desecration of churches and seizure of their property shows he was not a practising Christian. Charles may even have been Ragnald's baptismal name, in which case the *Karolus*/St Peter coins would have been a regal issue. A similar interpretation could also be placed on the enigmatic LVDO SITRIC inscription on a coin of Sihtric Caech, where *Ludo* is usually interpreted as an unknown title, but this could stand for a putative baptismal name *Ludovicus* (Stewart 1982a, 114, citing view of M.M. Archibald). In the face of Edward the Elder's advance through the Danelaw, it could have been politic for Ragnald to advertise a personal or dynastic association with the Carolingian king.

The pattern of die-linking in Ragnald's coinage suggests that the obverse (lower) die was the one with the mint-name and monogram or bow design, while the king's name and portrait, glove or hammer design was on the reverse (upper) die, that is, the one that took the hammer blows and so had to be replaced more frequently. Although unusual for an English coinage, where the mint-name is normally on the reverse, this arrangement is consistent with the preceding regal and Swordless St Peter issues at York. It seems to have come about through the York die-cutters wanting to be consistent in making the side with a circular inscription and small central cross the obverse and the two-line or other design the reverse, so that by the end of the St Peter coinage the mint/monogram side was on the obverse die and it continued to be so under Ragnald. Thereafter this arrangement was abandoned and on subsequent York issues the side with the mint-name was the reverse.

The restoration of the St Peter design, with the addition of a sword, could have been initiated by Ragnald at the end of his reign, but it is more likely that it was a decision taken by Sihtric when faced with the question of how to continue the coinage after Ragnald's death. The type must have been regarded as an important symbol of the York kingdom, despite the inferior weight standard to which the original St Peter coinage had fallen. Sihtric also produced a coinage in his own name, with designs that mirror three successive types of the Sword St Peters, but these were struck at a mint or mints in the Five Boroughs rather than York. The iconography of these issues, combining the sword with either a cross or form of Thor's hammer, maintained the balance of Norse and Christian symbolism introduced by Ragnald. The order of the three issues, each with distinct reverse designs, is not finally settled, although the balance of the evidence points to the Cross type

(Fig.81, 4) preceding the Thor's Hammer and Mallet (Fig.81, 5) types (Stewart and Lyon 1992, with a corpus of Sword St Peter coins). This is supported by the latest hoard of this period, from Thurcaston, Leicestershire, deposited c.925, for it contained two Sword St Peter and five Sihtric coins all of the Cross type, with three late Edward the Elder coins and two Arabic dirhems (Blackburn 2001b).

No coins are known of Guthfrith, king of Dublin, from the period of his brief attempt to secure York after the death of his brother in 927. Athelstan's conquest of York brought to a close this phase of Anglo-Scandinavian coinage, and the period of English rule that followed markedly influenced the subsequent Anglo-Scandinavian coinages, 939–54.

Athelstan and the later Scandinavian and English rulers of York, 927–54

Just as Athelstan razed to the ground the Scandinavian defences he found in York (*William of Malmesbury*, paragraph 134; Whitelock 1979, no.8), so he apparently made a clean sweep of the coinage. The currency in the northern Danelaw and parts of the Five Boroughs was incompatible with that of the rest of England as it was based on a different weight standard, and a burst of minting in the region would have been required to replace it. For this Athelstan introduced a novel type, with a church or reliquary on the reverse, struck by six moneyers (Blunt 1974, 88–93). The only coins that name York as the mint are ones by Regnald, who later became the sole moneyer there. The coins of the other moneyers are in a very similar style, but it is debatable whether they were produced at York or at mints elsewhere in the midlands, where at least two of the moneyers struck coins later in Athelstan's reign: Frotier at Shrewsbury and Turstan at Leicester (Blunt 1974, 88–9, 92). Regnald's coins of the *Church* type were not produced on a large enough scale for them to have replaced the Sword St Peter coinage on their own, and it is possible that the other moneyers were drafted in to assist with the recoinage. The discovery in excavations at the Coppergate site in York of a piece of lead with an impression of a reverse die of this type for the moneyer Adelbert supports the view that these were struck in York (*AY* 18/1, 55, *48*). After a short while the *Church* type was superseded by the *Circumscription Cross* (CC) type, for which Regnald was the only moneyer (Fig.82, 1), and then by a

Fig.82 *York coinage 927–47:*
(1) Athelstan, Circumscription *type, York; (2) Olaf Guthfrithsson,* Raven *type; (3) Olaf Sihtricsson,* Triquetra/Banner *type; (4) Sihtric,* Triquetra/Banner *type; (5) Ragnald II,* Cross Moline *type*

Bust Crowned (BC) type during which issue Regnald was replaced by Athelerd. The CC coins survive in large numbers and are remarkable for the variety of symbols and punctuation on them, suggesting an elaborate system of die control. The Latin forms of the mint name, EBORACE, maintained in the *Church* type, were replaced by the Old English EFORPIC on the CC and BC types.

On Athelstan's death, Olaf Guthfrisson (939–41), a nephew of Sihtric Caech, seized the opportunity to re-establish the Scandinavian kingdom of York. Once again the coinage was used for political propaganda. The plan must have been to oust English pennies from circulation and replace them with an overtly Anglo-Scandinavian coinage on the same weight standard as the Sword St Peter coins of the 920s (see below). The first type struck by Olaf, and perhaps continued under his cousin Olaf Sihtricsson (941–4/5), has one of the most dramatic coin designs in the English series. It shows a classic Viking symbol, a raven, with head turned left and outstretched wings (Fig.82, 2), and the inscriptions are in Old Norse: ANLAF CVNVNC ('King Anlaf', i.e. Olaf) and AÐELFERD MINETR ('Æthelferth the moneyer'). This coinage was struck on a substantial scale, with at least 36 specimens surviving and very little die-linking between them. The following issue (Fig.82, 3–4) also has Scandinavian motifs: a triquetra, a common element in interlace design and a motif that recurs on 11th-century Danish and Norwegian coins (Skaare 1976, 68–70), and a

triangular banner of distinctive Viking form found in Scandinavian metalwork and on some rare London coins of Cnut (Blackburn 1989b). Yet each of these designs can also be recognised in a Christian context: the raven is associated with St Oswald (a Northumbrian royal saint), the triquetra represents the Trinity in some 7th-/8th-century art, and the triangular banner on the coins is decorated with a cross. Again we can speculate whether the designers were subtly appealing to a dual audience. Did Archbishop Wulfstan's apparent alliance with Olaf Guthfrithsson (see p.313) ensure that the church continued to influence royal policy?

The final issue of this short period of Scandinavian rule, 939–44/5, is entirely Anglo-Saxon in design (a *Circumscription Cross* or *Cross Moline* type), while retaining Old Norse elements in the titles *cununc* and *monetr* (Fig.82, 5). The choice of type is interesting, for it is not one that Edmund (939–46) was using to any significant extent elsewhere in England, but in York it would undoubtedly have recalled the large *Circumscription Cross* coinage issued by Athelstan, which the two Olafs had apparently sought to demonetise. The *Triquetra* and *Cross* types were both struck in the names of three kings, Olaf Sihtricsson, Ragnald Guthfrithsson (943–4/5) and an otherwise unknown King Sihtric, implying that they may have ruled York jointly c.943–4. The true sequence of events seems to have been more complicated, however. The historical sources are confused and do not provide a complete account, but they suggest that Olaf, having made peace with Edmund and received baptism in 943, was ousted from York late that year by his cousin Ragnald. If so, Olaf must soon have returned for the *Anglo-Saxon Chronicle* records that both he and Ragnald were driven out of York by Edmund in 944/5 (Smyth, 1975–9 **2**, 110–14). This is not inconsistent with the coinage, but there are unresolved details such as how long Ragnald might have struck coins on his own and whether he was responsible for introducing the *Cross* type. And what was Sihtric's role in this affair? His coins are closely aligned with those of Olaf, sharing moneyers and varieties, so was he perhaps ruling jointly with Olaf early in 943, or did he come to power with Ragnald and merely take over Olaf's moneyers. The arrangement of the York coinage, although still complicated, has been clarified to some extent by the recognition that several types in the name of Olaf belong to the Scandinavian possessions in the Five Boroughs in the period 940–2 (Blunt, Stewart and Lyon 1989, 216–19). They emanate from at least three mints, Derby, probably Lincoln and perhaps Stamford, marking the final occasion on which Scandinavian authority extended south of the Humber.

Edmund, having restored Anglo-Saxon control of York, for the last two years of his reign struck *Hori-*

zontal (i.e. *Two-Line*) coins by the sole moneyer Ingelgar (Fig.83, 1), an arrangement which was continued by Eadred (946–55). The sources relating the final phase of Norse rule at York are also scanty and contradictory (see p.310). The conventional interpretation of events (reflected in Keynes 1999, 505) gives Eric Bloodaxe two reigns, 947–8 and 952–4, interrupted by Eadred, 948–50, and Olaf Sihtricsson, 950–2, but Sawyer (1995) has proposed an alternative sequence in which Eric would have only one reign, 950–952/4, preceded by a longer reign for Olaf, 947–50. He expressed the hope that the numismatic evidence might endorse one scheme rather than the other, but based on our present knowledge either arrangement could be accommodated. The conventional chronology will be followed here.

With the exception of Eric's final issue, the coins produced at York during the last periods of Scandinavian rule were Anglo-Saxon in design and in the form of their inscriptions. Eric's first issue (Fig.83, 2) continued the *Horizontal* type of Eadred, and while Olaf chose to differentiate his issues, he none the less selected designs of English origin: *Circumscription Cross*, reviving his own earlier issue, and *Flower*, after a rare type of Edward the Elder and Edmund from west midlands mints. A unique coin combining an

Fig.83 *York coinage 947–54:*
(1) Edmund, Horizontal *type; (2) Eric,* Horizontal *type; (3) Olaf Sihtricsson/Eadred mule,* Circumscription/Horizontal *types; (4) Olaf Sihtricsson,* Circumscription *type; (5) Eric,* Sword *type*

obverse die of Olaf with a reverse of Eadred (Fig.83, 3) offers corroboration for the view that Olaf succeeded Eadred in the later 940s. Eric's final type is also retrospective, but harking back to the coinages of the 920s, the Sword St Peter and Sihtric Caech's *Sword/Cross* issues. It is fitting, perhaps, that the very last Anglo-Scandinavian coins should display the sword so redolent of Norse culture, for in all other respects the Anglo-Scandinavian coinage had become indistinguishable from contemporary Anglo-Saxon currency.

Literacy and technical aspects of the coinage

The various influences and degree of innovation evident in the planning of the designs for the York coinages have already been touched upon. The translation of those plans into the final images or motifs seen on the coins relied upon the artistic skill of the die-cutter. The visual quality, and in particular the literacy, of the coins depended on the care he took in copying and re-copying the design, time after time. The standard achieved in the York series was variable. Even in the first York regal coinage, where the designer's input was exceptional and the general quality of die-cutting is high, the work is let down by the significant number of errors that crept into the legends. This partly arose from the need to shorten legends, such as EBRAICE CIVITAS and MIRABILIA FECIT, that were too long to fit comfortably on to a coin, but in the process inappropriate letters were dropped or inadvertently exchanged. It is also clear that rather than going back to the original model, the die-cutter would usually copy his own recent work, a standard practice that led to the perpetuation of mistakes. Thus EBRAICE quite soon becomes corrupted to EBIAICE, a form often found on the coins, or MIRABILIA to MIRABILA. Greater errors occur, occasionally with transposed or reversed letters. The number of mistakes in these legends is higher than one finds in Anglo-Saxon or Carolingian coinages, yet the die-cutter appears to have been making some effort to reproduce the inscriptions accurately, even if one suspects that he could not understand them.

By comparison, the standard of literacy on the succeeding St Peter and Ragnald I coinages down to Athelstan's conquest of 927 is quite abysmal. In most issues the legends are so corrupt that only the faint-est hint of the intended inscription can be discerned. Thus EBORACE becomes BORACE, BRACE, RACE, IIACE, BORAI, etc. in the Swordless St Peter series, while RAIENALT becomes RACIIODT, IACNOIT, ICAOCTI, etc. (cf. Keary 1887, 232–3, 239–44). In this period it seems that not only was the die-cutter quite unable to understand the inscriptions, but no one troubled to monitor his work after the initial model had been supplied. Similar poor standards of literacy are found on the Scandinavian coinages from the southern Danelaw, in both the imitative series and the St Edmund coinage (Smart 1985; Blackburn 2001a). While the literacy of a coinage is not a fair reflection of the ability of the general population among which it circulated, it may be a measure of the standard of literacy expected by the ruling administration. If so the difference between the Anglo-Saxon and Scandinavian administrations was considerable. The Scandinavian elite may well have relied more heavily on oral means of governing and legislating than the Anglo-Saxons, and this could be one reason why so few documents have come down to us from the Anglo-Scandinavian kingdoms. That is not to say that the Scandinavian administration was inferior in other respects; the general size and success of their coinages show otherwise. After Athelstan's conquest of York, the literacy of the coinage was raised to the normal Anglo-Saxon standard, and this was broadly maintained even through the later periods of restored Norse control. The poor literacy of the St Peter issues in particular perhaps suggests that the coinage was not then under the control of the church.

A distinctive feature of the production of coinage in Scandinavian York is the way in which the die-axes (i.e. the orientation of the obverse in relation to the reverse) are random. There seems to have been no co-ordination between the position of the two die faces. By contrast, on earlier Northumbrian coins and on coins from other Anglo-Saxon mints, the dies are normally aligned in a regular relationship (0°, 90°, 180° or 270°). An explanation for the difference can be found from surviving dies. The two York dies from the Coppergate excavations, one of the Sword St Peter issue (Fig.84) and one of Athelstan, have round profiles (*AY* 18/1, 33–41, 55–6, *43* and *49*). The three known late Anglo-Saxon dies from more southern mints — one of Lincoln of Æthelred II found at Flaxengate, Lincoln (Blackburn and Mann 1995), one of Norwich of Cnut from the Thames Exchange site in London (Archibald et al.1995) and an unidenti-

Fig.84 *Iron obverse die for Sword St Peter penny from 16–22 Coppergate. Length 91mm*

fied die from Mill Lane, Thetford (Blackburn and Davies forthcoming) — significantly have square profiles. When holding such dies and lining up their faces during striking it would be natural to align the square sides, with the result that most coins would have a regular orientation, as indeed we find. It is unlikely that the orientation of the dies particularly mattered to the Anglo-Saxons; it was merely a by-product of the technology of die-making. On the Continent most early medieval coinages have random die-axes, as at York, and indeed the only surviving Carolingian die, one from the town of Melle (*AY* 18/1, 44–5), has a round rather than square profile. It is notable, then, that in setting up the new mint for the York regal coinage c.895, the Scandinavians adopted a continental practice, rather than the usual English one. Moreover, this practice survived at York, not merely into the reign of Athelstan, but right down to the end of the 11th century.

The weight standard of the penny is another factor that sets the Anglo-Scandinavian coinages apart from contemporary Anglo-Saxon issues. Alfred had established the weight of the penny at c.1·6g, and this was maintained by Edward the Elder, though there was a gradual decline after that (Blunt, Stewart and Lyon 1989, 235–45, from which other data cited here is also drawn). The Frankish denier was somewhat heavier, set at c.1·75g for most of the 9th century, subsequently falling to a variety of regional standards in course of the 10th century (Dumas-Dubourg 1971, 30–40). The weight adopted for the York regal coinage, at c.1·3g, was significantly lighter than either, yet the degree of control was good (Metcalf 1987b, 390–6). It was comparable to the standard of c.1·35g used in the imitative coinages in the southern Danelaw (Blackburn 1990) and the earlier St Edmund coins (Blackburn and Pagan 2002). Interestingly, these standards reflected the weights of the Northumbrian and East Anglian coinages before the Viking conquest of the 860s, showing how local weight standards had survived Scandinavian domination and settlement. Yet it would have been simple for the Danes to have adopted the current West Saxon or Carolingian standard. The point is surely an important one, and contrasts with the general picture of discontinuity of institutions as shown by the law, the church and landholdings.

During the Swordless St Peter issue the weight of the penny fell dramatically to c.0·9g, a decline that has been associated with Viking defeat at Tettenhall in 910 (Dolley 1978, 27), although it may well have begun before that. Towards the end of the issue there was some restoration of the weight, with the rare *Karolus* and *One-Line* St Peter types following a standard of c.1·2g, and this was maintained in Ragnald I's coinage. The Sword St Peter types are in a similar or marginally higher weight range, so that they had broadly returned to the original standard of the York regal coinage 25 years earlier. After his conquest of York, Athelstan brought the coinage into line with the rest of England, with pennies weighing c.1·6g, but surprisingly this was done in two stages, with the first York issue, the *Church* type, being struck at an intermediate level of c.1·45g. A similar standard was used for two varieties of Athelstan's *Bust Crowned* type (NE II and III) in the east midlands, perhaps primarily for those areas that had remained under Scandinavian control striking coins of Sihtric Caech and St Martin until c.927.

On the restoration of the Scandinavian kingdom in 939, Olaf Guthfrithsson deliberately reverted to the Anglo-Scandinavian standard of c.1·2 g for the *Raven* type, and the *Triquetra* appears to be still lower to judge from the few surviving specimens. This represented a bold attempt to re-establish a distinctive independent coinage in terms of both design and monetary value, and it is no wonder that the *Raven* type appears to have been issued on a substantial scale if it was intended to replace the Anglo-Saxon coins circulating in Northumbria. By 943/4 the three York kings may have decided this policy was unsustainable, for the introduction of the more English *Circumscription Cross* and *Cross Moline* types was accompanied by an increase in the weight standard to c.1·35g, which by then was comparable to the contemporary coinage of Edmund in the Five Boroughs (NE I) as the Anglo-Saxon standard was declining. During the restoration of English control in 944–7, Edmund's and Eadred's York coins were struck at c.1·45g, and this was more or less maintained by Olaf Sihtricsson and Eric Bloodaxe during the final Scandinavian phases (947–8, 950?–954).

Excavations at 16–22 Coppergate in York yielded finds suggesting that two adjoining tenements (C and D) were involved in some form of minting-related activity during the 10th century (*AY* 18/1, 18–22, 33–45). These finds comprised the St Peter and Athelstan coin dies mentioned above and three pieces of lead sheet with impressions of dies, in contexts that revealed plentiful evidence of metal refining and metal working in gold, silver, copper alloy and iron, from litharge cakes, cupels, parting vessels, crucibles, ingot moulds, smithing slag and scrap metals (*AY* 17/6, 471–506; *AY* 17/7, 794–814). Two of the lead pieces show reverses of successive York issues of Athelstan — the *Church* and *Circumscription Cross* types — of different moneyers and the third shows an obverse and reverse of the *Horizontal Rosettes* type of Eadwig (955–9) (*AY* 18/1, *48, 50* and *59*). Various functions for these objects have been considered, including trial-strikings, weights, die records and customs receipts (*AY* 18/1, 37–40; Archibald 1984, 191; Blunt, Stewart and Lyon 1989, 247; Archibald 1991, 331–6; Williams 1999, 19). For the two Athelstan impressions on irregular-shaped pieces, trial-striking on a cheaper more malleable metal seems the most plausible explanation, although they could also have been preserved as a record of the dies issued. The Eadwig piece is a rather different object. Its form is unparalleled — a strip of lead sheet with one rounded and one pointed end, and bearing impressions of both obverse and reverse dies on one surface and a second obverse impression on the other surface. The dies are of a type used in the west midlands, while the moneyer is one recorded at Chester, although errors in the inscriptions suggest that these dies were not products of the usual die-cutter and could have been made elsewhere. What, then, was this item doing in York? Archibald (1991) argues, in the context of a group of at least 34 double-sided lead 'coins' of the later 11th and early 12th centuries from a wharf site at Billingsgate, London, that these were used for a form of customs control, and she suggests that some of the lead objects with die impressions from earlier periods may have had a similar function. In particular, she interprets the Eadwig piece from Coppergate as a tag that had been attached to merchandise perhaps in Chester and taken to York. Attractive as the customs receipt theory may be, it remains speculative as there is no documentary evidence of such a practice in England.

The evidence for Coppergate's involvement with some minting-related activity is focused on the 920s and 930s, extending into the third quarter of the 10th century if the Eadwig strip is interpreted in a similar light. In the context of iron smithing and general metal working, die-cutting rather than minting had been thought the most likely activity there, the worn dies having been returned for recycling (*AY* 18/1, 21–2). A parallel would be the Thames Exchange site in London, where four coin dies of the 11th and 12th centuries, although found in unstratified contexts, may plausibly be related to the presence of a die-cutter's workshop in the vicinity, since the dies had all been returned from mints outside London (Archibald et al. 1995). Yet Bayley's report on the non-ferrous metal working evidence from Coppergate shows that silver working was a prominent activity in Tenements C and D during the 10th century, with the most evidence concentrated in D (*AY* 17/7, 799–803, 815–16). The minting artefacts are divided between the tenements, with the St Peter die and the Athelstan trial piece of the moneyer Regnald in C, and the Athelstan die that had been used by Regnald and the Athelstan trial piece of Adelbert in D. Any of the three lead pieces could have been treated as scrap metal, as many pieces of lead sheet and other offcuts were found on the site, but this is particularly true of the Eadwig lead strip that came from the yard of Tenement D in a later 10th-/11th-century context.

Lead could be used for a number of purposes, but was required in considerable quantity for silver refining. No silver artefacts or scrap have been found, other than some coins, but the by-products and tools of the process suggest that wrought rather than cast objects were being produced, the metal being first refined and alloyed, then cast into ingots which were worked into sheet, rod or wire from which the products were made. This is just the process involved in minting, and there seems little reason to doubt that coins were being struck here. The Winton Domesday shows how the moneyers in Winchester operated from private tenements with forges that were mainly grouped in one area of the High Street, while their principal residencies were elsewhere (Biddle 1976, 397–400), and that may be the pattern observed in York. Indeed, it is tempting to think that one or perhaps both of these tenements belonged to Regnald, the dominant York moneyer of the period. The Æthelred II coin die excavated at Flaxengate, Lincoln, was also associated with intensive metal working activities, but these were predominantly in copper alloy, with only traces of silver working, suggesting less specialisation than at York if coin production was

also carried out there (Blackburn and Mann 1995). The later 10th-/11th-century site at Mill Lane, Thetford, that provided the most recent discovery of a coin die was likewise characterised as a site of prolific mixed metal working activity, with silver strongly represented (Blackburn and Davies forthcoming). If these sites do indeed represent moneyers' workshops, they shed interesting new light on the mixed nature of some moneyers' trade.

Moneyers and mint organisation

Certain distinctive features of the York Anglo-Scandinavian mint and its coinage have already been mentioned: the use of round-faced dies, irregular die-axes, a distinctive weight standard, strong Christian iconography, the regular inclusion of the mint-name, the absence of a ruler's name in several issues and the placing of the mint-name on the lower (obverse) die before the Sword St Peter issue. The omission of the moneyer's name during the first 30 years makes it difficult to see the type of mint organisation initially adopted by the Scandinavians. The reason for the omission may be because the mint was under the control of one individual and it was thought unnecessary to name him. When Athelstan in 927 introduced the practice of naming the moneyers at York, it becomes clear that York was quite unlike any other major English mint in having very often a single moneyer in charge. This was particularly true of periods when the mint was under Anglo-Saxon control, so that under Athelstan, Edmund, Eadred, Eadwig and Edgar there was normally one moneyer who issued most or all of the coins (Blunt, Stewart and Lyon 1989, 109, 117, 130–1, 147, 178–9). The same is also found in the *Raven* type of Olaf Guthfrithsson, but in the succeeding *Triquetra* and *Circumscription* types several moneyers are named, and it has been argued that each of the three co-rulers (Olaf, Ragnald II and Sihtric) may have had his own moneyer, even if in practice there is some movement of moneyers between kings. Although Edmund and Eadred restored the single moneyer arrangement, in the final Anglo-Scandinavian phase Eric and Olaf reverted to multiple moneyers by restoring some of those who had acted as moneyers during the previous Anglo-Scandinavian phase. After Edgar's coinage reform of c.973, York fell in line with other English mints of comparable size in having some 15–20 moneyers normally operating at any one time.

The presence of a single dominant moneyer at York during much of the 10th century may signal a fundamental difference in the organisation of minting there. At mints elsewhere it is thought that moneyers generally operated out of separate private workshops, as we have already seen documented for Winchester in the 11th century, though on occasion two or more may have shared resources. The centralisation of minting in a single mint building was brought about in most towns by the currency reform of 1180. In York a degree of centralisation may already have been in place during part of the 10th century, and the most obvious explanation for it would be that this was the practice employed when the Scandinavians first set up the mint in the 890s. Whether it was a Continental practice we cannot be sure, for while Carolingian coins name the mint but not the moneyer — as in Scandinavian York — this does not necessarily mean that Carolingian minting was not organised by groups of moneyers as in England.

The origins of the names can provide a clue as to how the moneyers were recruited (Smart 1986, 178–9). Of the thirteen moneyers named on the York coinage between 927 and 954, the majority (Regnald, Ascolv, Rathulf, Ba(ldri)c?, Durant, Rernart, Ingelgar and Wadter) have Continental Germanic (i.e. Frankish) or Old French names, while only two have names that are clearly Old English (Æthelerd / Athelferd and Leofic), one could be either Old English or Germanic (Ulfelm), one Germanic or Scandinavian (Farman) and one is uncertain (Avra). The most prolific moneyers for the Anglo-Saxon kings were Continental Germanic (Regnald and Ingelgar). Of the moneyers with English names, Æthelerd commenced under King Athelstan, but continued in office under Olaf Guthfrithsson, assuming Athelferd to be the same man as Æthelerd. The two other names that are English or possibly English only occur on coins of Scandinavian rulers. What is noticeable at York, as elsewhere in the Danelaw, is the small number of Scandinavian names. Clearly the Vikings did not promote their kinsmen in the field of coin production. But why so many Frankish moneyers? The high proportion found in the Danelaw, north and south, is quite untypical of the population generally, and it is thought to signal an influx of specialised Frankish craftsmen brought in by the Viking rulers to help run the mints. In the southern Danelaw they are present in the earliest phase of Scandinavian coinage, from the 880s and early 890s (Blackburn 1990), and their involvement appears to have been part of the original plan

for setting up the new mints. The skills of a moneyer are specialised, requiring technical and financial knowledge, and it is interesting to speculate how the Scandinavians might have recruited people with suitable experience from Francia. It is unlikely that such people could have been found among any followers that the Danish army may have attracted during its campaigning across the Channel, and so they must have been solicited through intermediaries in Francia. Were there, perhaps, Carolingian diplomatic delegations coming to the Danelaw to negotiate with and advise the new Scandinavian rulers? Moneyers were not the only specialists imported from the Continent, for Frankish potters also appear to have been recruited to modernise the pottery industry in the Danelaw, at Stamford and Torksey, during the late 9th or early 10th century (Sawyer 1998, 180).

The economic significance of the York coinage

It would be wrong to judge the scale of minting in different periods on the basis of the number of extant coins when their survival rate varies so enormously according to the hoards that happen to have been found. While the early York regal coinage has an extremely high survival rate thanks to the discovery of the Cuerdale hoard, many of the later Scandinavian coinages are poorly represented in the hoard material, particularly where they were in issue for only a short time. Fortunately, there is an objective way of assessing the relative output in different issues, if a die-study has been made. Providing the sample studied is large enough, there are statistical formulae that can be applied to estimate the number of dies originally used to produce the coinage, subject to certain reservations (Esty 1986).

Die-studies have been published for all the Scandinavian issues of York except the Swordless St Peter. The number of surviving coins and the number of obverse and reverse dies from which these were struck is set out in Table 5. From these figures it has been possible to estimate the total number of equivalent dies likely to have been used, which should give a broad indication of the relative size of each issue. In some cases the margin of error (indicated by the range in square brackets) is very wide because the sample is small, and for certain issues it is not even possible to produce any meaningful estimates.

Table 5 Number of surviving coins of York and the dies they are struck from

In the coinages before the Sword St Peter issue the side with the mint-name was normally on the lower die (see p.335) and has hence been treated here as the obverse.

In the 'Estimated dies' columns, the most probable estimate of 'equivalent dies' is given, and below in square brackets the range implied by the 95% confidence limits. The number of 'equivalent dies' means the total number of dies assuming that the unknown dies struck on average the same number of coins as those represented in the surviving material. Almost certainly they will have struck fewer, so the result will be an under-estimate of the original dies, but this is a fairer way of representing the likely size of the coinage. Calculations are based on Esty 1986, formulae J2, J3 and K1. For the early York regal coinage information about singletons and doubletons has not been published, and the estimates of dies are a guess.

Coinage	Length of issue (years)	No. of extant coins	No. of dies represented		Estimated total dies		Source of die-study
			Obv.	Rev.	Obv.	Rev.	
Early York regal	10	3,043+	c.250	c.400	c.275?	c.550?	Lyon and Stewart 1961
Swordless St Peter	15	c.200	n.a.	n.a.	n.a.	n.a.	–
Ragnald I	2	23	19	22	52 [28–400]	too uncertain	Blunt and Stewart 1983
Sword St Peter	6	83	38	56	48 [40–59]	95 [67–156]	Stewart and Lyon 1992
Athelstan	12	c.150?	n.a.	n.a.	n.a.	n.a.	–
Olaf *Raven* type	2	36	31	35	122 [68–550]	too uncertain	*CTCE*, 229–30
Triquetra type	2	20	19	20	too uncertain	too uncertain	*CTCE*, 231
Circumscription Cross/Cross Moline types	2	16	13	16	41 [21–444]	too uncertain	*CTCE*, 231–2
Eric *Horizontal* type	2	23	15	18	26 [17–54]	51 [31–152]	*CTCE*, 232–3
Olaf types	2	26	20	20	59 [34–233]	59 [34–233]	*CTCE*, 233–4
Eric *Sword* type	2	16	15	14	too uncertain	too uncertain	*CTCE*, 234

The early York regal coinage was very substantial, albeit that it lasted some ten years. If it was indeed the first coinage to be struck in Scandinavian Northumbria, there would have been a lot of 'foreign' coinage and bullion to be converted, the fruits of plunder and tribute over several decades. It would have required several tonnes of silver for its production (Stewart 1987, 349–54). Subsequent issues, however, would have relied primarily on trade to attract the necessary metal to York and to its mint. We have no figures for the Swordless St Peter issue, but Ragnald I's coinage seems to have been struck on quite a large scale, bearing in mind that it probably lasted for only a year or two. By contrast the Sword St Peter coinage was rather limited, for there is a good deal of die-linking among the surviving coins and the estimates are reasonably secure. The parallel coinage in the name of Sihtric Caech may have supplemented it to some extent, although the Bossall hoard suggests this barely circulated north of the Humber. The really surprising point to emerge from Table 5 is the size of Olaf Guthfrithsson's *Raven* type, with more than a hundred obverse dies employed in one or two years; it must have gone a long way towards replacing the Anglo-Saxon coinage put into circulation by Athelstan between 927 and 939. Subsequent issues were also substantial, although often the surviving sample is too small to provide a fair estimate of the dies in use. The *Triquetra* issue, in particular, could have been large, for there is virtually no die-linking among the 20 extant specimens. In the last two issues of Olaf Sihtricsson and Eric Bloodaxe, obverse and reverse dies seem to have been issued in equal numbers, while before that a ratio of two to one is implied by the estimates available.

It is clear that none of the coinages were merely token issues for political or propaganda purposes, and it seems that York was thriving economically, particularly during the periods of Scandinavian rule between 939 and 954. By way of comparison, after Edgar's monetary reform when there were regular periodic recoinages, the York mint is estimated to have used between 150 and 400 *reverse* dies per type for those types lasting five or six years and 50–100 for types lasting two or three years (Metcalf 1981, 84–5). This implies that during the period c.973–1050, when York ranked as the second or third mint in England, it normally used 20–60 reverse dies per year. More precise estimates will be available when Lean's die-study of the York mint has been published, but the preliminary results, as calculated by Lyon (pers. comm.), indicate that the number of reverse dies used annually between c.973 and 1066 was usually about 30–40, although at exceptional times it may have been as high as 70. It is impressive that most of the Anglo-Scandinavian issues seem to have equalled or exceeded the rate of die use at late Anglo-Saxon York.

Nature of currency in York and the northern Danelaw

For a full century before the Viking conquest, Northumbria had had a closed currency system based on the distinctive local stycas, which eventually became so base as to be made of pure brass. The silver coins of southern England rarely circulated north of the Humber, at least before the 870s, from when a few *Lunette* coins of Burgred, Æthelred I and Alfred have been found. Three have occurred at separate sites in York, and in a hoard from Lower Dunsforth, 22km north west of York (for finds mentioned in this section, see Appendix, pp.347–9). It is tempting to see these as part of the loot and tribute brought to the region by members of the Viking army when they returned to Northumbria with Halfdan in autumn 874 and subsequently settled the region in 875/6. However, with the political uncertainty of the preceding decade, and with stycas no longer be-

ing produced in York, southern coins could have begun to circulate among Northumbrians, especially traders in York. The Lower Dunsforth hoard, comprising a roleau of 30 pennies mostly or entirely of the *Lunette* type, is paralleled by the much smaller group of four coins from Gainford, Co. Durham (Blackburn and Pagan 1986, no.76). Both have a probable *terminus post quem* of 873/5. In any event, during the 870s and 880s people in Northumbria, who had been used to a plentiful money supply, must have found it increasingly difficult to conduct business as circulation of the old stycas declined and relatively few coins were being brought in from elsewhere. Other single-finds that may represent this period are two Alfred imitations from mints in the southern Danelaw found near Doncaster and near York, a Danish penny found in York and three Carolingian coins found at Kilham, Coxwold and York, though any of these finds might have been losses from the late 9th or early 10th century.

The Scandinavians were, of course, used to a money-weight economy in which coins were treated as silver bullion, together with ingots and ornaments, material to be cut up and exchanged by weight. By contrast, in the western coin-producing countries such as the Anglo-Saxon and Carolingian kingdoms, coins were generally trusted and accepted by tale (i.e. counted out) in transactions. There is ample evidence that the money-weight system was practised by Scandinavians in Britain. Mixed hoards containing local and 'foreign' coin — Arabic dirhems, and Carolingian and Anglo-Saxon pennies — often with cut ornaments and ingots, have been found in most areas of Britain settled by Scandinavians, the Cuerdale hoard being merely the largest and best-known example. In recent years 'foreign' coins, ingots and hack-silver have also become more numerous as single- finds from the same regions, best exemplified by the prolific site at Torksey, Lincolnshire. Another indicator of a bullion economy is the practice of 'pecking' or testing the coins and metalwork with a sharp knife to check the metal's purity (Archibald 1990), a feature found extensively in the Cuerdale hoard, but also observed, for example, in finds from the southern Danelaw in the period c.890–925.

From the northern Danelaw, taken for practical purposes as the present county of Yorkshire, besides the three Carolingian coins mentioned above, there are four single-finds of Islamic dirhems, a silver ingot from Easingwold (Blackburn and Bonser 1990) and two mixed hoards. The Goldsborough hoard, deposited c.920, contained 37 Arabic dirhems, three Anglo-Saxon coins and 14 pieces of silver ornaments. The Bossall hoard, deposited c.927, contained some 270 coins, mostly Viking issues, with some Anglo-Saxon and Arabic pieces, and ornamental silver. Both are of a classic Viking character, although of very different composition, presumably reflecting the economies of the areas in which they were assembled. Goldsborough, with no coins of the Danelaw and its ornamental silver essentially Irish (Graham-Campbell 1993), appears to have been brought intact from Ireland or north-west England (cf. the recent hoard from Warton, Lancashire). The much larger Bossall hoard also contained ornaments and hack-silver, but the coins were predominantly issues of the Vikings of York ranging from the odd piece of Cnut, through Swordless St Peter and Ragnald I to both issues of the Sword St Peter coinage. The few St Edmund coins present could have circulated on a par with the York issues, but the Anglo-Saxon element, struck to a heavier standard, and the two Arabic dirhems would have constituted 'foreign' money in the northern Danelaw, confirming Bossall's status as a hoard with a bullion element.

There is, however, other evidence to suggest that a more conventional coin economy was also operating, particularly in York itself. The very presence of a mint, producing a large well-regulated coinage, indicates an intention to run a managed currency in which the coins should be accepted by tale. Of the fourteen single-finds from York in the period c.895–954, only one can be classified as 'foreign' (a forgery of an Arabic dirhem). Nine are issues of Scandinavian York (Cnut two, St Peter six, Sihtric II one), two are arguably issues of the York Vikings struck at mints elsewhere ('Alfred' *Orsnaforda* type and Sihtric Caech), and two are Anglo-Saxon (Athelstan York and Eadred HT1 which may post-date 954). All of these could be regarded as legitimately circulating in York when they were lost. The 1856 hoard from Walmgate, York, reinforces this evidence. The hundred or more coins, so far as we can tell, comprised only Anglo-Scandinavian issues, and these were almost entirely of the Swordless St Peter type, with just a few St Edmund coins on a similar weight standard and perhaps one specimen of the earlier York regal coinage. This hoard has the classic features of a sum of money withdrawn from a well-managed monetary economy, one from which Anglo-Saxon or other 'foreign' issues had been excluded and earlier York coins had been replaced by the new St Peter coinage. We cannot be sure whether this was the result of a formal recoinage or occurred through the operation of Gresham's Law ('bad money drives out good', or in this case the lighter St Peter issue drove the York regal coins to the mint). The result was a fairly homogeneous currency within the city of York. In other parts of the northern Danelaw the York coinage also dominated the currency, as the rapidly growing body of single-find evidence shows. Thus of the seventeen post-895 single-finds from the rest of Yorkshire, twelve were York issues (York regal, six; Swordless St Peter, two; Olaf *Triquetra*, two; Ragnald II *Triquetra*, one; Eric *Horizontal*, one), one was a St Edmund and only four were 'foreign' (Arabic dirhems, three not identified, so perhaps from before 895). The only other hoard from York, a small group of four associated coins from the Coppergate excavations, illustrates the transition between the currency of Athelstan's reign and that of the restored Norse regime of Olaf Guthfrithsson. Two of the coins are heavy Anglo-Saxon pennies and two are coins of the *Raven* type that was intended to replace them.

The situation in the southern Danelaw was comparable, for there we find two hoards of c.915 dominated by later St Edmund pennies, accompanied by a few early St Edmund or St Peter coins (Blackburn 2001a; Blackburn and Pagan 2002). Parallels can also be drawn with Hedeby and Dublin, where the Scandinavian rulers established effective monetary control based on the local coinage within the town and its immediate hinterland.

It appears, then, that while in the earlier years of Scandinavian settlement in the Danelaw the economy probably functioned on the metal-weight or bullion system, with the establishment of a local coinage the rulers took measures to manage the currency, driving foreign coin and bullion out of circulation by insisting that it be reminted into the local coinage, and hence paying fees that benefited the state. In York this was soon implemented quite effectively, but elsewhere in the northern Danelaw there appears to have been a period of transition in which both types of economy co-existed. There is too little evidence to judge when transactions by weight ceased. Athelstan would surely have tried hard to stamp them out after the Anglo-Saxon reconquest of 927, and there is no sign of them after the restoration of Scandinavian rule in 939. The main evidence for their survival into the 920s is the Bossall hoard, but Graham-Campbell (1993, 83) has argued that this may have been exceptional, the hack-silver element perhaps representing treasure brought from Dublin by Sihtric Caech in 921 or through continuing contacts with Ireland in the years following. It does seem likely that a hoard the size of Bossall and one with a fairly long age profile represents a store of wealth rather than immediate currency. Yet the fact that new coins, 'foreign' coins and bullion were stored together, a phenomenon never found in the Anglo-Saxon or Carolingian kingdoms, shows that the owner perceived the various elements as forms of money appropriate to add to his savings. Again parallels from the southern Danelaw are relevant, for the recent Thurcaston hoard from Leicestershire, deposited c.925, contained a mixture of Anglo-Scandinavian, Anglo-Saxon and fragmentary Arabic coins, the latter only recently arrived from Central Asia. In the market-place the owner of such a hoard might well have sorted his money into different categories, for the local Viking issues should have been accepted at face value, while the 'foreign' coins and any hack-silver would have had to be weighed. The Anglo-Saxon coins were perhaps in an intermediate category and accepted at a standard rate, knowing that they could be passed by tale over the border in Mercia.

Conclusions

The Scandinavian kingdom of York, which lasted for some 60 years, is in many respects shrouded in mystery. The dearth of contemporary written evidence, even from external sources, means that for certain periods we barely know the names of its rulers, let alone its policies, achievements or institutions. One has to look to other sources, among which the coinage provides some of the clearest and best-dated evidence we have, shedding light on certain aspects of its administration, economy and political policies. Through these we can begin to glimpse what may have been a remarkably well-developed, sophisticated and successful state. How far the church in York contributed to this is a matter of debate. We should no longer think of the church as barely surviving in a hostile pagan environment, although its survival at York through the Scandinavian period is in itself a notable feat, for the coinage suggests that it had a

significant influence on policy and perhaps the administration. On the other hand allowance should be made for the ability of the Scandinavian ruling elite to develop political policy, engage in diplomacy and implement a strategy for the formation and development of an independent state.

We have seen that by the mid-890s (or a little earlier) the Scandinavians were able to re-establish a mint in York, perhaps with personnel recruited from the Continent. They produced a large coinage that was technically accomplished and innovative in many respects. The intellectual content of the designs is remarkable, and there can be no doubting the significance of the powerful Christian theme running through them. The audience is likely to have been not merely a domestic one, but the neighbouring Anglo-Saxon, Carolingian and British kingdoms as well, in a bid to persuade them that this was now a mature and civilised Christian state. In due course the message was modified, when in 919 Ragnald I faced the prospect of an Anglo-Saxon reconquest by Edward the Elder, in 939 Olaf Guthfrithsson celebrated the restoration of Scandinavian control and c.952 Eric Bloodaxe strove to hold on to power. They were moved, in each case, to appeal to Norse sentiments, though without abandoning the Christian ethic. Rarely in the early medieval period had coins been used for such overt political purposes.

Economically the York coinage was a considerable success, with annual output under the Scandinavians often equalling or exceeding that of the mint in the prosperous 11th century when York ranked as the second or third mint in the country. The period of lowest production appears to have been the mid-920s, perhaps because the northern Danelaw was politically isolated; yet the mint positively flourished during the later phases of Norse control between 939 and 954, coinciding incidentally with a period of intense activity on the Coppergate site. The Scandinavian rulers also made a reasonably good job of imposing a regulated currency, even if the traditional money-weight economy survived in some quarters until at least the 920s. The Scandinavian coinage had its weaknesses — not least in terms of literacy of the inscriptions — but overall it was an impressive achievement, which serves as a warning not to underestimate a society merely because we know little about it.

Appendix

Coin Finds from Yorkshire, c.870–954

Hoards

For fuller references to these hoards, see Blackburn and Pagan 1986, nos. 74, 94, 101, 108, 121; also available in an updated form on: www.medievalcoins.org/hoards/

Lower Dunsforth (St Mary's churchyard), N. Yorkshire (22km north-west of York), 1860. Found while digging a boundary ditch between the modern churchyard and School House. Some 30 coins mostly of the *Lunette* type of Burgred, Æthelred I and Alfred (fifteen listed: Burgred, six; Æthelred I, two; Alfred, seven), perhaps with the odd coin of Æthelberht of Wessex and Ceolwulf II of Mercia. If the latter was present, as suggested by a contemporary newspaper report, it would put the deposit date in the later 870s. A revised report will be published by the present author. No recorded container or other metalwork. Deposited probably c.873/5.

York (Walmgate), 1856. c.100+ coins, mostly St Peter type without sword (90+ and two halfpennies), with perhaps one York regal issue of Æthelwold (*Alvvaldus*), two pennies and a halfpenny of the St Edmund issue. No recorded container or other metalwork. Deposited c.915.

Goldsborough, N. Yorkshire (25km west of York), 1858. 40 coins: three Anglo-Saxon coins comprising a fragment of an exceptionally rare 'offering coin' of Alfred and two pennies of Edward the Elder's *Two-Line* type (not one as published by Vaux; pers. comm. Gareth Williams, who plans to republish the hoard), with 37 Arabic dirhems. Fourteen pieces of silver bullion, including a magnificent whole thistle brooch, predominantly if not entirely of Irish origin. According to different accounts, said to have been found in a 'small leaden chest' or an 'earthenware pot' (Graham-Campbell 1993, 83). Deposited c.920.

Bossall, N. Yorkshire (15km north-east of York), 1807. c.270 coins: mostly Vikings of York (Cnut, Swordless St Peter, Ragnald I and Sword St Peter), with some of St Edmund, Anglo-Saxon (Alfred, Edward the Elder and Athelstan), and two Arabic dirhems. Possibly in a lead chest with silver ornaments and hack-silver, of which only one arm-ring survives (Graham-Campbell 1993). Deposited c.927.

York (16–22 Coppergate), 1980. A pile of four coins: two of Athelstan (CR Chester and HT1 NE I), and two of Olaf Guthfrithsson's *Raven* type (*AY* 18/1, 52–5). Deposited c.940.

Single-finds

For more details of the following finds, illustrations and references, see the *Corpus of Early Medieval Coin Finds from the British Isles 450–1180* at: www.medievalcoins.org/emc/

1. Burgred, *Lunette* type a, London, moneyer Eanred, Early phase, style G (c.863–5). York (21–33 Aldwark), 1973.

2. Burgred, *Lunette* type d, London, moneyer Diarulf, Middle phase, style H (c.866–8). York (58–9 Skeldergate), 1974.

3. Burgred, *Lunette* type a, London, moneyer Diga, beginning of Late phase, style F (c.869–70). York (Tanner Row), 1961.

4. Lead weight implanted with a silver coin of the *Lunette* type a, probably in the name of Alfred, London, moneyer Dudda (c.873–5). Malton/Scarborough area, N. Yorkshire, 1998. Williams 1999, no.21.

5. Denmark, anon. penny, 'Wodan/monster' derivative, c.850, Ribe mint? (Malmer KG6), fragment 0·11g. York (16–22 Coppergate), 1980.

6. Carolingian, Louis the Pious, *Christiana Religio* type (822–40), denier. Kilham (Bridlington), E. Yorkshire, pre-September 1996 (Barclay 1997).

7. Carolingian, Charles the Bald or later (848–77 or later), Melle mint, 1·57g. Coxwold, N. Yorkshire, 1982–9 (Seaby 1992, 113).

8. Carolingian, Charles the Bald, *GDR* type (864–77, or later), obol, Palace mint. York (16–22 Coppergate), 1981. 0·45g, corroded.

9. Imitation of Alfred's *London Monogram* type (880s), southern Danelaw mint?, 1·14g, chipped. Doncaster, S. Yorkshire, 1987 (Archibald 1988).

10. Imitation of Alfred's *Two-Line* type (c.885–95), moneyer 'Ludig', southern Danelaw mint? Near York, 1988.

11. Imitation of Alfred's Oxford (*Ohsnaforda*) type (c.895–900), Five Boroughs or northern Danelaw mint? York (River Ouse), c.1740.

12. St Edmund issue, halfpenny, southern Danelaw, c.895–918. Some ten miles south of York, 1995.

13. Sigeferth, king of York (c.895–900), *CSiefredus Rex/ Ebraice Civi* type, York mint. 'Yorkshire, East Riding', pre-1998.

14. Æthelwold of Wessex, king of York (c.900–2), *Alvvaldus* type, York mint. North Ferriby, E. Yorkshire, 1985.

15. Cnut, king of York (c.900–5), *Cunnetti* type, York mint. York (Skeldergate), 1879.

16. Cnut, king of York (c.900–5), *Cunnetti* type, York mint. York (16–22 Coppergate), 1980.

17. Cnut, king of York (c.900–5), *Cunnetti* type, York mint. Pocklington, E. Yorkshire, 1993.

18. Cnut, king of York (c.900–5), *Cunnetti* type, York mint. Stamford Bridge, E. Yorkshire, 18 February 1990.

19. Cnut, king of York (c.900–5), *Cunnetti* type, York mint, 1·13g. Near Easingwold, N. Yorkshire, March 1990.

20. Cnut, king of York (c.900–5), *Cunnetti* type, York mint, 1·43g. Rufforth, N. Yorkshire, 1999.

21. Samanids, Isma'il b. Ahmad (892–907), copper forgery of a silver dirhem, Samarqand mint. York (16–22 Coppergate), 1980.

22. Samanids, silver dirhem, unidentified fragment, 892–999, probably early 10th century, 0·58g. Between Tadcaster and York, N. Yorkshire, by 1999.

23. Islamic silver dirhem, unidentified fragment, probably 9th–early 10th century. Kingston upon Hull, E. Yorkshire, by 1998.

24. Islamic silver dirhem, unidentified fragment, probably 9th–early 10th century, 0·91g. Scampston/ Rillington area, N. Yorkshire, 1999.

25. Islamic silver dirhem, unidentified fragment, probably 9th–early 10th century. N. Yorkshire, 2001.

26. St Peter issue, type Without Sword, early variant (c.905), York mint. York, 1859.

27. St Peter issue, type Without Sword, earlier variant (c.910), York mint. Near Doncaster, S. Yorkshire, 1988.

28. St Peter issue, type Without Sword, middle phase (c.910–15), York mint. York (16–22 Coppergate), 1980.

29. St Peter issue, type Without Sword, unidentified fragment, probably 9th–early 10th century. Middle phase (c.910–15), York mint. Beverley (Lurk Lane), E. Yorkshire, 1979–82.

30. St Peter issue, type Without Sword, later variant (c.915), York mint. York (St Mary Bishophill Junior), c.1961.

31. St Peter issue, type Without Sword, *One-Line* variant (c.917), York mint. York (Skeldergate), 1880.

32. Two or more St Peter issue, unspecified types, Without or With Sword (c.905–19, c.921–7), York mint. York (dredged from the River Ouse), c.1740.

33. Sihtric I 'Caech', king of York (921–7), *Sword/ Hammer* type, Five Boroughs mint. York (16–22 Coppergate), 1980.

34. Athelstan (927–39), *Circumscription Cross* type, moneyer Regnald, York mint. York (16–22 Coppergate), 1981.

35. Olaf Sihtricsson (941–944/5), AR penny, *Triquetra/ Banner* type, moneyer Farman, York mint, 1·03g.

Campsall, near Doncaster, S. Yorkshire, 1989 (Seaby 1992, 109).

36. Olaf Sihtricsson (941–944/5), AR penny, *Triquetra/Banner* type, moneyer Farman, York mint. West of Beverley, E. Yorkshire, 1994.

37. Ragnald II Guthfrithsson (943–944/5), AR penny, fragment, *Triquetra/Banner* type, moneyer Durant, York mint. Middleton on the Wolds, E. Yorkshire, 2002.

38. Sihtric II Sihtricsson, king of York (c.943–4), *Triquetra/Banner* type, moneyer Farman, York mint. York (16–22 Coppergate), 1981.

39. Eadred (946–55), *Horizontal* type (HT1), moneyer and mint uncertain. York (16–22 Coppergate), 1980.

40. Eric Bloodaxe, king of York (1st reign, 947–8), *Horizontal* type (HT1), moneyer Radulf, York mint. 'Yorkshire Wolds, between Malton and Beverley', N. Yorkshire, 1986.

The Inscriptions of Viking-Age York

By David N. Parsons

When in 1955 fire destroyed the historic water-front quarter of Bergen in western Norway, it not only reshaped the town, but also our understanding of literacy in the medieval period. The burnt site was given over to archaeologists, whose excavations turned up hundreds of wooden sticks bearing runic inscriptions, extraordinary not only for their numbers, but for the great range of their contents. Business transactions, ownership tags, love letters, poems, prayers, magical gibberish: all are represented in the casually carved texts that came from layers datable between the 12th and 15th centuries. Yet, although the cache was richer than anyone acquainted with the medieval inscriptions of north-western Europe could have imagined, it did not come wholly out of the blue. Scholars had long since observed that the angularity of runic script, with its general avoidance of horizontal lines, looked as if it might have been designed for cutting in wood, where curves are hard to cut and horizontals could be lost in the grain. From their invention by Germanic-speaking people some time before the 2nd century AD, runes may well have been commonly carved into wood. But wooden artefacts generally perish in the ground, and it has often been argued that the surviving evidence, predominantly on metal and stone, is likely to be untypical of what must have existed. The Bergen finds, which have since been supported by similar, if less extensive, discoveries in other medieval Scandinavian towns, like Lödöse (Sweden), Trondheim (Norway) and Ribe (Denmark), have been held up as representative of runic literacy that is largely lost but may have been widespread.

This was the line taken by a leading Norwegian scholar, Aslak Liestøl, who published an article in 1971 called 'The literate Vikings', in which he suggested that 'the majority of Viking Age Scandinavians — at least those of any standing, and those intent on making their way in life — were able to read and write' (Liestøl 1971, 76). He implied that the Bergen finds, although they are of rather later date, allow us to glimpse the everyday, practical, commercial and casual uses of literacy in the Viking Age (c.800–1100). If this were the case, one might expect that York — which, like Bergen, is archaeologically remarkable for

the excellent preservation of organic materials, including wood — would be rich in runic finds. Yet, to date, only a single undisputed rune-inscribed object has been found in the city. It is a wooden spoon, perhaps of the late 10th or 11th century, that came to light in 1884 in Clifford Street, during the rebuilding of the Quaker Meeting House (Waterman 1959, 85–6; Page 1969, 173; Page 1999, 170). The 'inscription' consists of just two runes, not even enough to allow us certainly to distinguish between the Scandinavian runic alphabet and the quite distinct Anglo-Saxon version. If the runes are Scandinavian, they read **nm** or **um**. If they are Anglo-Saxon, they are probably **cx**. Page (1999, 170) has suggested that the text may represent an owner's mark. Alternatively, if the Anglo-Saxon reading is the right one, **cx** might conceivably represent a Roman numeral (for this application of runes in a late Anglo-Saxon manuscript see Page 1995, 124). In the circumstances, any interpretation is clearly no more than guesswork.

Other possible runic inscriptions from York are equally unpromising. Page records a fragment of stone found beneath York Minster 'having traces of two runes so slight that we cannot tell which type [Anglo-Saxon or Scandinavian] they belong to' (Page 1971, 182; the stone does not appear to be noted by Lang et al. 1991). The same scholar also notes a bone comb-case from the city 'with a sequence of incised lines which 19th-century enthusiasts decided were runes', but which he groups with other 'rune-like' sequences (Page 1999, 94; the 'inscription' is illustrated at Waterman 1959, 90). On a charitable view, York might therefore aspire to three Scandinavian runic inscriptions (though no one could pretend that any of them is intelligible); on a more sober assessment, it has no certain examples, and does not feature at all in recent published lists of the Anglo-Scandinavian runic corpus (Barnes 1993; Holman 1996). If we wish to learn anything of the Vikings in York from epigraphy, we cannot simply read the runes: we shall have to find other angles of approach.

The first question to address is whether or not the virtual absence of runes from the city should be considered significant. If Bergen were to be our yardstick, then York certainly looks deficient, or significantly illiterate. The Bergen inscriptions do not come from a single 'library' site, the equivalent of which may so far simply have been missed at York; they appear to come from all over the medieval town (Seim 1988, 11). Surely, if literacy had functioned to the same extent and in the same ways in the two towns, the numerous excavations in different corners of York would by now have produced something to parallel the 600-plus runic finds from Bergen. It is probably safe to conclude that runic writing was less used in Viking-Age York than in Bergen and some other Scandinavian towns in the medieval period.

This, however, is an anachronistic comparison. Although Liestøl suspected widespread literacy in the Viking Age, so far no urban site — in Scandinavia or elsewhere — has produced finds of this date that come close to the scale of the Bergen discoveries. In the British Isles, the Viking town richest in runic finds is Dublin, where the total count of inscriptions found during extensive excavations in the 1970s and 1980s is just fifteen, two of which are classified as rune-like rather than truly runic (Barnes et al. 1997, 18–49; cf. Page 1999, 201 n.7). They are on wood and bone, and seem to belong to various dates between the second half of the 10th and the early 12th century. None approaches the length or interest of the more colourful Bergen texts, and none is certainly the practical work of a merchant or businessman (though one or two might be interpreted in this way). On the other hand, they come from at least three different excavated sites and must, like any such evidence, be interpreted as the tip of a larger iceberg (just as the surviving Bergen finds must represent a staggering number of inscriptions originally carved). Should thirteen to fifteen Scandinavian runic inscriptions from Dublin as against nought to three from York be regarded as a significant indicator of relative literacy? The question could be addressed to archaeologists, who may wish to compare the details of the excavated sites of the two cities, and to statisticians. But the numbers are probably too small for this to be a profitable line of enquiry.

If York's runic poverty is not so very remarkable when set in the context of towns in the wider Viking world, neither is it out of place in England. To date there are only some fifteen Scandinavian runic inscriptions to show for the centuries of political and cultural influence exercised by the Vikings and their descendants in this country (Barnes 1993, 33–4; Holman 1996, 14–85; cf. Page 1999, 204 and n.9). Moreover, of these fifteen, six were found in the south-east, outside (or, at best, on the very edge of) the Danelaw. One of the others, at Bridekirk in Cumbria, is carved in Scandinavian runes, but it records 12th-century English language not obviously influenced by Norse at all. A large proportion are barely legible, fragmentary or otherwise problematic. The nearest Scandinavian runic inscription to York is on a sandstone sundial found at Skelton-in-Cleveland (formerly in the North Riding of Yorkshire), almost 50 miles to the north. To the south, the nearest examples come from Lincoln, which boasts a cattle-rib with a rather inscrutable short message, and a comb-case made of antler, with the beautifully legible Old Norse text: **kamb:koþan:kiari:þorfastr**, 'Thorfastr made a good comb'. Lincoln is clearly to be envied such an intelligible inscription, but on such slight evidence it can hardly claim a demonstrably better-educated class of Viking settler than York.

It is not to be denied, of course, that in some parts of the Scandinavian world, at some periods of the Viking Age, there are considerable concentrations of surviving runic inscriptions: over 1,000 memorial stones in the Uppland district of Sweden, for instance; or, in the British Isles, over 30 stones on the relatively tiny Isle of Man. Yet distribution is in general very uneven (for memorial stones in mainland Scandinavia see the map in Palm 1992, 73; for an overview of runes in Viking colonies see Page 1971, 182–3; Page 1995, 195–6), and heavy concentrations are no less exceptional than absences elsewhere. The dearth of runes in York is not astonishing when set in contemporary context.

We might turn now to other, more tangible, evidence of inscriptions from early medieval York: the objects and stones that bear texts in Roman script. Unfortunately, again, this material is decidedly limited. Of the ten York items listed by Okasha in her *Hand-List of Anglo-Saxon Non-Runic Inscriptions* and two published supplements (Okasha 1971; 1983; 1992), at least six probably date from the period before the Viking settlements, while only one gives any record of vernacular language in the city during the Anglo-Scandinavian period. Nonetheless, although the latter, the St Mary Castlegate stone, naturally deserves special consideration here, the group as a whole is not without some interest, for it can (arguably) be seen to reflect important cultural change between the Anglian and Viking periods of the city's history.

Eight of the inscriptions mentioned by Okasha are on stone, and are also discussed in the third volume of the British Academy's *Corpus of Anglo-Saxon Stone Sculpture* (Lang et al. 1991). The latter assigns five of them, three memorial slabs from excavations at the Minster and two fragments of freestanding crosses found elsewhere in the city, to a period between the late 7th and early 9th centuries (Lang et al. 1991, 62–6 [*20–2*], 85–7 [*5*], 108–9 [*1*]; Okasha 1971 gives similar dates to the crosses [*147–8*], but regards the Minster slabs [*150–1, 153*] as of uncertain date). Higgitt (in Lang et al. 1991, 44–7) argues that there is reason to treat them as a coherent pre-Viking-Age group. He observes that all five 'are skilfully executed on well carved monuments', and that — although all are fragmentary — four of the five texts are clearly in Latin; the fifth simply preserves a personal name. The letter-forms on the stones, he suggests, are closely comparable to some varieties of display script employed in 8th-century Anglo-Saxon manuscripts, and the use of heightened language, poetic metre and occasional Greek lettering amongst the Roman seems to imply a sophisticated milieu for at least two of the inscriptions. All of this, Higgitt proposes, is appropriate to a literate ecclesiastical community such as that which fostered the famous scholar Alcuin (died 804). The inscription of the St Mary Castlegate dedication stone, attributed to the 10th or 11th century (Lang et al. 1991, 99–101 [*7*], Okasha 1971, *146*), is rather different. It is partly in Old English and its lettering, in Higgitt's view (in Lang et al. 1991, 47), consists of 'rather unrefined capitals'. Evidently, it belongs with a contemporary group of architectural inscriptions in Yorkshire in which laymen (apparently) are recorded as patrons of new, or newly restored, churches. Probably, as Higgitt suggests (ibid.), 'part of the function of these later inscriptions was to serve as secular symbols'.

This progression, from learned, Latinate and ecclesiatical to vernacular and secular, has been traced more widely in Northumbrian epigraphy (Fell 1994), and could be thought to reflect a general trend in Anglo-Saxon church organisation from the 9th century onwards. Control and influence, it has been argued, shifted away from the great ecclesiastical centres, the ancient minsters, and towards local par-

ish churches, often established under secular patronage (Blair 1988; cf. Blair 1995). Although this trend is not limited to the Danelaw and, as we shall see, there is not much that is Scandinavian in the St Mary Castlegate inscription, it is very likely that the Viking assaults of the 9th century were an important catalyst for these developments (cf. Blair 1988, 3; Dumville 1992, 29–54). If we are tempted to feel frustration at the virtual absence of Norse inscriptions from York, it is perhaps worth reminding ourselves that the pattern of finds across the region can be thought ultimately to depend on the Viking conquest.

Before turning to the dedication stone, we can briefly dispose of another three of York's early inscriptions. One appears on the famous helmet discovered at Coppergate in 1982 (*AY* 17/8). This is attributed on stylistic grounds to the 8th century, and bears a Latin text which Okasha (1992, 58–60 [*211*]) translates 'In the name of our Lord Jesus Christ, the Holy Spirit [and] God; and to all we say Amen. Oshere', where Oshere represents a syntactically unrelated Anglo-Saxon personal name, presumably that of the owner or maker of the helmet. There has been some dispute over the details of the interpretation, fuelled by the fact that there is at least one error in the Latin (cf. Binns et al. 1990; *AY* 1, 160–1). None the less, on any reading, the helmet is a fairly sophisticated, high-status production, which sits comfortably enough with the pre-Viking-Age group of inscribed stones. It is interesting, however, that Higgitt (in Lang et al. 1991, 45–6) argues that the script on the helmet contrasts markedly with that on the stones, possibly suggesting that it was produced outside York.

Then there are two more stones from the Minster. One is a memorial inscription in Latin (Lang et al. 1991, 75–6 [*42*], Okasha 1971, *152*), which might therefore be linked to the pre-Viking-Age group. Higgitt (in Lang et al. 1991, 46) argues, however, that its script and layout suggest an 'informality and lack of professionalism' that set it apart and may imply a rather later date, perhaps after the disruptions of the 9th century. The content of the inscription, however, is uninformative: it reads *Orate pro anima Costaun*, 'Pray for the soul of Costaun', where Costaun is apparently a personal name, or the beginning of a personal name, of uncertain origin (Lang et al. 1991, 76). Finally, the other Minster stone, which might be mentioned for completeness, is rejected by Lang et al. 1991 (p.118) as post-conquest (cf. Okasha 1971, *149*): the piece in question is a damaged sculpture representing the Virgin and Child, with an explanatory Latin text: S[AN]C[T]A MARIA.

The text of the St Mary Castlegate stone (Fig.85) reads as follows (for more rigorous transcriptions and detailed accounts, see Lang et al. 1991, 100; Okasha 1971, 131; Okasha 1983, 111):

> MINSTERSE
> ARD&GRIM&ÆSE:*O*
> MANDRIHTNESHÆ
> CRISTES&SCAMA
> E:MARTINI: &SCEC
> TI&OMNIVMSCŌR*V*
> *S*ECRATAESTAN
> *V*ISINVITA:ET
> AERIOÞEM
> *RÆ*TS*I*

Letters are lost from the ends of all of the lines, and the beginning of at least some. It is possible to restore the beginning of the text with some confidence:

... minster setton –ard & Grim & Æse on naman Drihtnes hæ– Cristes & Sancta Maria & Sancte Martini & Sancte C–ti & omnium sanctorum consecrata est ...

' –ard and Grim and Æse established [this] church in the name of the [holy?] Lord Christ and St Mary and St Martin and St [Cuthbert?] and of all the saints. It was consecrated ...'.

In the damaged end of the inscription *in vita* is clearly 'in life' but Higgitt (in Lang et al. 1991, 100–1) shows that various reconstructions of other fragments are possible. The use of Þ in the penultimate, and apparently Æ in the last visible line, suggests that the text may revert from Latin to Old English at the end.

As noted above, this inscription can be compared with others in the region. Most important is that carved around a sundial at Kirkdale (twenty miles north of York), the main text of which reads:

Orm Gamal suna bohte Sanctus Gregorius minster ðonne hit wes æl tobrocan & tofalan & he hit let macan newan from grunde Criste & Sanctus Gregorius in Eadward dagum Cyning & in Tosti dagum Eorl

Fig.85 *St Mary Castlegate dedication stone. Height 495mm*

'Orm, son of Gamal, bought St Gregory's church when it was utterly ruined and collapsed, and he had it built anew from the ground for Christ and Saint Gregory, in the days of King Edward and Earl Tostig' (Lang et al. 1991, 163–6 [*10*], Okasha 1971, *64*) (Fig.86).

The dating formula places the rebuilding between 1055 and 1065. Another text states that it (presumably the inscribed sundial) was made by Hawarð and Brand the priest. As at Castlegate, therefore, the stone commemorates the patron of the church and records the dedication. Where the Castlegate stone uses both Old English and Latin, Kirkdale is wholly in Old English. Particularly interesting in the present context are the personal names: Castlegate's Grim, certainly, and Æse, possibly, are names of Old Norse origin, as are Kirkdale's Orm, Gamal, Hawarð and Brand. Yet the small fragment of Old English at Castlegate and the longer specimen from Kirkdale offer very little other evidence of linguistic influence from Old Norse. Although several late, 'non-classical' features can be identified in the Old English of Kirkdale, nothing in

Fig.86 *The Kirkdale sundial (above) and details of the inscriptions (left)*

the texts that have been quoted is easily explained as due to a Norse admixture. Only in a third short text at Kirkdale, cut into the semi-circle of the sundial, is there a possible Nordicism: the word *solmerca* in the sentence *Þis is dæges solmerca æt ilcum tide*, 'this is the day's "sun-marker" at every hour', may represent Old Norse *sólmerki*, though this word is otherwise only recorded in the sense 'sign of the zodiac', not the 'sun-marker, sundial' that would best suit the context (Page 1971, 193–4).

There are other examples in the East Riding of late Anglo-Saxon inscriptions which commemorate people with Scandinavian names but use Old English little, if at all, influenced by Old Norse (Okasha 1971, *1, 41*; cf. Higgitt in Lang et al. 1991, 46; Page 1971, 191–3). The St Mary Castlegate stone should be considered in this context. In an influential paper entitled 'How long did the Scandinavian language survive in England?', the Swedish scholar Ekwall argued that these inscriptions showed that Scandinavians in the area had given up their language in favour of Old English before the Norman conquest (Ekwall 1930). Page, on the other hand, disputes their evidential value: he points out that Norse personal names may have been widely adopted by English people as a matter of fashion, and cites documented cases of Norse-named people from predominantly English families (Page 1971, 192). In light of this, it becomes very difficult to isolate any evidence that would demonstrate that the descendants of the Viking settlers had given up the Old Norse language: our ignorance on the question of how long the language was spoken is great.

Nonetheless, the inscription from Skelton-in-Cleveland, briefly mentioned above, is interesting here. Like several of the other Yorkshire instances, it accompanies a sundial, and has a text in Roman script and vernacular language. Though too little of the inscription remains for its message or purpose to be deciphered, it seems likely that the stone belongs to the region's late Anglo-Saxon vogue for architectural inscriptions, especially on sundials (though cf. Holman 1996, 80 who finds arguments for a post-conquest date). The Skelton stone is extraordinary, however, because the language of the Roman-script text is very likely Old Norse, and because the stone also bears an inscription (unfortunately even more fragmentary) in Scandinavian runes. This looks rather like a Scandinavian reflex of the tradition represented at Castlegate, Kirkdale and elsewhere in rather more English form, despite their Norse personal names. If this is right, Skelton indicates that Scandinavian settlers *could* assimilate to the local Christian culture of late Anglo-Saxon Yorkshire without losing their language, and that they were not excluded from the section of society that could afford to commission monuments. These observations may be relevant to consideration of the St Mary Castlegate stone, though conditions in the great urban centre of York may have differed considerably from those on the coast of North Yorkshire.

What we can certainly deduce from the Castlegate inscription is that, despite centuries of Norse rule and high-status cultural influence in York, Old Norse had not become a required language for public statements. This is hardly a surprise: after all, the inscription may well post-date the final re-establishment of English political control over the city in 954. In fact it is not unlikely that English would have retained some respect throughout the Viking period, since one crucial Anglo-Saxon institution, the church, survived and managed to absorb the Scandinavian influx. Episcopal lists demonstrate that the see of York remained intact throughout the upheavals of the 9th century (Dumville 1992, 31, cf. Hadley 1996, 78–80), and at least one of the late 9th-century Viking rulers at York was reputed to be a Christian (see pp.311, 318). Early in the 10th century epigraphy illustrates the point: the coins issued by Frankish moneyers on behalf of the Norse authorities after c.900 bear Christian iconography and Christian inscriptions in Latin, such as DNS DS REX for *Dominus Deus Rex* (see p.329) (Grierson and Blackburn 1986, 320–2). Not only the

Christianity, but the very decision to issue a coinage, and, of course, the use of Roman script for the legends, indicate a willingness to adopt the culture of the subjugated people, a tendency — whether fuelled by faith or pragmatism — which may also have played a significant role in the Scandinavians' adoption of the English language (cf. Hines 1991).

The only direct, contemporary evidence for the use of Scandinavian language in York comes from coins issued between 939 and 944 in the name of King Anlaf. On them the royal title is given as *cununc*, for Old Danish *kunung*, and the word for 'moneyer', usually Latin *moneta*, is given as *minetr*, presumably a form of Old Norse *myntari* (cf. Grierson and Blackburn 1986, 324). Of course, the widespread, popular use of Old Norse in the city is proved by its later-recorded street-names (see pp.357–71). Inscriptions on other materials unfortunately add nothing to this evidence. The only find recorded by Okasha that remains to be mentioned is an ivory seal-die, possibly of early post-conquest date, which was discovered at Aldwark in 1973 and reads *Sig[illum] Snarri theolenarii* 'the seal of Snarri the tax-gatherer' (Okasha 1983, 103 [*184*], cf. Okasha 1992, 74). Snarri is almost certainly a Scandinavian name, though we have observed that this need tell us nothing of his language or national background; as Fellows-Jensen observes (see p.359), Scandinavian names remained fashionable in York until about the end of the 12th century.

Conclusion

The epigraphic evidence for Viking-Age York is very slight, and this chapter has necessarily been an exercise in explaining absences, exploring contexts and joining widely separated dots. Most conclusions are necessarily going to be speculative, though one deduction seems a robust one: extensive excavations in well-preserved deposits have by now surely demonstrated that Viking-Age York did not use literacy in the same way, or on the same scale, as medieval Bergen. Whether it is significantly short of runes by comparison with broadly contemporary Viking towns like Dublin or Lincoln is less clear. It is perhaps possible that at Dublin a 'purer' Norse linguistic community survived for longer than at York, where from the beginning trade may generally have involved both English and Scandinavian merchants, and where written communication in Scandinavian runes and Old Norse may therefore have been of limited value. It may simply be that literacy in the towns was generally limited, and that York archaeologists have so far been unlucky in hunting for the relatively few inscriptions that would have been left lying around.

Page has speculated on possible reasons for England's general shortage of Viking monumental inscriptions (1971, 195):

the Norse settlers may have belonged in the main to social classes with no tradition of setting up memorial stones, or the English church to which so many inscriptions are linked may have exerted influence against the use of an alien tongue and in favour of the language traditionally employed for vernacular texts.

Both of these factors may well have had a part to play, and the second — as we have seen — could be thought to be exemplified by inscriptions like the St Mary Castlegate stone and Kirkdale sundial, erected by prominent members of Anglo-Scandinavian society. An attractive hypothesis is that the Scandinavian community of York relatively quickly embraced not only the religion but also the language of the Anglo-Saxons, at least in formal, high-status usage (the everyday use of Old Norse reflected in the street-names would perhaps have persisted longer). On the other hand, the evidence of the Skelton-in-Cleveland sundial hints at the possibility that Norse-speakers could erect stones using their own language (and alphabet) within the region's Anglo-Scandinavian monumental tradition. The Skelton stone is a unique piece, too fragmentary to be well understood, but it serves as a useful reminder that we still have very little precise knowledge of the interaction between Old English- and Old Norse-speaking communities in the centuries after the Viking conquest of the Danelaw.

The Anglo-Scandinavian Street-Names of York

By Gillian Fellows-Jensen

The street-names of any town or city reflect the history of the settlement in question. Many of the younger names are often self-explanatory, commemorating as they do events of national or local importance, or people whose lives have in some way been influential for the development of the nation or the town. The city centre of York, for example, was opened up by the insertion between 1835 and 1840 of the broad *Parliament Street*, which cuts directly across the medieval tenement pattern (RCHMY **5**, 173), while *Station Road* has in turn led to the old railway station, built within the walls on the site of a Dominican friary in 1839, and the new railway station, built outside the walls on the site of a large Roman cemetery between 1869 and 1877. Nor does it seem too hazardous a guess to suggest that *Wellington Row* was named in celebration of the victory at Waterloo in 1815. George Hudson (1800–71), once known as the 'railway king', 'made York a major railway and commercial hub' (*Encyclopædia Britannica*, 15th edn, V 181). It is not surprising, therefore, that, in spite of the frauds with which he later became involved, the city should have renamed *Railway Street* as *George Hudson Street* in 1971 (RCHMY **3**, 100).

It is not only such relatively modern figures as the Iron Duke and the Railway King, however, who are commemorated in York street-names. Occasionally the specific or defining element of a medieval street-name is a personal name whose bearer can be identified with a reasonable degree of certainty so that the approximate date of the coining of the name in its present form can be determined. *Davygate*, for example, was almost certainly named after the David who was the son of the John le Lardener of York to whom the land there had been given back in 1137 in connection with his holding of the office of lardener, with responsibility for exercising jurisdiction over the royal forest of Galtres, supplying the king's larder with venison and other game, keeping the measure of the king's corn, selling the corn and making distraint for the king's debts (*EYC* **1**, 243). The name Davygate is a good illustration of the fact that the street-name-forming element *gate*, from Scandinavian *gata*, was still current in York in the 12th century, a fact that is of great relevance for any attempt to as-sess the extent of Scandinavian influence on the city's street-names.

Dating the coining of names

The *terminus post quem* for the coining of Scandinavian names for streets in England must be assumed to be the date when the Danes occupied the various settlements. York was conquered by the Danes in 866 (*AY* 1, 71–2). In 876, when the Vikings settled in Yorkshire and began to cultivate the land there, they had learnt from earlier unfortunate experiences with the city's defences and it is generally thought that they extended these and built new walls around an area down towards the River Foss (*AY* 1, 164–5; *AY* 8/3, 274–7), although it has recently been argued that the physical expansion of the city southwards and southeastwards towards the rivers Foss and Ouse may have begun earlier under the protection of the authorities of the Anglo-Saxon cathedral (Norton 1998, 27–8). It would nevertheless seem to have been in the period under Viking rule that York developed into an important trading centre.

Unlike York, Lincoln had not been exploited by the Viking 'great army' for their winter quarters but after the occupation of Mercia in 877, the city fell into Danish hands and from then on it began to flourish as a trading centre (Vince 2001, *passim*). Silver Street, joining the south and east gates of the upper part of the city, was constructed towards the end of the 9th century (Sawyer 1998, 179) and another Lincoln street, Flaxengate, appears to have been established about the year 900 (Hall 1989, 179). It is uncertain, however, whether the city's development might not first really have gathered speed after its submission to Edward the Elder in 918 or even as late as after its reconquest by Edmund in 942. The English kings, however, only demanded to be recognised as overlords in the Danelaw and they allowed the Danes to live there according to their own laws, so it seems reasonable to accord responsibility for Lincoln's commercial development to the Danes.

For the four remaining of the Five Danelaw Boroughs the evidence is less clear but it has been conveniently summarised by Richard Hall (1989, 201–5). It seems likely that the Vikings found a pre-existing centre of occupation with natural potential for development at all of these, but whether or not this development took place in the four decades between their takeover by the Danes who settled in the region in 877 and their recapture by the Anglo-Saxons in 917 cannot be determined with certainty on the basis of the archaeological and historical evidence available. Although their development is certainly not comparable in scale with that of York or Lincoln, and there is little archaeological evidence of Scandinavian influence on their evolution, their Scandinavian street-names do suggest that the Danes must nevertheless have played a not insignificant role in it.

Unlike York and Lincoln, Norwich does not owe its status as one of the most important cities in medieval England to an origin as a Roman fortress. The development of the city would seem to have been the result of the merging of a number of separate settlements between about 850 and 925, presumably largely under the Danes, who began their attacks on East Anglia in 865, settled there in 880 and ruled the region until 917 (Ayers 1987). The main evidence for Danish influence on the development of Norwich is once again provided by the numerous street-names of Scandinavian origin. In this connection it is significant that the English reconquest of Norwich would seem to have put a more effective brake on the spread of Danish linguistic influence than was the case in the cities further to the north.

In preparation for this article I have compared the street-names in Danelaw cities with those occurring in two cities in southern England which had contact with the Danes at a later period (Fellows-Jensen 1997). London played a major role in the struggle against the Danes in the late 10th and early 11th centuries. The defences of the city were in good order and its garrison able to withstand even lengthy campaigns. The citizens eventually submitted to Svein Forkbeard in 1013 but Svein died before he could consolidate his hold on the kingdom. The struggle continued between Æthelred's son Edmund, and Svein's son, Knut, until they eventually came to terms. Edmund retained Wessex, while Knut received all England north of the Thames. The citizens of London bought peace with the Danes, who took up their winter quarters there. After the death of Edmund on

30 November 1016, Knut was chosen as king. London does not seem to have played a major role as royal seat in his reign or those of his sons and Knut was buried in Winchester, where he had taken up residence with a large following. Neither London nor Winchester has any Scandinavian street-names, probably because it was after the period when these cities developed as administrative and commercial centres that the Danes settled there (Ekwall 1954; Biddle and Keane 1976).

Documentary evidence for dating

The documentary sources are unfortunately unable to provide much help in dating the coining of the street-names. The description of the topography of towns and cities in *Domesday Book* is restricted to references to some specified churches and occasionally to such a locality as *macellum* 'the flesh-market' in York (GDB 298a; C/3). It would also seem to have been rare for streets to be mentioned by name in Anglo-Saxon charters and in any case comparatively few charters survive from Yorkshire and the Danelaw. The oldest records of English street-names that I have come across are all from Winchester, where five names occur in documents from the 10th century (Biddle and Keene 1976, 231). Two of the streets are named in a set of bounds from Winchester dated to the year 909 (Sawyer 1968, no.1560). These are: *on þa ceap strǽt* 'market street' (now High Street) and a lost *on þa strǽt midde*, perhaps 'middle street'. *Ceap strǽt* also occurs as *Cypstrǽte* in a document from 996 (which survives in a 12th-century transcript; Sawyer 1968, no. 889). This document also names two other streets: *andlang flǽscmangara strǽte* 'fleshmongers' street' (now Parchment Street) and *to Scyldwyrhtana strǽte* 'shield-makers' street' (now Upper Brook Street). A document from 990 (also surviving in a 12th-century transcript; Sawyer 1968, no. 873) names *on Tænnere-stret* 'tanners' street' (now Lower Brook Street/Tanner Street). If we can take these five street-names as being typical of the 10th century, they reveal that street-names tended to refer to the situation of the street (*mid*) or its function (the others). It will appear below that both these types of name were also of common occurrence in York and the other Anglo-Scandinavian towns.

There is no reason, then, why many of the street-names we find in York should not have been coined in the 10th century, even early in the 10th century, but we cannot be certain that they were. In Norwich, which was certainly recaptured by the English in 917 and where there would not seem to have been Danish immigration later than that (cf. Insley 1979, 56–57), it is certain that many of the Danish street-names must have been coined before this date. English-speaking inhabitants would hardly have chosen *-gate* as the generic for new street-names in Norwich unless there was already an established body of *gate*-names that could form the models for analogical naming. It seems unlikely that the Danes who remained in the city continued to speak Danish or to be at all linguistically influential there. The Scandinavian personal names which did remain in use in East Anglia for some time appear in the anglicised forms that were normal in the early years of settlement and show no traces of the developments that are evidenced in Scandinavian personal names in York, for example.

The nationality of the inhabitants in the towns

Danish settlers would seem to have continued to flock to the northern Danelaw throughout the 10th century (Fellows-Jensen 1998, 31). A general idea of the percentage of the population of the towns that was of Scandinavian birth or descent can be gained from the personal names known to have been borne by the citizens in the 10th and 11th centuries. Studies of the names borne by moneyers in England between 973 and 1016 have shown that 70% of the York moneyers bear Scandinavian names, 40% of those in Lincoln, 13% in Norwich and only 4% in Winchester (Smart 1973). *Domesday Book* reveals that of the named householders in 1065, 57% of those in York bear Scandinavian names, 82% in Lincoln, where the total figures are small, and less than 4% in Winchester. We cannot, of course, be sure that a man bearing a Scandinavian name was of Scandinavian birth or even descent but in York and Lincoln, at least, it seems likely that he was. It is also worth noting that several of the Scandinavian names borne by *Domesday* tenants in York appear with a contracted form in *-kil* or *-kel* of the element *-ketel*, e.g. *Turchil, Rauechil, Vlchel*. Such contracted forms first became common in Danish after about the year 1000, so these men seem likely to have been fairly recent immigrants for whom it may still have been natural to speak Danish and to use forms of names that were current in the Danish homeland (Fellows-Jensen 1998). My study of Scan-dinavian personal names in sources from Lincoln-shire and Yorkshire has shown that Scandinavian names continued to occur quite frequently until about the year 1200 but by that date they had been ousted from popularity by the comparatively restricted corpus of names of Continental-Germanic or biblical origin that had been introduced by the Normans (Fellows-Jensen 1968, lxi–lxiv). It is, of course, unlikely that men in these two counties bearing Scandinavian names as late as the year 1200 were Scandinavian born or Scandinavian speakers and their names probably simply reflect family traditions.

Analogical formations in *-gate*

The case is similar with the use of the generic *-gate* in street-names. Once this word had gained a foot-hold in a town, the workings of analogy would ensure that it could continue to be used. It was, in fact, employed even in the 20th century. The name *Dean-gate* was given to a road constructed in 1903 along the south side of York Minster to ease the traffic flow in the area (Hall 1988, 244). With streets originally made centuries ago, however, it can sometimes be very difficult to date at all closely the coining of their names or to identify the specific or defining element of these. One of the most well-known and most puzzling street-names in York is that of the shortest street in the city, *Whipmawhopmagate*, which is first recorded as *Whitnourwhatnourgate* in 1505. Several explanations have been proposed for this name. The most satisfactory of these would seem to be that suggested by Angelo Raine (1955, 61), namely that the specific is made up of the dialect expressions 'whitna' and 'whatna', both meaning 'what kind of?', probably giving in combination a meaning such as 'Why on earth do you call this a street?'. It is unlikely that this name is much older than its first written occurrence.

For the historian of street-names it is unfortunate that the element *gata* remained in currency for so long because it is the frequency of occurrence of street-names in *-gate* that is responsible for the very Danish impression made by York on its visitors and the similar impression made by other cities in eastern England with many street-names in *-gate*, particularly Lincoln, Norwich, Nottingham, Leicester and Stamford, and even by the Norman foundation of King's Lynn. It is also noticeable, on the other hand, that there is no instance of a street-name in *-gate* in London or Winchester, in spite of Danish activity there at a later period. There are no street-names in -*gate* in Chester in north-west England either, although other names there point to Scandinavian influence in the city. This may reflect the fact that the settlers there were predominantly of Norwegian rather than Danish origin.

Street-names in medieval cities

In an attempt to explain differences between the street-names in York and those in other cities that were occupied by the Scandinavians, as well as cities not subject to Scandinavian influence in the 9th and 10th centuries, I have compiled a database of over 4,000 street-names recorded before c.1500. The name-forms are derived from various detailed treatments of street-names by philologists and historians, all the result of serious scholarship but some more up-to-date than others. Works treating of York are: Lindkvist 1926, 345–94; Smith 1937, 275–300; Raine 1955; Palliser 1978, 1–16; of the Five Boroughs, Derby: Cameron 1959, 447–51; Nottingham: Gover, Mawer and Stenton 1940, 14–22; Lincoln: Cameron 1985; Leicester: Cox 1998; Stamford: Perrott 1979, 413–19. From East Anglia works treating of Norwich are: Sandred and Lindström 1989; of King's Lynn: Owen 1984. A book devoted to the street-names of London is Ekwall 1954. The street-names of Winchester have been treated by Biddle and Keene 1976, 231–39, and those of Chester by Dodgson 1981, xlvii–li, 1–84. The forms of street-names will be quoted in this chapter without specific references to the books and articles from which they are taken except when scholars differ on significant points. I shall also have occasion to refer to a few medieval street-names from other towns in England and Scandinavia. In these cases the relevant references will be cited in connection with the discussion of the names.

The street-name generic *gata*

The element *gata* (f.), which occurs in England in the sense 'street (in a town)' is a typically Scandinavian element, although it is related to German *Gasse* (f.), which has the sense 'narrow street or alley'. The element *gata* is thought originally to have had a meaning such as 'opening, way out' and perhaps to be associated with Modern English *gate*, but in Scandinavian sources from before c.1500 it is only recorded with the meaning 'a road or street', predominantly one that is bounded on either side by fences (e.g. a fenced path for cattle), by trees (e.g. a

path cut through a wood or forest), by buildings (e.g. a street in a town or other urbanised settlement) or by human beings (e.g. a path slashed through opposing forces). It would also seem to have had a more general sense of 'road' or 'highway'. It is certainly used in Scandinavian sources to translate the Latin terms *via* 'way', *platea* 'a broad way or street in a city' and *semita* 'path or lane' (cf. the files of the *Dictionary of Old Norse Prose* in Copenhagen).

We cannot be sure about the frequency of occurrence of the element *gata* in street-names in Scandinavia in the Viking period because of the almost complete lack of medieval records of these names but, to judge from the sources available, it would seem that *gata* was the word most frequently employed for a street in towns in Denmark and Sweden, whereas more commonly occurring elements in Norway are *almenning* and the loanword *stræti* from Latin *via strata* 'paved way', borrowed through the medium of a West Germanic language that is generally assumed to have been Frisian but may perhaps have been English. This Latin loanword also occurs in street-names in Denmark and in the south-western parts of present-day Sweden that once formed part of Denmark, but apparently not in Sweden proper.

The street-name generic *stræt*

In England the element *stræt* was first only employed with reference to Roman roads but it came to develop the general sense 'paved way' and to be used of roads other than Roman ones, particularly urban roads, being employed, for example, to gloss Latin *platea* (Smith 1956 **2**, 161–2). It is by far the most frequently occurring element in the names of major urban streets everywhere in England except in the towns where *gata* gained a strong foothold: York, Lincoln, Norwich, Leicester, Derby, Nottingham. In each of these towns there are only a handful of early names in -*stræt*. This is at least in part because *stræt* would seem to have been employed in a more restricted way than *gata* in the early period, normally being used to denote a major thoroughfare. There are, for example, only 54 names in -*stræt* in London sources from before about 1500 as against 176 names in -*lane*, denoting a 'lane or narrow road'. It would seem to be of significance that the specifics of the four early instances of street-names in -*stræt* in York are either definitely or possibly of Scandinavian origin and I shall therefore pause to examine these four names before continuing the discussion of the names in -*gate*.

York street-names in -stræt (Fig.129s)

The first record of the name *Coney Street* is as *Cunegestrate* 1153 x 1158; this and other early forms confirm that the specific is the Danish appellative *kunung* 'king' rather than the cognate English word *cyning*. The name originally denoted not only the present Coney Street but also the streets now known as Lendal and Spurriergate so that it formed the main route from the old fortress area to Ouse Bridge and the south, running outside the site of the south-western wall of the fortress. David Palliser has suggested that it may have been the first street in York to be paved and to be given a name whose Latin form *via regia* or *strata regia* later became the common term for all the main streets in urban settlements in England (Palliser 1978, 8). This suggestion seems quite likely and it is interesting that the name, to judge from its specific, would seem to have been coined by the Danes, although the road may well have been in use in the Anglian period (*AY* 7/2, 153).

Blake Street, first recorded as *Blaicastret* between 1150 and 1160 (*EYC* **1**, 201), probably has as its specific the Scandinavian verb *bleikja* 'to bleach' and hence refers to a place for bleaching. The name has an exact parallel in *Blegstræde*, the name of a street in Holbæk in Denmark, while a Copenhagen street-name of similar significance, *Blegdamsvej* 'bleaching-ground road', has achieved fame as the setting for Lars von Trier's Danish cult-film 'The Kingdom', which opens with an eerie scene of ghostly bleachers at work swilling cloth in the ponds that stood there before the construction of the *Rigshospital*, the hospital whose nick-name *Riget* gave the film its title. There is little evidence for the presence of water that could have been used in the preliminary process of bleaching in York's Blake Street, although somewhere along the street there was a side-lane or passage called *Fountain Lane* (*Funtaynesgayle* c.1277; see p.368), which may have taken its name from some public well or spring there (Raine 1955, 118). Blake Street may, of course, simply have been a bleaching ground where cloth was exposed to dry in the sunlight. It curves across the south-western corner of the fortress between the north-west and south-west gates, ignoring any Roman alignments. This corner of the fortress area was presumably uninhabited at the time of the construction of the street, which may have taken place as early as the 7th century (Norton 1998, 25; *AY* 7/2, 158), and it may have been the Anglians who first exploited it for bleaching.

North Street is first recorded as *Nordstreta* in a document written c.1090 (RCHMY **3**, 96). Its specific, which can equally well be of Danish or English origin, probably refers to the fact that the street ran in a northerly direction from Micklegate at Ouse Bridge; it is said to have formerly included what is now Tanner Row (Palliser 1978, 13). It is one of the main streets on the west side of the Ouse and may represent a survival of part of the Roman road running down to the Roman equivalent of Ouse Bridge and of a Roman riverside road (*AY* 7/2, 166).

The most problematic of the four names in -*stræt* is *Finkle Street*, which is first recorded as *Finclegayle* 1361 and as *Fynkullstrete* between 1381 and 1384. This late 14th-century form is the earliest attestation of the name Finkle Street anywhere in England. In an ambitious and wide-ranging article Richard Coates has discussed the 35 or so instances of this name in England, all of which are found in an essentially north-easterly distribution area (Coates 1995). Although a few loose ends in his argument still remain to be tied, Coates's explanation of the name seems to me to be the best one proposed so far. He examines the various more or less satisfactory explanations proposed hitherto, including Lindkvist's formally satisfactory but nevertheless unlikely suggestion that the specific was the rather rare West Scandinavian personal name *Finnkell* and Ekwall's 'lovers' lane' theory, which compared the name with *Grape Lane* (*Grapcunt Lane*, 1329), the name of an alley not far away from Finkle Street in York (Ekwall 1959, 47–53). Coates ironises over Ekwall's omission to explain in what way *groping* differed from *finkling* and points out that the lost *Finkle Street* in Lincoln, which is described as a *via regia*, could hardly have been a particularly well-adapted locality for urban lovemaking. On the other hand, the fact that this name has been lost and the street tentatively identified with Rosemary Lane may suggest that the description as a *via regia* was erroneous. Coates's conclusion is that the specific of all the Finkle Streets is the term for the plant 'fennel' (Latin *fœniculum*), in a form derived from the ancestor of modern Danish *fennikel*, that the street-name is thus probably of Danish origin and that it was carried from York to other towns and cities in the north-east, occurring in anglicised form as Fennel Street on the fringes of the Finkle-area, for example in Manchester, Warrington and Loughborough. The main problem with this explanation is that the plant-name never appears with *i* in the first syllable in

Danish sources, while the Latin plant-name in the form *finiculus* is glossed as *finugl* in some Old English glosses (Pheifer 1974, 25) and spellings such as *finkle* occur in English dialect sources. Coates argues that the street-name refers to the well-known medicinal properties of fennel, both for driving out wind and as a diuretic, so that the street-name could have had a significance similar to that of London's *Pissinge Alley* 1574 (Ekwall 1954, 176), possibly with reference to the characteristic, if not offensive, smell of fennel. It should also be noted that fennel was not found in the Anglo-Scandinavian cesspits at Coppergate (A.R. Hall, pers. comm.), though it was present in faecal deposits from medieval Bedern (*AY* 10/5, 620). It should be emphasised that in the earliest occurrence of the name Finkle Street in York the generic is in fact the more appropriate Scandinavian term *geil*, a word meaning 'alley' that dropped out of use at a fairly early date and was probably therefore replaced in the York name by the more common -*strete*. At present, Finkle Street is an alley leading into St Sampson's Square from Little Stonegate. It may simply have been an alley with an unpleasant or strong smell. In 1750 it was known as *Mucky Pig Lane* (RCHMY **5**, 172). Palliser has noted that there is evidence for another *Finkle Street* in York in earlier times (*Fynkul Strete* 14th-century), which is now lost but which is perhaps to be identified with Museum Street (Palliser 1978, 9). In spite of the comparatively late attestation of the name in York, it seems likely that it is this York name which is the original source of inspiration for the other names discussed by Coates. Among these are found, in addition to the lost Finkle Street in Lincoln, present-day *Finkelgate* in Norwich, of which the earliest form is *Fenkelstret* 1566 and whose present form shows a modern substitution of -*gate*.

Since the appearance of Richard Coates's article, my attention has been drawn by Peter McClure to the fact that Finkle Street is of quite common occurrence in street-names in English towns and villages in post-medieval times, particularly in the East Riding of Yorkshire, and this would suggest that it had a general significance that would be appropriate in most such settlements, for example 'back street'. In these numerous young occurrences, at least, the naming seems most likely to be analogical, perhaps without too much thought being paid to the original name or to the connotative significance of the name. Peter McClure also notes that *Fenekyl, Fenechil'* occurs as the by-name of *Aldusa Fenekyl,* who held property in

Bridlesmith Gate in Nottingham in the 13th century (Foulds 1994, nos.508, 509, 512), and that this surname might lie behind the Nottingham *Fink Hill Street*, first recorded in 1744, even though Fink Hill Street was situated at some distance from Bridlesmith Gate. It may well be that the Finkle Streets in England do not all share the same origin but I would think it reasonable to say that most of these streets were so named either because there was some generally accepted significance for the compound or because one of the early Finkle Streets was so famous or notorious that it became the model for analogical naming.

Of the Five Boroughs it is only Derby that has a fair number of early recorded names in -*stræt* and none of these has a specific of Scandinavian origin so the only reason to suspect that any of these might be of Danish coinage is that *Bridge Gate*, first recorded as *Brig(g)estrete* between 1233 and 1248, has forms in *Briggegate* and the like from 1331 and it is the form in -*gate* that survives until today. There are two names in -*stræt* with early records in Lincoln: a lost *Old Street* (*le Ald stret'* 1304) and a lost *Humber Street* (*Humberstrete* 1219 x 1229), which may have been the name given to the Roman road known as Ermine Street, where it traverses the fields to the north of the city on its way to the Humber.

There is one name in -*stræt* in Nottingham which seems likely to be old: *Stoney Street* (*Stanstrete* 1218), whose specific is Old English (OE) *stān* 'stone'. It was one of the main thoroughfares of the medieval city and perhaps one of the first streets to be paved.

Norwich has four streets with names in -*stræt* that are recorded fairly early: *Bishopgate* (*Holmestrete* 1107 x 1116), whose specific is the Scandinavian appellative *holmr* 'island', referring to *Cowholme*, an area of grassland or water-meadow on both sides of *Holmestrete*; *Ber Street* (*Berstrete* 1135 x 1154), which was the road running from the Castle to the main entrance to the city from the south. Its specific has been explained as OE (Anglian) *berg* 'hill, mound' but could equally well be the cognate Scandinavian word. *Fye Bridge Street* (*Fibrigestrete* c.1200 etc., *Fibriggate* 1200 etc.) was an important thoroughfare that originally extended from Tombland to the city wall in the north. The specific is the OE bridge-name *Fifbrig'* of uncertain significance. The name may have been coined by Danes employing the element *gata*.

St Andrew's Street (*in Wimere street* 13th century) has as specific a Norman personal name *Wímar(d)*, functioning as the name of a leet. It is borne by an important road running through the centre of the city. All of these early names in *-strǽt* in Norwich may have been coined by Danes. The appellatival specific of one is Scandinavian and of the second either Scandinavian or English, while the last two names incorporate earlier place-names as their specifics.

Most of the fairly numerous names in *-strǽt* in King's Lynn are not recorded until late in the 16th century and seem likely not to have been coined until *street* had become the normal term for a major thoroughfare throughout England, even where *gata* had previously been the favoured term.

In Kingston-upon-Hull, which was not founded until 1219, it appears that in the 14th century major streets had names in *-strǽt*, e.g. *Humberstrete* 1333, now Humber Street, and *Chaumpaynstrete* 1342 'the road to the open country', now Dagger Lane, or less frequently in *-gata*, e.g. *Markedgate* 1321, now Low Gate, and *Blackfriargate* 1381, while narrower streets had names in *-lane*, as was the case in London. There was, however, a certain amount of variation in the elements of the names. *Halestrete* 1321 had become *Fynkelstrete* by 1415 and is now Finkle Street (see p.361), while *Hull'streth* 1303 had become *Highegate* by 1443 and is now High Street (Smith 1937, 210–12).

The York evidence certainly points to the Danes as coiners of the names in *-strǽt* and the same can be said of several of the names in Norwich and a few of those in other towns, while a few of the names discussed may be early English coinages and several others post-medieval ones. Some support for the theory that it may have been Danes who coined at least the name Finkle Street in York is provided by the fact that in Denmark, unlike in other European countries, the element corresponding to Old English *strǽt* has always been employed of the smaller streets in the towns (Jørgensen 1999, 279).

Street-names in *-gata* in York (Fig.129s)

We have now seen that names in *-gata* could be coined as late as the 16th century and incorporate specifics of non-Danish origin, and that *gata* could replace *strǽt* as the most popular generic for the names of major streets in records in areas where *gata*

was the more commonly occurring element, sometimes only temporarily but sometimes permanently. It is therefore time to examine the specifics of the names in *-gate* in York as a body to see whether it is possible to distinguish names coined by Danes from names that are more likely to be analogical formations, coined by English speakers perhaps centuries after Danish had ceased to be spoken in the city.

There are 35 street-names in *-gata* in York which are recorded in sources from before 1400: three in the 11th century, sixteen in the 12th, ten in the 13th and six in the 14th. Some of these names were probably coined after the Anglo-Scandinavian period on analogy with older names in *-gata*. This is certainly the case with Davygate mentioned earlier. Other names which might be thought to be comparatively young are those containing the names of saints and referring to churches, i.e. *Gillygate* (*via sancti Egidii* 1145 x 1161, *sayngiligat'* 1330), which runs outside the city wall to the north-west. The small church dedicated to St Giles, the guild church of the skinners, stood here until the 16th century and must have been in existence by the mid-12th century at the latest (Raine 1955, 269–70). *Petergate* (*vicus Sancti Petri* 1189 x 1195, *Petergate* 14th century), however, is one of the chief roadways of York, running from Bootham Bar past York Minster to King's Square on a line coinciding roughly with one of the main Roman streets through the fortress area, the *via principalis* (Hall 1994, 34; Ottaway 1995, 13; *AY* 7/2, 151–2). This name seems likely to be old. Its specific presumably refers to a church dedicated to St Peter, as was the case with the hastily erected wooden church in which King Edwin was baptised in 627, as related by Bede (*AY* 1, 132–4) and the *monasterium* that was burned down in 741 (*AY* 1, 144). These churches were probably in the vicinity of the Norman and later medieval Minster.

A name which can certainly be assumed to be old is *Stonegate* (*Steingate* 1148 x 1175), containing Scandinavian *steinn* 'stone' and presumably referring to the paved Roman street through the fortress, the *via praetoria*, which ran along approximately the same line (*AY* 7/2, 152, 154). This may be compared with the lost name *Stainegate* (*Staynegate* 1226 x 1228) in Lincoln.

The three names recorded in the 11th century can also be presumed to be old. They are all contained in a single charter in the York Minster Library Archives (L 2(1), pt 1, fo.61r) that has been dated between 1070 and 1088; significantly they all denote streets outside the fortress area. *Monkgate* (*Munecagate*) 'monks' street' is the name borne by a broad street outside the north-eastern fortress wall which leads to Monk Bar and the Minster and is the main approach to the city from the north-east. It has been suggested that this was a street used by heavy traffic for parking outside the city (Raine 1955, 276), and, although this idea is perhaps rather anachronistic, it is not inconceivable that heavy farm wagons sometimes had to remain outside the city. An interesting fact about this name is that the specific is the English form of Latin *monachus* 'monk', i.e. *munuc* in the genitive plural *muneca*. Perhaps the name is a partial scandinavianisation of an older English name. This suggestion is supported by the fact that the street was constructed in connection with the closing of the Roman northeast gateway and the opening up of Monk Bar, possibly by the cathedral authorities in the Anglian period (Norton 1998, 22–3; *AY* 7/2, 159).

The other two names recorded in this 11th-century charter are borne by streets in the part of the city south-east of the Foss that was first enclosed by the medieval walls in the 12th century, namely the Walmgate area. The name *Walmgate* (*Walbegate*) is borne by the continuation of Fossgate south of the Foss that runs to Walmgate Bar and the road to Hull. The specific is not easy to explain but would seem most likely to be an otherwise unrecorded hypocoristic personal name, OE *Walba* or Scand *Valbi*, short forms of names such as OE *Waldbeorht*, Scand *Valbjörn*, *Valbrandr*. The other street south-east of the Foss to be named in this document is *Fishergate* (*Fiscergate* 1070 x 1088; *Fiskergate* in other sources). This street corresponded not to the diverted route followed by the western end of modern Fishergate but to Fawcett Street and the southern end of George Street (Palliser 1978, 9). The variation in spelling of the first element makes it uncertain whether it was originally OE *fiscere* or Scand *fiskari* but it is certain that it is the occupational term meaning 'fisherman'.

Of the three names recorded in the 11th-century document, Monkgate and Fishergate both belong to one of the oldest and largest categories of medieval street-names, that containing occupational terms, while Walmgate with its anthroponymical specific is something of an odd-man-out. Street-names with a personal name as specific, generally a surname, became very common in later centuries but there are comparatively few early street-names containing personal names. A significant one is *Goodramgate* (*Gutherungate* 1177 x 1181), an example of a road in the old fortress area that cuts across the lines of the Roman streets there (*AY* 7/2, 159). The specific is a Scandinavian personal name, feminine *Guðrún* or masculine *Guðþormr*. The person in question cannot be identified but it seems likely that he or she was of Scandinavian descent. The only other example of an early York street-name with a personal name as specific is *Besingate* (*Besynggate* c.1260), probably identical with the present Bishophill Senior in the *colonia* area and most likely containing the personal name *Besing*, a derivative of Scand *Besi*, very probably the name of the *Besing Betemarched* who had owned property before 1180 in Lounlithgate, a side-street to Bishophill Senior (Palliser 1978, 5).

Returning to the occupational terms, we find six Scandinavian terms: **barkari* 'tanner' in *Barker Hill* (*Barkergate* c.1230), now St Maurice's Road; **heymangari* 'hay-seller' in *Haymongeregate* 1240, now Shambles; *kjötmangari* 'flesh-seller' in *Ketmangeregate* 1194, now probably St Saviourgate (Palliser 1978, 14) or perhaps St Andrewgate (Raine 1955, 55–6); *koppari* 'cup-maker, turner' in *Coppergate* (*Coppergate* c.1120 x 1135); *plógsveinn* 'ploughman' in *Blossom Street* (*Ploxwangate* 1241); and *skjaldari* 'shield-maker' in *Skeldergate* (*Sceldergata* 12th century; RCHMY **3**, 100).

Three of these names I have discussed elsewhere in connection with studies of crafts in York (Fellows-Jensen 1979a; *AY* 17/16, 3226–7). The occupational term **barkari* would not actually seem to be recorded in Old Scandinavian sources but there is an obsolete Danish term *barker* meaning 'tanner' and the verb *barke* in the sense 'to tan with an infusion of bark' occurs in Danish sources, although it only survives in modern Danish in the past participle *barket* in expressions such as *en barket næve* 'a horny hand' and *barkede sejl* 'tanned sails' and in Old West Scandinavian sources in the by-name *barkaðr* 'with horny skin'. There are a couple of instances of the occupational term *barker* in citations in the *Oxford English Dictionary*, in one of which it appears as a kind of synonym for 'tanner'. It has been pointed out to me by A.R. Hall (pers. comm.) that *barker* was originally an occupational term for someone who strips bark from trees for the tanners. It is interesting to note that the York street-name *Tanner Row* is first recorded as *Barker rawes* in 1524. The specific of this name would seem to have been replaced by the English word *tanner* once the term *barker* had become obsolete. It should also be noted that both York streets which are shown by their names to have been occupied by tanners are situated near or outside the city walls and with easy access to the rivers Foss and Ouse respectively. Tanning was a smelly process and required access to running water.

Shield-makers also needed to soak the leather they employed for strengthening their shields. Skeldergate runs along the bank of the Ouse in the *colonia* area and may, in part, represent a Roman riverside street (*AY* 7/2, 156). It should be noted that streams ran along both *Scyldwyrtana stræt* 'shield-makers' street' and *Tannerestret* 'tanners' street' in Winchester (Biddle and Keene 1976, 287). Palliser (1978, 15) draws attention to what he refers to as an ingenious recent suggestion that the specific of Skeldergate might be a Scandinavian word *skelde* meaning 'shelf'. I have not, however, been able to find any record of such a word and can only assume that it might be an anglicised form of the common noun *skjöldr* (m.) 'shield'. The forms found in all the recorded forms of the street-name could then only reflect the genitive singular *skjaldar* of this word. There is no instance to my knowledge of the word *skjöldr* being used in a sense such as 'shelf', while the English term *scyld-wyrhta* is certainly found in the 10th-century Winchester street-name, showing that shield-makers were of sufficient significance to have their own quarter in a city. I therefore find no reason to doubt that shield-makers plied their trade in Skeldergate.

The Scandinavian occupational term *koppari* is associated in the written West Scandinavian sources with the terms *kistasmiðr* 'a kind of joiner' and *laggari* 'a kind of cooper'. *Koppari* may have been used with a general sense such as 'turner' or 'joiner' but the finds of wooden cups, spoon-bits and cores of wood on the site excavated at Coppergate (*AY* 17/13) suggests that the term may well have had the specialised sense 'cup-maker' here.

Of the two terms in -*mangari*, one, *kjötmangari* 'meat-seller', is recorded in Old Scandinavian sources and forms the specific of the name of one of the major streets in Copenhagen, *Købmagergade* (*Køthmangerstrede* 1475) and of a lost street in Roskilde (*Kødh-mangherestrædith* 1306). *Heymangari* is not recorded in Scandinavian sources and it may, in fact, be an English term. The English term *flæsc-mangere*, identical in meaning with *kjötmangari*, occurs in street-names in Winchester (*to flæsmangare stræt* 996) and Chester (*Flesmongerlone* 1100 x 1160), while *iren-mongere* 'ironmonger' occurs in street-names in Norwich, London and Chester, and *stokfiscmonger* in *Stokfisshmongerrowe* 1373 in London. The *mangere* element in both English and Scandinavian is ultimately a loan from the Latin substantive *mango* 'trader, dealer'.

Blossom Street (*Ploxwangate* 1241), probably containing the Scandinavian occupational term *plóg-sveinn* 'ploughman', is a wide and spacious road outside the south-eastern wall of the *colonia* area. Its great width would have made it possible for a horse or cattle-market to have been held along it (RCHMY 3, 62).

Three of the names in -*gate* contain occupational terms of English origin. *Colliergate* is first recorded as *Coliergate* in 1303–4 and its specific is the Middle English (ME) term *colier* 'charcoal-maker or -dealer'. Its site near the Shambles would suggest that the colliers would be more likely to be dealing with their wares there than processing them, although it may originally have run along a wide open space (RCHMY 5, 117). *Nedlergate* 1394 was once an alternative name for the Shambles and must refer to the presence of needle-makers there. Some needles were manufactured from bone and the needlers may have exploited the plentiful supply of bones from the Shambles. Finally, *Baggergate* (*Bagergate* 1241), running outside the city along the south-western wall and now called Nunnery Lane, probably contains the ME appellative *baggere* 'badger, hawker, pedlar'. The name had become modified to *Beggargate Lane* by the 16th century either as a result of confusion between *bagger* and *beggar* or because there was a ME word *badger* that had the meaning 'beggar' (Palliser 1978, 4).

The last two of the York names in -*gate* containing terms for human beings are the two names whose specific is the Scandinavian national term *Brettar* 'Britons': *Bretgate* on the north-eastern side of Walmgate near the city wall (*Brettegata* c.1145 x 1155), now Navigation Road (RCHMY 5, 167), and a *Bret(t)egate* recorded c.1249, now Market Street and Jubbergate. The name *Jubbergate* results from the prefixing of another national term, ME *Jewe* 'Jew' to original *Bret-gate* at some time before 1280, when the street is referred to as *Joubrettegait* (RCHMY **5**, 121, 149). Palliser has noted that Jews did hold property here and that the street was not far from the synagogue (Palliser 1978, 7). It is impossible to be certain to whom the term 'Britons' refers here but I am inclined to think that they were Britons who came in company with Viking settlers from Cumbria, although they might possibly have been survivors from the British kingdom of Elmet, which had been subjugated by the English between 616 and 632 (Jones 1967; Fellows-Jensen 1972, 21), or Bretons who had taken up residence in York in the wake of the Norman conquest (Hall 1996, 58).

Two or three names in *-gate* contain as specifics terms for animals. The genitive *hjartar* of Scand *hjörtr* (m.) 'hart, stag' is found in *Herteregata* 1175, now Friargate. It is difficult to explain the significance of the term 'hart' in the name of a small street running down to the Ouse so it would perhaps be more satisfactory to treat the specific as the Scandinavian personal name *Hjörtr*, an interpretation supported by the fact that the specific occurs in the genitive singular, although, as noted above, personal names are rare as the specifics of early names in *-gate*. The specific of *Haver Lane* (*Havergate* 1170 x 1184), a lane or road in the marsh, can be explained as the animal term *hafr* (m.) 'he-goat' or the plant term *hafri* (m.) 'oats' or the personal name *Hafr,* identical in origin with the animal term.

The third name in this group is more certain to contain a Scandinavian animal term. The genitive plural *hunda* of *hundr* (m.) 'dog, hound' occurs in *Hungate* (*Hundegat* 1116 x 1156), which runs from St Saviour's church to the River Foss. This name is one of several of identical form which occur in England, not all probably having the same significance. A detailed study of ten Hungate names, six occurring in towns and four in rural areas, has suggested two probable interpretations (Fellows-Jensen 1979b). The name may have indicated a street where dogs of some value were kept, presumably the hunting dogs of a secular lord or bishop; alternatively, it may have been a derogatory name for an insignificant street or a street of bad repute. The York Hungate runs through an area of marshland reclaimed from the Foss by the construction of an embankment. This was earlier thought to date to the Anglo-Scandinavian period (Richardson 1959, 59–61) but it is now considered that it may have evolved through several phases of accretion during the Anglo-Scandinavian and/or early Norman periods (*AY* 8/3, 276). Angelo Raine has pointed out that there is also documentary evidence that the butchers from the Shambles used to throw out on to the waste ground here the parts of carcasses that could not be sold and that this attracted many dogs to the place (Raine 1955, 80–3). Reports from the church of St John Baptist in Hungate reveal that it could sometimes be impossible to hear the service there because of the noise of dogs on the dung-heap and that it was difficult for the priest to get through service because of the vile smell.

The same street-name occurs twice in Lincoln in the forms *Hungate* (*Hundegatam* 1126) and *Old Hungate* (*Aldehundegate* 1275); in Nottingham in *Hounds Gate* (*Hundegate* 1325); twice in Norwich in *Hundegate* 1257, now Prince's Street, and *Hundegate* 1320, now Waggon and Horses Lane; as well as in Market Weighton in Yorkshire in *Hungate* (*Hundegate* 1285).

The York Hungate would seem to bear a derogatory name and derogatory names seem particularly liable to be carried from one town to another, as in the case of Finkle Street discussed above (pp.361–2). There is little to suggest that the other Hungates had an inferior status, however. Lincoln's Hungate is described as being a *regia strata* and the two Norwich streets are near the centre of the town, while Nottingham's Hounds Gate is a major street running between the castle and St Peter's church.

Three York street-names in *-gate* have as their specifics names of localities to which they lead: the two major rivers and a hidden gateway. These names are all likely to be old formations and they are recorded in 12th-century sources: the River Foss in *Fossgate* (*Fossagata* 1122 x 1137), the River Ouse in *Ousegate* (*Usagata* 1120 x 1133) and the lost name of an old entrance to the city in the south-eastern wall, **lounlith* < Scandinavian *laun-hlið* 'secluded gateway' in *Launelidgate* 1180 x 1195, now Victor Street (RCHMY **3**, 59). There are two names whose specifics are terms for natural features which might here have had the function of place-names: Scandinavian *kjarr* 'marsh' in *Cargate* (*Kergathe* 1191 x 1210), now King Street, running down to the Ouse, and Scandinavian *nes* 'headland', referring to the ridge of high ground running parallel to the Ouse in *Nessgate* c.1154 x 1174, now Nessgate and Castlegate. The Castlegate portion of this street is first recorded with this name in the 14th century. It led to the principal castle, a structure begun in 1068 (Palliser 1978, 7). It is referred to as *Castelgate Street* in 1358. It is significant that the specific is a word of French origin that was introduced to England by the Normans together with the castles themselves. Another specific which is probably ultimately of French origin is that of the lost street-name *Buttegate* 1259, 'road leading to the butts for archery practice'. The ME word *butte* originally referred to the embankment on which the targets were placed. The etymology of the French word *but* is uncertain but it may be identical with the French word for 'stub' and its form influenced by another French word, *butte* 'rising ground, knoll'. Altogether it would seem that the street-names Castlegate and *Buttegate* must post-date the Viking period.

The last small group of names in *-gate* to be discussed is that in which the specifics are adjectives. *Micklegate* (*Myglagata* 1161 x 1184) contains the Scandinavian adjective *mikill* 'great'. Very appropriately it is borne by the main thoroughfare from Ouse Bridge to Micklegate Bar. There is also a *Micklegate*, now known as High Street, in Lincoln. The opposite to *mikill* is *lítill* 'little', the specific of *Lytlegata* 1161 x 1184, now St Martin's Lane, a side-street to Micklegate in York. The specific of *Holgate* (*Holgate* 1368) is the Scandinavian adjective *holr* 'hollow', referring to a road that has been hollowed out by much traffic. The same street-name occurs in Leicester, Stamford, Lincoln, Nottingham and twice in Norwich, as well as quite frequently as a place-name in Normandy in the form *Houlgate*. The final adjective to occur in a York street-name in *-gate* is English *niwe* 'new' in *Newgate* (*le Neugate* 1328). This street-name also occurs twice in Norwich, as well as being of frequent occurrence in Denmark in the form *Nygade*, with the cognate Danish adjective *ný* appearing instead of *niwe*.

Scandinavian generics other than *-gata* in York street-names

What distinguishes York from the other towns which have many street-names in *-gate* is the variety of Scandinavian generics which occur in its street-names. In addition to *-gata* these are: *bogi* 'bow' (1), *búð* 'booth' (1), *garðr* 'enclosure' (1), *geil* 'narrow alley' (14), *lending* 'landing-place' (5), *steinn* 'stone' (1) and *toft* 'plot of land' (1). Of these generics *búð* oc-

curs once in a Nottingham street-name but none of the other Scandinavian generics occurring in York street-names re-appears in street-names in the English towns whose names I have studied. On the other hand, a few additional Scandinavian street-name generics make scattered appearances elsewhere: *dík* 'dyke, ditch' in Nottingham (1), *hergata* 'army road' in Lincoln (1) and *skeið* 'track' in Leicester (1). Street-names containing *dalr* 'valley' in Derby (1) and Norwich (1), in *deill* 'share of land' in Lincoln (1) and *holmr* 'island' in Lincoln (1) are simply to be looked upon as topographical place-names functioning as street-names. I would argue that the greater variety of Scandinavian street-name generics in York points to a greater number of Scandinavian settlers and longer-lasting Scandinavian occupation there than further south, where English rule was restored earlier.

I shall look first at the street-names in *-geil* and *-lending* in York and then go on to treat the generics which only occur in a single name there.

Street-names in *-geil* (Fig.129s)

The word *geil* (f.) 'narrow alley' would seem to have been typically Norwegian in medieval Scandinavia, that is, in sources from before about 1500. It occurs more frequently than *gata* in Norway for roads bounded by fences and the occurrences in York would seem to point to the presence of Norwegians there, probably in the period when the York Viking kingdom had important commercial links with Dublin. In York the generic *geil* would seem to have been used of a narrow lane between houses. It should be noted that the first occurrence of the name *Finkle Street* is as *Finclegayle* 1361 (see p.361).

A small group of *geil*-names have specifics associated with domestic animals: *Nowtgail* (*Noutegayle*, 1405), now George Street, contains the Scandinavian appellative *naut* n. 'cattle'. The street leads from Walmgate to the city wall and, appropriately enough, the site of the post-medieval cattle-market, which was moved there in 1605 (Raine 1955, 299), but this relocation cannot account for the coinage of this Scandinavian name. Perhaps cattle were earlier put to grass out there. The medieval *Swinegate* (*venella que dicitur Swyngaille* 1276) has as its specific either the Scandinavian appellative *svín* n. or the cognate English word. The course of the street corresponds not to that of modern Swinegate but to that of Little

Stonegate. It was probably named from being the city's swine-market (Palliser 1978, 15), a function it retained until 1605 (Raine 1955, 174). The present *Feasegate* is first recorded as *Fesegayt*, probably erroneously for *Fesegayl*, in 1259 and as *fesegayl* in 1299. The specific of the name is Scandinavian *féhús* n. 'cowhouse'. The street runs from Market Street to St Sampson's Square. Cattle were earlier kept here, presumably because the food-market and the Shambles were not far away.

A rather larger group of names in *-geil* have other miscellaneous living creatures as their specifics. The Scandinavian term *fótlauss* 'footless' or 'legless' was used to denote a cripple. It occurs as the specific of *Footless Lane* (*Fothlousgayl'* 1218 x 1220), which has been identified with the modern Museum Street. It was certainly situated near to St Leonard's Hospital, for it is recorded in the hospital chartulary as *Ffotles gate juxta portam aquaticum* (Raine 1955, 128) and its name is probably to be associated with crippled people seeking alms and food here (Palliser 1978, 9).

Two street-names in *-geil* contain the Scandinavian appellative *þurs* (m.) 'troll, giant': *Thursegayl* 1191 x c.1210, now Cumberland Street, running down from Clifford Street to the Ouse, between *Cargate* and *Hertergate*, and *Thursegail* 13th-century, a lost lane off St Martin's Lane, which ran down to the Ouse upstream of Ouse Bridge. It seems likely that this name had a derogatory or derisory significance in both locations (Palliser 1978, 16).

Four names in *-geil* in York have as their specifics ME occupational terms and may thus first have been coined after the Viking period, although they may be originally Scandinavian formations that were anglicised at a later date by the substitution of an English specific. *Fetter Lane* (*Feltergayl* c.1280; *Feltergate* 1299), a side-street to Skeldergate, contains ME **feltere* 'felt-maker' and *Girdlergate* (*Glovergail* c.1250; *Girdelergate* 1381 x 1384), later renamed Church Street, originally contained ME *glouere* 'glover'. The presence of felt-makers in York is confirmed by an undated 12th-century charter, in which a grantee and a witness were both felters who apparently lived in Davygate (Raine 1955, 127). The fact that the name *Glovergail* was replaced by *Girdlergate* points to replacement of glovers by girdlers here at a period when the generic *geil* had dropped out of currency.

A lost *Trichur Lane* off Fossgate is first recorded as *Trichurgail* 1301. The specific must be the term *trichur* 'trickster, cheat', a loan in Middle English from Old French *tricheor*. The lane was presumably dark and unsavoury, and perhaps to be compared with *Finkle Street*, whose first record is as *Finclegayle* (see p.361). The name *Trichurgail* suggests that it was possible to form a name in *-geil* as late as the period in which French loanwords were entering the English language (in the three centuries after the Norman conquest), although *trichur* may simply have replaced an earlier specific, in the same way as the Scandinavian generic *geil* was itself later replaced by English *lane* in this street-name. *Inchegayle* (*Inthegaile* c.1260) is the name of a lane off Fishergate. It is difficult to explain but Palliser quotes a suggestion made by Margaret Gelling to the effect that the specific might be ME *enche* 'manorial servant, workman'. This word is not common but it is well-evidenced in minor place-names in Berkshire and Gloucestershire. The suggestion would undoubtedly be more attractive if the word occurred in minor names in Yorkshire but I have no better interpretation of the name to offer.

Related to the street-names in *-geil* containing occupational terms are two other names which point to commercial activities. These are: *Bakehouse lane* (*Bacusgail* 1312), containing OE **bæchús* 'bake-house', and *Fountain Lane* (*Funtaynesgayle* c.1277), containing Old French *fontein* 'fountain, spring'. Fountain Lane was somewhere off Blake Street and it may have been so named because it led to some public well whose water would have been employed in the bleaching process of the bleachers of Blake Street (see p.361).

The picture presented by the street-names in *-geil* in York as a group is not very clear. Several of the names have specifics which are either certainly or possibly of Scandinavian origin and these are likely to have been coined in the Anglo-Scandinavian period of the city's existence. The same may apply to the names with Old English specifics, and the Middle English occupational terms may simply reflect replacement of Scandinavian terms. Most intriguing are the two names with French specifics which must post-date the Norman conquest and suggest that *geil* remained current as a name-forming specific longer than might have been expected from its absence from other towns and its comparative rarity in York.

Street-names in -lending (Fig.129s)

The Scandinavian term *lending* (f.) denotes 'a landing-place', 'a place at which one can land from a vessel'. It is found in five street-names with early records in York, all borne by small lanes running down to the Ouse. Four are on the north-eastern bank. *St Martin's Lane* (*Vicus qui dicitur Sancti Martini Lending* c.1170 x 1199) runs from Coney Street to the Ouse past St Martin's church, thus accounting for the specific. *St Leonard's Landing* (*Saynt Lenard Lendyng* 1391) was a staithe close to St Leonard's Hospital and the site of the modern Lendal Bridge, to which stone for building the Minster was brought from the Tadcaster quarries (Raine 1955, 146). The name *Fish Landing Lane* (*venella que dicitur fischelendyng* 13th century) contains OE *fisc* 'fish'. It eventually came to be used both for a lane and for the fish quay to which it led, the lane running from the churchyard of St Michael's Spurriergate to the Ouse. *Swine Landing* (*Sywinlending* 1300) was probably also used both for the quay at which the pigs (OE *swin*, Scandinavian *svín*) were landed and the lane leading from the Ouse to Coney Street and the market at Swinegate. *Lime Landing Lane* (*le Lymelendiyng* 1375) runs from North Street to the south-western bank of the Ouse, where lime (OE *lim*, Scandinavian *lím*) was landed.

Of these five names in *-lending*, three have specifics that could well have been either Old English or Scandinavian originally, the words for 'pig', 'fish' and 'lime', while the other two contain the names of churches near to which they were situated. The church of St Martin is mentioned in *Greater Domesday Book* (*æcclesiam Sancti Martini* GDB 298b; C13) and the name of St Leonard's Hospital was changed to this form from its older name, St Peter's Hospital, in the reign of Stephen (1135–54). It is impossible to determine the date of the coining of the street-names in *-lending* but it must be significant that the generic is of Scandinavian origin. It would seem that these landing-places (or at least some of them) were developed for use in the Scandinavian period. Others may have been constructed at a later date and named on analogy with the earlier ones.

Other Scandinavian generics in York street-names (Fig.129s)

These other generics only make one appearance each in York street-names and it seems most likely that the names in question were coined in the Danish period. The generics will be treated here briefly in alphabetical order.

The word *bogi* (m.) 'bow' is compounded with the Scandinavian specific *steinn* (m.) 'stone' in the name *le Staynbowe* 1276, later *white Freeres lane* 16th century, and until 1952 a dark, narrow passage leading from Fossgate to Hungate was known as *Stonebow Lane*. It is not known to what architectural feature the name originally referred but it cannot have been to the Carmelite Friary here, the construction of which was not begun until 1295 (Raine 1955, 62). Patrick Ottaway has suggested tentatively that the stone arch in question may have been part of the remains of the Roman amphitheatre which he has argued was perhaps situated between St Andrewgate and St Saviourgate (Ottaway 1993, 33–4). It is interesting to note that an English parallel to this name occurs in Lincoln, where the name *Stonebow* (*ad Stanboghe* 1147), a compound of OE *stan* and *boga*, was borne by the principal Roman gate of the city, which probably stood slightly to the north of the present arch (Cameron 1985, 40).

The street-name *Bootham* (*Bouthum* c.1145 x 1161, *Butham*, *Budum* c.1150 x 1161) reflects the dative plural form *búðum* of Old West Scandinavian *búð* (f.) 'tent, booth, small house' and can be translated as 'at the booths' (Palliser 1978, 6). This may well have been where the booths of travelling Scandinavian merchants were erected in the Anglo-Scandinavian period, for the road runs north away from the city through the gate known as Bootham Bar (Lindkvist 1926) but it seems more likely that the booths of craftsmen or tradesmen lined this route out of the city. The form taken by the generic in this place-name is typically West Scandinavian and points to coinage by Norwegians rather than Danes, although *búð* was the form of the word current in North Jutland as well as in Norway in the Viking period. The normal Danish form of the word, *bōth*, appears four times as a simplex place-name with a secondary Middle English plural in *-es* in southern Lancashire and Cheshire, e.g. *Booths* (Fellows-Jensen 1985, 62). There is a lost street-name in Nottingham, *The Shoemakers Booths*, which occurs with early spellings pointing both to West Scandinavian *búð* and East Scandinavian *bōth*, namely *ye Coruezar Bowthes* 1435, containing Old French *corvisier* 'a worker in Cordovan leather' and with the *ow* in the generic being a reflex of *ú*, and *the Shoemak-*

ers Booths 1486 (Gover et al. 1940, 20–1). The element *bōth* enters into a few Danish street-names, e.g. *Klædebodern* 1377, a name referring to the booths or small houses from which cloth was sold and which was later transferred to a *kvarter* or district in the city (Jørgensen 1999, 160–1). In Norway *búð* occurs in a number of compound words indicating the function of the booth in question, e.g. *járnsmiðabúð* 'ironsmiths' booth', *saltbúð* 'salt booth' and *ölbúð* 'ale booth'.

Coney Garth (*Kuningesgard* c.1270) contains East Scandinavian *kunung* 'king', as found in *Coney Street* (see p.361), and is traditionally considered to be the site of the palace of the Scandinavian rulers of the Viking kingdom, a structure which might have incorporated the south-eastern gatehouse of the Roman fortress (Palliser 1978, 8). Since the Norman kings and their successors, as well as the Earls of Northumbria, had their royal residences at other sites, the most likely explanation of the name is that the Viking kings had their residence here until 954 (Hall 1991, 92; 1994, 54).

The street-name *Dublinstones* (*Divelinestaynes* 1233 x 1239) was borne by a lost quay on the south-west bank of the Ouse and the lane leading to it from North Street. The name has recently been revived by the city. The specific is the Celtic place-name **dubhlinn* 'black pool' by which the Vikings and subsequently the English always referred to the chief city of Ireland, which was, and is, known to Irish-speakers as *Áth Cliath* 'the ford of the hurdles'. The generic is the Scandinavian word *steinn* 'stone', with a secondary Middle English plural in *-es*. The name would seem to have denoted the place on the Ouse where Dublin goods were at one time loaded and unloaded (Hall 1994, 39). Alfred P. Smyth has suggested that the fact that the landing-place was on the south-western bank of the Ouse in the *colonia* area might indicate that it is to be dated to late Anglian or early Norman times, when Dublin ships, although welcomed for their cargoes, may have been suspect on political grounds (Smyth 1975–9 **2**, 236–7). It has indeed been argued on the basis of archaeological evidence that the chief anchorages for commercial shipping in Scandinavian York lay along the Foss rather than the Ouse (Richardson 1959; Radley 1971), although Anglo-Scandinavian occupation of the *colonia* area would seem to have been dense. A combination of documentary and archaeological evidence points to its commercial importance at this period as the main point of entry for merchants from London and the south, the site of an important harbour and the city's shipbuilding yards, as well probably as that of the hall of the Gild Merchant (Palliser 1984).

The final Scandinavian generic to have been observed in a York street-name is *toft* (f.) 'building plot', which occurs more frequently in settlement names than in street-names. It was not until the 1920s that *toft* began to be employed fairly frequently as a generic in street-names in Denmark and this was at the same time as field-names and artificial field-names also began to be employed to denote streets, often in new estates whose street-names commemorated the fields on which they had been built. The York street-name *Toft Green*, however, which is first recorded as *Kingestoftes* 1227, with a secondary Middle English plural in *-es*, is a much earlier instance of *-toft* as a street-name generic. The specific is the Middle English and modern form of OE *cyning* and refers to the presence here c.1133 of a king's house and a royal free chapel (Palliser 1978, 16). The land, which had belonged to the king, has in more recent years been occupied by the old railway station and the offices of British Railways but in medieval times there had been an open space and a Dominican friary, and later a horse-market and a dung-heap. A parallel to the street-names has been noted in Denmark in the form of *Kongens Tofte* in the town of Nakskov (Lindkvist 1926, 361).

Hellekeld

One final name will be mentioned here that is not strictly a street-name but rather that of an urban property in King's Square. It is referred to as *Tenementum super Hellekeld* in 1376 (Raine 1955, 43). The buildings in question would seem to have been constructed on top of a spring that had been called **helgakelda* or 'holy spring' by the Danes. This name occurs in several localities in Denmark, where it is used of springs whose waters were thought to have healing properties. The name was certainly brought to Yorkshire by the Danes, for it is borne by one of the wapentakes in the North Riding of Yorkshire, *Halikeld* (*Halichelde* 1086), which took its name from that of its meeting-place, *Hallikeld Spring* (*Halikeld'* 1202; Smith 1928, 218–19). The York property in question now backs onto the street known as *Pump Court*. The pump referred to is presumably the replacement for the original spring.

Scandinavian generics occurring in English towns other than York

The generic *dík* 'ditch' occurs in the name of the lost *Town Dyke* in Nottingham (*le Toundyk* 1390), compounded with the OE specific *tūn* (f.), here in the post-Viking sense 'town'.

In Lincoln there is a compound in *-gata*, namely *hergata* (f.) 'army road', which functions as a generic in the street-name *Midhergate* c.1227, later Dovecote Lane, now Orchard Street in the west of the city, just outside the city wall (Cameron 1985, 87). It is presumed that this generic denotes a road suitable for the passage of an army, in this case a road leading southwards from the castle.

A rather specialised generic, *skeið* (f.) 'race-course', occurs in a lost street-name in Leicester, *The Skeyth* (*le Sckeyth* 1316), an alternative name for Sanvey Gate (*sand+weg+gata*), which ran from the north gateway of the town north-eastwards along the outside of the wall to its northern angle and was early used for horse-racing (Cox 1998, 61–2, 144).

Conclusion

It is impossible to ascribe precise dates to the coining of the Anglo-Scandinavian street-names in York or the other cities, for very few of them are recorded in sources earlier than from the 12th or 13th century and for many of them the earliest records are even later than this. It seems likely, however, that a substantial body of Scandinavian names had been coined in the 10th and 11th centuries so that a close-meshed network of streets with Scandinavian names had been established before the Norman conquest. It has been noted above that in York streets even outside the city walls were being given names in *-gata* by the end of the 11th century.

The evidence from Norwich, which was recaptured by the English much earlier than was York, shows how the Danes there had been able to establish *gata* in use as the regular word for a city street in the course of the comparatively short period of their occupation, since there is no evidence for the survival of the Danish language there.

Subsequently the names coined in the Anglo-Scandinavian period in all the English cities were modified as circumstances changed. New names in *-gata* were coined by English-speaking people who employed English words as the specifics or even French loanwords but retained *gata* as the generic because of the workings of analogy.

The occurrences of Scandinavian occupational terms such as *barkari* 'tanner', *koppari* 'cup-maker' and *skjaldari* 'shield-maker' in York street-names show that the network of streets was being laid down at a period when Scandinavian craftsmen were at work in the city and a Scandinavian language was still in use. The same may well apply to many other York names with specifics of Scandinavian origin, although some of the Scandinavian terms were borrowed into the local dialect and the names may have been coined by English-speakers. The case is similar with the comparatively few street-names containing Scandinavian personal names. These names may have been borne by men and women who were English-speaking and probably looked upon themselves as being English.

In spite of these necessary reservations, however, it can be claimed that the survival of the many street-names in *-gata* and other Scandinavian elements has made no less significant a contribution to our knowledge of the early history of York than has the survival of the stones and mortar of the Romans.

Setting People in their Environment: Plant and Animal Remains from Anglo-Scandinavian York

By Allan Hall and Harry Kenward

Introduction

For the past millennium, the inhabitants of the centre of York have, whether they knew it or not, been living on top of a compost heap in which are preserved all kinds of remains of Anglo-Scandinavian and early post-conquest life. The preservation of this mass of organic matter has come about because, for reasons which are not fully understood, the deposits show anoxic waterlogging — in other words they have remained moist, and decay has been inhibited by lack of free oxygen. Later citizens must often have encountered these 'peaty' deposits and wondered about some of the more recognisable biological remains, as well as the numerous artefacts, surviving in them. However, it was not until the early 20th century that the value of all this material in investigating the past started to be appreciated (see p.294).

Early observations

There are a few early allusions to plant and animal remains from Anglo-Scandinavian York, as well as to the nature of the deposits containing them. Over a century ago, it had become clear that the centre of York was the repository for an important archive of plant and animal remains from the early medieval period. Benson (1902) observed deposits at 25, 26 and 27 High Ousegate, some of which — to judge from their character and from the evidence of later excavations — were surely of Anglo-Scandinavian date. He wrote (p.64) that 'the material [exposed] was a black warp deposit, matted with brushwood, pieces of leather, bones and horns of cattle, sheep, pigs, goats, etc., tusks of boars, cut antlers of red and fallow deer, and occasionally oyster shells. A thin light-coloured strawy band, two inches deep, occurred here and there, and gave out a strong odour that savoured of manure. The deposit was very compact and could be cut vertically, and on digging into it vapours were emitted similar to steam.' By analogy with the 16–22 Coppergate excavation, such deposits accumulated in the 10th–13th/14th centuries.

Benson's comments also embody an early attempt to interpret the formation of the deposits (p.65): 'the site of the excavation has been subject to floods, warp being deposited, and vegetation growing between times to be entombed by warp with recurring floods. The district was a swampy one; the leg bones of a stork or heron were found. The area has been raised by warp deposits and in later times the road was heightened five feet, may be as a barrier between the two rivers when in flood. The depth of this warp deposit has not been reached, although penetrated three feet below present level of digging.' Ramm (1971), evidently influenced by these early comments, perpetuated the 'warp' theory when he wrote at some length on the supposed evidence for late and post-Roman flooding. In particular, he cites (ibid., 183) a late 19th-century account of finds of Viking (and Anglian) date at the Friends' Meeting House between Clifford Street and Castlegate: 'under the finds "was heather and ling" indicating an open site in what had been the middle of the closely packed civilian area south of the fortress. Heath is the vegetation that might be expected to grow over silt left behind after the floods had receded.' Sadly, this last statement is untenable: heath is almost the *last* kind of vegetation to colonise such deposits and it is very much more likely — given all subsequent studies in the city — that the sequence at the Friends' Meeting House included heather (ling is the same plant!) imported by the Anglo-Scandinavian inhabitants of the area for one or more of many purposes. It is worth mentioning here that vegetative remains of heather, *Calluna vulgaris* (L.) Hull, have been recorded from as many as 173 contexts at 16–22 Coppergate, sometimes in considerable quantity, and from twelve layers at 6–8 Pavement; a 20–30 mm thick layer of heather was also recorded at 21–33 Aldwark (Seaward and Williams 1976; *AY* 10/2). That there is no clear evidence for flooding in York in the Anglo-Scandinavian period will be argued below.

History of biological analyses

The earliest report on plant or animal remains from Anglo-Scandinavian York that was more than anecdotal in nature was that by Godwin and Bachem (1959) on plant material from Richardson's excavations in Hungate . They studied plant macro-fossils from a pit fill and five 'levels' (layers), dated as 'Late Anglo-Saxon' or 'Anglo-Danish' from a brushwood and clay bank; in all, eight samples were examined, though no details of their size were published. The samples contained a wide range of uncharred material including wetland taxa and weeds of cultivation, especially cornfield weeds and nitrophiles, but also some *Prunus* stones and several grassland plants. Hop and ?flax were both present, but the tentative identifications of seeds of 'vegetables' are rather suspect. Indeed, a number of the taxa were not regarded by the original authors as necessarily satisfactorily identified at the level of species and this, and the lack of accurate dating, makes this early work of rather limited value, other than as a demonstration of potential.

The 'rescue' excavations of the 1970s–1980s can be seen as the period in which the study of plant and animal remains from archaeological deposits in York evolved from a marginal to a central role. Much of the stimulus for this came from Peter Addyman and Paul Buckland during the earliest years of York Archaeological Trust's work in the city, and by 1975 there was sufficient momentum for the Ancient Monuments Laboratory of the then Department of Ancient Monuments and Historic Buildings to establish and core-fund the Environmental Archaeology Unit at the University of York to undertake the routine analysis of a wide range of biological remains and archaeological sediments from York's extensive excavations. Anglo-Scandinavian material figured prominently in these early projects, starting with 6–8 Pavement but mainly through the large-scale investigations at 16–22 Coppergate in the period 1976–81. This was a time when techniques for sampling, for processing, and for analysis were all being developed and it is for this reason that Kenward and Hall wrote in 1995 (*AY* 14/7, 437) 'the ill-formed theoretical base for work on biological remains from urban deposits in existence ... meant that the investigations ... were essentially an exercise in exploratory data gathering with *post hoc* "interpretation". Only when a substantial proportion of the work had been completed ... [could] the authors ... begin to construct hypotheses...'. Urban environmental archaeology is a discipline which still requires a great deal of fundamental research.

Since the advent of 'developer-funded' archaeology in the 1990s, opportunities for studying biological remains from the usually rather deep-lying Anglo-Scandinavian levels in York have become extremely limited. Indeed, it is something of an irony that the city's (and for that matter the nation's) policy with regard to preservation of its below-ground heritage was in part born out of the problems encountered at a site where there happened to be excellent water-logged preservation of Anglo-Scandinavian occupation deposits (but an inadequate provision for sampling and post-excavation analysis), viz. at 1–9 Micklegate. As Table 6 shows, interventions in the last decade have generally yielded at most only one or a few samples of Anglo-Scandinavian date, the most important being those from St Saviourgate, Layerthorpe Bridge and 4–7 Parliament Street (preservation of delicate plant and invertebrate remains at the last-named site was as good as or better than anything observed at 16–22 Coppergate). The fall-off in numbers of samples from Anglo-Scandinavian deposits subjected to biological analysis over the past three decades has been dramatic: there have botanical analyses of over 500 contexts from sites excavated in the 1970s, but only 50–60 from both of the two succeeding decades. However laudable the policy of in-ground preservation, the failure to collect samples when opportunities arise is, in academic terms, reprehensible, especially if there is a long-term threat to at least some of the deposits (Kenward and Hall 2000c; Kenward and Hall forthcoming).

What are the deposits made of?

As the passages from Benson and Ramm quoted above indicate, the question of how these thick organic occupation deposits dating to the Anglo-Scandinavian period in York formed and subsequently survived the vicissitudes of a millennium of burial is an important one. That the deposits were, in most cases, clearly not laid down in water or by the agency of flooding means that they formed subaerially (although some pit fills must have been saturated as they formed). Parallels in nature are accumulations of peat in fens and bogs where ground water conditions or levels of precipitation are such that plant and other organic matter steadily builds up because deposition rates are faster than rates of decay. It is not surprising, therefore, that the more richly organic deposits at sites like 16–22 Coppergate were commonly termed 'peats' during the earlier stages of excavation. A better analogy, though, is with a garden compost heap which has been poorly constructed and is consequently insufficiently well drained and aer-

Table 6 Sites with Anglo-Scandinavian deposits in York for which some analysis of plant and/or invertebrate remains has been made. References marked * are archaeological reports with passing references to biological remains but no detailed account of results concerning their study

Site name	References	Nature of site	Size of corpus of samples
Hungate (1949)	Godwin and Bachem (1959)	one pit fill and five 'levels' (layers), dated as 'Late Anglo-Saxon' or Anglo-Danish, and coming from a 'brushwood and clay bank'	very small
6–8 Pavement (1972.21)	AY 14/4	?floors associated with wattle structures	modest
21–33 Aldwark (1973–4.6)	Seaward and Williams (1976); Greig (1983); AY 10/2*	layers of brushwood and moss	very small
58–9 Skeldergate (1973–5.14)	Tomlinson (1989a)	mostly pit fills, but phasing not certain	small
5–7 Coppergate (1974.8)	AY 14/4	deposits of uncertain nature associated with wattle; probably Anglo-Scandinavian	modest
site adjacent to 1–5 Aldwark (1976–7.15)	Kenward (1986); Kenward and Robertson (1988); Hall (1988); AY 10/2*	?Anglo-Scandinavian bank deposits and pit fills	small
16–22 Coppergate (1976–81.7)	AY 14/7	various deposits associated with post-and-wattle and plank buildings and their surroundings	very large
118–26 Walmgate (1978–9.8)	Tomlinson (1989b); Kenward and Hall (2000b)	floors, pit fills and external layers	modest
5 Rougier Street (1981.12)	AY 14/6	a pit fill and its timber lining	very small
36 Aldwark (1983.1)	Tomlinson (1989c)	two ?soil deposits; assessment only	very small
24–30 Tanner Row (1983–4.32)	AY 14/6	five contexts, mainly from a timber-lined pit (dated C11–12)	very small
46–54 Fishergate (1985–6.9)	AY 11/2	three pit fills dated late C10/first half C11	very small
7–9 Aldwark (1985.5)	McKenna et al. (1988); Tomlinson (1989d)	fills of two pits, ?Anglo-Scandinavian	very small
22 Piccadilly (1987.21)	Carrott et al. (1995)	mostly waterside dumps; assessment only	small
1–9 Micklegate (1988–9.17)	O'Connor (1990); Dobney et al. (1993); Kenward and Hall (2000a)	various deposits associated with ?post-and-wattle buildings and their surroundings	modest
Adams Hydraulics, Phase I (1990–1.13)	Alldritt et al. (1990)	one levelling/'agricultural' deposit; evaluation only	very small

Site name	References	Nature of site	Size of corpus of samples
104–12 Walmgate (1991.21)	Carrott et al. (1992a)	pit fills; evaluation only	very small
Carmelite Street (1991.9)	Carrott et al. (1991)	one linear cut fill; evaluation only	very small
41 Piccadilly (1992.18)	Dobney and Hall (1992)	one dump deposit; evaluation only	very small
38 Piccadilly (1992.4)	Carrott et al. (1992b)	two build-up deposits overlying a cobbled surface; evaluation only	very small
North Street (1993.1)	Carrott et al. (1993a)	dump deposits; assessment only	small
148 Lawrence Street (1993.11)	Carrott et al. (1994a)	one pit backfill; evaluation only	very small
9 St Saviourgate (1995.434)	Carrott et al. (1998a)	pit fills; assessment only	small
All Saints' Church, Pavement (1995.47)	Hall et al. (1998)	occupation deposits from boreholes; assessment only	very small
St George's School (1995.1)	Buckland (1995); Hajnalova and Charles (1995)	occupation deposits; evaluation only (by ARCUS); dating not wholly certain	very small
Foss Bridge/Peasholme Green/ Layerthorpe Bridge (1996–7.345)	Hall et al. (2000b)	riverside dumps and features (dating frequently imprecise)	modest
Davygate (1997.102)	Carrott et al. (1997)	a single dump deposit; evaluation only	very small
2 Clifford Street (1999.256)	Hall and Kenward (2000b)	probable external accumulations	very small
41–9 Walmgate (1999.941)	Johnstone et al. (2000)	mainly floors and associated make up; assessment only	small
4–7 Parliament Street (1999.946)	Hall and Kenward (2000a)	some perhaps middens, but all probably pit fills	very small

ated: decay of plant matter is slow and the heap fails to compost properly.

Of course, the Anglo-Scandinavian deposits in York are not entirely derived from the decay of plant and animal remains, and in some cases have no perceptible organic content. It is worth considering how the inorganic component originated. Some is clearly artefactual — pottery, the debris of brick and tile, and building stone. This is true even of the fine mineral particles, which under the microscope can be often be seen to be fragments of fired material. Much of the sand grade and finer sediment may have accumulated in an essentially natural way, through wind-blow and trample, or by excavation from the underlying natural deposits. Another source would have been the erosion of Roman building stone and mortar. Probably the bulk of the mineral sediment, however, was imported, either deliberately as make up or accidentally with plant resources and perhaps turf. 'Clay layers', often actually silts or clay silts, have been recorded fairly often, having been used as levelling or packing. The origin of these materials has not yet been investigated, though some undoubtedly was dug up from the underlying moraine. Some clean sands may have been brought from further afield, although some beds of well-sorted sands occur in places in the moraine within the limits of the early town.

Many deposits with a silty texture (often perceptible as a silky or soapy feel between the fingers) have proved on closer investigation to be ash. Most of this presumably was wood ash and, indeed, fragments of wood charcoal are often dispersed through it. Further investigation of such deposits may reveal ash derived from peat, but this is a neglected area of research in York. Charcoal itself, presumably mainly derived from fuel, is abundant in many Anglo-Scandinavian deposits, sometimes forming an appreciable component (Fig.87).

Wood as a component of the build up

If we consider the materials contributing the bulk of the organic build up at sites like 16–22 Coppergate, 6–8 Pavement and so on, it is evident that uncharred wood and timber in one form or another is often significant. Apart from structural material, and smaller fragments which may represent decayed structures or artefacts, debris from woodworking was at times and in places an important contributor to bulk and water retention in deposits. Although probably very much under-recorded archaeobotanically (to judge from records made during excavation at Coppergate, for example), wood chips — fragments up to about 25mm in maximum dimension, often in thin flakes or wedges, and distinguished by having one or more straight cut edges — have been quite frequently noted in assemblages of plant remains from Anglo-Scandinavian sites (Fig.87). Given the preservative qualities of tree bark employed by tanners, one might wonder whether the presence of so much tannin-rich material (especially bark, but to a lesser extent also wood) was not a major factor in the 'self-preservation' of these richly organic occupation deposits, as alluded to in connexion with bracken- and leather-rich deposits at Vindolanda on Hadrian's Wall by Seaward (1976). This is certainly an area where some simple experimental studies could easily be made. Fig.87 also indicates how frequently bark may be recorded in these occupation deposits.

Other components of build up

For many of the organic deposits, studies of the plant remains and parasite eggs have shown that a major component was faeces, whilst in numerous others concentrations of dyeplants have been recorded (both are discussed further below).

The volume of human faecal material at 16–22 Coppergate has been estimated by Kenward and Large (1998b) as over 45m³. The volume of compressed faeces, largely human, buried in those areas of York with Anglo-Scandinavian anoxic waterlogging must be enormous. Assuming there is about 100ha of Anglo-Scandinavian waterlogged deposits in the city and (perhaps dangerously) that Coppergate (with an area of 0·1ha) is typical, the total volume of buried faeces could be of the order of 45,000m³ (but see p.493). To this can be added an enormous quantity of plant material originating in dyeing processes, to judge from the amounts of material interpreted as dyebath waste at Coppergate and other sites (see pp.395, 404).

Bone is another very significant component of the deposits, although its volume is perhaps rarely as great as the subjective impression gained during excavation. Nevertheless, it is estimated that some millions of bone fragments, contributing many cubic

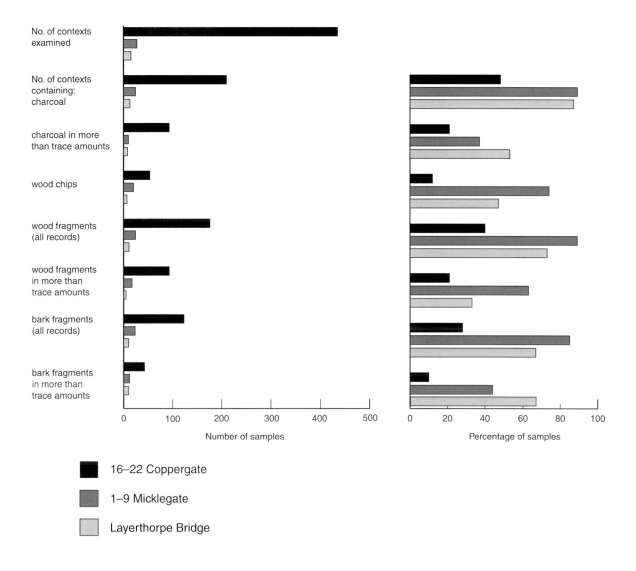

No. of contexts
examined

No. of contexts
containing:
charcoal

charcoal in more
than trace amounts

wood chips

wood fragments
(all records)

wood fragments
in more than
trace amounts

bark fragments
(all records)

bark fragments
in more than
trace amounts

0   100   200   300   400   500

Number of samples

0   20   40   60   80   100

Percentage of samples

■ 16–22 Coppergate

■ 1–9 Micklegate

□ Layerthorpe Bridge

Fig.87 Records for charcoal, wood chips, wood fragments in general, and bark fragments in samples from which plant remains have been studied from Anglo-Scandinavian deposits from three sites in York

metres to the accumulated deposits, were recovered from excavations at 16–22 Coppergate, if both hand-collected and sieved material are considered.

While some layers consist of only one kind of material, it is not surprising that many, perhaps most, contain a mixture of components of various origins. Disentangling the complex mixtures of biological remains (and other material) in these more heterogeneous deposits is one of the more challenging aspects of environmental archaeology, but it is essential if environment and activity in the past are to be elucidated.

An astonishing diversity of evidence

It has been established that a great variety of materials contributed to the build up in Anglo-Scandinavian York. For the biological remains, the quality of preservation in many of the deposits has been such that extraordinarily — even bewilderingly — long lists of plant and insect remains have often been compiled from studies of only a kilogramme or two of raw sediment. Thus, for example, more than 30 of the insect assemblages from 16–22 Coppergate each included over 100 species of beetles (out of perhaps 900 beetle species recorded from the site as a whole, and out of about 3,800 on the modern list for the British Isles). For the plant remains, as many as 82 taxa of vascular plants have been recorded from a single sample (again from 16–22 Coppergate), out of a total for the site as a whole of 431 (for comparison, nearly 3,000 plant species are established in Britain at the present time).

Why have so many species been found? For the plants, the explanation lies principally in their exploitation by human beings, who brought a wide range of plant materials to York for many purposes, and also imported larger or smaller amounts of even more plant species incidentally with plant or other resources (e.g. woodland moss and turves). For the insects, other explanations must be sought. Undoubtedly, numerous insects were also brought accidentally with plant resources, water and turf. However, many species were established in the town, taking advantage of a range of habitats created by human activity. Unique insect communities arose which are not paralleled in nature (Kenward and Allison 1994a). Species which are normally rare in natural habitats were able to prosper — those which reproduce rapidly as an adaptation to patchy, short-lived habitats, such as dung, found huge concentrations of habitat, and slowly reproducing species normally found in small numbers in stable, long-term habitats were also able to build up large populations.

Structural materials

The first impression gained by a visitor to Anglo-Scandinavian York would doubtless have been of a vast expanse of crowded buildings in what was one of the largest urban centres of the period. What were these buildings made of? And where did the building materials come from?

Excavation answers the first of these questions in broad terms. Post-and-wattle buildings have been recorded at various locations, notably at 6–8 Pavement, in the Period 4B levels at 16–22 Coppergate, and at 1–9 Micklegate. A later stage of building at Coppergate (Period 5B) employed massive oak planks and uprights, as did buildings at 25–7 High Ousegate (Benson 1902; *AY* 8/3, 247), King's Square (Stead 1968; see Fig.75, p.299) and 1–9 Micklegate. The quantities of roundwood required for wattle buildings (not to mention all the ancillary structures such as fences, screens and pit linings) must have

been very large, to extrapolate from the amounts surviving in the ground. The above-ground structures would have a short existence before the ravages of moulds and perhaps also insects led to their collapse: Hall et al. (*AY* 14/4) suggested a lifetime of 10–15 years, so that there would have been a continuing need for replacement. The environmental impact of winning all this wood is considered below (pp.411–18). The spider beetle *Tipnus unicolor* (Piller and Mitterpacher), or at least its rarity, may offer further evidence for the short life of buildings (see p.400).

The broad nature of the structures at this period is thus well established, but some details are not. Outstanding amongst these lacunae is continuing uncertainty as to the nature of the roofs. When the report on plant and invertebrate remains from 16–22 Coppergate was written, this question was merely touched on. More evidence has since come to light; combined with work on various sites elsewhere, this has clarified the picture somewhat. Kenward and Hall (*AY* 14/7, 723–4) discussed the records of brushwood at Coppergate and considered the possibility that at least some of it represented layers from within roofs. Similarly, evidence for turves might point to the use of this material in roofing (ibid., 724–5).

While the case for brushwood as a component of roofing is still weak, that for turf roofs has strengthened somewhat. Perhaps the best indicator that turf was used frequently in Anglo-Scandinavian York is the heath grass, *Danthonia decumbens* (Fig.88). This rather short-growing grass (typically 10–40cm tall) is widespread on poorer soils, especially sandy or peaty, often damp, substrates, particularly on heaths and moors. That the cleistogenes (fertile spikelets forming in the culm bases rather than on aerial stalks) were recorded from some contexts at Coppergate suggests the basal parts of the plant found their way into the deposits; routes for this include turves, but also gut contents from herbivores such as sheep which crop closely. In the absence of any clear evidence for gut contents, and in view of some records of heathland insects (and a variety of heathland plants), the importation of *Danthonia* in grass sods is a distinct possibility (see further discussion by Hall 2003). Heather might be brought for a variety of purposes but some records of roots and basal twigs of this plant, and of mosses from heathland surfaces, might suggest the use of turves rather than cut heather. For one of these cases, it was specifically sug-

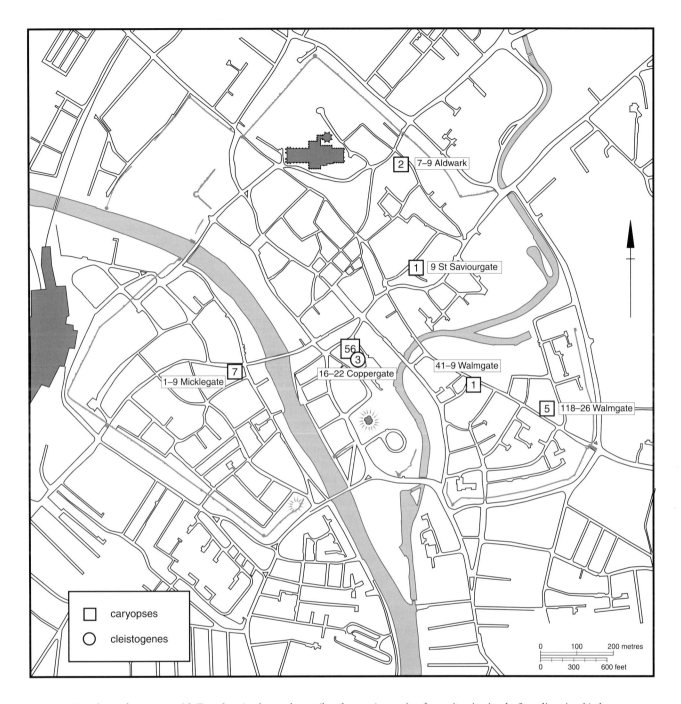

Fig.88 *Numbers of contexts with* Danthonia decumbens *(heath grass) remains from sites in Anglo-Scandinavian York*

gested that a range of typical heathland/moorland insects in the deposit had probably been imported in cut turf (*AY* 14/7, 611).

Heathland/moorland insects, mostly *Ulopa reticulata* (Fabricius) and *Micrelus ericae* (Gyllenhal), were recorded from a small number of contexts at Coppergate. As there was no indication of an origin in peat,

turf was favoured as a likely source for these remains (ibid., 724). The argument for turf is greatly strengthened by the lack of records for these insects from Period 3 (see Table 17, p.415), when buildings were insubstantial. The evidence for the importation of peat to Anglo-Scandinavian York is minimal (pp.414–16), in contrast to the numerous records for Roman York, and its fairly frequent occurrence in post-conquest deposits, e.g. at a site in Bedern (*AY* 10/3) and at two sites in Swinegate (Hall et al. 1991; Carrott et al. 1994b). Ants from heathland were found at nearby 6–8 Pavement during the preliminary investigation (Buckland et al. 1974), but heath/moor insects were present only in traces in the main series of samples (*AY* 14/4, 221); inspection of the database for the site shows that most of the records were of *Strophosomus sus* Stephens. This rather large weevil seems much more likely to have arrived in turf than in cut vegetation since it drops from vegetation when disturbed. Importation of specimens caught in spider webs on heather is just possible, however.

The very fragmented remains of 'outdoor' insects found in floor deposits of some of the houses at Coppergate (*AY* 14/7, 550, 555, 557, discussed 736), may have originated in turf roofs. The cycles of changes in moisture status and the action of scavengers may gradually have reduced the corpses in turf to particles small enough to filter down as dust. If this explanation is correct, there should be parallel evidence from fragmented plant remains, and we may have a much-needed tool in the difficult campaign (conceptually) to reconstruct ancient roofs. Unfortunately, other explanations for the presence of fragmentary insects cannot be ruled out; for example, bats reduce insect cuticle to minute fragments (e.g. Swift et al. 1985), and commensal rodents may do the same.

Perhaps the most likely materials to have been used for roofing in Anglo-Scandinavian York are 'Norfolk reed' (the common reed, *Phragmites australis* (Cav.) Trin. ex Steudel) and cereal straw. The archaeobotanical evidence for the former is sparse, whilst for the latter there is abundant 'proxy' evidence in the form of seeds of cereal weeds together with some vegetative material which may be the undecayed remnants of straw culms. In no case, however, has a large concentration of cereal straw been recorded — somewhat contrary to expectations, given the excellent state of preservation of so much plant material in the town at this period. Some records of remains of the saw-sedge *Cladium mariscus* (L.) Pohl (Fig.89) may point to the use of this plant as thatching material; perhaps the most convincing examples are those of charred and uncharred leaf fragments from Layerthorpe Bridge and charred leaf fragments from 1–9 Micklegate and 41–9 Walmgate. This last-mentioned site also yielded some possible evidence for cereal

straw thatch in the form of partly charred ('toasted') remains of oat spikelets and for straw fragments with a coating of fine black particles, probably soot; some similar part-charred material was seen in two contexts at 2 Clifford Street.

If thatched roofs were used in Anglo-Scandinavian York, they might have have needed an 'underlay' of some kind, perhaps turf or brushwood, laid over a system of timbers or roundwood poles as in the tradition of the Northern Isles of Scotland (e.g. Fenton 1978), the Hebrides (e.g. Geddes 1955), and parts of north and west England and Ireland (e.g. Buchanan 1957; Evans 1974). However, only at 16–22 Coppergate has a deposit of brushwood been found which could be interpreted as a collapsed roof — though it might equally be argued that such material would, under normal circumstances, have been used for fuel after it had been stripped from the roof, and thus would mostly not enter the archaeological record.

The 'sooty' straw from 41–9 Walmgate has been mentioned but the fact that this is the only record of sooted material is a matter for note. On the assumption that Anglo-Scandinavian buildings had open hearths with at most a small opening in the roof for smoke to escape, the insides of roofs should have become heavily smoke-blackened (cf. Letts 1999) and debris from such roofs ought, preferentially, to survive in the fossil record. It might also be argued that roofs would frequently have caught fire, yet no layers of charred thatching materials have been found (the charred saw-sedge leaf material, cf. Fig.89, was dispersed amongst other components of the deposits in which it was found and may merely represent saw-sedge used as fuel; cf. Rowell 1986).

Many of the 'dry decomposer' insects found in Anglo-Scandinavian buildings (e.g. *AY* 14/7, 671–2) would have found thatch a congenial habitat (Smith 1996). Much the most abundant beetle in floors at Coppergate was *Lathridius* (probably mostly *L. pseudominutus* (Strand)), very likely to have lived in thatch, but also in floors and walls. Whether insects would have been deterred from living in the superstructure by smoke contamination is uncertain (Smith et al. 1999).

The presence and condition of timber, wattle and basketwork may be indicated by insect remains, and timber beetles are a constant in Anglo-Scandinavian

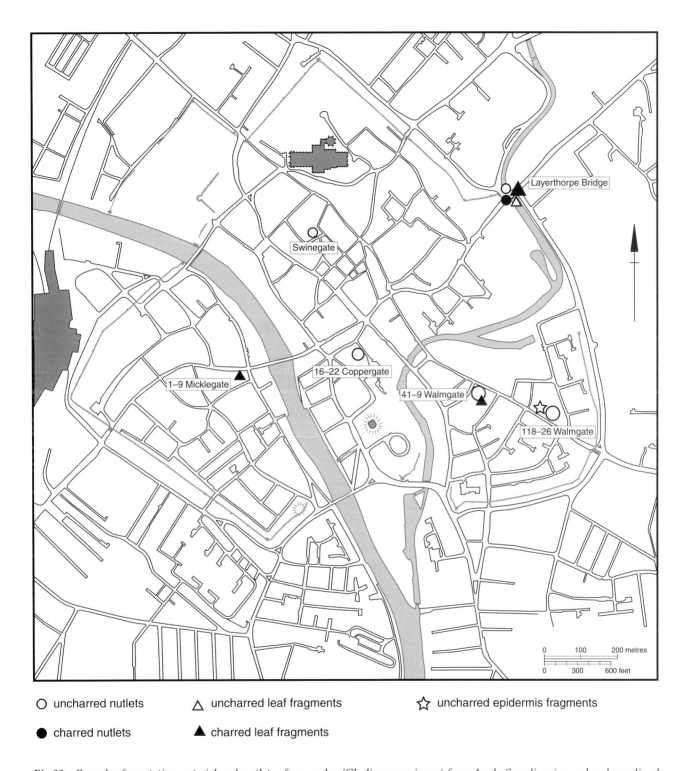

○ uncharred nutlets   △ uncharred leaf fragments   ☆ uncharred epidermis fragments

● charred nutlets   ▲ charred leaf fragments

Fig.89   *Records of vegetative material and nutlets of saw sedge* (Cladium mariscus) *from Anglo-Scandinavian and early medieval sites in York. The size of the symbol provides a guide to the frequency with which remains were recorded*

deposits in York. Kenward and Hall (*AY* 14/7, 658) listed the insects associated with wood which were recorded from Coppergate: twenty species were considered particularly likely to have exploited structural timber or wattle. Some, notably the woodworm beetle *Anobium punctatum* Degeer (from almost two-thirds of the contexts for which insects were quantified), *Ptilinus pectinicornis* (Linnaeus) (from more than one in ten contexts), and the powder-post beetle *Lyctus linearis* (Goeze) (from about one-fifth of the

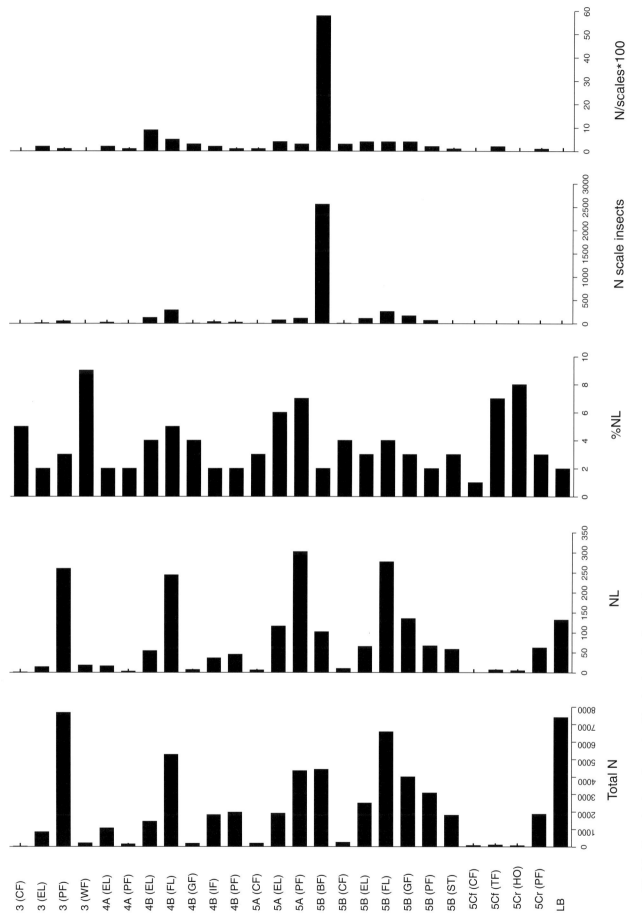

Fig.90 *Records of wood-associated beetles from Anglo-Scandinavian deposits at 16–22 Coppergate and 6–8 Pavement (LB) by period and feature type. For key to abbreviations, see Table 10, p.393*

382

contexts) were clearly established on the site, and some other species were quite frequent (e.g. *Grynobius planus* (Fabricius)).

A. punctatum and *L. linearis* are capable of causing considerable damage to timber, although not in proportion to the paranoia that has been generated by the pest control industry! They were, however, most unlikely to have caused appreciable damage to any but (ironically) the best-constructed and longest-lived buildings in the past, fungal decay of timbers at ground level probably being the factor limiting the life of most (*AY* 14/4, 190; *AY* 14/7, 722–3 and see above, p.376). Perhaps significantly, there was no concentration of wood-associated beetles in and around the buildings at Coppergate (Fig.90). Even in long-lived Roman, medieval and post-medieval buildings, it is likely that insects caused relatively little structural damage. Woodworm takes many decades to weaken large timbers significantly, and the death-watch beetle (*Xestobium rufovillosum* (Degeer)), cause of much alarm to modern building conservators, damages timbers immensely slowly and would rarely have concerned people in the past, except superstitiously (the adults knock their heads against the inside of the pupal cell, producing what is said to be a disturbing sound in a silent room).

Gracilia minuta (Fabricius) is a small black longhorn beetle which bores in fine twigs, and is well known from wickerwork (Duffy 1953, 195; Hickin 1975, 241). It is fairly often recorded from Anglo-Scandinavian York and, when it occurs in large numbers, as in one pit fill at Coppergate (*AY* 14/7, 520), it probably indicates the presence of material such as basketwork. At Coppergate it occurred in seventeen contexts, suggesting that it was well established in the town. Another longhorn beetle, the attractively patterned *Phymatodes alni* (Linnaeus), is so frequently found (e.g. 29 contexts at Coppergate; *AY* 14/7) that it, too, surely must have lived in basketwork or, more probably, in wattle or light roof supports.

Scale insects (*Chionaspis salicis* (Linnaeus) and *Lepidosaphes ulmi* (Linnaeus)) were abundant in some layers of Period 4B at Coppergate, doubtless originating from wattle in walls and perhaps in furniture and roofs including brushwood (Fig.90). They were also sometimes immensely abundant in brushwood layers amongst the 'backfills' (heterogeneous series of apparently dumped deposits) in the Period 5B

structures. The scale insects are fairly firmly attached to the host twigs and branches, and only likely to be released in large numbers over a long period of time, suggesting an origin on structural wood rather than firewood which would presumably have been quickly used up. Another route by which scale insects may have entered the deposits is via the stripping of bark from twigs prior to their use for purposes such as basketry; the bark may well have decayed preferentially or have been overlooked.

A range of other materials may have been used in finishing structures, among them textiles and skins. Moss would have been invaluable in packing cracks in walls and such a use might explain why small amounts of moss were observed in so many surface-laid deposits at Coppergate, although evidence from remains of standing structures for moss used in this way is lacking. Moreover, Anglo-Scandinavian York has not provided evidence of the double-skinned wattlework 'cavity-wall' construction employed in 7th-century buildings at Deer Park Farms, Co. Antrim, N. Ireland (Hamlin and Lynn 1988, 44–7).

Conditions and activities within buildings

The first issue to be confronted in discussing what it was like inside Anglo-Scandinavian buildings in York is whether the excavated 'floor' deposits relate to the use phase or abandonment (or low-grade use) of the structures. Obviously, if they do not represent the litter accumulating during use they cannot provide evidence for human activity and living conditions. It has been argued that floors are the one place where there should *not* be accumulation, but the present authors do not agree: such a view is too coloured by modern attitudes. We suggest that in a culture where organic waste was produced in huge quantities, and where floors were damp, there would inevitably have been a net accumulation of biological (and other) remains on floors, even if they were occasionally swept or scraped off. The arguments have been rehearsed elsewhere (*AY* 14/7, 725). Hall et al. (*AY* 14/4) offered a model of the way mineral and organic material may have accumulated on Anglo-Scandinavian floors, which clearly shows how much debris may build up; analogous deposits in Iceland and Greenland are discussed by Amorosi et al. (1992) and Buckland et al. (1994).

Before discussing the debris of occupation, it is worth considering whether any of the archaeological deposits represent 'made' floors, that is, material used to make a level living surface. It was suggested in the account of the 6–8 Pavement site (*AY* 14/4) that made floors and periods of accumulation in use could be distinguished, and in a few cases mineral-rich floor layers at Coppergate may represent material used for levelling. There is, of course, always the possibility that sediment used for levelling may be richly organic and contain abundant fossils, having been excavated from earlier occupation deposits. The redeposition of identifiable remains certainly can occur in this way (a notable case being at the Magistrates' Courts site in Kingston-upon-Hull; Hall et al. 2000a). The secondary deposition of delicate organic remains is discussed by Dobney et al. (1997).

Is it possible to determine the quality and use of buildings from biological remains in their floors (and in deposits which can be argued to contain waste cleaned from floors)? First of all, it must be emphasised that it is important to avoid regarding litter accumulating on floors as evidence of low-quality occupation — it is the *nature* of the build up which matters. It should be possible to distinguish clean from filthy living conditions using insect remains, their value lying in the wide range of species capable of exploiting the many kinds of habitats created by human life, combined with the fact that the animals concerned are not deliberately exploited by humans. If a *community* of insects requiring a particular habitat is present in the deposits formed on a house floor, then it is very likely that the habitat existed in the house; the main exceptions to this are where earlier material has been imported to make up floors — which should be detected through careful excavation in most cases — and where turf has been used. If fauna from within houses can be identified, then conditions within the buildings, and something of their construction, can be determined.

An extremely distinctive group of species has been repeatedly detected in house floor deposits, both subjectively (*AY* 14/6, 398–9; *AY* 14/7, 662–7) and objectively (Carrott and Kenward 2001). For ease of discussion (and despite the dangers of circular argument) this group is termed 'house fauna'. The species assigned to this group are only likely to be found together in fairly dry litter with some mould growth, and many have been recorded in modern buildings

(at least of the kind normal until the mid 20th century; Kenward and Allison 1994a).

The Anglo-Scandinavian period at 16–22 Coppergate has provided classic examples of house fauna assemblages. Unfortunately, house fauna communities evidently developed in structures used to house livestock as well as those used primarily by people (Kenward and Hall 1997), so that it is essential to determine which kind of use is represented. This is generally not too difficult since there is a characteristic suite of organisms which signal stabling — one which is conspicuously rare in those parts of Anglo-Scandinavian York investigated bioarchaeologically.

House floor deposits may be encountered in situ or as dumps; in the latter case, it may be necessary to disentangle very mixed communities including post-dumping decomposer successions. Large quantities of house fauna, presumably from floor clearance but perhaps sometimes introduced as residual material in backfills, were observed in some pit fills at Coppergate (*AY* 14/7).

The gross condition of the floors at Coppergate (in Periods 4B and 5B/5C), indicated by the predominance of house fauna, was generally best described as rather damp, but certainly not wet. There were, however, some occasions when insects indicating rather more foul conditions became established, perhaps as a result of particular activities. In some cases, flies indicating very unpleasant conditions, including the housefly *Musca domestica* Linnaeus and stable fly *Stomoxys calcitrans* (Linnaeus), occurred in substantial numbers in the post-and-wattle buildings of Period 4B (*AY* 14/7, 548, 564). The range of insects recorded suggested that it was cosy and well sheltered within these structures. It can be argued that the floors of the Period 4B post-and-wattle buildings were certainly domestic, the evidence including the presence of both human fleas and lice. The relative rarity of human lice in the Period 5B floors, together with other evidence, perhaps suggests that the floor deposits represented workshops, and it is possible that if these buildings had any domestic function, then the occupants lived on an upper floor. Human fleas were frequently recorded and sometimes abundant in floors of both periods (and in many other deposits) at Coppergate, representing a minor nuisance which would have been unavoidable in houses of this kind.

The kinds of materials which may have been deliberately scattered onto floors to sweeten them and to provide a dry and somewhat absorbent living surface include rushes, bracken, leaf litter, wood chippings, straw, hay and moss. Fossil remains likely to have originated in one or more of these materials are variously recorded from floor deposits in Anglo-Scandinavian York, though never in high concentrations. Rush seeds, for example, as a proxy for the use of the whole cut plants as litter, are present in many cases but usually in low concentrations, in contrast to the large numbers of rush seeds from floors of post-conquest medieval date at some other sites (e.g. Magistrates' Courts site, Hull; Hall et al. 2000a). Indeed, in the three cases where rush seeds were abundant in floors at Coppergate, the species concerned was the short-growing toad rush (*Juncus bufonius*) whose seeds are much more likely to have arrived on muddy feet than with cut rushes. It may well be, in fact, that the rather well-drained floors at this site were not conducive to the preservation of plant remains from litter in a recognisable state, though insects were not particularly strongly decayed. The organic content of the floors of Period 4B at Coppergate was close to 40%, testifying to the presence of a great deal of humified plant material. Studies of the differential decay of delicate plant and animal remains under varying depositional conditions must be seen as a priority in understanding the taphonomy of floors, and of course of archaeological deposits in general. As an aside, we would also argue strongly for the routine recording of material forming the matrix of archaeological deposits rather than merely the identifiable remains present as 'inclusions', even if the former are listed only at a rather superficial level, such as 'bark fragments' or 'herbaceous detritus'.

The same arguments about decay patterns apply to waste matter which found its way onto floors, either accidentally or through deliberate discard. Evidence of food remains is largely restricted to bones and the more robust kinds of plants; hazel nutshells, for example, were recorded from most of the floors at Coppergate and Pavement (and seem likely to represent debris from 'snacking'). Other waste which became incorporated into floors included dyeplants, which were occasionally abundant, wool cleanings (indicated by sheep parasites), wood chips and ash. A substantial proportion of accumulation indoors may, however, have resulted from the trampling of mud from outside, incidentally accounting for a

range of biological remains in addition to the toad rush seeds mentioned above. The flow of material was probably two-way, since a greater thickness of accumulation would surely be expected unless there was at least some attempt to scrape or sweep out buildings at intervals. The abundance of 'house fauna' in deposits adjacent to buildings and in some of the pits at Coppergate may point to such clearance.

While it seems likely that earth floors were the norm in Anglo-Scandinavian York, there is some evidence from the excavation record for plank floors (e.g. the charred remains of planks from Structure 5/5 at Coppergate). Such floors could be kept completely clean, although litter and especially insects might accumulate beneath them, having fallen through cracks. The subterranean insect fauna recorded from a gully within one of the Period 5B buildings at Coppergate (*AY* 14/7, 607) suggests that this cut was covered.

It seems likely for Period 4B at Coppergate, at least, that the buildings were people's homes, especially given the range of artefacts recovered, and the records of hearths, food remains and human lice. Many of the activities in these houses are discussed elsewhere (principally in sections dealing with craft and food). One 'activity' which may be mentioned here is sleeping. Excavations in other Viking-Age towns have revealed structures within buildings which gave every sign of being beds (e.g. in Dublin; Wallace 1992). The evidence in York is much less clear, although one of the Coppergate buildings (on Tenement D in Period 4B) may have had benches or beds against both walls. The Early Christian buildings at the Deer Park Farms site in Co. Antrim had what (on excavational evidence) seemed to be bed areas, and this was supported by the biological analyses (Allison et al. 1999a; 1999b). No such evidence was obtained at Coppergate, although the sampling regime was (with 25 years' hindsight) not ideally suited to detecting zonation within buildings.

Most of our evidence for life indoors in Anglo-Scandinavian York inevitably has come from the major excavation at Coppergate. The identification of 'floors' at 6–8 Pavement (*AY* 14/4) was far less clear because of the limited lateral extent of the excavated trenches and, although many of the layers probably formed during occupation, some may have been make up and others external layers. However, if it is assumed that the Pavement deposits were mainly floor build up, it appears that conditions in the structures at the site were broadly like those at Coppergate. The relative abundance of some insects varied, but not in an ecologically consistent way. There may perhaps have been a greater tendency towards occasional episodes of 'foulness' at Pavement and in Period 4B at Coppergate.

Floors of post-and-wattle buildings of the Anglo-Scandinavian period were also revealed by excavation at 1–9 Micklegate, although there was only limited sampling and analysis. The biological remains were broadly similar to those from 'floor' deposits at Coppergate and Pavement, and suggested reasonably dry buildings. Preliminary analyses of the small number of samples from deposits interpreted as floors at 41–9 Walmgate indicated that these, too, were acceptably dry, though moister here and there. The floors never yielded seething assemblages of house fauna like those seen at other sites, suggesting that they were used in different ways. Unfortunately, detailed analysis was impossible because the samples had degraded during more than two decades of storage prior to examination.

Analyses to date have given some indications as to the range of conditions and uses of floors of this period. However, there is clearly much unrealised potential and, should further examples be revealed, a far more intensive sampling strategy should be adopted in order to allow for spatial analysis and statistically significant comparison through time within single buildings and between buildings and sites.

The floors of some buildings in both of the main Anglo-Scandinavian structural phases at Coppergate had been cut into. In Period 4B there were large pits, one with fills including abundant honeybees, *Apis mellifera* Linnaeus (*AY* 14/7, 765–7). In Period 5B there were gullies cut into floors, one of them apparently having been used to dispose of waste water (since it contained resting eggs of water fleas, presumably imported in water; *AY* 14/7, 595–6), and another perhaps having been covered (and consequently colonised by subterranean species). The function of these pits and gullies is far from clear and most of the fills appear to represent floor litter which had spilled into them (or perhaps filtered through floorboards) or had been deliberately dumped.

The lack of evidence for large-scale flooding in Anglo-Scandinavian York has already been mentioned. On a more local scale, were there occasions when either the local water-table rose or rainfall was so heavy that drainage failed and the 'basements' in the Period 5B buildings at Coppergate flooded? The presence of gullies within the buildings might at first sight suggest that this was the case but in two cases (both in Tenement B) these cuts appear to have been entirely within the buildings (*AY* 14/7, fig.157). It seems likely that they were associated with some craft activity, textile processing being much the most likely. Perhaps they were just soakaways for waste liquor; there is nothing to suggest that they were related to livestock kept in the buildings (cf. Fenton 1978, 117ff.). Even the gullies which exited the buildings (Tenements C and D) seem as likely to have been used to carry effluent as to have been intended as flood drains. Like the entirely internal gullies, those on Tenements C and D sometimes contained abundant dyeplant debris, perhaps from the emptying of dye vats.

The outlines of the Period 5B buildings at Coppergate contain a series of more or less level deposits referred to as 'backfills'. While some of the lower of these may in fact be floor deposits (*AY* 14/7, 596), most do, on both stratigraphic and biological evidence, seem to have been dumps, although of a variety of different kinds. They give no clear evidence that they represent a change of use of the buildings, such as to the housing of livestock.

The evidence in the ground for the wooden structures in Anglo-Scandinavian York does not offer a clue as to how well lit and ventilated they were. In theory, the quantity and structure of outdoor background insect fauna in floor deposits should give clues as to how open structures were, following arguments presented by Kenward (1985), but there is a problem in determining how outdoor remains entered structures. Many of them may have been imported in one way or another rather than having flown in through openings. The large quantity of highly comminuted remains of outdoor insects found in some floors at Coppergate (*AY* 14/7, 736), for example, seem unlikely to have arrived on the wing, and these animals perhaps came from the roofs (see p.380) or were imported in materials of some kind. It was formerly thought that the presence of large numbers of certain waterside beetles was evidence of open-sided structures, the insects drifting in on the breeze as they migrated in swarms, but (however improbable it may appear) these beetles are now believed to have lived in the buildings (see, for example, *AY* 14/7, 733). Bearing in mind the many ways in which outdoor insects might be brought into a building, it now seems much less likely that background fauna can be used in a positive way to indicate an open construction. On the other hand, very restricted faunas in floors may stand as evidence of a firmly closed structure (e.g. the Roman wooden store building with abundant grain pests at Coney Street, York; *AY* 14/2), but no unequivocal examples from the Anglo-Scandinavian period have been found. At best, a few of the internal deposits of Period 5B buildings at Coppergate may fall in this category.

External surfaces and the external environment

There is inherently a particularly strong bias against the existence of a fossil record for surfaces in cleaner, drier places in towns. Preserved remains at such sites may often represent atypical circumstances; there is always a danger of misinterpretation consequent upon over-representation of foul conditions for taphonomic reasons: filth, where abundant, will often have been self-preserving. It is important to draw a distinction between conditions in open areas such as yards, gardens and streets, where people would normally be experiencing the environment at first hand as they went about their daily lives, and those in disposal areas, which would presumably be avoided and where rapid accumulation of organic matter might favour preservation. This section deals primarily with the former; the latter are considered on pp.394–5.

Reconstruction of conditions and activities in yards and other open areas by any means presents considerable difficulties. Soils will have been disturbed, and any plant remains may represent materials imported for a variety of reasons and by various routes. Invertebrates may thus represent the best hope for ecological reconstruction. The deposits formed on the external surfaces themselves may be of little value in this respect (although they may be important for wider reconstruction where there is good preservation). In many cases there appears to have been much informal dumping, which introduced a wide variety of remains from elsewhere. Open areas are likely to have been rather dry and well drained, often disturbed by human activity or by livestock, particularly chickens and pigs, so that there was strong decay of biological remains, making preservation unlikely.

Remains of value in reconstructing surfaces are thus more likely to be found in pits and other cuts, although under some circumstances there may be surface preservation. The Anglo-Scandinavian material at Coppergate (*AY* 14/7) provides a good case in point for, while external surface deposits contained larger numbers of well-preserved insect (and other delicate) remains than is the case at most sites, it was rarely clear whether they had originated in situ. Indeed, the presence of distinct house fauna assemblages here and there in deposits formed on external surfaces strongly indicated dumping or scatter from within the nearby buildings, and botanical evidence showed that some layers were rich in dyeplant waste (*AY* 14/7, fig.196). It did appear, however, that the concentrations of fly puparia found scattered in surface layers had developed where they were found, indicating short-lived patches of very foul material such as dung or moist food waste, and rarely were there beetle communities suggesting rather longer-lived rotting matter. Some insects associated with weeds were considered too abundant in the assemblages from the site as a whole to be present by accident (ibid., 654), and it seems that some plants, particularly crucifers, nettles and docks and/or knotgrasses, were able to survive. There was also a limited non-phytophagous (plant-feeding) open ground fauna, consisting of ground beetles and others able to survive where a few scattered plants or piles of loose debris provided shelter. Some other plants were at least occasionally able to gain a foothold, but do not have characteristic insects associated with them; plants such as fat hen (*Chenopodium album* L.) are also large seed producers so it is difficult to judge whether the abundant seeds of these weeds can be translated into a luxuriant growth or a few poorly grown but still seed-prolific specimens.

Most of the phytophages recorded in Anglo-Scandinavian York may have been imported in moss, turf, cut vegetation, water, brushwood or dyeplants, as well as being 'background fauna' which arrived on the wing and in bird droppings. The abundance of one genus of weevils seems not to be so easily explained: *Sitona* species were repeatedly recorded and had a strong statistical association with house fauna at Coppergate, suggesting either that they were brought with materials used in houses or were attracted to them in some way. Some *Sitona* may have been imported with peas and beans, for several species feed on these plants. Alternatively, they may have been imported with dyer's greenweed, since at least a few species have been found on it. These weevils are regarded as a component of 'hay' fauna (Kenward and Hall 1997), but there is only limited evidence for such material being brought to York in the period considered here. It is worth mentioning that *Sitona* species were very frequent in medieval floor and dump deposits at the Magistrates' Courts site, Hull (Hall et al. 2000a), and, although their origin was not clear, it appeared most likely that they had arrived with pulses.

Shells of snails, mainly the large garden snail *Helix aspersa*, were rather often found at Coppergate and although some were undoubtedly of modern origin (*AY* 14/7, 472, 526, etc.), others appeared to be ancient, supporting the hypothesis that disturbance did not completely sterilise the yard areas. In general, though, disturbance seems to have been intense, not least as a result of the digging of pits and ditches and through dumping. It may be that much of the town was sterilised in this way, but that a flora of opportunistic weeds appeared almost immediately disturbance ceased and quickly contributed to a 'seed bank' forming in the deposits and which was the source of new plants at some later stage. The rate at which vegetation can re-appear in apparently sterile environments was amply demonstrated during phases of non-excavation at Coppergate when the ground quickly became colonised by dense stands of annual weeds.

So, as a source of information about surface conditions, we are largely thrown back on cut fills. This means it is necessary to attempt to determine the likely origin of the various components of what are often very complex assemblages from the fills of wells, ditches and pits. Pits in some cases may be rather effective in sampling the biota of the surroundings, especially insects. If there is water in them, then small or inept species may land on the surface by accident and be trapped, while larger walking insects may fall in and drown. The 'pitfall' effect appears to have operated for some Anglo-Scandinavian pits at Coppergate (*AY* 14/7, 567–8, 614, 627).

While the open areas at Coppergate appear mostly to have been sterilised by intensive use during the Anglo-Scandinavian period (see above), there is a little evidence that at some stages there was development of more stable vegetation to the rear of the site (*AY* 14/7, 624–7). The cut containing the Anglian helmet (*AY* 17/8) appears likely to have been a well, whose fills may date to the Anglo-Scandinavian period, the biota suggesting open disturbed ground with annual and perennial weeds, plant litter and perhaps dung. Some of the pits in the backyards at 16–22 Coppergate gave somewhat similar evidence, although in rather less clear form. Animals may possibly have been kept in these backyards and at times maintained a short turf by grazing. The lowest and uppermost parts of the succession in one of the trenches at 6–8 Pavement (*AY* 14/4) were thought perhaps to have been external deposits on the evidence of the plant remains, but this was not clearly supported by the insects. In the assemblages as a whole from Pavement, as at Coppergate, there were rather few phytophages likely to have originated in yards and alleyways, other than crucifer and nettle feeders, and even these were present only in small numbers. Nothing suggested the presence of livestock at the Pavement site with any certainty.

Given the relative paucity in the fossil record of insects associated with the sorts of weeds likely to have grown in the Anglo-Scandinavian town, were stands of weeds established on the sites? If not, how do we explain the abundant weed seeds? One or more of the following explanations may account for this contradiction: (a) that isolated plants (or localised patches) produced the seeds (the taxa concerned are typically prolific seed producers) but supported relatively few insects; (b) that the seeds entered in the faeces of livestock; (c) that the seeds fell from plants growing on roofs (either 'live' turf or poorly maintained thatch); (d) that they were wind-blown or trampled to the site from further afield; (e) that they grew in brief periods of neglect; (f) that they originated in whole mature plants cut during ground clearance; (g) that the seeds originated in backfill soil containing a seed bank slowly accumulated over a long period; or (h) that most of the weed seeds were brought with some plant material such as straw or hay. Amongst the plant-feeding insects, nettle-feeders were particularly well represented. Unfortunately, the data are not adequate to determine statistically whether numbers of nettle-feeders and nettle 'seeds' are cor-

Table 7 Records of (a) fruits of stinging nettle and annual nettle (all records, and those where the semi-quantitative abundance score was greater than '1', a 'trace') and (b) of nettle-feeders from 16–22 Coppergate; for plants, numbers of contexts are translated into percentages (in parentheses) for those periods for which large numbers of contexts were examined. There was no significant association between the records of nettle fruits and insects (p >> 0.05)

(a)

Period	No. contexts examined for plants [no. pit fills]	U. dioica >1		all U. dioica		U. urens >1		all U. urens	
		all	pit fills	all	pit fills	all	pit fills	all	pit fills
3	89 [54]	15 (7)	8 (9)	61 (69)	36 (40)	14 (16)	9 (10)	69 (78)	46 (52)
4A	12 [3]	4	–	8	1	2	–	11	2
4B	148 [29]	7 (5)	2 (1)	76 (51)	14 (9)	11 (7)	9 (6)	110 (74)	23 (16)
5A	47 [19]	1 (2)	–	27 (57)	9 (4)	2 (4)	–	35 (74)	12 (6)
5B	96 [41]	3 (3)	2 (2)	53 (55)	26 (25)	3 (3)	3 (3)	63 (60)	31 (30)
5Cr	24 [22]	1	1	14	12	5	4	23	20

(b)

	Period/number of individuals					
	3	4A	4B	5A	5B	5Cr
Heterogaster urticae (Fabricius)	17	2	19	4	28	10
Trioza urticae (Linnaeus)	3		1			
Trioza urticae (nymph)			(1)		(1)	
Brachypterus glaber (Stephens)			2		1	
Brachypterus urticae (Fabricius)			1		2	
Brachypterus sp.	8	2	7	6	3	3
Apion (Taenapion) urticarium (Herbst)	3					
Cidnorhinus quadrimaculatus (Linnaeus)	12		5		6	
Total	43	4	35	10	40	13
Total period N	36463	2648	16230	18652	39356	3473
Percentage nettle insects	0.1	0.2	0.2	0.1	0.1	0.4

related in archaeological assemblages at Coppergate (Table 7).

In terms of visual impact, trees are important, and they also provide shade and raw materials. Were trees a significant feature of Anglo-Scandinavian York? As far as the evidence from the plants themselves is concerned we can adduce the few records for stumps or roots of elder (*Sambucus nigra* L.) from Coppergate (Table 8a); the living plants they represent may also go a long way to explaining the abundance of elder

seeds in so many deposits (Table 8b). Elder is, of course, one of the most successful colonists of nutrient-rich soils in the vicinity of human occupation. Many of the seeds from other trees and shrubs may also have come from within the town, though those with edible fruits have routes via consumption by humans or other animals.

Another source of imported tree seeds would have been the abundant woodland moss brought to the site. Most of the insects associated with living trees

Table 8a Records of elder (*Sambucus nigra*) stumps or roots from 16–22 Coppergate

Context	Period	Nature of material
18659	3	roots
34753	3	roots
36098	3	stump/root
34967	4B	branching trunk/stump, max. diam. 10cm (part of fence line)

Table 8b Records of elder (*Sambucus nigra*) seeds from Anglo-Scandinavian deposits in York. Percentages in brackets indicate very low numbers of contexts examined

Site	No contexts examined	No. contexts with elder seeds	%	No. with more than traces	%
6–8 Pavement	55	51	93	2	4
5–7 Coppergate	18	11	(61)	0	0
site adjacent to 1–5 Aldwark	8	8	(100)	3	(38)
16–22 Coppergate	430	340	79	33	8
118–26 Walmgate	17	16	(94)	3	(18)
5 Rougier Street	2	1	(50)	0	0
24–30 Tanner Row	5	1	(20)	0	0
46–54 Fishergate	3	0	0	0	0
7–9 Aldwark	7	7	(100)	5	(71)
22 Piccadilly	6	4	(67)	1	(17)
1–9 Micklegate	27	11	41	0	0
Adams Hydraulics, Phase I	1	0	0	0	0
104–112 Walmgate	3	2	(67)	0	0
North Street	9	8	(89)	1	(11)
9 St Saviourgate	10	8	(80)	5	(50)
All Saints' Church, Pavement	5	5	(100)	0	0
Foss Bridge/Peasholme Green/Layerthorpe Bridge	15	12	(80)	2	(13)
Davygate	1	1	(100)	1	(100)
2 Clifford Street	5	4	(80)	1	(20)
41–9 Walmgate	7	5	(71)	1	(14)
4–7 Parliament Street	4	2	(50)	0	0

recorded in Anglo-Scandinavian York seem likely to have been imported with moss. On the other hand, the small bark beetle *Scolytus rugulosus* (Müller) offers a small hint that fruit trees were grown in the town. It was recorded from five of the samples from 1–9 Micklegate, usually as single individuals. It was also recorded from three contexts at Coppergate (*AY* 14/7, 658), although undiagnostic fragments seem likely to have been included in the 23 records of '*Scolytus* sp.' from that site. According to Balachowsky (1949) it is associated with Rosaceae, on domestic forms of which it may be a serious pest, and is only extremely rarely known to occur under the bark of other woody plants. (A wide range of woody rosaceous plants was recorded from the Coppergate site, though mainly as remains of fruits or seeds and of course quite probably imported to the site — as discussed above.) While the specimens may have emerged from rosaceous firewood, or even from hawthorns growing in the town, it is tempting to suggest that there were fruit trees of some kind here and there, perhaps in the very hypothetical 'gardens' where the bees (see p.397) were kept.

There is no clear evidence from the biological remains for cultivation at any of these sites. The three plants contributing vegetables to the diet of the Anglo-Scandinavian inhabitants of York — leeks, peas and field beans — all seem likely to have been grown on a small scale, perhaps in gardens or 'allotments' rather than on a field scale, but there seems to be no easy way of proving this. Broadly speaking, the insect remains offer no evidence of cultivation at any of the sites although several species often found in cultivated areas were present, some being fairly frequent.

Open water on sites *versus* imported water

A reliable water supply is crucial for human settlement. The quantities required in Anglo-Scandinavian York for consumption by humans and livestock, and for craft and industrial processes, must have been enormous. Most parts of central York are within relatively easy reach of one of two rivers, the Ouse and Foss, both of which seem likely to have flowed throughout the year in the Anglo-Scandinavian period, so far as we can judge.

Was the water potable? The water in both rivers was probably passably clean when it reached York, although the Foss, at least, was used for processes which would have caused substantial pollution: there is good evidence for Anglo-Scandinavian tanning at the Layerthorpe Bridge site (Hall et al. 2000b, and see p.407). Further analysis of deposits at 22 Piccadilly may provide more information concerning the Foss. To date, the only deposits indicating dumping along the Ouse have been observed at North Street (Carrott et al. 1993a), but samples from them have so far only been examined in a very cursory way. A hint as to water quality comes from riffle beetles (various

members of the family Elminthidae, including the very rare *Macronychus quadrituberculatus* Müller; Kenward and Hall 2000a), all of which require clean, moving water. Small numbers have been recorded from Anglo-Scandinavian deposits at 1–9 Micklegate and Coppergate. While these beetles may have flown to the sites and died there, it appears far more likely that they were brought in river water. Unfortunately, they may have been washed down from cleaner reaches rather than having lived in the York area. Records of freshwater mussels (*Unio* and *Anodonta* spp.) from Coppergate also suggest reasonably clean water, assuming that they were not imported from elsewhere. O'Connor (1984, and in *AY* 14/7, 780) has postulated that changes in the relative abundance of *Unio tumidus* Philipsson and *U. pictorum* (Linnaeus) through the Anglo-Scandinavian period at Coppergate may possibly indicate degradation of water quality by pollution as the town increased in size, the more pollution-tolerant *U. pictorum* becoming relatively more frequent. Clearly further research, using riverine sediments, is required to address this significant aspect of past human impact; the study of lead from alluvial deposits at North Street by Hudson-Edwards et al. (1999), which shows a slight increase in lead levels from the 10th century onwards, forms a useful start.

Many of the freshwater plants and invertebrates recorded from Anglo-Scandinavian deposits in York seem likely to have been brought with water intended for one use or another. Records of true aquatic plants (as opposed to emergents which might be cut for some reason, for example with reed for thatch) are extremely sparse (Table 9). Certain water beetles are common in occupation deposits of this period (particularly *Helophorus* and *Ochthebius* species), but the former, at least, is a conspicuous component of the 'background fauna' of insects arriving in flight. Another group clearly originating in water are the cladocerans (water fleas, particularly *Daphnia* spp.). These little animals are represented by their ephippia, which are resistant eggs formed in the body of the adult. They are fairly common in deposits accumulating under various circumstances, ranging from floors to cesspits. At Coppergate they may have been under-recorded, but nevertheless were found in over 60 contexts (Fig.91; Table 10). The greatest concentrations were in deposits associated with structures of Period 5B, particularly in a gully inside Structure 5/3 on Tenement B, where they were accompanied

Table 9 Records (numbers of contexts) from which aquatic plants (counted in groups POTA, LEMN or CHAR, cf. AY 14/7, 678) were found at Anglo-Scandinavian sites in York; some other taxa, e.g. *Oenanthe* spp., which are counted in other groups, too, are not included here

	Chara sp(p).	*Lemna* sp(p).	*Lemna trisulca* (sterile fronds)	*Potamogeton* sp(p).
Groups	CHAR	LEMN	LEMN	POTA
6–8 Pavement		2		
'1–5' Aldwark		2		
16–22 Coppergate				4
104–12 Walmgate	1			
North Street			1	
Layerthorpe Bridge				1

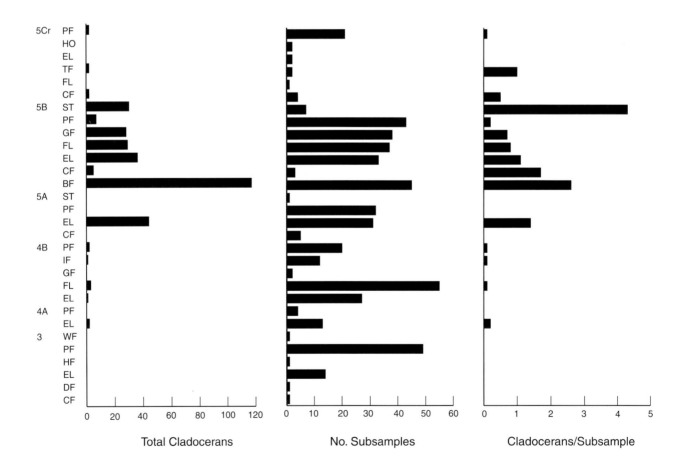

Fig.91 *Records of cladocerans from 16–22 Coppergate by period and feature type. For key to abbreviations, see Table 10, p.393*

Table 10 Records of cladocerans from those samples from 16–22 Coppergate where the number per sample was greater than 3

Key for Table 10 and Figs.90–1
BF = backfills; CF = non-specific cut fills; DF = depression fill; EL = external layers; FL = floors; GF = gully and ditch fills; HF = hearth fill; HO = post-hole fills; IF = fills of cuts within structures ('internal' fills); PF = pit fills; ST = associated with structures; TF = trench fill; WF = well fill

Period	Feature Type	Context	Sample	Subsample	No. cladocerans
5A	EL	8282	257	/1	30
5A	EL	8290	261	/T	9
5B	BF	15361	776	/T	7
5B	BF	15470	815	/1	23
5B	BF	15470	815	/C	6
5B	BF	15471	816	/1	12
5B	BF	15471	816	/2	12
5B	BF	15471	816	/3	12
5B	BF	15526	827	/1	30
5B	BF	15530	831	/1	6
5B	EL	15583	908	/T	18
5B	EL	21478	1711	/T	15
5B	FL	15559	872	/1	6
5B	FL	14297	70506	/1	6
5B	GF	15560	851	/1–3	9
5B	GF	15560	852	/1–3	6
5B	GF	15581	857	/1–3	7
5B	ST	8730	375	/(1)	15
5B	ST	8730	375	/2–3	15

by more water beetles than might reasonably be expected indoors (*AY* 14/7, 595–6).

These records of water fleas in what were clearly surface (or in the case of the gully, internal) deposits, are surely indicative of the disposal of waste water, the ephippia or live adults containing them having been brought with supplies. It might be argued that records of these animals from cuts in the open may indicate populations living in open water, but in at least some cases they seem to indicate waste disposal. At 4–7 Parliament Street (Hall and Kenward 2000a) a sample from a cut fill provided seven aquatic beetles and bugs, and numerous cladocerans. Bearing in mind the extremely foul nature of the deposit as inferred from other evidence, these freshwater crustaceans seem most unlikely to have lived in situ in the cut, since the water would have been intolerably polluted. They therefore seem much more likely to have been deposited in waste water (from dyeing, perhaps), or entered via faeces, having been inadvertently ingested. Our understanding of the sources of water on occupation sites such as these would be greatly enhanced by identifying a wider range of water fleas (Cladocera and Ostracoda), as well as diatoms (which are unicellular green algae often sensitive to water quality).

Although York is well provided with rivers, and the Anglo-Scandinavian sites which have been investigated for waterlogged plant and invertebrate remains in any detail are located no more than 200m from them, other water sources should be considered. Structures which were unequivocally wells have not been recorded. A Period 3 feature at Coppergate described as a barrel well consisted only of a single barrel and may have had various uses. Cut 6422 at Coppergate was perhaps the only other really well-like feature of the period (but note that it was only 2m deep, not 4m as implied by the incorrect scale on fig.167 of Kenward and Hall's account in *AY* 14/7). However, there is no evidence from the flora and fauna of the thin, level, basal deposits that it had served as a well. There may have been shallow pit-like wells. Some of the pits at Coppergate lacked evidence for the disposal of foul waste and appear on the basis of the insect remains to have been left open for a long period and sometimes to have contained water. Such pits were identified at the rear of the site in Period 5C (*AY* 14/7, 627); the pit containing the Anglian helmet (*AY* 17/8) may be another example. They may have provided water, but equally they may represent cuts abandoned on a change of use or ownership. If water was obtained in this way, it would be very likely to contain water fleas and beetles such as *Helophorus* and *Ochthebius*.

The question of water supplies is a difficult one. Higher water-tables in the Anglo-Scandinavian period may have provided springs locally on the slopes of the moraine underlying the town (see p.370). Roman drains and culverts may still have carried clean water which could be tapped here and there; the system contained flowing water in places at least to the 1970s (Phillips 1985, 57–9). We may find that systematic analysis of faecal deposits believed to originate from humans and from livestock shows, for example from the abundance of water fleas or the nature of the diatom flora, that the quality of water drunk by these two groups differed.

Waste disposal

Much of what has been excavated in Anglo-Scandinavian York consists of waste of one kind or another, and most of what we know about the town has been discovered by analysing it. Some of the richest sources of waste material, of course, are the fills of pits.

Twenty-five years of study of the fills of pits in Anglo-Scandinavian York lead us to believe that their primary function was for waste disposal. With the possible exception of the 'wells' mentioned above, there is no clear evidence for any other 'primary use'.

Were pits *exclusively* used for waste disposal? Possible uses would be as drainage sumps, for processes such as dyeing and tanning, and for storage. Pit storage seems extraordinarily unlikely in what seem always to have been rather moist deposits, although one or two cuts within buildings may conceivably fall in this category (perhaps more in the nature of cellars than traditional storage pits). One example of this is cut 22557 in the wattle building on Tenement C in Period 4B at Coppergate (*AY* 14/7, 557–60) — an almost cellar-like feature which incidentally contained large numbers of honeybees.

Bearing in mind the very large scale of wool processing at Coppergate it is possible that lined pits were used for dyeing. Corroborative evidence in the form of clay linings, the remains of skins used as liners, or stones used as pot boilers, is absent, however.

On balance, then, it must be accepted that pits were dug specifically for waste disposal. The argument that the elaborate wicker linings present in many of them represent excessive effort for such a use is spurious, since cesspits, at least, would have had a substantial life during which there was a pressing need to avoid collapse (*AY* 14/7, 747–8).

Many pits were clearly cesspits on the basis of bioarchaeological analysis of their fills, which are characterised by assemblages rich in cereal 'bran', food remains such as fruitstones and pips, eggs of intestinal parasites, and fish bones which carry evidence of having been chewed and of having passed through the digestive tract. A component of large, branching mosses, presumably material used as toilet wipes, is often associated with this faecal material. Where insects are numerous in such deposits they are typically dominated by species favoured by extremely foul conditions, including various flies (*AY* 14/7, 746–7). Some of the pit fills at Coppergate appear to have been so foul that they could not be colonised by beetles, only a very restricted range of specialised flies being able to exploit them. Where large populations of insects were able to develop, it is likely that the fills had been exposed for a considerable period, with implications for human health (see below).

Some waste was certainly dumped onto surfaces. At Coppergate there was evidence, particularly from fly puparia, for patches of foul matterbut large quantities of dyebath waste were occasionally tipped onto the ground to judge from spreads of 'burgundy' coloured material which proved on closer examination to be rich in madder root fragments. The deposits dated to Period 3 at this site appear to represent accumulation in an area lacking substantial buildings but used for industrial purposes (there were numerous hearths) and for waste disposal both into pits and onto surfaces (AY 14/7, 509–27). Of course a proportion of waste may have been carried away from occupation areas and in this respect it is unfortunate that it has not been possible to carry out full analyses of what have been interpreted as Anglo-Scandinavian waterside dumps at the 22 Piccadilly and North Street sites.

Various stages in textile processing would have required large quantities of water and, if the relevant processes were carried out on properties rather than at the river edge, there would have been a need to dispose of what would often have been foul waste water. This may be the reason why some of the ditches or gullies excavated at Coppergate were dug; it seems unlikely that they would have been necessary for carrying away rainfall on soils which would have absorbed water freely, although it is just conceivable that there was local groundwater seepage which needed to be carried away. If this was the function of these ditches and gullies it would explain why dyeplants were so often abundant in the fills (cf. AY 14/7, fig.196b). Clearly these ditches were dug for drainage since none formed tenement boundaries.

Feeding the inhabitants of Anglo-Scandinavian York

A consideration of the diet of the inhabitants of the Anglo-Scandinavian town implies three principal questions: what was eaten (and drunk)? how was food obtained? and was the diet conducive to good health? The first of these is relatively easily, if incompletely, answered. Plant, invertebrate and vertebrate foods are considered separately. For all of these categories, the evidence is broadly consistent from all of the sites studied, but the enormous corpus of material from Coppergate dominates our view. Anglo-Scandinavian York appears to have covered a considerable area, of which we have estimated up to 100ha may have deposits of varying thickness with waterlogged preservation.

In this context, it is worthwhile considering how large the population of Anglo-Scandinavian York may have been. An attempt by Kenward and Large (1998b) to calculate how many people's faeces might have been disposed of in pits of Anglo-Scandinavian date at Coppergate is relevant here. Their conclusion — which was regarded as highly tentative — was that around two people per tenement were, on average, living at the site. This estimate appears low, but it was argued that allowance must be made for periods without evidence of houses on the site (although pits were still dug during these), under-estimation of the degree of decay and compaction of faeces, and the likelihood of disposal off site. Against these was set the biological evidence that many of the pits, or layers in them, did not consist entirely or even in part of faecal material. Following this reasoning we may calculate on the basis of the volume of faeces preserved by waterlogging (see p.376) that of the order of 6,000–10,000 people on average lived in the town — excluding those who lived in areas without waterlogged preservation and any within the 'waterlogged area' whose faeces were removed from it. For another view on population see pp.320–1.

Plant foods and fungi

Although biased in favour of the more readily preserved remains — nutshells and fruitstones rather than soft foods like vegetables — the archaeological record for Anglo-Scandinavian York is rich. The results presented by Kenward and Hall (AY 14/7) for Coppergate (see especially their table in fig.191m, pp.685–9) provide the basic list for plant foods; from the records from other sites in the town we can add only one more plant, lentil, *Lens culinaris*, though it seems very likely that the few charred remains (from 2 Clifford Street and 24–30 Tanner Row) were in fact reworked from underlying Roman deposits.

Cereals and fruits form the bulk of the fossil remains of plant foods for this period in York, the former largely as 'bran'. Most of the bran is not more closely identifiable than 'wheat/rye', though bran or whole uncharred caryopses of barley and oats have also been identified. In the case of charred grains, all these four cereals have been recorded, with wheat and barley by far the most commonly observed, though no cereals were ever abundant (Table 11). The long list of fruits includes many which would not be considered a regular part of the diet of most people today, notably

Table 11 Records of charred cereal grains from Anglo-Scandinavian York (minor categories such as the few records for chaff of various kinds have been excluded)

Taxon	No. contexts	% (of 631 contexts examined)	No. contexts with more than a trace	%
Avena sativa (cultivated oats)	33	5	2	0.3
Avena sp(p). (oats)	136	22	5	0.8
Hordeum sp(p). (barley)	177	28	3	0.5
Secale cereale (rye)	61	10	4	0.6
Triticum 'aestivo-compactum' (bread/club wheat)	203	32	5	0.8
Triticum sp(p). (wheat)	36	6	1	0.2

sloes (*Prunus spinosa*), hawthorn (*Crataegus*), rose (*Rosa*) and rowan (*Sorbus aucuparia*). These wild-collected fruits must have been a vital source of, for example, vitamin C, though we have no clue from the fossil record as to how they may have been used. Storage or preservation in some way for use beyond the autumn would have greatly enhanced their value, even allowing for an inevitable reduction in vitamin C content. To judge from their frequent occurrence in deposits rich in foodstuffs, seeds of flax (linseed, *Linum usitatissimum*) were also a regular part of the diet, providing valuable fatty acids and, were it needed, a natural laxative!

The list of vegetables is limited. Two pulses (if we discount lentil) have been recorded: pea and field bean, both of which might have been eaten fresh in season or, perhaps more likely, have been dried for use throughout the year. The delicate leaf tissue of leek will usually have decayed and, even when preserved, may not always have been recognised during analysis. How far other green leafy plants may have contributed to the diet is difficult to judge; this is certainly an avenue for future study, concentrating on the identification of epidermis fragments from those cesspit fills with the best preservation by anoxic waterlogging.

Food flavourings are a very prominent group within the plant remains from Anglo-Scandinavian York and indicate that a wide range of seasoning was available. Seeds of coriander, celery, dill and opium poppy seem most likely to have been used in their own right, whilst those of summer savory presum-ably represent the whole fresh or dried herb. Summer savory is today used in northern Europe with field beans, and thus perhaps we are seeing a tradition extending at least as far back as the 10th century. As for possible flavourings for drinks, both hops and bog myrtle are recorded and seem likely to have been used (they would act as preservatives as well as flavourings); in no case, however, have very high concentrations of either plant been found which might indicate waste from making beer or other drinks.

A group of organisms, many of which are edible but which are scarcely known in archaeology, are the fungi (no longer considered by most biologists to be plants). There is a strong tradition of eating a wide range of mushrooms throughout much of Europe, including Scandinavia, and they represent an excellent source of flavoursome food, both on their own and in combination in dishes such as stews. Although most edible fungi are soft and decay quickly, it is conceivable that fragments of the fruiting body might be recognised in suitable deposits. Spores from such fruiting bodies might be more likely to survive in the ground, but unfortunately they are probably insufficiently distinctive in their size, shape and ornamentation to be identifiable with certainty to types which might have been eaten. One group with rather distinctive spores, however, are the puffballs, some of which make good eating. Remains of giant puffball (*Calvatia gigantea* (Batsch: Pers.) Lloyd, formerly *Langermannia gigantea*) have been noted from Anglo-Scandinavian Coppergate (*AY* 14/7, 527, the identification now confirmed by Professor Roy Watling).

Though this material had aged beyond the point where it could be eaten, and the fungus has a variety of uses (Pegler et al. 1995, 14–17), it is hard to believe that the succulent, and (when suitably prepared) delicious, young fruiting bodies were not exploited for food. The other species of macro-fungus identified from Anglo-Scandinavian York, the bracket fungus *Daedalea quercina* (L.) Pers. (again, the identification can now be regarded as certain), is surely too leathery to have been eaten and was probably brought attached to wood.

Invertebrates as food

Marine shellfish are abundant in Anglo-Scandinavian deposits in York. At Pavement mussel and oyster shells were numerous (*AY* 14/4, 180), although it was not clear whether they were thrown onto floors or derived from redeposited sediment used in levelling, and at 5–7 Coppergate there were smaller concentrations. Enormous numbers of shellfish valves were recovered from 16–22 Coppergate, mostly by hand collection (*AY* 14/7, especially 690 and 756–8; O'Connor 1984). Oysters (*Ostrea edulis* Linnaeus) were predominant (groups of twenty or more individuals were recovered from over 200 contexts). There were much smaller numbers of mussels (*Mytilus edulis* Linnaeus) and cockles (*Cerastoderma edule* (Linnaeus)), and some records of winkles (*Littorina littorea* (Linnaeus)) and whelks (*Buccinum undatum* Linnaeus). Even allowing for possible under-representation of the smaller species and for differential decay of mussel shells (which break down in the soil), oysters seem to have been by far the most heavily exploited shellfish. Clearly marine molluscs, especially oysters, were a significant resource in Anglo-Scandinavian York, although no guess can be made as to their proportional contribution to diets. It is not known how shellfish were brought to the town — presumably by ship — but were they fresh or at least sometimes preserved in some way?

One context at Coppergate gave substantial numbers of a range of small marine molluscs, either from fish guts or from a catch of shellfish which had not been sorted before it was brought to York (*AY* 14/7, 756–7).

Freshwater molluscs may also have been exploited. Valves of *Unio* and *Anodonta* species were 'surprisingly numerous' at Coppergate (*AY* 14/7, 757;

O'Connor 1984), where exploitation as food is argued for the former, although the small size of the *Anodonta* valves was regarded by O'Connor as possibly indicative of their collection for some other use, perhaps as scoops. The very common 'garden snail' *Helix aspersa* is one of the few terrestrial invertebrates known to have been exploited for food in the British Isles. It is quite often recorded from Anglo-Scandinavian York. O'Connor (1985) considered that it was 'an opportunist detritivore exploiting the debris of human settlement' at Coppergate, and there is no evidence that it was eaten. *H. aspersa* hibernates in clusters, so the groups of shells recorded should not be assumed to have been deposited by humans (and many of the shells were clearly modern, see p.388).

Honeybees were very frequent, and sometimes abundant, in Anglo-Scandinavian deposits at Coppergate (*AY* 14/7, 706–7) and they have been repeatedly recorded from other sites (e.g. at 1–9 Micklegate, 2 Clifford Street and 4–7 Parliament Street). These records, and others from British archaeological sites, are discussed by Kenward (in press). Two deposits at Coppergate yielded large numbers of bees, clearly either the result of the killing or natural death of a hive or of prolonged deposition of corpses adjacent to a hive. At the three other sites mentioned there seem to be too many records to be accounted for by accidental deaths unless there were hives nearby (Table 12). However, other means of entry for bees need to be evaluated: firstly, their ingestion with food (having been contaminants in honey); secondly, ejection during the extraction of honey from combs (or in subsequent purification); and thirdly, extraction during purification of wax. The superb preservation of some of the bees from 4–7 Parliament Street might suggest a direct entry rather than a route involving processes such as heating and straining. The effect of passage through the human gut requires study. Clearly bees, and probably bee-keeping, had a significant place in Anglo-Scandinavian York. This is not surprising, since honey would have been the only significant source of sugar prior to the importation of sugar from the tropics later in the medieval period. (According to Smith (1882), sugar cane was first known in India, whence it is said to have been brought to Europe by the Venetians about the middle of the 12th century, and was early cultivated on the islands of the Mediterranean. Afterwards it was introduced to Spain and Portugal, and also the Americas, becoming firmly established by mid 16th century.)

Table 12 Records of bees (*Apis mellifera* and Apoidea sp.) from Anglo-Scandinavian deposits in York.

Key: * = count includes semi-quantitative records and totals in fact much higher; A mel = *Apis mellifera*; Apoid = Apoidea sp., probably *A. mellifera*. The number of records for 16–22 Coppergate given here is larger than given in *AY* 14/7, 706–7, because further analyses have been carried out.

Site name, code and reference	date, feature types	as	contexts	individuals
41–9 Walmgate (Johnstone et al. 2000)	?Anglo-Scandinavian layer and pit fill	?A mel	1	1
		Apoid	1	1
4–7 Parliament Street (Hall and Kenward 2000a)	Anglo-Scandinavian yard deposits	?A mel	1	1
		A mel	3	8
16–22 Coppergate (*AY* 14/7; details in *Technical Reports*)	Anglo-Scandinavian: wide range of feature types	?A mel	2	2
		A mel	55	1377*
		Apoid	155	199*
1–9 Micklegate (Kenward and Hall 2000a)	Anglo-Scandinavian layer and pit fills	A mel	6	7
		Apoid	6	6
2 Clifford Street (Hall and Kenward 2000b)	Anglo-Scandinavian deposits	?A mel	1	1
		A mel	1	3
All Saints' Church, Pavement (Hall et al. 1998)	?Anglo-Scandinavian deposit (pile hole)	A mel	1	1
Layerthorpe Bridge (Hall et al. 2000b)	Anglo-Scandinavian river deposits and dumps	Apoid	6	6
7–15 Spurriergate (Hall et al. 2000c)	11th-century pit	A mel	1	1

One important use of honey must have been in making fermented drinks like beer and wine and, of course, mead. The last of these would leave no clear record in the ground, but beer might be detected by the remains of concentrations of plants used for flavouring, and wine by the presence of concentrations of seeds of various fruits, perhaps accompanied by their skins. As noted above, no very high concentrations of such remains have been observed in Anglo-Scandinavian deposits: remains of the fruits of hop are frequently recorded, though usually in modest numbers, whilst the large quantities of seeds of a wide variety of wild fruits are invariably found in faecal deposits. The hop fruits may represent the use of this plant in dyeing or as a medicinal plant, for example.

A second bee product, wax, may be mentioned here. Like honey, it must have been important and have had a wide range of uses. Kenward and Hall (*AY* 14/7, 766) discuss the records from Coppergate

of numerous fragments of wax and a wax ball bearing the marks of twine. One aspect of this invaluable material which might be investigated further is its purification (given that this might have been the source of concentrations of bees).

Vertebrate foods

There is abundant evidence, in the form of bones, for the consumption of vertebrates in Anglo-Scandinavian York, although the only published account relating to bones of this period is for selected material from 16–22 Coppergate (*AY* 15/3) (see Table 20, p.428). At this site, remains of cattle always formed the largest component, especially in the Period 3 material; in Period 5B, by contrast, there was a much wider range of wild birds (although most were present in very small numbers) and a higher proportion of pig bones (ibid., tables 39–40, and see Fig.92). Overall, there was nothing to suggest that wild birds and mammals contributed significantly to the diet. Fish, on the other hand, seem to have been eaten frequently, with herring and eel two of the most important. The wide range of fish represented can be judged from *AY* 15/3, table 56; they included sturgeon, salmon, trout, pike, cod and haddock. Clearly both freshwater and marine resources were being exploited.

O'Connor suggested that the livestock remains gave no evidence for organised butchery and that beasts may have been 'brought in and slaughtered as required and shared amongst several households, the role of butcher being taken by whomsoever ... had a sharp knife and a rough idea of how to use it.' It will be interesting to see if this pattern is repeated throughout Anglo-Scandinavian York (see pp.435–6).

Food preservation and storage

Food storage is essential to a stable urban economy, given that most plant foods, including staples, are produced seasonally in temperate regions, but the bioarchaeological evidence from York at this period gives no clear indication of how any materials were preserved. Grain storage is one obvious topic to be explored in view of the abundance of evidence for cereals in the town. The best indication of how cereals may have been stored comes from the records of grain pests. These beetles were very abundant in Roman York, e.g. at Coney Street (*AY* 14/2), Skeldergate (*AY* 14/3) and Tanner Row (*AY* 14/6). In complete contrast, they were definitely not a significant problem in cereal storage in the Anglo-Scandinavian period in York, and in fact may have been wholly absent. Even if the few grain beetles recorded from samples of this date were contemporaneous (which the authors doubt), they were clearly so rare as to be insignificant. No assemblages of insects consisting of likely communities of potential 'native' grain pests have been found either, although many generalist species which were commonly present in Anglo-Scandinavian York were recorded from stored grain in the 19th and early 20th centuries (see, for example, Hayhurst 1940; Hinton 1945).

It is postulated that the rarity of specialist grain pests was a consequence of non-centralised grain storage and distribution systems radically different from those of the Roman and post-conquest periods. We can perhaps envisage grain storage at the level of sacks or jars in individual tenements where even

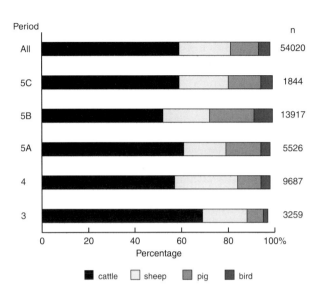

Fig.92 *Hand-collected vertebrate remains from Anglo-Scandinavian deposits at 16–22 Coppergate*

if infestations arose the pests would be unable to move on to other stores. The substantial number of fragments of rotary querns (41) found in Anglo-Scandinavian levels at 16–22 Coppergate (*AY* 17/14, table 255) certainly points to local milling of grain rather than a supply of flour to households from a centralised store.

As already noted, small numbers of remains of grain pests *have* been found in deposits dated to this period: at Pavement (*AY* 14/4, 185), Coppergate (*AY* 14/7), 2 Clifford Street (Hall and Kenward 2000b), and a single *O. surinamensis* from a pit fill of uncertain date, possibly Anglo-Scandinavian, at Walmgate (Buckland 1995). These records are all suspect in some way, with contamination in the laboratory as a depressingly likely source, while residuality of Roman remains, intrusion by later material and incorrect context dating are also possible. For the Pavement site it was suggested that they were contaminants from Roman material which was being processed at the same time, while at 16–22 Coppergate residuality, contamination in processing, later intrusion and incorrect dating were all possible (*AY* 14/7, 760–1). This latter site offers a cautionary lesson — early in analysis grain pests were found in a rather large number of contexts given preliminary Anglo-Scandinavian dates, but a (blind) request for a more careful evalu-

399

ation of dating moved almost all of them to the post-conquest period and revealed others to have been cut by later features! The Clifford Street samples were processed at a time when samples rich in grain pests from other sites were also undergoing analysis, and there is also the possibility of reworking, given the presence of Roman pottery through the Anglo-Scandinavian deposits at Clifford Street. It may be thought that a degree of special pleading is being applied in an unwillingness to accept these records as authentic, but the dangers of this are more than outweighed by the seriousness of incorrectly assuming that they were contemporaneous. Why are the grain pests never at all common in these deposits when they typically develop large populations when they infest grain?

Why are grain pests, specifically, singled out as likely contaminants? The reason is that they are recognisable as not 'belonging' to the Anglo-Scandinavian fauna. Most of the Roman and post-conquest fauna (and much of the flora) is identical in character to that of Anglo-Scandinavian settlement and so would not be recognised as such when residual or contaminant. So far as redeposition of Roman remains is concerned, Roman pottery is common in later deposits (*AY* 16/5) so there is no reason why other remains should not also be residual (cf. Dobney et al. 1997). One species which may also occur as residual remains in Anglo-Scandinavian deposits is the spider beetle *Tipnus unicolor*. This robust and easily recognisable species is characteristic of old and slightly damp buildings. It was common in Roman York (e.g. at Skeldergate, *AY* 14/3), but then very rare until the post-conquest period. As Table 13 indicates, *T. unicolor* was commonest at Coppergate in Period 3, when there were no buildings in the excavated area, then rare, and only began to increase in abundance again in Period 5C. This pattern of abundance may have resulted from re-deposition of Roman remains in the earlier period, the beetle perhaps re-establishing itself when buildings of relatively good quality had been present for some time. The abundance of this spider beetle in the small isolated Early Christian settlement at Deer Park Farms, Co. Antrim (Allison et al. 1999a and 1999b; Kenward and Allison 1994b), appears to undermine this line of argument, but may have been a result of the long life of that settlement or of climatic differences.

Storage of some other plant products will have been straightforward: hazelnuts, walnut, linseed, field beans, peas and other dried 'seeds' such as the flavourings dill, celery seed and coriander, would all survive for many months in a dry place. Crab apples probably remained edible for quite long periods, too, and may have been dried. For the soft fruits such as raspberry, blackberry and bilberry, storage beyond a day or two would only have been possible by cooking (when they could have kept for some days) or, for the longer term, with the use of large quantities of honey or in the form of ferments. The one certain

Table 13 Records of the spider beetle *Tipnus unicolor* from Anglo-Scandinavian and post-conquest deposits at 16–22 Coppergate by period

Period	*Tipnus*			
	no. individuals	in no. subsamples	Period total no. samples N>20	Individuals/100 subsamples
3	8	6	68	12
4A	1	1	18	6
4B	1	1	114	1
5A	0	0	60	0
5B	4	4	190	2
5Cf	0	0	3	0
5Cr	1	1	28	4
6	3	2	14	21

'leaf' vegetable available to the inhabitants of Anglo-Scandinavian York, leeks, would presumably have stood in the ground through much of the winter. Honey, itself, is an excellent energy source which would have kept more or less indefinitely.

Vertebrates would have presented fewer problems of seasonality, since at least a few individuals of domestic livestock would have been available for slaughter and consumption fresh throughout the year. Similarly, at least some wild mammals and birds could have been hunted in every month, although as noted on pp.398–9 they appear not to have been used on a large scale. We know of no bioarchaeological or artefactual evidence for storage of the meat of mammals and birds in Anglo-Scandinavian York, even though the tradition of smoking meat is well established in Scandinavia. Fish, too, would have been available to catch all year round, although their quality and the ease with which fishing could be carried out would vary. Preservation of excess meat and fish is of course desirable and common in most European cultures. While much fish was probably brought to York fresh (running boats up the Ouse on the tide), the strong Scandinavian tradition of fish preservation by pickling, drying and smoking would lead us to expect that such preserved products were also available. Detecting pickled fish, presumably filleted, at the point of consumption would be difficult unless characteristic suites of flavourings were recognised. Dried and smoked fish might be recognised by the proportions of post-cranial to cranial bones, and the particular cranial bones present.

Studies of plant and animal remains in Anglo-Scandinavian occupation deposits in York have given us extensive lists of ingredients but we can say little about how the ingredients were prepared and cooked, and how they were associated into dishes and meals. Even when a range of foods are found together in a discrete patch of faeces, for example, they may represent successive meals or mixing during deposit formation. Perhaps the only evidence for a prepared food is the discovery of fragments of charred material which appears to be bread from Coppergate (20 records), 1–9 Micklegate (3) and 2 Clifford Street (1). Records of zonation of burning in bones might give clues as to how joints were cooked, but no systematic analysis has been made. Fruitstones up to about 12mm in maximum length seem often to have been swallowed, to judge from the quantities observed in faecal deposits in pit fills, though whether they were eaten fresh or cooked cannot be determined from the remains. Likewise small fish bones seem to have been swallowed fairly often, the remains bearing characteristic evidence for crushing during chewing and acid etching in the gut (AY 14/7, fig.193a). That these bones survived digestion indicates that they had not been cooked for long periods (cf. AY 14/4; Nicholson 1993). Again, patterns of burning of fish bones might suggest means of cooking.

Human health

As pointed out by Kenward and Hall (AY 14/7, 758), human remains of Anglo-Scandinavian date are uncommon in York so that direct observation of skeletons cannot be used to deduce pathological conditions, and thus indirect evidence must be sought. This evidence may be in the form of conclusions as to the quality of diet, or indications of toxins or pathogens.

Judging from the food remains discussed above, the townspeople had a rich and varied diet available to them, overall. Whether individual diets were good throughout the year is another matter, and probably impossible to ascertain given the fact that the deposits analysed were almost always formed over weeks, months or years, and that debris representing different components of the diet may have had different disposal routes. Faecal layers in which fruitstones are rare may suggest the possibility of vitamin C deficiency, but only if green vegetables were not being consumed in quantity (the evidence for leafy vegetables is currently restricted to leek).

The possibility that the large quantities of corncockle seeds present in cereals may have had a deleterious effect on health was mentioned by Kenward and Hall (AY 14/7, 758); it clearly deserves further study. Peas and/or beans appear to have been contaminated by the bean weevil *Bruchus rufimanus*, which has frequently been found in cesspits in the town, doubtless having been swallowed with cooked pulses. The effect of low-level contamination by this and other insects (perhaps including aphids, cf. Hall et al. 1983b), was probably negligible, however, since quite high levels of insect contamination of food can be tolerated (Venkatrao et al. 1960).

As mentioned above, material interpreted as human faeces has been widely recorded in Anglo-Scandinavian deposits in York both in primary contexts (typically pit fills), and occasionally as reworked faecal concretions, and this is some of the best evidence available regarding health. It is characterised by the presence of high concentrations of wheat/rye (*Triticum/Secale*) 'bran', usually accompanied by a suite of other plant remains likely to have been ingested in food. These include seeds and sometimes other parts of fruits like blackberry, sloe and apple and, where preservation is very good, even seed coat fragments and other tissues of pulses (peas and beans) and leaf fragments of leek. With the bran in these deposits, almost invariably, are abundant eggs of the intestinal parasites whipworm (*Trichuris*) and roundworm (*Ascaris*) (e.g. *AY* 14/7, 696–7, 758–9). Infestation by these two nematode gut parasites was probably very common, perhaps ubiquitous. The numbers of eggs were sometimes large so that individuals may have carried heavy burdens of parasites at times, with an inevitable effect on the well-being of individuals whose health was challenged by some other factor. No other internal parasites have been unequivocally recognised from Anglo-Scandinavian York, although identification of the rather featureless eggs of, for example, liver flukes, is very difficult.

Infection by the common nematode gut parasites occurs all too easily. Vast numbers of eggs are produced by both *Ascaris* and *Trichuris* (e.g. Markell and Voge 1976, 240, 261), and they remain infective for some time. The exposure of faeces in pits is attested by evidence from some sites (for example Coppergate), and it is likely that parasite eggs, as well as disease-causing micro-organisms, were dispersed by insects as a consequence (Kenward and Large 1998b). Infection by drinking water seems possible where wells or other sources of water were close to cesspits or contaminated ditches.

Despite the negative effects of gut parasites and contaminant corncockle seeds, the typical Anglo-Scandinavian alimentary tract will have enjoyed a diet rich in roughage, much of it in the form of 'bran' so that transit times were low and we can suggest that diseases such as diverticulitis and bowel cancer were rare. The liveliness of digestive systems is attested by the abundance of fruitstones (and sometimes fish bones) which had plainly been voided in faeces.

People may have carried gut parasites without realising it, but some other invertebrates would have had a tangible effect on humans, namely fleas, lice, flies and ticks. The last of these groups is represented only by rare records of the sheep tick *Ixodes ricinus* (Linnaeus), which attacks a wide range of warm-blooded animals. In addition to being irritating, *I. ricinus* can carry Lyme disease (caused by spirochaetes) and may have been favoured by higher temperatures in the Anglo-Scandinavian period (Lindgren et al. 2000). Human fleas (*Pulex irritans* Linnaeus) were very common at Coppergate, especially in deposits associated with buildings (they were recorded from 197 contexts; *AY* 14/7, 698–703), and have regularly been recorded from other sites of the period. The fact that only one human flea was recorded from the Pavement site may be ascribed to failure to recognise their remains during that early study. Clearly fleas were at least a minor nuisance, and they may have been vectors of disease. A few fleas of dogs and rodents have also been recorded, and they too may have been annoying and potentially injurious to health.

Human lice (*Pediculus humanus* Linnaeus) were also fairly frequent at Coppergate, with records from nearly 60 contexts, particularly in floors of Period 4B (*AY* 14/7, 698–700). *P. humanus* has occurred regularly in small numbers at other sites, and the absence of early records undoubtedly reflects non-recognition. The frequency with which these very delicate insects are now recovered from suitable archaeological deposits suggests that they were extremely common, perhaps ubiquitous. Oddly, the numerous bone combs recovered from Coppergate, in particular, all appear to have had teeth too coarsely set to have functioned in combing nits (*AY* 17/12, 1923–34). By contrast, what were clearly nit combs are described by Schelvis (1991; 1992; 1998) and Fell (2000), and a fine-toothed boxwood comb of post-conquest date from Coppergate is described by Morris (*AY* 17/13, 2309–12). Although in themselves a minor irritation, *P. humanus* is known to carry human disease. It is perhaps only a matter of time before the pubic louse, *Pthirus pubis* (Linnaeus), is discovered in Anglo-Scandinavian York, since it is now known from Roman and medieval Carlisle (Kenward 1999a).

A single bedbug, *Cimex lectularis* Linnaeus, was recorded from Coppergate, and seems more likely to represent the form associated with humans than that found on pigeons. If so, bedbugs either survived in Britain from the Roman period (for which there are a few records) or were re-introduced, quite possibly by the far-travelling Vikings. Bedbugs are probably disadvantaged by the more flimsy kind of human dwelling, and may not have been able to become abundant until well into the post-conquest period, when the general standard of urban buildings improved.

O'Connor (*AY* 15/3, table 54) gives Anglo-Scandinavian records for the black rat, *Rattus rattus* Linnaeus, from Coppergate, and it appears very likely that the animal was established at least on the fringes of the town. We do not know whether plague struck York at this period but the presence of black rats obviously makes it possible. We need to search for remains of the plague flea, *Xenopsylla cheopis* (Rothschild), although plague can also be spread by other species, including human fleas and fleas associated with rodents, some of which have been recorded from Coppergate.

Several species of flies known to carry disease, including the housefly and stable fly, have been identified from Coppergate, where they were sometimes abundant (*AY* 14/7, 762–3). The numerous beetles living in cesspits may also have carried a range of pathogens (Kenward and Large 1998b). Fly puparia from Anglo-Scandinavian York have not been studied systematically, but species of medical importance were certainly both ubiquitous and abundant. Various biting midges and mosquitoes must have been common, too, but it has not yet been practicable to identify the abundant remains of the group to which these flies belong. An attempt to investigate these would be worthwhile in view of the ability of some of the species to carry disease, particularly malaria, which may have been a constant threat in a town fringed by marshland and, it is suspected, with a climate warmer than that of the 20th century.

Textile working

One of the consistent features of plant assemblages from Anglo-Scandinavian sites in York has been the presence of plants likely to have been used in certain stages of textile working, especially dyeing and mordanting. The presence of one of them, dyer's greenweed (*Genista tinctoria* L.), was signalled during very early work on insect remains from Pavement, when material of the weevil *Apion difficile* Herbst, which feeds almost exclusively on this plant, were recognised (Kenward et al. 1978, 63). Subse-

quently, a suite of taxa was found at 16–22 Coppergate comprising dyer's greenweed, madder (*Rubia tinctorum* L.), woad (*Isatis tinctoria* L.) and the clubmoss *Diphasiastrum complanatum* (L.) J. Holub (as *Diphasium complanatum*, *AY* 14/7, 709–15 and 767–9). Some other plants recorded at that site might also have served to provide dyestuffs (ibid., 770–1). Incidentally, the *Apion* proved to be very common, too. As a further aside, it may be mentioned that insects in addition to *Apion difficile* may have been imported with the large quantities of *G. tinctoria* and other dyeplants obviously utilised in Anglo-Scandinavian York, but they are difficult to recognise unless they are abundant or alien. In particular, *Sitona* species and a range of other *Apion* species, both of which genera are rather numerous in deposits of this date, may have been brought with *G. tinctoria*, host to at least some species in both genera (Hoffmann 1958, 1768) (see, however, the discussion of the possible origin of *Sitona* with peas and beans, p.388).

Remains of some or all of these plants were subsequently recorded from other deposits of Anglo-Scandinavian date in the city and, indeed, the clubmoss, in particular, has become something of a 'marker fossil' (with the caveat that it may in some cases be reworked); the distribution of records for these plants is shown in Fig.93. It is worth remarking here that small amounts of some of these dyeplants were discovered in the 1990s in the dried residues from the samples from 6–8 Pavement originally examined in 1977 (Hall 1998, 6); clearly it is important to retain at least some material from excavations for future study to check for remains which are not recognised or not identifiable initially.

That dyeing was one of the processes in textile working which took place within the city is clear from the concentrations of dyeplant material in many of the deposits, especially at Coppergate (cf. *AY* 14/7, 709–10, 712–13). In many other cases, however, only traces of material were recorded and it seems likely that we are dealing with a 'background' of debris spreading from an epicentre in the Coppergate/Ousegate area (and with another focus at 1–9 Micklegate), though of course we still only have records from a few sites (Fig.93). Although dyeing must have taken place along with the various other processes involved in turning raw fibres into finished garments, the precise way in which dyeing was undertaken remains obscure. Thus, no vessels survive which

(a)

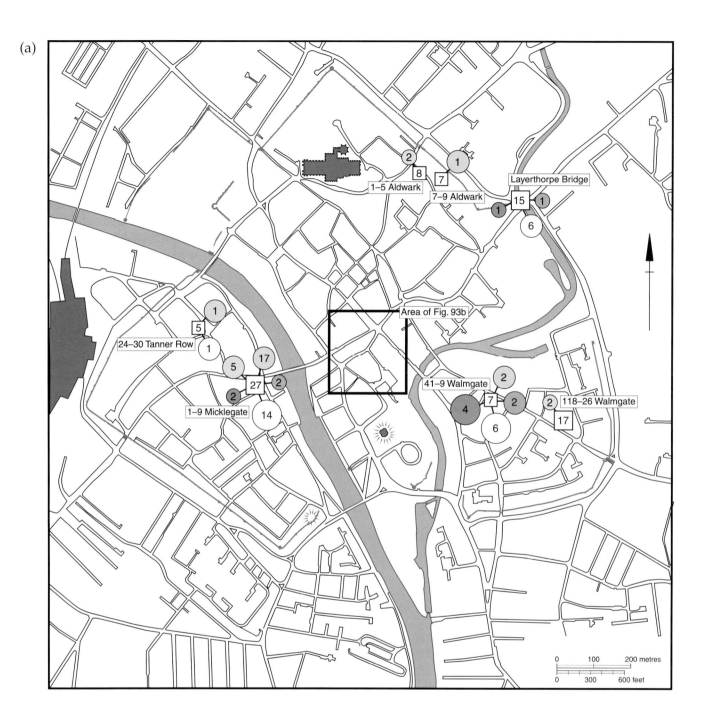

1–5 Aldwark
7–9 Aldwark
Layerthorpe Bridge
Area of Fig. 93b
24–30 Tanner Row
1–9 Micklegate
41–9 Walmgate
118–26 Walmgate

0   100   200 metres
0   300   600 feet

might have served for dyeing large hanks of wool, let alone lengths of cloth. Cardon and du Chatenet (1990) record the former practice of dyeing with woad in pits or gullies. This may explain the records of concentrations of remains interpreted as dyebath waste in the fills of some cut features, though none was noted as having the kind of waterproof lining one presumes would be necessary for such a use. In any case, it is difficult to see how these could be distin-

guished from cuts into which dyeplant material had simply been discarded from vats or other vessels.

Between them, the three main dyeplants — woad, madder and greenweed — will have provided the three primary colours and from these most intermediate shades. The red colouring matter from madder (mainly alizarin and pseudopurpurin) and the blue of woad (indigotin) match the evidence for these

(b)

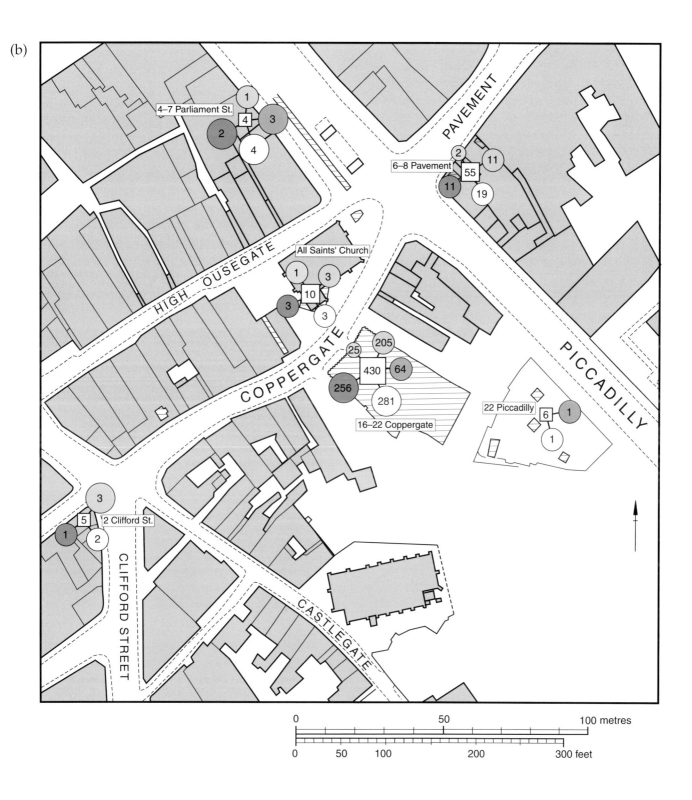

Fig.93 (above and facing) Evidence from Anglo-Scandinavian York for plants used in dyeing and mordanting. The central square in each 'constellation' gives the number of contexts examined (and the size of the symbol provides a crude measure of the scale of investigation thus: smallest, 1–9 contexts; medium, 10–99 contexts; largest, >99 contexts examined). The peripheral symbols show the numbers of contexts in which remains of the plants were recorded: white, clubmoss (Diphasiastrum complanatum (L.) J. Holub); green, dyer's greenweed (Genista tinctoria L., though note that this plant dyes yellow unless used with another dye); blue, woad (Isatis tinctoria L.); yellow, weld (Reseda luteola L.); and red, madder (Rubia tinctorum L.). The size of these peripheral symbols reflects the proportion of investigated contexts which contained the taxa in question, though of course, for sites with relatively few samples, the importance of the remains may sometimes be exaggerated by this device (e.g. for Tanner Row, where the taxa were each recorded in one of only five samples). The scale adopted for these is: small, recorded in 1–9% of contexts; medium, 10–49%; and large, present in 50% or more

substances from studies of dyestuffs on textile fragments (*AY* 17/5). This indicates that dyeing took place locally — whilst the yellows (from genistein) from dyer's greenweed (and perhaps other plants, of which the most likely is weld or dyer's rocket, *Reseda luteola*, Fig.93) fill a gap resulting from the non-survival of these substances on textile fibres which have been buried in the ground.

The clubmoss appears to have been imported specifically for use as a mordant, for these primitive plants have been shown to accumulate aluminium (e.g. Hutchinson and Wollack 1943), one of several metals whose ions act on certain dyestuffs to make them more light- and wash-fast and to alter the colour they produce. In the absence of alum (potassium aluminium sulphate), which was presumably not available to dyers in the Viking world unless there was trade with those areas where alum could have been produced at that period (probably only the eastern Mediterranean, cf. Singer 1948), such a raw material would have been invaluable and this must explain the importation of a commodity almost certainly collected in the wild from some part of Scandinavia or northern central Europe. Although important in later centuries, the 'local' alum industry of north-east Yorkshire did not begin to become established until the early 17th century (Pickles 2002).

The quantities of dyeplant (including clubmoss) recovered at 16–22 Coppergate (and variously at almost every other site with Anglo-Scandinavian contexts in central York) — which must represent a fraction of the total amount originally used, given losses to decay and presumed disposal away from the sites excavated — incline one to wonder whether dyeing was not being practised on an almost 'industrial' scale; if so, it would certainly require large-scale trade to support it.

The kinds of textile raw materials for which there is evidence in Anglo-Scandinavian York from yarns or textile fragments have been considered by Walton Rogers (*AY* 17/11) and that author also mentions archaeobotanical evidence for achenes ('seed') of hemp and for seeds, capsule debris and 'scutching waste' of flax from Coppergate. These fibre plants were presumably retted in the vicinity, though the only good evidence for this activity is the later material of clumped flax stem fragments (with seeds and capsule debris) from a medieval river deposit at Layerthorpe Bridge (Hall et al. 2000b).

Turning now to animal fibres, the working of wool is well attested by remains of this fibre as staples or clumps of raw wool, as well as fragments of yarn and woven textiles (*AY* 17/11), and a range of textile-working artefacts at Coppergate. Studies of insects have contributed substantially to our knowledge of wool processing, revealing it to have been a common and widespread activity. In view of this, and given the number of 'small finds' of wool of various kinds, the lack of records of raw wool fibres from samples analysed for biological remains is quite surprising. This might be taken to indicate that wool came to Coppergate ready cleaned; however, there are numerous records of the very distinctive adults and puparia of sheep keds, *Melophagus ovinus* (Linnaeus), and sheep lice, *Damalinia ovis* (Schrank), or both, from the Anglo-Scandinavian period in York as a whole. These remains are considered to have been deposited as a result of wool (or fleece) cleaning, and many of them are from deposits which were clearly domestic floors, although the insects (especially the robust ked puparia) seem to have been scattered widely, perhaps with floor sweepings. There is a strong impression that the remains of adult keds, which appear to have very weak cuticle, are in most cases recovered only because they remained within the extremely tough puparia until released during sample processing (something also suggested by Robinson 1981, 204); this explains how they may have become dispersed without decaying.

It is perhaps worth mentioning here that the sheep parasites at Coppergate are statistically very closely correlated, in their occurrence in deposits, with *Apion* species (probably including numerous unrecognised *A. difficile*) and with some scarabaeid dung beetles (*Geotrupes* spp., *Aphodius prodromus* Brahm and *A. granarius* (Linnaeus)). One possible explanation for the latter association is that wool cleanings, including sheep 'dags' (wool matted with dung), fell onto floors or were discarded immediately outdoors and attracted the dung beetles. Human fleas were positively correlated with these dung beetles, too, and it seems possible that slovenliness in leaving wool cleanings on floors provided a nutritionally rich substratum for flea larvae. The association of all these insects may reflect the fact that cleaning and dyeing were carried out in the same place.

Tanning and leather working

The importance of leather to the Anglo-Scandinavian inhabitants of York is evident from the study undertaken by Mould, Carlisle and Cameron (*AY* 17/16), founded on the large corpus of well-preserved material of leather offcuts and finished leather artefacts from Coppergate, Piccadilly and Bedern. However, the location of the tanners' establishments where the hides and skins were converted into leather has for a long time been a matter of debate.

Benson (1902, 64) described pits in High Ousegate which he thought to have been used for tanning: 'Amidst this subsoil were a number of horizontal timber balks, about 9" x 9" rebated, and a quantity of piling ... these indicate that the area was the site of tan pits ... The pit towards High Ousegate rested on a twelve-inch bed of puddled clay, the centre pit had a nine-inch bed of yellow sand, whilst the one at Coppergate end had, at the bottom, a lime deposit five inches in thickness' [*sic*]. This interpretation as tan pits has subsequently been questioned and the structures reinterpreted as cellared buildings (*AY* 8/3, 238–50).

Subsequently, some biological and other evidence from deposits rich in leather offcuts at 6–8 Pavement led Buckland et al. (1974) to postulate that early processes in leather making (i.e. hide cleaning and then tanning) might have been practised at this site. However, most or all of the materials such as fine charcoal and ash, as well as the plant and insect remains they discuss, are quite likely to have had some other origin, and were frequent in contemporaneous deposits at Coppergate for which there is absolutely no reason to suppose an association with tanning. Moreover, the abundant leather offcuts at Pavement (considered in *AY* 8/3) indicate a later stage in the utilisation of leather, either its working into articles in the buildings or the use of offcuts from elsewhere as litter on house or stable floors, the latter seeming to be a reasonable interpretation to be placed on leather offcuts in many cases (Hall and Kenward 1998).

Part of the evidence of Buckland et al. (1974) for hide preparation (necessary prior to tanning) at Pavement was the record of a single specimen in each of the four samples of the beetle *Trox scaber* (Linnaeus); later analyses showed it to be present in nearly half of the samples from this site, but mostly as single individuals and in a few cases as two. These are consistent with the data from 16–22 Coppergate but in contrast to those from Anglo-Scandinavian and early medieval deposits at Layerthorpe Bridge where it was present in 30 of the samples at a mean frequency of 3·6 per sample when present, and was sometimes very numerous. Moreover, many of these samples also yielded high concentrations of decayed bark fragments and also sclereids — clusters of lignified cells which form in some kinds of bark, and which are resistant to decay, being released as the bark decomposes (these will certainly have been overlooked in material examined prior to 1999). In the case of Layerthorpe Bridge, we are probably dealing with redeposited waste from tan pits. It may be significant that, though never abundant, small (2–35mm) scraps of uncut leather were recorded from seven of the eleven contexts at this site which contained bark and sclereids. The recognition of tanning waste using plant and invertebrate remains is discussed by Hall and Kenward (2003), who also consider suites of remains indicative of various other craft activities.

Vertebrate resources had other uses in craft and industry, notably horn, antler and bone in the making of a variety of artefacts. The importance of these materials is highlighted by MacGregor et al. (*AY* 17/12), who include combs, pins, knife handles, needles, thread reels, spindle whorls, skates, box lids, and so on.

Livestock, their food and their parasites

Although most of the faecal deposits at Coppergate, for example, are thought to be of human origin (and at Pavement a discrete human stool preserved by mineralisation was studied by Jones in *AY* 14/4), some contexts have been described as perhaps containing or consisting of pig faeces on the basis of a low ratio of *Trichuris* to *Ascaris* eggs, and in at least one case measurements of *Trichuris* eggs suggested *T. suis* (of pigs) might have been present (*AY* 14/7, 759 and 778–9). Such a ratio has been said to be indicative of pig, rather than human, faeces (Taylor 1955), although this assertion requires objective testing. Subsequently, some material examined as part of a project to draw together the information discussed here has given some more support to this idea: samples from 4–7 Parliament Street (Hall and Kenward 2000a), for example, were found to have low

Table 14 Records of uncharred ('waterlogged') cereal or cereal/grass chaff from Anglo-Scandinavian sites in York

Site	Record	No. contexts examined	No. cases	No. cases with more than traces of remains
16–22 Coppergate	Cerealia indet.)	430	29	9
	Gramineae/Cerealia)		8	2
1–9 Micklegate	Cerealia indet.)	27	6	3
	Gramineae/Cerealia)		2	0
North Street	Gramineae/Cerealia	9	1	0
2 Clifford Street	Gramineae/Cerealia	5	1	0
41–9 Walmgate	Cerealia indet.	7	1	0
4–7 Parliament Street	Cerealia indet.	4	4	4

Trichuris to *Ascaris* ratios and, whilst rich in wheat/ rye 'bran' and other food debris, also contained substantial concentrations of uncharred cereal chaff (Table 14), something which is unlikely to have formed more than a small component of human food but which is very typical of animal feed.

Support for the presence of pigs, or at least their uncleaned skins, at Coppergate is provided by small numbers of records of the pig louse *Haematopinus apri* Goreau. However, in no case were these lice especially abundant (cf. one of the house floors at the Deer Park Farms site, Co. Antrim; Kenward and Allison 1994b). It is worth mentioning here that *H. apri*, now found on wild boar, appears to have been the louse of British pigs in the medieval period, probably only being replaced by *H. suis* (Linnaeus) when modern pig varieties were introduced. *H. apri* is now extinct in Britain (*AY* 14/7, 778).

There were also (in addition to numerous sheep lice) lice from cattle, goats, horses and cats, but again in small numbers and certainly not providing evidence that these animals lived on the site.

With regard to the keeping of livestock in the town, it has been suggested by Kenward and Hall (2000b) that conditions resembling those in an old-fashioned farmyard may have existed at 118–26 Walmgate. The buildings may have been byres or stables, and the food remains may have represented either domestic occupation or the feeding of livestock

with scraps (or both); pigs seem the most likely animals to be kept at a site such as this. Pigs might well be fed cereal cleaning waste, accounting for the records of chaff and whole or fragmentary seeds of cornfield weeds, and might produce ambiguous evidence in the worm egg record (either by recycling human faeces or through their own infections). The Walmgate area of York may represent an early stage of urban settlement, with crowded smallholdings which would eventually be subdivided into tenements to form an urbanised area of the kind seen closer to the centre of York at this period (and as discussed for the Norwegian town of Bergen (Krzywinski and Kaland 1984) (see also p.495). This is clearly a topic for further research using structural and bioarchaeological evidence.

For the Roman and post-conquest periods in York there is good evidence for the stabling of horses (or other equines), in the form of large quantities of stable manure, a material whose identification in archaeological deposits is discussed by Kenward and Hall (1997). By contrast, clear identification of stable manure is conspicuously rare for the Anglo-Scandinavian period, suggesting real differences in the importance of horses. Stable manure may be recognised by combinations of plant remains from cut vegetation, typically grassland, various materials used as absorptive litter (which may include bracken, moss, peat, wood chips and perhaps even leather), insects imported with 'hay' and other materials, insects favoured by foul but open-textured rotting matter, and, in the

Roman and post-conquest periods, grain pests from cereal feed. The probable absence of grain pests in the 5th to mid-11th centuries may make it harder to recognise stable manure, but the combination of other components should still be diagnostic.

Although a few samples at the Pavement and 16–22 Coppergate sites contained quite large numbers of insects which would have been favoured by stable manure, they may equally have exploited other rather foul decaying matter, and they were not accompanied by unusually large quantities of plants considered typical of stable manure. One exception was a very deep narrow wattle-lined cut (6422, to the rear of Tenement D on the Coppergate site in Period 5B) which conceivably started life as a well but was eventually used as a repository for stable manure amongst other fills (*AY* 14/7, 611–13). Thus it appears that horses were not normally kept stabled in what is the archaeologically best-known part of York. Might they have been kept in the open? It has been suggested, albeit on rather limited evidence, that the area to the rear of the Coppergate site may, in Period 5C, have been grazed (*AY* 14/7, 624–7). Perhaps this was the kind of place where horses were kept in paddocks, or tethered. Even if horses were kept indoors, stable manure may only very rarely have been allowed to accumulate or have been dumped on occupation sites. Perhaps it was too valuable as manure to be wasted. On the other hand, urban stabling needs large quantities of imported food in the form of hay and cereals, not easily available in a decentralised economy, so that animals were left outdoors where there was at least limited grazing. Certainly horses entered into the life of Anglo-Scandinavian York, for artefacts associated with horses were quite frequent at Coppergate (*AY* 17/6, 704–9; *AY* 17/14, 2558–9; see also *AY* 15/3, 152, 183–4).

Perhaps the most likely livestock to be have been kept within the Anglo-Scandinavian town are chickens, and certainly bones of domestic fowl are well represented in assemblages of vertebrates. In view of this, the complete lack of records of lice and fleas parasitic on chickens is odd. It was suggested in *AY* 14/7 that some of the shallow 'scoops' recorded at Coppergate may have been produced by the scratching and dust-bathing of chickens; a modern parallel is discussed by Dobney et al. (2000). Geese, too, seem likely to have been kept, but again have left no evidence in the form of parasites. Eggshell was fre-

quently recorded in occupation deposits at Coppergate and elsewhere, but no identification has been made and no entire 'lost' eggs appear to have been recorded.

Quite large numbers of bones of cats and dogs have been found in deposits of the Anglo-Scandinavian period in York, and a single cat louse (*Felicola subrostratus* (Burmeister)), was reported from Coppergate (*AY* 14/7, 596).

Vermin and their parasites

The status of wild (or domestic) animals as vermin is a matter of some subjectivity. Among the mammals from Anglo-Scandinavian deposits at Coppergate listed in *AY* 15/3 (table 54) bank vole, field vole, water vole, wood mouse, house mouse and black rat might all, under some circumstances, be regarded as pests, and one suspects that cats might be, too. Of these species (and ignoring the moot case of cat), only house mouse and black rat were represented by more than a few bones. It is suspected that, had sieving been carried out on a much more systematic basis, the status of all of these species at Coppergate would be much clearer. It is worth noting that a few individuals of fleas found on rats and mice (*Nosopsyllus fasciatus* (Bosc) and *Ctenophthalmus nobilis* (Rothschild)) were also recorded from Coppergate. Both may carry diseases of human beings, and *N. fasciatus* is certainly implicated as a plague transmitter, as is the human flea. It seems unlikely that any birds would have been regarded as a nuisance, on the assumption that tender greens and cereals were not being cultivated in the town.

The influence of the rivers

The rivers Ouse and Foss were clearly important in determining the location of Jorvík, through its accessibility by water for trade in a period when ships were the principal means of long-distance transport. This would have been at least as true for the Scandinavian colonists as for the Romans who sited *Eboracum* for its strategic value 800 years earlier. It used to be suggested that the reason why so much organic matter is preserved in archaeological deposits in York is that it was regularly soaked by floodwater (and see discussion on p.372 concerning Benson's and Ramm's comments on flooding), but there is no good evidence from sediments or biological remains to support this. Although aquatic and waterside organisms are fairly common in occupation depos-

Table 15 Proportion of aquatic insects (adult beetles and bugs) from Anglo-Scandinavian sites in York

Site	%NW
6–8 Pavement	1.4
118–26 Walmgate	1.8
16–22 Coppergate	1.4
1–9 Micklegate	1.9
41–9 Walmgate	1.9
2 Clifford Street	0.4
4–7 Parliament Street	2.7

its, there are far more plausible explanations for their presence than flooding to a level which would be surprising even today, when run-off into the rivers is enhanced by artificial drainage above York and when both rivers have been narrowed so much that the escape of flood water is impeded. This said, were any areas ever subject to flooding? Of the sites for which significant bioarchaeological analyses have been made, that at 1–9 Micklegate seems the most likely to have been in danger of inundation. However, there were no more remains of riverine plants and invertebrates than at sites on higher ground (indeed, the former are always rare; see Table 9, p.392). Thus, the proportion of aquatic insects, for example,

fell only slightly above the mean for those sites for which data are available (Table 15); the highest value came from 4–7 Parliament Street, one of the most elevated of the sites, and variations may depend primarily on the amount of water imported. The river level in the Roman period was estimated by Hall et al. (*AY* 14/3) to lie below 4m OD, well below the level of Anglo-Scandinavian occupation here, and it seems entirely possible that it had not risen significantly by the 9th century (Kenward et al. 1978, fig.40; Tooley 1990; Long et al. 1998).

Salt-marsh and estuarine habitats

Records of macrofossil remains of some obligate salt-marsh plants from Anglo-Scandinavian York (Table 16) have, together with those for similar plants from Roman deposits, posed something of an interpretative problem. If they arrived from salt-marsh vegetation in the vicinity, we have to allow that the rivers in York were not only tidal at least as far as the city (*fide* Briden 1997) but also sufficiently saline for halophyte plants to become established along the high water mark (most are plants only found in such habitats). Another hypothesis is that these remains arrived in the city incidentally with vegetation cut or grazed from salt-marsh, i.e. with hay or in herbivore dung. If the latter is the explanation, then we must assume that animals reached York on the hoof from salt-marsh grazing within the time required for

Table 16 Records of salt-marsh plants from Anglo-Scandinavian York (numbers of contexts); remains were 'waterlogged' unless otherwise indicated

	Armeria maritima (Miller) Willd. (calyx)	*Aster tripolium* L.	cf. *A. tripolium*	*Juncus gerardi* Loisel.	*J.* cf. *gerardi*	*J.* cf. *maritimus* Lam.	cf. *Limonium* sp(p). (calyx)	*Triglochin maritima* L.	*T. maritima* (charred)
6–8 Pavement		1							
5–7 Coppergate	1								
1–5 Aldwark					1				
16–22 Coppergate			4	19	16	2	1	3	
9 St Saviourgate				1					
Layerthorpe Bridge								1	
41–9 Walmgate		2			1			2	1

complete transit of salt-marsh plant material through their guts. Tracing the changes in the lower Ouse and the Humber should not be too difficult using sedimentological and bioarchaeological studies, providing suitable sections can be located.

Marine littoral invertebrates, and some estuarine and salt-marsh ones, may provide a tool for tracing the extent of marine influence into estuaries in the past. However, as an ecological grouping they are not without their complications. *Ptenidium punctatum* (Gyllenhal), a small beetle primarily associated with seaweed on the strandline, was found in large numbers in some Anglo-Scandinavian layers at Pavement and Hall et al. (*AY* 14/4, 181–2) have discussed the significance of this species at length, concluding that it probably exploited some specialised kind of decaying matter on the site. Rather remarkably, the species was not found at the nearby (and one would have imagined very similar) Coppergate site (*AY* 14/7, 747). There is a record of *P. ?punctatum* from an evaluation of medieval deposits in the Gowthorpe, Finkle Street and Micklegate area of Selby (Carrott et al. 1993b), from the supposed Kirk Dyke, in company with a rather unusual assemblage of insects and not far from the tidal River Ouse. In the absence of the York records this might have been interpreted as evidence of saline water, but obviously this is not the only possible explanation. Another marine littoral insect which adapted itself to habitats on occupation sites in the past was the fly *Thoracochaeta zosterae* (Haliday), whose puparia are often abundant, especially in deposits interpreted as cesspit fills (Belshaw 1989; Webb et al. 1998).

The rural landscape and the environmental impact of resource winning

York did not exist in isolation: it was dependent on the local landscape for its raw materials and food supply. One vital source of information about the rural hinterland of a town like York should be extractable sequences of peat laid down in wetland areas. Peat deposits can be regarded in two ways: firstly, their very existence stands as evidence of the nature of the local landscape and of the availability of a resource; secondly, and potentially more important, bioarchaeological information concerning conditions at the time of deposition is locked up in them.

The only published information from a natural site near York is for Askham Bog a few kilometres south-west of the city, where two studies of pollen in sequences of peat have been made (Kenward et al. 1978; Gearey and Lillie 1999). Unfortunately the upper part of the stratigraphy at this wetland site has been disturbed by human activity (including peat cutting, perhaps as early as the Roman period, and dike cleaning). Consequently the top metre of sediments, in which the Anglo-Scandinavian period should be recorded, cannot be reliably dated (Gearey and Lillie 1999, table 7.2). However, fen peat was probably still abundant in low-lying areas around York, despite Roman depredations (in fact, Roman cutting of raised bog peat probably promoted regrowth of fen peat). Peats have frequently been observed within York's presumed catchment, for example in ditch sections. The only bioarchaeological investigations of any of these peats, other than that at Askham, were work at Thornton, some 20km south-east of York, where deposits dated to the first half of the first millennium AD were analysed for insect remains by Hill (1993), and an assessment of thin but extensive Bronze Age peats at North Duffield, about the same distance to the south of the city. Prehistoric peat was recently discovered at a site in St Paul's Green, only a few hundred metres to the west of the city centre, but here it is clear from the stratigraphic record that it became buried during the Roman period. It seems likely that any peat resources close to the city would either have been buried or worked out during the first half of the first millennium.

In the absence of direct information from natural in situ deposits, can we deduce anything of York's rural environs in the Anglo-Scandinavian period? A variety of biological remains in occupation deposits in the town may provide indirect evidence for this, although of course precise location and quantification of natural and semi-natural habitats and land-use types detected in this way will be very difficult. Some vegetation types, notably woodland, heathland/moorland, various kinds of wetland, and pastureland, seem likely to have been present near the town to judge from the quantity of plant remains representing them, and to a lesser extent from the evidence of the insect remains. There are obviously dangers in arguing that quantity indicates proximity: some of the dyeplants, for example, seem far more likely to be imported than of local origin. The distance over which materials were carried would be determined by their value as resources.

Timber and woodland management

There can be little doubt that the inhabitants of Anglo-Scandinavian York made a considerable impact on woodland, presumably in the environs of the town (though see comments in previous section); the huge quantity of timber surviving — from brushwood and wattle to large oak planks and posts — stands as evidence for the importance of woodland to the economy. The question of how far this resource was carefully managed to remain sustainable is less easily answered. On the face of it, the large quantities of poles used to make wattle and wicker structures at Coppergate, as well as the many turned wooden objects formed from stems with a diameter within Rackham's (1976) definition of 'underwood' (cf. *AY* 17/13, 2101), stand as evidence for woodland managed by rotational coppicing. However, studies of the numbers of annual rings and the diameters of the poles from Coppergate do not give a clear indication of a cyclical management regime: there is not an overwhelming predominance of specimens of similar age, as might be expected for material cut from a large stand of systematically coppiced woodland from which rods were cut at regular intervals. As Figs.94–5 show, most of the stems of hazel and willow used for wicker structures fell in a rather

broad age range, so whilst coppicing (and possibly pollarding) may — perhaps must — have been practised, it did not follow a regular regime but was probably opportunistic (or, and much less plausibly, the roundwood used at Coppergate came from a series of managed woodlands with very different rotations).

Botanical analysis has revealed the use of woodland moss on a large scale at some sites. Given the low rate of regeneration of moss, the impact on woodland of harvesting this crop must have been marked. Moss-carpeted woodland floors would soon have been replaced by leaf litter or even bare soil or, where felling had occurred, by a ground flora of vascular plants, followed by eventual regeneration of trees and shrubs (where damage to seedlings by grazing herbivores was prevented). This impact would have been augmented by the effects of running pigs in woodland. The continuing availability of such mosses into the later Anglo-Scandinavian period and beyond suggests either that the area of woodland available was enormous, so that these effects were diluted, or that moss was a sufficiently valuable commodity to have been transported over considerable distances. There is, however, nothing amongst the insect records from moss-rich layers to suggest importation from continental Europe. The kinds of mosses recorded through the sequence at 16–22 Coppergate show no particular pattern, with the same major taxa recorded throughout.

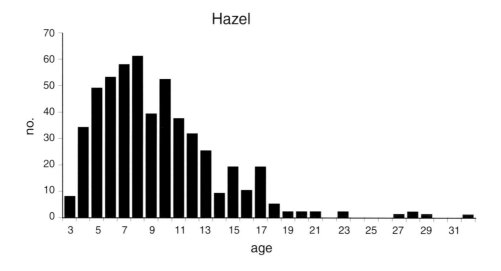

Fig.94 *Distribution plot of roundwood ring counts for all hazel specimens from wicker and wattlework structures from Anglo-Scandinavian deposits at Coppergate*

Many kinds of plants and insects were certainly brought to the town incidentally in woodland moss. At Coppergate, for example, some of the Anglo-Scandinavian pits gave a substantial number of woodland insect species, including the small stag beetle *Sinodendron cylindricum* (Linnaeus), while in a few cases it has been suggested that landsnails were been imported in this way (*AY* 14/7, 514–15, 545, 576, 661, fig.183). A component of plants other than mosses from woodland floors was regularly recorded, at least from Coppergate, the most conspicuous being wood sorrel (*Oxalis acetosella* L.), of which seeds, abscission plates from the bases of the leaf stalks, rhizome fragments, stem epidermis, and even hairs from the stems, were all recorded. This plant must surely either have been imported incidentally with moss or with leaf litter. A similar route is suggested for the leaves (and perhaps also seeds) of holly (*Ilex aquifolium*). It seems contradictory to have collected moss for sanitary purposes in which large prickly leaves were present, so moss intended for other purposes (possibly filtering or packing), or even leaf litter, for example as a flooring material, may account for some of this woodland component. Holly leaves were quite frequent in pit fills but not strongly correlated with remains indicating faeces. Perhaps they were picked from the moss before its use but ended up in the same repository.

Not all the wood brought to Anglo-Scandinavian York was destined for structures or artefacts. Much must have been used as fuel, so that its quality would have been rather less important. It is suspected that a proportion of the wood-associated insects recovered from occupation sites was brought with collected firewood (although some may then have colonised decaying structural timbers). Some bark beetles and dwellers in epiphytic moss probably arrived in this way. The bark beetle *Leperisinus varius* (Fabricius) has occasionally been found in archaeological deposits under circumstances leading to the suspicion that it emerged from logs, probably of ash (*Fraxinus*), intended for firewood; ash burns particularly well when green by comparison with other woods and so might have been favoured. Ash is rather common in Anglo-Scandinavian York, for example at 1–9 Micklegate (Dobney et al. 1993; Kenward and Hall 2000a) and at Pavement (*AY* 14/4, 185), while there were records from about 50 Anglo-Scandinavian contexts at Coppergate (*AY* 14/7). Ash was, however, at least sometimes used for structural timber. Wood for fuel would also be a source for some corticolous mosses, especially, for example, *Ulota*, recorded from 100 contexts at six Anglo-Scandinavian sites.

Studies of woodland history are perhaps inclined to concentrate on stands of woodland or the spaces

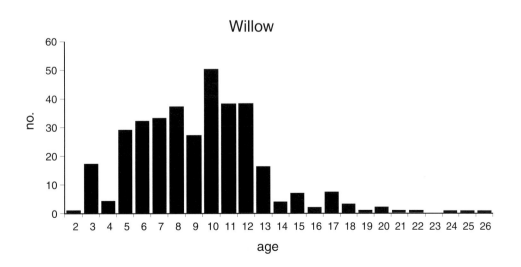

Fig.95 *Distribution plot of roundwood ring counts for all willow specimens from wicker and wattlework structures from Anglo-Scandinavian deposits at Coppergate*

in between, with rather little consideration of the transitional habitats afforded by woodland margins and their linear versions, hedgerows. These are the places where no doubt much of the wild plant food in the form of nuts and berries was gathered by York's Anglo-Scandinavian inhabitants and they would perhaps have been subject to less control by landowners than the forests and fields they bounded.

Heath and bog

Heathland and moorland is well represented amongst the plant remains from Anglo-Scandinavian York; indeed, if the remains of heather described by early workers (Benson 1902; Ramm 1971) were correctly identified, this plant is one of the more conspicuous components of deposits in York at this period. Heather, and a suite of others likely to have grown with it on heathland and moorland, were frequently recorded at Coppergate, for example (*AY* 14/7, 653), although many of these plants are not restricted to acid soils. The table in *AY* 14/7, fig.181, omitted *Vaccinium* from the list; it was recorded from 31 contexts at Coppergate as seeds and from a few others in the form of fruit epidermis fragments and 'tori', the rounded plates from the apex of the fruit. The last of these is probably diagnostic for *V. myrtillus*, the bilberry. The source of these remains might be only a few kilometres from the town if areas of heathland had developed on the poorest sandy soils (as at Strensall and Skipwith Commons), although Baines (1840) notes that heather grew then as close to the city as the Heslington 'Tillmire', an area of common land just to the south of York. The question of the date at which the heaths around York first developed is one which remains to be answered. In particular, we might ask whether turf cutting, starting with the construction of the first Roman fortress but perhaps resumed with renewed vigour in the period we are considering here, caused soil degradation and hastened the process of acidification.

In what form were the heathland resources brought into York? Apart from the fruits of bilberry brought as food, the more obvious possibilities for the vegetative remains are turf, heather plants brought whole for thatching, cut heather shoots selected for dyeing or for artefacts such as besoms, and heathland mosses (for similar purposes to those from woodland and, like them, containing various biological remains as contaminants). Various strands of evidence are relevant here. Generally speaking, heathland insects (mostly the froghopper *Ulopa reticulata* and the weevil *Micrelus ericae*) are rare in Anglo-Scandinavian deposits in York (Table 17), especially by comparison with some Roman sites, and certainly very much less frequent than heather. This perhaps suggests that heather, at least, was imported largely as whole plants or cut material (from which most insects would have tumbled during collection). If turves were used regularly in large quantities, a wide range of insects would be predicted to have been brought, either sheltering in the litter layer or as corpses which had died some time before the turf was cut.

Ants from heathland were found at the Pavement site during the preliminary investigation (Buckland et al. 1974), but heathland/moorland insects were present only in traces in the main series of samples (*AY* 14/4, 221); as mentioned on p.380, most of the records were of the weevil *Strophosomus sus*, perhaps offering a hint of the presence of turves.

One beetle which deserves mention at this point in view of its frequent occurrence in Anglo-Scandinavian York (and in many other archaeological deposits) is the small chafer *Phyllopertha horticola* (Linnaeus), which is found far more often than its present-day distribution and abundance in the York area would lead us to expect. Either it was far more common in the past or its importation was favoured in some way, or perhaps both. It is mentioned here because it is likely to have been imported in turf or cut vegetation (Kenward et al. 1992, 8). It is a rather bumbling insect, and seems quite likely to be caught up in cut plants. Since it is most common on acid soils, it may well have been brought with heather or heathland turves.

Another aspect of the exploitation of peatland is represented by the records for the moss *Sphagnum*, leaves and shoots of which have been observed at several Anglo-Scandinavian sites in York (Table 18). That these were brought as fresh or dried moss rather than as fossils in peat is suggested by the paucity of records of peat (and a complete lack of examples of peat composed of *Sphagnum* itself). A further piece of negative evidence in this respect is the absence of one particular species, *S. imbricatum*, formerly an important peat-forming species (e.g. Daniels and Eddy 1990; Green 1968), very widely recorded in

Table 17 Records of heathland insects from Anglo-Scandinavian deposits at 16–22 Coppergate. The numbers of contexts where more than 19 adult beetles and bugs of the groups used in calculating statistics for each period are as follows: P3, 49; P4A, 4; P4B, 90; P5A, 42; P5B, 141; P5Cf, 3; P5Cr, 21. There were no records of heathland insects from Periods 3, 4A and 5Cf.

Taxon	Period	no. contexts	no. individuals
Rhacognathus punctatus (Linnaeus)	5B	1	2
Macrodema micropterum (Curtis)	5B	2	5
Scolopostethus decoratus (Hahn)	5B	1	8
Strophingia ericae (Curtis)	5B	1	2
Ulopa reticulate (Fabricius)	4B	1	5
	5A	2	4
	5B	12	53
Bradycellus ruficollis (Stephens)	5B	1	2
Lochmaea suturalis (Thomson)	5B	2	7
Strophosomus sus (Stephens)	4B	1	1
	5A	2	14
	5B	2	5
	5Cr	1	2
Micrelus ericae (Gyllenhal)	4B	7	22
	5A	1	3
	5B	8	28

Table 18 Records for *Sphagnum* and for peat from Anglo-Scandinavian York

Site	No. contexts examined	No. (%) contexts with remains of *Sphagnum*	No. contexts with peat recorded
'1–5' Aldwark	8	2 (25)	
16–22 Coppergate	430	22 (5)	
118–26 Walmgate	17	5 (29)	
5 Rougier Street	–	–	1: burnt peat fragments (?reworked)
7–9 Aldwark	7	5 (71)	
1–9 Micklegate	27	4 (15)	
104–12 Walmgate	3	1 (33)	
9 St Saviourgate	10	5 (50)	1: peat fragments
All Saints' Church, Pavement	5	1 (20)	
Foss Bridge/Peasholme Green/ Layerthorpe Bridge	15	5 (33)	1: ?burnt peat fragments 1: detritus peat fragments
41–9 Walmgate	7	2 (29)	1: ?peat/mor humus

Table 19 Records of waterside/aquatic-marginal/reedswamp plant taxa (counted in group PHRA, though not necessarily exclusively so) from Anglo-Scandinavian York (number of contexts from which remains were recorded)

	6-8 Pavement	118-26 Walmgate	1-5 Aldwark	16-22 Coppergate	24-30 Tanner Row	7-9 Aldwark	22 Piccadilly	1-9 Micklegate
Alisma sp(p).	20		2	28		1		1
Apium nodiflorum (L.) Lag.			4	1		3		
Baldellia ranunculoides (L.) Parl.				2				1
Caltha palustris L.	15	1	1	19				
Cicuta virosa L.	1			1				
Cladium mariscus (L.) Pohl.	25	6		10				
C. mariscus (vegve fgts)								
Eleocharis palustris s.l.	45	12	5	237 + 2ch	1	6	1	14 + 2ch
Eupatorium cannabinum L.				1				
Glyceria cf. *fluitans* (L.) R. Br.				1				
Hippuris vulgaris L.				1				
Hydrocotyle vulgaris L.	7	1		6				
Iris pseudacorus L.	4	1		23				1
Juncus subnodulosus Schrank			1	5				
Lycopus europaeus L.	17	3		11				1
Lythrum salicaria L.			1	5				
Menyanthes trifoliata L.	15			67		1		3
Oenanthe aquatica (L.) Poiret in Lam.	2			2 + ?3				1 + ?5 + ?1ch
Oe. fistulosa L.	2 + ?3	1		1 + ?2				
Oe. fluviatilis (Bab.) Coleman								
Oe. lachenalii C.G. Gmelin				2 + ?1		2		
Phragmites australis (Cav.) Trin. Ex Steudel				3				
Ph. australis (culm nodes or fragments)	1			6				
Ranunculus lingua L.	1			1				
Scirpus lacustris s.l.				4				
Scirpus maritimus/lacustris	10	2		18	1			1
Scutellaria galericulata L.	3			1			1	
Solanum dulcamara L.				4				
Sparganium sp(p).				2				
Typha sp(p).	6			7				

post-conquest medieval deposits in York as well as in Hull. Indeed, more generally, it has been noted in at least 102 archaeological contexts from 31 sites, mostly in central and eastern Yorkshire (A.R. Hall, unpublished data), for example at Blanket Row, Hull (Carrott et al. 2001), and from post-conquest Coppergate and medieval deposits at Bedern, York, but not from the Anglo-Scandinavian period.

Wetland

Plant taxa from wetland habitats, other than true aquatics (see pp.391–2) or acid bog plants, occur from time to time in Anglo-Scandinavian deposits in York (Table 19). The tall emergent waterside taxa included in this group have usually been considered to have arrived with cut vegetation for thatch or litter of some

Table 19 (*contd*)

	104-112 Walmgate	North Street	9 St Saviourgate	All Saints' Church	Layerthorpe Bridge	2 Clifford Street	41-9 Walmgate	4-7 Parliament Street
Alisma sp(p).		2	1					
Apium nodiflorum (L.) Lag.								
Baldellia ranunculoides (L.) Parl.		1						
Caltha palustris L.							1	
Cicuta virosa L.								
Cladium mariscus (L.) Pohl.					1ch		3	
C. mariscus (vegve fgts)					1 + 2ch			
Eleocharis palustris s.l.	2	3	1	4	7 + 1ch	3	6	1
Eupatorium cannabinum L.								
Glyceria cf. *fluitans* (L.) R. Br.								
Hippuris vulgaris L.								
Hydrocotyle vulgaris L.		2						
Iris pseudacorus L.							2	
Juncus subnodulosus Schrank								
Lycopus europaeus L.				1				
Lythrum salicaria L.								
Menyanthes trifoliata L.		1			2 +1ch		5	
Oenanthe aquatica (L.) Poiret in Lam.							?1	
Oe. fistulosa L.								
Oe. fluviatilis (Bab.) Coleman					1			
Oe. lachenalii C.G. Gmelin					2			
Phragmites australis (Cav.) Trin. Ex Steudel								
Ph. australis (culm nodes or fragments)								
Ranunculus lingua L.			1					
Scirpus lacustris s.l.				1				
Scirpus maritimus/lacustris								1
Scutellaria galericulata L.								
Solanum dulcamara L.								
Sparganium sp(p).					1			
Typha sp(p).		1						

kind (e.g. Kenward et al. 1978). The numbers and amounts of these plants are usually small, however, and in no cases have deposits formed largely from cut waterside vegetation been observed. A few fen insects have been recorded (e.g. *Dromius longiceps* Dejean), but these are as likely to have arrived on the wing (or even with water) as in cut vegetation.

Wetland insects are common in occupation deposits in the town, but the more abundant species (e.g. *Carpelimus bilineatus* Stephens, *C. fuliginosus* (Gravenhorst), *Anotylus nitidulus* (Gravenhorst) and *Neobisnius* sp.) undoubtedly lived on the sites, apparently often within buildings (*AY* 14/7; Kenward and Allison 1994a; Carrott and Kenward 2000).

Arable and pasture

Evidently large parts of the surroundings of Anglo-Scandinavian York were still in a semi-natural state (as defined by Kenward and Allison 1994a, 56, following Rackham 1989, 226), as heathland, woodland and wetland. However, unless there was a substantial long-distance trade in cereals and livestock, arable and pasture must have made up a large proportion of the landscape in order to provision the inhabitants of the town. Cereals were presumably grown locally, though there is no evidence from the cereals themselves or their weed contaminants to confirm or refute this. In so far as they can be used as soil indicators, the weed seeds point to exploitation of neutral to acid soils, rather than those formed on chalk or limestone. Most of the local soils, where not too wet, would have been suitable for arable cultivation. Similarly, most would also have supported pasture, including those inundated in winter (and such areas seem likely to have been largely devoted to grazing, at least while any hay crop was not standing). Pastures not subjected to heavy grazing seem the most likely source for the very large quantities of dyer's greenweed which were brought to the town in the Anglo-Scandinavian period, though it is not impossible that the plant was deliberately cultivated or even imported from further afield to supply the needs of the urban dyers. Edlin (1951, 133) notes that the plant was sometimes cultivated in the past — in the case he cites, in south-east England.

Two of the dyeplants, madder and woad, must surely have been cultivated to provide the enormous quantities of dyestuff needed; the location of the fields remains quite unknown, however. Both may be grown in the York area today, though madder seems to require shelter to succeed and may well never have been a viable field crop, even allowing for higher summer temperatures. Woad is more likely to have been a field crop at this latitude (it was, for example, grown with teasels in the Selby area in the 19th century, according to McMillan 1984) though there seems to have been no persistent tradition of growing it much further north in England than south Lincolnshire during the second half of the second millennium AD. Either or both may have been brought from much further afield, even from overseas. As remarked elsewhere, the one plant used in Anglo-Scandinavian York which must surely have been imported from abroad is the clubmoss *Diphasiastrum complanatum*, presumably brought from Viking homelands in Scandinavia or northern Germany. It is inconceivable that it was cultivated.

Climate

Dark (2000) has summarised evidence for the pattern of climatic change during the first millennium AD. The Anglo-Scandinavian period was probably warmer than present-day on a range of evidence (Kenward in press).

Bioarchaeological evidence from York concerning climatic change has been alluded to elsewhere (e.g. *AY* 14/7, 781). The nettlebug *Heterogaster urticae* (Fabricius) had a southerly distribution in the mid 20th century, yet has been very regularly recorded from Anglo-Scandinavian York: there were, for example, eight records from Pavement (*AY* 14/4, 219) and 64 from Coppergate (*AY* 14/7, 489). Although plant materials may have been imported in bulk from further south or even from overseas, it is quite impossible to believe *H. urticae* was carried with such frequency without being accompanied by a range of other thermophilous insects, so it must have been a very common denizen of the nettlebeds of Viking-Age York. The return of the nettlebug to the York area in the late 1990s, as global temperatures increased, seems to demonstrate the sensitivity with which it responds to climate.

Some other species with possible climatic implications were noted from Pavement and Coppergate, and from more recent excavations. *Anthicus bifasciatus* (Reitter) has been found at three sites and *Acritus homoeopathicus* Wollaston was recorded from Pavement; both have southerly distributions in Britain at the present-day. *Anthicus antherinus* (Linnaeus), found at 1–9 Micklegate (Kenward and Hall 2000a) and provisionally recorded from Coppergate, is known from southern England, as far north as Derbyshire (Buck 1954). All three are associated with decomposing matter and may have been favoured by artificial habitats, so it is uncertain whether they were responding to generally higher temperatures or by the special conditions of the Anglo-Scandinavian town. The significance of some *Platystethus* species which are north of the distributions given by Hammond (1971) is not certain; the apparent recent restriction of their distribution is probably a mixture of modern under-recording (P.M. Hammond, pers. comm.) and a greater abundance in the north of England in the past. *Phymatodes testaceus* (Linnaeus), *Eurydema oleracea* (Linnaeus), and *Cryptolestes duplicatus* (Waltl) were all recorded from 1–9 Micklegate but are not normally found so far north today; *E. oleracea* has also been found in a late Anglo-Scandinavian deposit at 118–26 Walmgate. The possibility that these insects were imported rather than reflecting local climate is discussed below.

The method of recording adopted for insect remains from most of the sites considered here was intended to maximise archaeological reconstruction rather than to obtain large numbers of records of rarities, so information about some climatically significant species may have been lost; it would be useful to return to stored specimens to search for such species.

Trade: distance and volume

Biological remains offer evidence of trade of various kinds over short and long distances. Trade may be considered at several levels, but in the context of a discussion of Anglo-Scandinavian York will be divided into *regional* trade (say, beyond a few hours journey from a site but within northern England) and *long-distance* trade (beyond this, but particularly overseas). The procurement of materials from areas within one day's round journey is not considered in this section. Generally speaking, trade within a single geographical area may be difficult to detect using biological remains, since the fauna and flora can be expected to have been fairly uniform. Exceptions will be importation of materials not locally available: marine, high moorland and chalkland resources fall in this category for York. Marine shellfish and crustaceans were obviously, of necessity, imported to the town (p.397) and are clear evidence of trade links unless it is believed that occupants of the sites always went to the sea in person!

Trade over longer distances is perhaps more interesting to archaeologists and biologists alike. Some invertebrates were introduced dead, as in the case of the Red Sea cowrie *Cypraea pantherina* (Solander) from the 16–22 Coppergate site (*AY* 14/7, 781), showing saw marks and probably used in manufacturing some form of personal decoration. Imported insects (and most other invertebrates) are very unlikely to be found unless they become established at least locally, although rare cases may occur. Osborne's (1971) record of the longhorn beetle *Hesperophanes fascicu-*

latus Falderman from Roman Alcester, probably imported from the Mediterraean, provides an example, but no parallels are known from the Anglo-Scandinavian period. It has been suggested above that some, at least, of the dyeplants were imported from beyond the immediate surroundings of York, perhaps from further south (madder and woad) or certainly from overseas (clubmoss). Such importation may conceivably account for the presence of insects which have a southerly distribution in Britain today (see p.418). Importation of madder and woad from continental Europe is a possibility, although at least a few non-British insects might be expected to have been brought with them and encountered at Coppergate or Micklegate if this was the case. The clubmoss was almost certainly brought from Scandinavia or northern Germany, areas which support numerous readily identifiable beetles and bugs which are not found in the British Isles. The fact that such insects were not found at Coppergate where the clubmoss was enormously common may seem surprising at first, but *D. complanatum* grows as creeping stems rather than as clumps which would shelter insects, and was presumably dried and to some extent cleaned before making the journey across the North Sea, reducing the likelihood of insects being transported with it.

It is notable that the 1–9 Micklegate site has provided a rather larger number of 'unusual' insect remains *pro rata* than the large body of samples from Coppergate. This may be a real phenomenon, but it is just conceivably an artefact of a further ten years of experience and improved rapid identification skills. However, the former site was close to the main Ouse waterfront, where the presence of large quantities of imported materials may inevitably have led to the importation of insects. Three of these, *Phymatodes testaceus*, *Cryptolestes duplicatus* and *Eurydema oleracea*, seem to be likely candidates to have been imported with raw materials from southern England or the continental mainland (including the southern fringes of the Baltic) to this riverside site: the first two with wood and the last with woad (Kenward and Hall 2000a). All may have originated locally, however, if temperatures were higher or a wider range of natural habitats existed.

Land-use zonation

Sufficient sites of Anglo-Scandinavian date in York have now been investigated at least on a small

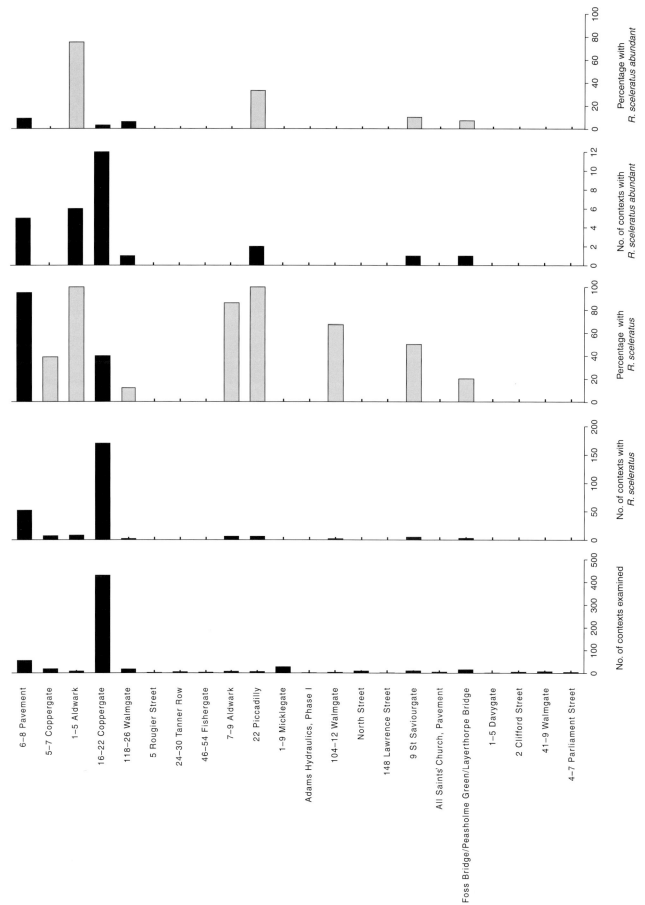

Fig.96 *Records of Ranunculus sceleratus from Anglo-Scandinavian sites in York. Some percentages are based on very small numbers of samples and these are shown in light tone*

scale for us to begin to search for systematic differences in their biota and to construct hypotheses about variations in living conditions and human activity.

It seems probable that the area represented by the 16–22 Coppergate excavation was densely built at the street frontage, at least from Period 4B onwards, and that the tenement yards were intensively used in all periods. The buildings at Pavement appear to have had a character broadly similar to those of Period 4B at Coppergate, but we have no first-hand information about conditions in the open areas associated with them. There are hints from the plant remains at Pavement that the area behind the buildings had open access to the River Foss. There were very abundant achenes of celery-leaved crowfoot (*Ranunculus sceleratus* L.) in many deposits from that site which seem likely to have been introduced by the trampling of mud from an area of disturbed but at least seasonally wet ground. The introduction of these seeds by flooding or in buckets of river water seems unlikely in view of the relative rarity of other aquatic organisms. The different recording methods employed over the years make it difficult to demonstrate objectively, but *R. sceleratus* was certainly by no means so prominent at Coppergate, either because the riversides differed between the two sites, or (more probably) because there was less direct traffic between the river and the occupation area at the latter site (Fig.96).

The small area investigated at 5–7 Coppergate probably represents a very disturbed but rather muddy yard area, whilst the few assemblages from All Saints' Church, Pavement, closely resemble many of those from 16–22 Coppergate. By contrast, the material from 4–7 Parliament Street (Hall and Kenward 2000a) has given an overall impression that that site was in some respects unlike anything studied at 16–22 Coppergate, especially if it is accepted that the three 'dumps' examined really formed on surfaces and not in unrecognised large pits. (Cuts on the scale of those seen in what may well be equivalent tenements fronting the Ousegate-Pavement line at 44–5 Parliament Street would not necessarily be recognisable as such in sections in an excavation as small as that at 4–7 Parliament Street.) Nevertheless, it seems possible that the 4–7 Parliament Street site lay in an area with poorer drainage than was experienced at 16–22 Coppergate and 6–8 Pavement; it was well above the slope to the river seen at those two sites on what may have been an undulating plateau

with drainage impeded by Roman earthworks and walls. The deposits appear to have formed far from the street frontage, considerably removed from the likely position of houses, and so may represent an area where the foul conditions generated by keeping livestock (probably pigs, see pp.407–8) would be tolerated.

Plant and insect remains from 1–9 Micklegate, the only site so far to yield large numbers of Anglo-Scandinavian deposits south-west of the Ouse in York, were essentially very similar to those from 16–22 Coppergate. The numbers of samples from other sites in this area (24–30 Tanner Row and 5 Rougier Street, cf. *AY* 14/6) are too few to form the basis for any meaningful comparison.

Recrossing the river, the site at 2 Clifford Street, although only studied on a very small scale, appears to have differed from those in Micklegate, Coppergate and Pavement, even though it lay barely 100m from 16–22 Coppergate. While the rather sparse plant remains were generally much like those from many deposits at Coppergate, two of the five assemblages were unusual in having prominent components of material preserved by charring and consisting in large part of cereal grains or spikelets, primarily oats. At 16–22 Coppergate, for example, there were only two contexts (out of 430) from which more than traces of charred oat grains or spikelets were recorded (a third context yielded quite large amounts of uncharred oat spikelets but came from a sequence of deposits representing perhaps the best evidence at Coppergate for stable manure, cf. p.409).

By contrast, charred oats were frequent at 118–26 Walmgate (Kenward and Hall 2000b) and 41–9 Walmgate (Johnstone et al. 2000), and part-charred material of the kind noted at Clifford Street was also recorded at 41–9 Walmgate (Fig.97). Whatever the source for this material, we may be beginning to see a pattern emerging in which two foci — in the Coppergate/Pavement area, and perhaps another area including 1–9 Micklegate — contrast with those more 'peripheral' sites characterised by the presence of concentrations of charred and part-charred oats (with the Clifford Street site having deposits of both types). One possible explanation is that roofing types, assuming the material represents thatch, differed, the more inflammable straw thatch perhaps being frowned upon where settlement was densest and replaced by

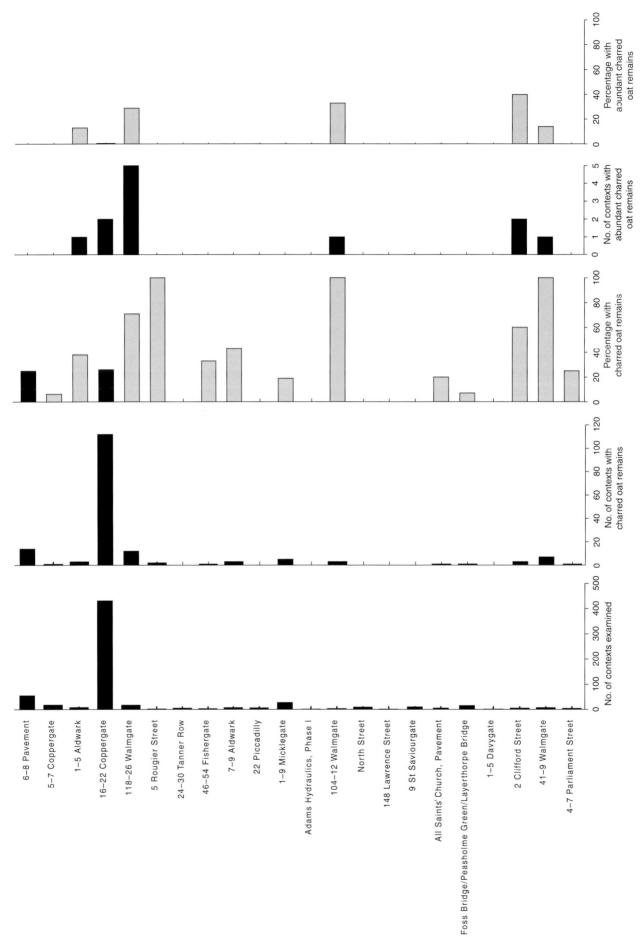

Fig.97 *Records of charred and uncharred oats from Anglo-Scandinavian York. Some percentages are based on very small numbers of samples and these are shown in light tone*

turf or some other material (cf. p.378). Another possibility is that chaff-rich oats were abundant at these 'fringe' sites because they were fed to livestock. In either case, there would have been sufficient of the material for a proportion of it to have been accidentally charred.

Perhaps the most outstanding feature of the (admittedly small corpus of) samples from 118–26 Walmgate is the almost complete lack of any evidence for the suite of plants used in textile dyeing seen at almost every other site in York with Anglo-Scandinavian deposits (Kenward and Hall 2000b; Fig.93, p.404). Yet some of these dyeplants were recorded from contemporaneous deposits around 200m away at 41–9 Walmgate (Johnstone et al. 2000), albeit in very small amounts. Perhaps the former site — the one so far investigated which is furthest from the 'epicentre' of dyeplant use and disposal in the city centre — was simply too far for remains to arrive by accident, and textile dyeing was not an aspect of the local economy in the Walmgate area.

The assemblages from 118–26 Walmgate showed other, more subtle, characteristics which differentiated them from those from the town centre. The floors never yielded seething assemblages of house fauna like those seen at the other sites, suggesting that the buildings were used in different ways. One possibility is that conditions resembling those in an old-fashioned farmyard existed there, as suggested on p.408, the buildings being byres or stables, and the food remains representing either domestic occupation or the feeding of livestock, probably pigs, with scraps. The Walmgate area of York may represent an early stage of urban settlement, with crowded smallholdings, perhaps originally farmsteads, which would later be subdivided into tenements.

Moving to the area east of the town centre, developer-funded excavations at 9 St Saviourgate revealed excellent preservation of Anglo-Scandinavian organic deposits which unfortunately have to date only been submitted to assessment (Carrott et al. 1998a). Even so, it is clear that this site presented an environment different from anything seen at Coppergate and Pavement, although perhaps with some affinity to the 4–7 Parliament Street site. Annual nitrophile weeds were very abundant in the assemblages from a series of Anglo-Scandinavian pit fills from St Saviourgate, suggesting conditions not unlike a poorly kept farm-

yard; this impression is strongly reinforced by records of large numbers of dung beetles (*Aphodius* spp.). We may tentatively suggest that the site was either far enough from the town centre or, like 4–7 Parliament Street, sufficiently removed from buildings for activities which would generate very unpleasant conditions to be tolerated. It is to be hoped that this material can be subjected to detailed study before it degrades in storage.

Moving further east, very foul conditions certainly seem to have existed along the banks of the Foss in the vicinity of what is now Layerthorpe Bridge. As noted on p.407 Anglo-Scandinavian deposits from an excavation here consistently gave evidence for very decayed bark and large numbers of the beetle *Trox scaber*, together considered to indicate the presence of waste from tanning (Hall and Kenward 2003). This process would have generated extremely foul effluent, and tanning has rarely been tolerated close to (at least the more refined) dwellings in the past.

Land-use zonation is clearly a topic for further research using structural and bioarchaeological evidence; we are perhaps obtaining the beginnings of an understanding of the way different areas of Anglo-Scandinavian York were used, paralleling results from Roman Carlisle (Kenward 1999b).

The beginning and end of Anglo-Scandinavian York

All that has been discussed above relates in large part to the heyday of Anglo-Scandinavian York. Taking a chronological view, we may ask, firstly, what the Scandinavians found when they came to York, secondly, how the town evolved through time, and thirdly, from the bioarchaeological point of view, what impact the Norman conquest had.

With regard to the first of these questions, there is limited structural and artefactual evidence for an Anglian presence in the centre of York, and certainly nothing to suggest a thriving town. All of the bioarchaeological analyses made to date tend to support this. The rare deposits yielding well-preserved biological remains which seem connected with the Anglian period — the pit containing an Anglian helmet at Coppergate (*AY* 17/8) and some pit fills at a site between Bedern and Aldwark (*AY* 14/5) — are subject to doubt as to dating. The helmet pit has been argued to have been infilled in the Anglo-Scandinavian period (*AY* 17/8). The pits at Bedern gave a radiocarbon date in the Anglian period, but it has been suggested that they may have incorporated later material (*AY* 3/3, 150). In either case, the plant and invertebrate remains from the Bedern pits suggest no more than low-density occupation, perhaps in a rather damp corner of what had been the Roman fortress. How did the pattern of occupation in York arise? Were small tenements laid out essentially *de novo*, or did they develop organically from less heavily subdivided holdings, perhaps farmsteads, whose insubstantial remains have yet to be discovered?

One approach to the question of the mode of development of Anglo-Scandinavian York may be to use insects strongly associated with human dwelling areas (synanthropes), which Kenward (1997) has postulated increase in their diversity with time in any given settlement. Inspection of the data for 16–22 Coppergate phase by phase does not show any significant increase with time, so that the town had either been established for some time before the earliest period (3) in that area, or had been preceded by farmsteads with a well-developed synanthrope fauna, paralleling the rich fauna seen in deposits at the tiny isolated rath site at Deer Park Farms, Co. Antrim (Kenward and Allison 1994b; Kenward et al. 2000). It would be enlightening to examine the synanthropic fauna of samples dated to the very earliest phases of Anglo-Scandinavian culture across York to determine whether there was an initial stage with a limited range of species, as may have been the case at Viborg, Denmark (Kenward 2002).

It has been argued that the Fishergate area may represent the Anglian *wic*, but such bioarchaeological evidence as has been recovered suggests that this area was only intermittently occupied; the investigated area again appears not to have developed into a significant settlement. It thus appears likely that the Scandinavian brigands, traders or settlers who came to the desirable spit of elevated land between the Ouse and the Foss in mid 9th century themselves brought about the development of a town in the modern sense. York in Alcuin's time may only have been a tight-knit ecclesiastical community and its lay associates — it is hard to believe that a more densely urban settlement could have existed without leaving clearer traces in the archaeological record.

As to the development of Jorvík through the mid 9th to mid 11th centuries, it is too soon to try to draw any conclusions. The course of events at Coppergate is well documented, but there is insufficient information from elsewhere. Among the pressing questions regarding the growth of York is whether it developed primarily as a trading and craft centre, through urban spread, or whether at least some areas were initiated as agricultural settlements which gradually succumbed to urbanisation.

As far as the 'end' of Anglo-Scandinavian York is concerned, the Norman conquest is surprisingly hard to detect bioarchaeologically. Although it has not yet been possible to carry out more than an assessment of most of the early post-conquest material, it appears that in many respects life continued unchanged. A notable exception is the apparently abrupt appearance of grain pests, surely related to the establishment of central storage as part of the new politico-economic control system (although the extent to which the changing abundance of and methods of husbandry for horses was a factor requires critical evaluation). Even here, however, the precise timing of the arrival of these insects is uncertain: did they come first in grain supplies supporting the conquest (as seems to have been the case in the early Roman period), or did they gradually establish themselves in large stores over a longer period of time? More substantial changes had occurred by the later medieval period, a range of plant foods including the imported fig and grape appearing in large quantities, and the insect fauna showing appreciable modification, presumably as buildings became cleaner and drier.

Future research

We have alluded in many places in this discussion to those areas where bioarchaeological research into Anglo-Scandinavian York could be concentrated in future. Much of this research is predicated upon the survival of York's superb archive of delicate biological remains preserved by anoxic waterlogging. Unfortunately, this resource may be under threat from the effects of past and future development, and perhaps of climatic change. Kenward and Hall (2000c; forthcoming) have argued that at least the superficial deposits in York may be undergoing irreversible decay. It is important that their hypothesis is put to the test as soon as possible, and if there is any doubt as to the stability of the deposits there should be a two-pronged strategy: to alter ground conditions in an attempt to halt further decay; and to make very detailed investigations of representative sites in case that attempt fails.

That said, what should our future priorities be? Firstly, it is essential to maximise the information obtained from those deposits which are destroyed legitimately within the course of the planning process by focusing on research priorities and ensuring that sampling and recording are appropriate. The 5% destruction sanctioned within York's implementation of PPG16 should be seen as providing opportunities for investigation rather than as an excuse for removing deposits with only cursory examination. Developer-funded excavations can provide the material for future research, but developers cannot be expected to fund that research. Thus, synthetic programmes based on samples from well-excavated evaluations need to be sufficiently well thought out to attract funding from research councils or English Heritage.

Secondly, we would urge that the time has come for a major programme of research excavation on the scale carried out at 16–22 Coppergate between 1976 and 1981, taking advantage of the important lessons learnt over the last quarter of a century. The questions which bioarchaeology poses today were not thought of 25 years ago, and the sampling and analysis strategies were, as an inevitable consequence, limited. To give two examples, we now realise that floor deposits should be sampled in great detail in order to investigate changes through time and use of internal space, and that analysis of the way pits were used may be better served by investigating the interfaces between fill layers than by studying only the 'pure' middles of contexts. Techniques of biomolecular analysis are now known to offer an opportunity to extend greatly our understanding of the resources used on sites (for a recent review see Brothwell and Pollard 2001), and the desire to monitor the success of in-ground preservation has emphasised the need for accurate records of the preservational condition of biological remains (e.g. Kenward and Large 1998a). Ideally, detailed excavation should be carried out in several zones of the city, for example in the Skeldergate riverside area, along Walmgate, in the Parliament Street area, and in the town centre on the fringes of the area with extensive organic preservation, in order to test for occupation which did not generate the 'compost heap' seen in the Coppergate/Pavement area.

The environmental archaeology of Anglo-Scandinavian York seems generally to be considered to have been the subject of a great deal of investigation. In one sense this is so but, as will be clear from the foregoing, the work carried out so far has (with rare exceptions) concentrated on the Coppergate/Pavement area, and, in truth, only one extensively excavated site (16–22 Coppergate) has been more than cursorily investigated. Although a substantial number of samples from 6–8 Pavement and 5–7 Coppergate has been studied, both sites were excavated in small trenches whose archaeology was not entirely clear, limiting their value and, in the case of 5–7 Coppergate, leaving dating rather uncertain; of course even radiocarbon dating was very crude at that time, relying on whole-sediment radiocarbon assay rather than single-item AMS dating. Studies of other sites with deposits of the period have been minor, or funds have not yet been made available to study them. A selection of the material from 1–9 Micklegate was examined, representing the only other substantial corpus of information. Work on the archive of unprocessed sediment samples from the 9 St Saviourgate, North Street and 22 Piccadilly sites is of the highest priority, and this material should be investigated before it decays in store.

We suggest the following as particular areas for research into Anglo-Scandinavian York:

What climatic change, if any, occurred immediately before and during the period? Was the climate conducive to easy travel and successful agriculture, including growing warmth-demanding plants such as madder?

What did the incoming Scandinavians find on the site of Jorvík? Were Roman buildings still in use?

Was there functional zonation? How representative is a site such as that at 16–22 Coppergate of the town as a whole? Is the zonation suggested by the spatial distribution of evidence for dyeplants borne out by areas so far uninvestigated?

Were some areas of 'high status' (cleaner and better cared for) and consequently poorly represented in the record?

Are variations in preservation primarily related to ground conditions or to organic input?

Did some structures and possibly areas of the town have a primarily domestic character, while others were purely used for craft, industry and trade?

A list of smaller-scale topics for investigation would be huge, but might include:

What roofing materials were used?

Was beekeeping a common urban pastime?

Can we extend the known ranges of activities and materials exploited through studies of biological remains?

What were the rivers and their fringes like?

Can studies of marine molluscs elucidate their origin and patterns of exploitation and supply?

Lastly, York did not exist in isolation in the Anglo-Scandinavian period. It needs to be placed in its local, regional and international setting. As far as rural sites are concerned, there is effectively no information from any group of organisms, and detailed studies of Saxon/Anglo-Scandinavian rural sites in the region must be seen as a particularly high priority, to address a broad range of questions, especially those concerned with provisioning, with comparisons of urban and rural conditions, and with the effects of changes of political control on the way of life at isolated farmsteads. Location and palaeo-environmental studies of rural and natural sites within its hinterland are a high priority; we know next to nothing of producer sites for this thriving urban settlement. Investigation of trade in biological raw materials (such as dyeplants) over greater distances is also crucial and will demand changes in the approach to identification of insects, at least.

In addition to giving a picture of local landscape and change through time, rural sites (and natural deposits, for which no significant post-Roman material appears to have been studied) will also be important as a source of information about climate, providing large insect assemblages can be recovered; the evidence for temperatures higher than those of the 20th century from towns is strong, but largely depends on a single species (p.418).

Bioarchaeological studies have completely changed the way we look at the Anglo-Scandinavian period in York and elsewhere, but clearly there are many new avenues to be explored, and a great deal of consolidation of existing knowledge to be undertaken.

Animal Bones from Anglo-Scandinavian York

By T.P. O'Connor

Department of Archaeology, University of York

Introduction

This chapter provides an overview of the current state of knowledge regarding vertebrate animals in and around York in the Anglo-Scandinavian period. The great majority of the available evidence derives from 16–22 Coppergate (*AY* 15/3), with smaller amounts of data from a number of excavations around the city. The aim is not to describe the data at length, but to review the information inferred from those data under several thematic headings. Examination of the material from Coppergate began as the excavation neared its end, early in the 1980s. At that time, our knowledge of urban zooarchaeology in Britain rested on just a few major studies (e.g. Exeter, Maltby 1979; Southampton, Bourdillon and Coy 1980; Baynards Castle, London, Armitage 1977), and little or nothing was known about Anglo-Scandinavian husbandry. The intervening 30 years has seen the publication of many substantial assemblages from 8th- to 15th-century urban contexts across northern Europe (e.g. Birka, Ericson et al. 1988; Ribe, Hatting 1991; Waterford, McCormick 1997; Lübeck, Rheingans and Reichstein 1991; Compiègne, Yvinec 1997). With that increasing information has come some shift in emphasis from data such as the relative abundance of different taxa and changes through time, to more thematic questions of supply and demand, and the value of animal bones in discussions on the emergence of towns and their associated social structures (e.g. Bourdillon 1994; O'Connnor 1994; Crabtree 1990). This review therefore revisits previously published material, and incorporates additional data in a synthesis of evidence from York as a whole, and in regional comparisons. Practical methods are not discussed at length here: they are detailed by site in the appropriate fascicules of *AY* 15/1–5, and reviewed in *AY* 19/2.

Materials

Excavations at 16–22 Coppergate (1976–81.7) generated an enormous archive of animal bones, of which an estimated 50% was from, broadly, Anglo-Scandinavian deposits. The great majority of that archive was retrieved by hand-collection during excavation, with a much smaller, though still significant, quantity retrieved by the bulk-sieving of sediments on 1mm mesh, followed by sorting of the >2mm fraction. Work on the bones began in parallel with studies of the pottery and other dating evidence, and the analysis of the stratigraphic record. Accordingly, the first published work was based on a selection of the better-dated and larger assemblages (*AY* 15/3). Subsequently, the larger remaining assemblages from Anglo-Scandinavian deposits were assessed and recorded. The strategy of recovering some bones by hand-collection and some by sieving became the standard for subsequent YAT excavations in York (*AY* 19/2, 98–112).

Material from 1–9 Micklegate (1988–89.17) was recovered in particularly difficult circumstances, from surface deposits and pit fills associated with Anglo-Scandinavian post-and-wicker structures. The remains of small vertebrates from the pit fills were the subject of a special taphonomic study (Piper and O'Connor 2001). Although the Micklegate assemblage is quite small, preservation is very good, and the close association with structures makes this an important assemblage. Anglo-Scandinavian deposits were sampled during excavations at 9 St Saviourgate (1995.434), with particularly substantial assemblages from two Anglo-Scandinavian pits. Although this material has been the subject of an assessment, not a full analysis, the results are sufficient to be incorporated into this synthesis (Carrott et al. 1998). Further material of Anglo-Scandinavian date has been recovered from excavations on Layerthorpe, where deposits of refuse and leather working debris appear to have accumulated within the channel of the Foss, and a small assemblage from 76–82 Walmgate (1987.33). Further 9th- to 10th-century material has been recovered from excavations in North Street (1993.1), and has been subject to an assessment, not a full record (Dobney and Jaques 1993).

Excavations at 58–9 Skeldergate (1973–5.14) yielded modest bone assemblages, which are reported in *AY*

15/1, 16–19. These assemblages are from 'soil' deposits, and the circumstances of their deposition are not clear. An Anglo-Scandinavian/Norman phase was recognised at 24–30 Tanner Row (i.e. Period 9, 1983–4.32; *AY* 15/2, 68–9), though little material was recovered that is relevant to this synthesis. The material attributed to Period 4a at 46–54 Fishergate (1985–6.9), dated to the first half of the 11th century, is late Anglo-Scandinavian, though the striking thing about this site is the lack of evidence of occupation in the late 9th and 10th centuries.

In short, much rests on Coppergate, with some additional material from elsewhere, not all of it fully recorded. Large though the Coppergate archive is, its predominance means that much of what we think we know about the zooarchaeology of Anglo-Scandinavian York rests on evidence from a few tenements along one street, and the synthesis should be read with that in mind.

Thematic overview

To give structure to this part of the text, the information recovered from York animal bones is reviewed under four headings: animal husbandry; distribution and deposition; fishing and fowling; and

pets and pests. These four categories are intended to explore, respectively, the production of staple animal resources, their circulation and utilisation within the city, the acquisition of animal resources beyond the realm of agriculture, and the place of animals in people's homes and lives.

Animal husbandry

Table 20 summarises the abundance of bones of the major taxa in Anglo-Scandinavian assemblages from York discussed in this paper. The predominance of cattle bones is striking; they comprise 59% of all identified hand-collected bones from Periods 3 to 5C at Coppergate (*AY* 15/3, 151, table 40). In Anglo-Scandinavian assemblages from 1–9 Micklegate, cattle comprised 61% of identified fragments; 67% and 59% in Trenches 2 and 3 respectively at 9 St Saviourgate; and 72% in the small assemblage from 76–82 Walmgate. Though not fully quantified, cattle bones comprised the majority of Anglo-Scandinavian assemblages from North Street. This predominance of cattle is obviously accentuated by the reliance on hand-collection of bones. For comparison, in samples from Micklegate sieved and sorted to 2mm, cattle comprised only 40% of identified specimens. None the less, the predominance of cattle is too marked to

Table 20 Numbers of identified specimens in hand-collected assemblages from Anglo-Scandinavian deposits. Note that the 'All Anglo-Scan.' category for Coppergate includes material in addition to that allocated to Periods 3 to 5C

	Cattle	Sheep	Pig	Other	Bird	Fish	Total
16–22 Coppergate							
All Anglo-Scan.	31872	11722	6536	1297	2485	108	54020
Period 5C	1095	384	254	22	89	–	1844
Period 5B	7257	2757	2616	181	1050	56	13917
Period 5A	3382	1006	802	103	227	6	5526
Period 4	5541	2645	930	135	426	10	9687
Period 3	2255	606	228	108	62	–	3259
1–9 Micklegate							
All Anglo-Scan	727	149	159	85	51	13	1184
76–82 Walmgate	190	41	17	14	3	–	265
9 St Saviourgate							
Trench 2	141	37	9	20	4	–	211
Trench 3	165	92	19	4	2	–	282

be argued away, and we have to ask what agricultural regime would have produced a surplus of adult cattle.

Dairy production might be expected to generate a death assemblage in which male calves surplus to breeding requirements and elderly cows culled from the dairy herd are most abundant. Calves are infrequent in the York assemblages, though culled calves may have been disposed of on the farm, at point of production, rather than being brought into town, so it might be erroneous to argue from their absence alone. However, even if we propose that calves were disposed of outside the town, the adult cattle seen in York are, on the whole, not particularly old; rather they are mostly adults aged between about three and five or six years, plus some second- and third-year beasts. That seems an unlikely profile for culled dairy cows, which are likely to be much older cows, too old to breed or lactate reliably. Kill-off patterns typical of dairy production clearly can be detected in urban assemblages. Medieval material from Bedern shows exactly the 'calves plus old cows' profile predicted here (*AY* 15/5, 384–7), and a shift towards older cattle detected in the assemblages from 13th-century deposits at Coppergate might also represent an increase in the keeping of dairy cows (ibid.). The material from Bedern stands out from medieval York as a whole, and there are several grounds for believing that this institution derived its cattle and sheep from populations other than those that supplied the rest of the city (*AY* 15/5, 395–7, 409–10). None the less, it serves to show that the mortality profile that might be predicted from a dairy herd *can* be detected in urban debris, and therefore that the absence of that mortality profile in data from for Anglo-Scandinavian York can be used to argue against specialised dairying.

Further afield, Viking-Age and Norse sites in Orkney and the Hebrides typically yield death assemblages in which young calves are abundant (e.g. Bond 1998, 100; Noddle 1997, 235–7). We can be confident, therefore, both that cattle-based dairy production was practised in some parts of the British Isles where there was Scandinavian influence, and that the death assemblages typical of that production can occur at urban sites, as well as at rural sites of production. The evidence does not prove that cattle in the vicinity of York in the Anglo-Scandinavian period were never used as dairy animals, only that this was not the dominant form of agricultural production.

Specialised meat production can probably be ruled out as well. If cattle production were optimised for meat, we would expect a predominance of young adults, killed as their growth rate declined. Assuming that Anglo-Scandinavian cattle grew appreciably more slowly than modern beef cattle, that point might not have been reached until the cattle were two to three years old. On that assumption, we might expect the mortality profile from a beef herd to show a predominance of mandibles in which the third molar was just erupting and coming into wear. Some of the cattle in assemblages at Coppergate and Micklegate were around 18 months to three years old at death, old enough to be full-grown and productive in terms of meat, but only just becoming productive in terms of milk or offspring. However, the great majority were appreciably older, indicating that they were kept as adults for some productive purpose other than meat alone. Fig.98 summarises the age at death data for cattle from Micklegate and Coppergate. In general, the two assemblages are similar in having the great majority of specimens in the subadult and older categories, although there is a higher proportion of elderly cattle (seven to eight years plus) in the Micklegate assemblage. The observed age profiles would have allowed a steady increase in herd size, the adult cattle 'paying back' their grazing with two or three offspring before death. If this was a priority, then it was maintained throughout the Anglo-Scandinavian period: there is no substantial change in the mortality profiles from the late 9th to early 11th centuries. The exceptional preservation of leather artefacts and manufacturing waste at Coppergate serves as a reminder that cattle were important for their hides, too. Hides were clearly used somewhat selectively, as 'calf' leather predominates in artefacts of this period, although the correlation of 'calf' with dental age categories is problematic (*AY* 17/16, 3234–5).

The most plausible interpretation of the age at death data, and the predominance of cattle in Anglo-Scandinavian assemblages, is to suppose that cattle fulfilled a mixed function, probably with the emphasis on maintaining numbers of adults as breeding stock and for haulage of ploughs and carts. Additionally, of course, cattle produce the dung necessary to maintain crop yields. If cattle were important for dung and traction, that implies an appreciable need for tilled fields and therefore for crop production. In the original publication of evidence from Coppergate,

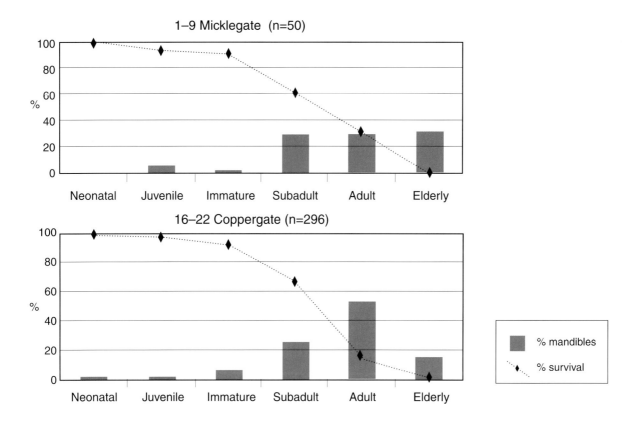

Fig.98 *Age at death distribution for cattle from 16–22 Coppergate and 1–9 Micklegate, based on dental eruption and attrition. Age groups are as used and defined in* AY 15

the observation was made that this multi-purpose husbandry 'is what might have been predicted for a system based on independent small farmers' (AY 15/3, 163). In retrospect, that interpretation is an over-simplification. If renders and other obligations required farmers to provide livestock, or to provide a plough team, both of those obligations would tend to predispose towards the keeping of prime adult cattle, in addition to older working cattle for use on the farm. If our understanding of Anglo-Saxon England from historical sources can be projected into the Anglo-Scandinavian north, it is likely that most, if not all, of those engaged in animal husbandry and farming in general were bondsmen of some form, owing renders and allegiance to a lord. That social and economic stratification need not have precluded the 'private' ownership of livestock by farmers, the husbandry of which would probably have been subject to different objectives than the husbandry of the lord's livestock. A detailed exploration of this subject is beyond the remit of the present chapter, and it is doubtful that historical sources for Anglo-Scandinavian

Yorkshire would provide a clear answer. For the present purposes, there are grounds for allowing that some of the movement of livestock into York may have been by direct trade, and some by redistribution. Differences in the bone assemblages from 8th-century Fishergate and late 9th- and 10th-century York have been argued to indicate a shift towards a greater economic independence on the part of the urban population (O'Connor 1994). The likely complexity of the economic context, and the possibility that the Anglo-Scandinavian period saw marked changes in social and economic relations, make it necessary to interpret the urban assemblages with due caution.

Another issue related to animal husbandry is the use of woodland as wood-pasture. The scale of timber construction in Anglo-Scandinavian York makes it quite clear that mature woodland was accessible within a practicable distance. We know little about the management of such woodland (but see Hill 1994), though cattle are well suited to grazing open woodland, and it is possible that some of York's beef derived from extensively managed 'park' cattle. Studies of plant macrofossils and invertebrate animal remains from Coppergate have produced numerous records of woodland taxa (*AY* 14/7, 656–61), and it is clear that woodland mosses were brought into the city. Moss would offer a ready mode of transportation for seeds and snails, though mud and plant debris attached to cattle would serve equally well as a vector (see pp.389–91). Again, this is a topic that merits further investigation, in part through archaeobotanical work in the region, and in part through historical reference to woodland pasturing.

The place of sheep in this proposed regime is around the edges, as useful grazers of uncultivated rough grassland, and of harvest aftermath. The relative abundance of sheep in Anglo-Scandinavian assemblages is generally low (Table 20): just 22% of identified hand-collected specimens at Coppergate, 13% at Micklegate; 16% at Walmgate; 18% in Trench

2 at St Saviourgate, but 33% in the two pits in Trench 3 at St Saviourgate. Recovery bias does not entirely account for these low percentages: at Micklegate, sheep and sheep/goat specimens comprised 13% of hand-collected assemblages, and 12% of sieved assemblages. Either wool production was relatively unimportant, and finds of textiles and related artefacts suggest otherwise (see pp.474–5), or it took place at a sufficient distance from York that only small numbers of sheep entered the city's food supply. Age at death data consistently show a predominance of adult sheep, though with some site-to-site differences. Fig.99 summarises the attribution of mandibles to age classes for Micklegate and for Coppergate. Taken with the more detailed breakdown of the Coppergate data in *AY* 15/3, 173, table 48, the results show the presence of generally younger sheep at Micklegate (mostly one to two years old) than at Coppergate (mostly two to four years old). Although the two samples differ considerably in size, the difference is highly significant (Table 21). The two sites may have been access-

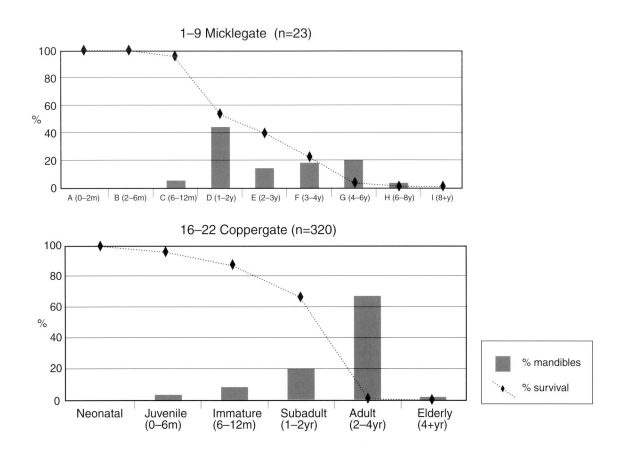

Fig.99 *Age at death distribution for sheep from 16–22 Coppergate and 1–9 Micklegate, based on dental eruption and attrition. Age groups for Coppergate are as used and defined in* AY *15; those for Micklegate follow Payne. Approximate calendar age equivalents are given to facilitate comparison. See also Table 21, p.432*

Table 21 Absolute numbers of sheep mandibles from Anglo-Scandinavian contexts at 16–22 Coppergate and 1–9 Micklegate in broad age classes (see Fig.99). Despite the substantial difference in sample size, the age distributions are significantly different (chi-squared = 45.74; 4 degrees of freedom; p < 0.01)

	0–6 months	6–12 months	1–2 years	2–4 years	4 years+	Total
16–22 Coppergate	10	27	64	215	4	320
1–9 Micklegate	0	1	10	7	5	23

1–9 Micklegate

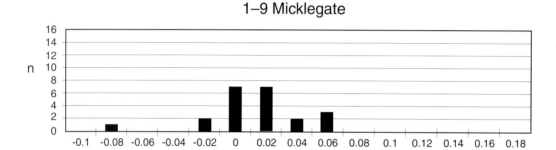

76–82 Walmgate

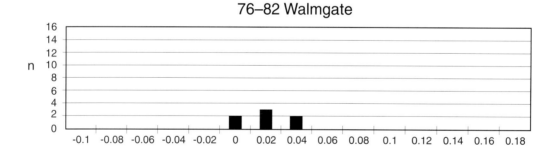

16–22 Coppergate

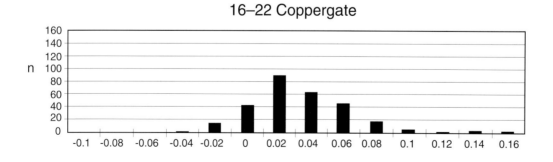

Fig.100 Log-ratio comparisons of the lengths of measurable adult caprine bones from 1–9 Micklegate, 76–82 Walmgate and 16–22 Coppergate, using a modern sample of Shetland ewes as the zero standard

ing different sources, both of them producing adult sheep for mixed meat and wool production, but with the Micklegate source perhaps tending more towards the provision of prime young adults for meat. That difference could reflect differences between the two neighbourhoods in terms of the rights and obligations of their respective populations, a topic that cannot be addressed through animal bones alone.

There is some tenuous evidence that these sheep were quite diverse in size and appearance. Sheep horncores from Coppergate showed a considerable variation in size and morphology, with no obvious division into 'male' and 'female' forms, perhaps in-dicating that variation due to sexual dimorphism was exceeded by other phenotypic variation. If sheep came to the city from a number of different sources, between which there was little exchange of livestock, then we might expect to see appreciable variation in the urban sample. Specimens of polycerate (four-horned) sheep have been found at Coppergate and St Saviourgate. In Figs.100–1, size variation in sheep bones from Coppergate, Walmgate and Micklegate is investigated by means of a log-ratio comparison. This procedure makes best use of small datasets, such as that from Walmgate. The standard measures used in this comparison are the means for a sample of modern Shetland ewes given by Davis (1996). The

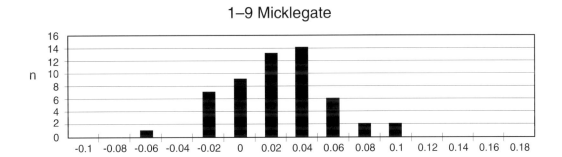

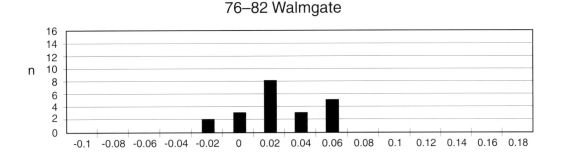

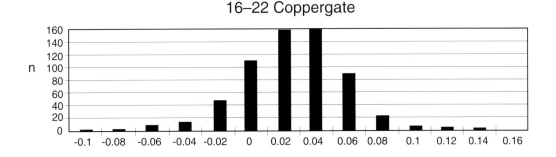

Fig.101 *Log-ratio comparisons of the widths of measurable adult caprine bones from 1–9 Micklegate, 76–82 Walmgate and 16–22 Coppergate, using a modern sample of Shetland ewes as the zero standard*

comparison on width measurements shows little difference between the samples, but on length measurements, the Coppergate sample shows a slightly higher mode than the sample from Micklegate. A difference in lengths but not breadths could have a number of explanations, amongst them differences in the ratio of males to females in the two samples. Fig.102 compares the sheep metacarpals from the Coppergate sample with the Shetland standards. The Coppergate sample includes quite a number of specimens that are appreciably more long and slender than the Shetland ewes, and it is therefore quite possible that these specimens are wethers (castrated males). Comparison with the Shetland specimens does not *prove* that the Coppergate specimens are, case by case, male or female. However, the results shown in Fig.102 would be consistent with a high proportion of wethers in the Coppergate sample. As the sample consists of fully fused metacarpals, it represents sheep older than about one-and-a-half years.

That inference takes us back to the question of husbandry regimes. Taking the differences between Coppergate and Micklegate in bone morphology shown in Figs.100–1 and in age at death distribution shown in Table 21, we might wonder whether the higher proportion of second-year sheep in the Micklegate sample were disproportionately ewes. If so, that would account for the less elongated bone morphology seen in the Micklegate sample. That interpretation is not implausible, if an aim of sheep husbandry around York was to raise wool, and there was no particular pressure to increase the size or number of flocks. In that case, some young ewes might have been disposed of as surplus to breeding requirements in their second year, their metacarpals having just fused. They would have yielded their first and best clip of wool, leaving the majority of grazing land to the more productive wethers. The wethers would then have been gradually culled in their third and fourth years, having given two or three clips of wool, and with their wool yield and quality beginning to decline. That interpretation rests on a little evidence and a lot of supposition, but is open to testing as and when more evidence becomes available on the sex and age structure of sheep samples from York. Whether we should expect the expanding population of York and an increased demand for wool and cloth to have an effect on the mortality profiles is debatable. Wool is readily transportable, and any

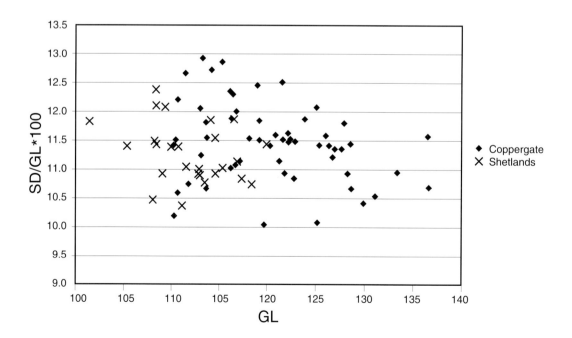

Fig.102 *Scattergram of length against an index of relative shaft breadth for sheep metacarpals from 16–22 Coppergate, plotted against a sample of modern Shetland ewes*

increased demand generated by York might more readily have been met by trading in wool from further afield, rather than by increasing the numbers of sheep kept in the immediate vicinity of the city.

Pigs might have been kept around the city in small numbers. The relative abundance of pig bones (Table 20) is generally higher at sites where house structures indicate dense occupation (Coppergate 12%; Micklegate 15%) than at Walmgate (6%) or St Saviourgate (7%). Some specimens of neonatal pigs have been recovered, indicating the presence of breeding sows, and the irregular attrition noted on the lower first molars of some Coppergate pigs might be symptomatic of stalled pigs chewing sticks and stones out of boredom and frustration. If pigs were part of the urban scene, rather than part of the general agricultural economy, the gradual rise in their relative abundance through the 10th and 11th centuries might reflect changes in the provisioning of the city (O'Connor 1994, 144–5). Whatever their point of origin, most of the pigs were slaughtered during their second year, though with no particular concentration on narrow age-categories, such as was seen in Anglian material from Fishergate (*AY* 15/4, 249–51), and no evidence of markedly seasonal slaughter.

Distribution and deposition

One of the questions raised above is how far the supply of meat to York was subject to decisions taken by individual urban households or farmers, and how far controlled by a higher social tier such as estate owners or those acting for the regal or ecclesiastical powers. Consistency of butchery practice might be one indicator of central provision, having arisen through the activities of independent specialist butchers, the prototype of the medieval guilds, or because much of the meat supply was managed through slaves or other dependent personnel answerable to a lord or higher power. In fact, there is not much evidence of such consistency at Coppergate or Micklegate, although some 'butchery marks' are seen quite frequently. The longitudinal splitting of long bones was particularly evident in material from North Street, and was the most commonly recorded form of butchery on cattle humeri, radii, femora and tibiae from Coppergate. The cleaving of vertebrae in the median sagittal plane, consistent with the splitting of carcasses into sides, was seen in most samples. In all cattle vertebral centra recorded from Anglo-Scandinavian Coppergate, sagittal cleaving was noted in 166 out

of 363 specimens of cervical vertebrae (45·7%), but only 103 out of 564 lumbar vertebrae (18·3%). The difference between those figures probably indicates that some sagittal-plane cutting took place after the carcass had been reduced to a number of large pieces. Subsequent subdivision of the spinal column is shown by transverse cutting in 33·9% (123 out of 363) of cervical vertebrae and 22·9% (129 out of 564) in lumbar vertebrae. It is quite difficult to distinguish the dismantling of carcasses and removal of meat, such as a butcher might undertake, from subsequent chopping of bones to extract marrow or to reduce those bones for the stock-pot, processing that might be domestic. Anglo-Scandinavian York has produced none of the large-scale chopping-up of bones such as is seen in Roman deposits (*AY* 15/2, 82–3). The balance of evidence suggests that there was little central control of distribution and butchering within the city. The butchery evidence shows enough diversity to be consistent with much of it taking place at the household or neighbourhood level, perhaps by whoever had the tools and sufficient expertise.

One deposit (4374) at 9 Blake Street (1975.6), probably of (?late) Anglo-Scandinavian date, gave an assemblage that essentially comprised six cattle skulls, over 30 cattle metapodials, and 50 first phalanges (O'Connor 1986b, 9). Most of the cattle skulls had massive depressed fractures in the frontal region, consistent with a lethal blunt instrument injury. This Blake Street assemblage is evidently a deposit of primary butchery waste. A generally similar, but less restricted, assemblage was recovered from pit 3007 at 9 St Saviourgate. Otherwise, Anglo-Scandinavian York shows little indication of selective disposal of bone debris. Coppergate and Micklegate had bones in pits, bones trodden into surface dumps of refuse and bones in levelling deposits under structures. Even contexts closely associated with structures at these two sites contained cattle cranial and foot bones. It appears that the debris from different stages of carcass reduction was usually disposed of rather unsystematically into whatever dumps or holes in the ground happened to be available at the time. Apart from the isolated examples described above, we have little positive evidence of selective deposits of, for example, skulls and feet, or the negative evidence of assemblages conspicuously depleted of heads and feet. What that might indicate is that heads and feet were not regarded as 'waste' at the original point of butchery.

An interesting example of the butchering of pigs comes from Period 5B deposits in Tenement B at Coppergate. Pig bones from floor and backfill deposits in Structure 5/3 show a particularly high proportion of foot bones, whereas the admittedly quite small sample of pig bones from the adjacent Structure 5/4 is markedly depleted in head and foot bones, with abundant bones from the legs and limb girdles (*AY* 15/3, 179–80). To put that into percentages, 3rd and 4th metapodials made up 67% of pig limb and girdle elements from Structure 5/3 deposits, but only 15% in Structure 5/4. The assemblages from the two Structures are almost complementary, and the deposits concerned appear to have sampled the systematic butchering of several dozen pigs, though whether in one event or several closely spaced events it is not possible to say.

Apart from the unfortunate pigs of Tenement B, it appears that debris from primary butchery at Coppergate and at Micklegate became re-acquainted with household debris, and therefore that bones were distributed with meat and so perceived as having either food or other value. Many cattle long bones have been chopped roughly to open up the marrow cavity, also indicating the food value of the bones. A point to watch for in subsequent work on Anglo-Scandinavian sites in York might be the presence of butchered cattle cranial and foot bones in unambiguously domestic waste contexts, necessitating context-by-context assessment of bone assemblages closely associated with domestic structures. Such associations certainly seem to have occurred at Coppergate, and arguably at Micklegate. If confirmed elsewhere, they would point to quite an intensive utilisation of cattle carcasses, not necessarily through a desperate need for meat but perhaps because of a cultural inclination to maximise the use of a carcass.

One value of bone is as raw material for artefacts (see pp.469–72). There is some antler working debris from Coppergate, Micklegate and North Street, though not on the scale seen in some contexts at Fishergate and at Clifford Street (*AY* 17/12), and no evidence of antler working at St Saviourgate. The small assemblage from Walmgate included five fragments of worked red deer antler. Apart from antler, bone *per se* is well represented in artefacts, including a lot of objects made from unspecified mammalian compact bone. These objects are typically pins or other elongated objects cut from thick, flat, straight

pieces of bone. The bones concerned could be cattle or horse, probably metapodial or tibia shafts. Pig bones are commonly represented amongst the artefacts, both as 'needles' fabricated from fibulae, and as 'toggles' made from metapodials. These artefacts illustrate the extent to which bones were put to use. Taken with the butchery evidence, they show that cattle carcasses, especially, were used down to the last gasp.

Fishing and fowling

Bird and fish bones from Coppergate were the subject of special studies by E.P. Allison and A.K.G. Jones respectively, and particular attention was paid to their recovery. As a consequence, the very large volume of fish and bird material from this one site tends to dominate the record for Anglo-Scandinavian York as a whole. The results from Micklegate are generally consistent with those from Coppergate, and other Anglo-Scandinavian deposits have yielded insufficient material to make any useful comparison. Table 22 gives a full list of bird taxa identified from Anglo-Scandinavian deposits in York.

The birds show the familiar mixture of domestic taxa (chickens, geese), presumably hunted wild taxa (e.g. waders, crane, wild geese and ducks, black grouse), urban taxa (e.g. corvids), and 'accidental' taxa that fit none of these categories (e.g. short-eared owl). The hunted taxa show a predominance of those that form large flocks in winter on wetland areas. Although the identification of duck and goose bones to species is problematic, some species have been identified with due caution that are likely to have been winter visitors only, such as barnacle goose and teal. The washlands ('ings') of the Ouse and Derwent valleys are close enough to York for those taxa to have been hunted directly by York people, though this assumes that distance from York was the only parameter determining accessibility. A notable exception are the auk species that first appear late in the Anglo-Scandinavian record for Coppergate, and become a distinctive feature of 11th- and 12th-century assemblages in York and Beverley. Guillemots and razorbills are maritime taxa, coming ashore to breed in colonies, and the specimens recovered from York were probably acquired by trade with the east coast.

Both the frequency and the occasional abundance of corvid taxa, notably jackdaw and raven, are consistent with the evidence that Anglo-Scandinavian

Table 22 A list of the bird species identified from Anglo-Scandinavian deposits at 16–22 Coppergate and 1–9 Micklegate. The list excludes higher-level taxa. Other sites of this date in York have produced only domestic fowl and goose bones

		Coppergate	Micklegate
Mute swan	*Cygnus olor*	*	
Whooper swan	*Cygnus cygnus*	*	
Pink-footed goose	*Anser brachyrhynchus*	*	
White-fronted goose	*Anser albifrons*	*	
Domestic/greylag goose	*Anser anser*	*	*
Barnacle goose	*Branta leucopsis*	*	*
Brent goose	*Branta bernicla*	*	
Mallard	*Anas platyrhynchos*	*	
Teal	*Anas crecca*	*	
Tufted duck	*Aythya fuligula*	*	
White-tailed eagle	*Haliaeetus albicilla*	*	
Red kite	*Milvus milvus*	*	
Buzzard	*Buteo buteo*	*	
Goshawk	*Accipiter gentilis*	*	
Sparrowhawk	*Accipiter nisus*	*	
Black grouse	*Lyrurus tetrix*	*	
Domestic fowl	*Gallus gallus*	*	*
Coot	*Fulica atra*	*	
Crane	*Grus grus*	*	*
Golden plover	*Pluvialis apricaria*	*	
Grey plover	*Pluvialis squatarola*	*	
Woodcock	*Scolopax rusticula*	*	
Guillemot	*Uria aalge*	*	
Razorbill	*Alca torda*	*	
Short-eared owl	*Asio flammeus*	*	
Rock/Stock dove	*Columba livia/C. oenas*	*	*
Wood pigeon	*Columba palumbus*	*	
Jackdaw	*Corvus monedula*	*	
Raven	*Corvus corax*	*	

York provided ample opportunities for scavengers. The importance of organic refuse in urban food webs, and thus in the urban environment, has been discussed at length elsewhere (O'Connor 2000b). The refuse accumulations that became the thick, richly organic deposits typical of the archaeology of this period probably did much to determine the characteristics of the urban biota, from the numerous flies and beetles to the scavenging white-tailed eagles.

The fish tell a number of stories, and Table 23 lists the taxa identified from Anglo-Scandinavian samples. Assessment of the relative abundance of fish taxa is problematic because different taxa differ appreciably in the number of bones in the skeleton, or in the pro-

portion of those bones that can be confidently identified, a point that is discussed further in *AY* 15/5 (pp.398–401). Accordingly, the abundance data discussed here refer to the recorded assemblages of bones and should not be directly equated with the relative abundance of fish. Furthermore, this analysis takes account only of changes of relative abundance of such magnitude that anatomical biases alone are an insufficient explanation. That said, the assemblages from Coppergate are dominated by eel bones. Through the 10th century, there is a marked rise in the relative abundance and relative frequency of herring, and subsequently of offshore marine taxa, notably cod and other gadid species (*AY* 15/3, 195–8). In 10th- to early 11th-century deposits at Micklegate,

Table 23 List of fish taxa identified from Anglo-Scandinavian samples from 16–22 Coppergate and 1–9 Micklegate. Some identifications to Family have been omitted, and '?' records are only included if that species has not been positively identified from the same site

		Coppergate	Micklegate
Thornback ray	*Raja clavata*	*	
Sturgeon	*Acipenser sturio*	*	
Shad	*Alosa* sp(p).	*	*
?Sprat	*?Sprattus sprattus*	*	
Herring	*Clupea harengus*	*	*
Grayling	*Thymallus thymallus*	*	
Salmon	*Salmo salar*	*	*
Trout	*Salmo trutta*	*	
Smelt	*Osmerus eperlanus*	*	*
Pike	*Esox lucius*	*	*
Carp family	Cyprinidae	*	*
Barbel	*Barbus barbus*	*	
?Gudgeon	*?Gobio gobio*	*	
?Tench	*?Tinca tinca*	*	
?Bream	*?Abramis brama*	*	
Roach	*Rutilus rutilus*	*	*
?Rudd	*?Scardinius erythropthalmus*	*	
Chub	*Leuciscus cephalus*	*	
Dace	*Leuciscus leuciscus*	*	*
Eel	*Anguilla anguilla*	*	*
Whiting	*Merlangius merlangus*	*	*
Cod	*Gadus morhua*	*	*
Saithe	*Pollachius virens*		*
Haddock	*Melanogrammus aeglefinus*	*	
Burbot	*Lota lota*	*	
Sand eel	*Ammodytes tobianus*		*
Perch	*Perca fluviatilis*	*	*
Horse mackerel	*Trachurus trachurus*	*	
Mackerel	*Scomber scombrus*	*	*
3-spined stickleback	*Gasterosteus aculeatus*	*	
Flatfish	Pleuronectidae	*	*
Flounder	*Platichthys flesus*	*	

herring bones outnumbered those of eel, with the next taxon (cod) only one-tenth as abundant as eel. There would appear to be some variation in the deposition of fish bones from site to site, therefore. The change seen through the 10th century at Coppergate seems to show an extension of the area fished from York, from the lower reaches of the Ouse, into the Humber basin, then into North Sea inshore waters. Deeper-water marine fish, such as ling, haddock and conger eel, only become a regular feature of York assemblages from the 12th century onwards (e.g. see *AY* 15/4, 263–7). Apart from eels, river fish are represented mostly by pike and cyprinids, the latter often

not identifiable beyond the level of Family, and these taxa are most abundant in late 9th- to early 10th-century assemblages. Two estuarine taxa of note are shad, present in late 9th-century samples from Coppergate and from Micklegate, and smelt. The latter species was present in Micklegate samples, and, though never particularly abundant at Coppergate, occurred in an appreciable number of samples, particularly from the earlier part of the 10th century.

The early Anglo-Scandinavian assemblages from Coppergate are also typified by the frequent, though never particularly abundant, presence of barbel, burbot and grayling, species that require well-oxygenated water with little suspended sediment. The low relative abundance of these taxa is at least in part a consequence of the anatomical effects outlined above, and their frequency is probably a more useful parameter to consider (see O'Connor 2001a for further discussion of quantification of sieved assemblages). From the mid-10th century onwards, they become less frequent, and disappear from the record by the end of the Anglo-Scandinavian period. Changes in relative abundance could be an arithmetical consequence of changes in the relative abundance of other taxa, the data being interdependent. However, the disappearance of certain freshwater taxa from deposits in which fish bones are otherwise well represented requires another explanation. Assuming for the moment that these fish are from the Ouse-Foss system, we might infer from their presence and absence an increasing pollution of the rivers around York as the settlement grew. The deposition of refuse into the rivers, coupled with increased sediment input through run-off from unvegetated and unstable road and backyard surfaces, could have led to a rise in suspended sediment and a fall in the oxygen content of the water. In parallel with the decline in 'clean water' fish, the hand-collected freshwater molluscs from Coppergate show a decline in the freshwater mussel *Unio tumidus* and a rise in *U. pictorum* (*AY* 14/7, 780). Modern data indicate that *U. pictorum* is the more tolerant of silty, poorly oxygenated water, so the freshwater mussels are consistent with the inferences drawn from the fish bones (see p.391). Furthermore, the simple comparison of counts of valves of two mollusc taxa does not suffer from the arithmetical and anatomical uncertainties attendant on the fish bones.

Although river pollution remains the most credible explanation of the observed data, two other possibilities should be considered, as neither can be absolutely ruled out at this point. The first is a base-level change in the Ouse-Foss system, reducing the gradient of the river and effectively moving the 'grayling zone' upstream from York. On this model, grayling, barbel and burbot would have become unavailable in the immediate vicinity of York, their place being taken by cyprinid taxa typical of more 'downstream' stretches of lowland rivers. To test this possibility, we need well-dated river levels at York or indirect evidence such as the sequential raising of riverside structures. The second possibility is that the change in the fish recovered from York marks a change in the river systems that were routinely fished. If the Derwent contributed to York's supply of freshwater fish early in the 10th century, but not later, then much the same change in 'clean water' taxa might be apparent in the data. We might think that an implausible explanation, but it cannot be ruled out on evidential grounds, and would be difficult to test directly.

Pets and pests

Amongst the animal bones from sites in York are the remains of those species with which people most intimately shared their lives, voluntarily or otherwise. Dogs are a frequent find, and Anglo-Scandinavian dogs from York show some variation in size and build. The very small 'lap-dogs' seen in Roman assemblages are not known from the Anglo-Scandinavian town, though Fig.103 shows a group of quite small dogs, around 35cm in shoulder height. A larger group is represented by specimens around the size of a modern Border Collie (shoulder height around 55cm). A few specimens defy confident identification as dog or wolf: a tibia and two metapodials from Coppergate are from animals that could be either species. On Fig.103, those three specimens are around the size of a modern Alsatian. Given that recent biomolecular studies have thrown doubt on the species distinction of dog and Eurasian grey wolf (Tsuda et al. 1997), our inability to classify an isolated bone as one or the other is hardly significant. There were some very large canids around Anglo-Scandinavian York; whether they were big dogs, captive wolves, tame wolves or dog/wolf hybrids can not be determined from the bones alone. What can be said is that the great majority of the dog bones were those of adults, and furthermore that sufficient whole or part-skeletons have been recovered to indicate at least the occasional deliberate burial of dogs. These two observations would seem to indicate that dogs were cared for and treated differently to the more utilitarian animals. Very little pathology was noted on the dog bones. One specimen showed marks of butchery: a fragment of occipital bone that had been cut away from the anterior part of the skull.

Bones of cats have been recovered quite frequently from Anglo-Scandinavian deposits, though seldom in any abundance, and generally as dispersed bones rather than skeletons. Furthermore, quite a high proportion are of subadult cats, an observation that has been made in other urban contexts (O'Connor 1992; 2000b). The high subadult mortality and lack of evi-

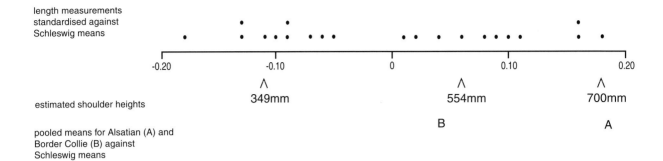

Fig.103 *Length measurements of dog bones from Anglo-Scandinavian Coppergate, plotted as log-ratio values, taking the sample means of dog measurements from medieval Schleswig as the zero standard (Spahn 1986). Pooled values for a modern Border Collie (B) and a modern Alsatian (A) are given, with shoulder heights reconstructed from three of the Coppergate specimens using the regression equations given by Harcourt (1974)*

dence for careful disposal point to cats occupying a different role to that of dogs, and the evidence is more consistent with a largely feral population of cats than with 'pet' cats under close management and care. Several cat skulls and mandibles from Anglo-Scandinavian deposits at Coppergate, Micklegate and St Saviourgate bear fine knife-cuts consistent with skinning, and sieved samples from Coppergate Periods 4 and 5 included concentrations of cat phalanges, such as might have been retained on a pelt. This need only indicate the occasional, opportunistic use of cat skins. If cats were more systematically exploited for their skins, as some colleagues have suggested (McCormick 1997), then we might expect to have found greater concentrations of cat bones (i.e. less frequent; occasionally abundant), such as the deposit reported recently from Cambridge (Luff and Moreno Garcia 1995). An interesting comparison is with Birka. Phases 6, 7 and 8 at this site (approximately late 9th to late 10th century) yielded numerous bones of animals apparently taken for their fur, but whereas foxes, martens and squirrels were largely represented by skull and foot bones, cats were represented by all parts of the skeleton, with no knife cuts noted on the skulls, leading Wigh (2001, 119–20) to conclude that the cats were not systematically skinned.

A general survey of the frequency of taxa across the Anglo-Scandinavian deposits at Coppergate (Scott 1984) showed that cat bones were significantly more frequent in Period 4 and 5 deposits in Tenements A and B than in the same periods in the other tenements. This distribution could be interpreted in either of two apparently conflicting ways. If we ac-

cept the evidence that cats lived in Anglo-Scandinavian York largely as feral animals, then the distribution of their bones might indicate that Tenements A and B were less consistently and intensively occupied by people than the other tenements, thus allowing at least some periods of time during which feral cats could move in, breed and die. Conversely, the opposite suggestion has been made, that cats are an indicator of 'hearth and home', and thus that Tenements A and B were the more consistently domestic part of the site (*AY* 15/3, 186). For the moment, the mortality and taphonomic evidence is more consistent with feral cats than with 'pet' cats, and so with Tenements A and B being the part of the Coppergate site where those populations were more common. That assumes, of course, that the distribution of dead cats indicates the distribution of live ones, but as cats appear not to have been eaten, and to have been used for fur rather intermittently, we have no good reason to posit any consistent spatial translocation between life, death and burial.

Anglo-Scandinavian York had rats and mice. Bones recovered by sieving confirm the presence of black rat (ship rat) at Micklegate and from the end of the 9th century onwards at Coppergate, the species having been present in Roman York, but absent from 8th- to early 9th-century occupation at Fishergate. House mice appear to have been in York from the late 2nd century onwards, apparently without a break. The relative frequency of the two species differs consistently at most sites in York where both are present, with house mouse generally at a much higher relative frequency than black rat. In all Anglo-

Scandinavian samples from Coppergate, house mouse was identified in 64 out of 234 samples, giving a relative frequency of 0·27, compared with 0·08 for black rat (19 out of 234 samples). To consider that in more detail, rat bones were generally more common in samples from the 'back' of the site, away from the street frontage, or from Period 3 deposits, before the development of structures and tenements that came to characterise the site in Periods 4 and 5 (Fig.104). This could be taken to indicate an avoidance by rats of the most intensively occupied parts of the site, though the predation of rats by cats, and consequent deposition of rat corpses away from the life-range of the rats, could complicate this interpretation.

Work to date on the remains of small vertebrates other than fish has focused on the interpretation of small bone assemblages in terms of the urban environment. In order for such interpretations to be credible, it is essential to understand the taphonomic pathways by which the remains of mice, frogs and so on have entered pit fills and surface accumulations of refuse. Sieved assemblages from Micklegate formed a pilot study to determine whether the sur-

face condition of small bones in pit fills could be used to differentiate those that accumulated through small animals becoming trapped in pits from those in which small bones were secondarily deposited with refuse or other materials. The results from Micklegate showed that secondary deposition was common, and therefore that the small vertebrates did not necessarily reflect the environment immediately around the pit in question (Piper and O'Connor 2001). Furthermore, it appeared that downward vertical movement of bones had occurred in some deposits, and therefore that at least some accumulations of small bones might not indicate an original accumulation of small vertebrate corpses. In short, our interpretations to date of small bones from sites such as Coppergate have been called into question.

The presence of quite large numbers of frog bones in the fills of some Coppergate pits had been taken to indicate that frogs lived, perhaps even bred, in water-filled pits that, by inference, must have lain open for some months at least. However, the Micklegate study indicates that two taphonomic mechanisms might be operating. The first is the secondary deposition into pits of refuse that had accumulated elsewhere, and had been used by frogs as a place in which to hibernate or as a place of shade and moisture in summer, leading to the secondary deposition of frog corpses into the pit. The second is the post-depositional concentration of small bones by downward movement. The richly organic deposits that are typical of this period appear to be far too dense and coherent to allow such movement. However, that is their texture and porosity when excavated. As originally laid down, these deposits probably included quite substantial lumps of organic material, and could have been essentially clast-supported, with large pore spaces through which small bones could have been moved by gravity and water. The downward movement of bones would have ceased at the interface with less porous, matrix-supported, mineral sediments, hence the concentrations of small bones at the base of pits, or towards the base of organic fills that are underlain by deposits composed largely of silts and clays (*AY* 19/2, 207–10). Secondarily redeposited assemblages of frog bones, in particular, can be distinguished from primary deposits of frogs by the differential loss of fragile skeletal elements, notably the parasphenoid, and by the dispersal of elements of single individuals. In short, the interpretation of small vertebrate assemblages from sites such as

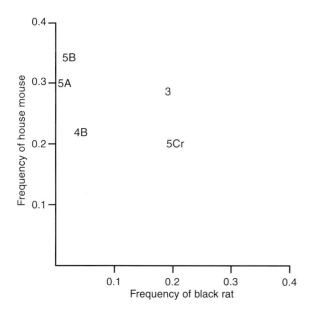

Fig.104 Relative frequency of bones of house mouse and black rat in samples from 16–22 Coppergate. Rats were more frequent early in the Anglo-Scandinavian sequence (Period 3) or at the 'back' of the site (Period 5Cr), in contrast to the frequency of house mice. Note that these are relative frequency data, and therefore independent. The apparent negative correlation is not a statistical artefact

Micklegate and Coppergate is both more difficult and more interesting than has previously been allowed, and should be approached with some caution until the taphonomic processes involved are better understood. Research continues on this subject. Early results indicate that assemblages of small bones from pits at different sites in York have quite different taphonomic trajectories, requiring site-by-site, or even pit-by-pit, interpretation.

Regional comparisons

Crude comparisons of relative abundance have, of necessity, to be conducted with caution, not least because of the interdependence of the data. Inter-observer variation in the process of identification and recording will lead to inter-site variation that has nothing to do with animal husbandry or deposition. Different depositional contexts will tend to predominate at different sites, too, possibly leading to further variation in the data if some taxa are more likely to have been deposited in, for example, pit fills than in extensive surface dumps. We can only make such comparisons in very general terms, but even those generalities might be informative if they enable us to recognise, for example, major geographical or cultural trends.

Table 24 compares the relative abundance of major taxa at a range of 8th- to 11th-century sites across north-west Europe. Not all of these sites have a Scandinavian component, and the nature of the sites varies from urban settlement at York, Lincoln and Hedeby (Viking-Age Denmark), to high-status farmsteads at Eketorp III (Öland, Sweden) and North Elmham Park, Norfolk. Some Middle Saxon sites are included, to give a 'pre-Viking' comparandum for the English material, and a group of eastern European 'Slavic' sites is included to allow the examination of geographical trends beyond the sphere of Scandinavian influence.

The first point to make is that a modest predominance of cattle bones — about 40–50% cattle — typifies most of the Anglo-Scandinavian sites, and the Middle Saxon assemblages from early towns. Exceptions to this generalisation are Anglo-Scandinavian York, with around 60% cattle, and three of the East Anglian sites (North Elmham Park, Brandon, Wicken Bonhunt) with a predominance of either sheep or pig. The figures for Brandon and North Elmham Park are quite similar, and probably reflect the high-status role of these two rural sites. Wicken Bonhunt stands out for its high proportion of pigs, unparalleled in Britain, and probably indicating a specialised function for this enigmatic site. Otherwise, the relative abundance of taxa seen in Late Saxon and Anglo-Scandinavian assemblages is a continuation of that seen in Middle Saxon towns, the predominance of cattle being somewhat greater at York. Widening the comparison, York is in a '60%+ cattle' group that includes the two 'Viking' towns in Ireland, and one early town in the Netherlands. As Deventer cannot be argued to have been particularly 'Scandinavian', the predominance of cattle at these sites may have more to do with a similarity in their function as regional centres for trade and exchange than with any cultural affiliations.

The two Orkney sites in Table 24 show much the same spectrum of relative abundance, with cattle the most numerous taxon, but not heavily predominant. What the simple bone counts conceal is a major difference between the utilisation of cattle in the Northern Isles and in mainland Britain at this time. In the Anglo-Scandinavian assemblages, and at Waterford and Dublin, the great majority of cattle remains in the towns were from adults, with small numbers of one- and two-year-old individuals. At Skaill and Buckquoy, and in other assemblages from Orkney and Shetland, a high proportion of the cattle are immature, young calves apparently slaughtered as part of a dairying strategy. This is not a distinctively 'Viking' strategy, but a continuation of a husbandry regime that has its roots arguably in the Middle Iron Age in Orkney and Shetland.

What these data seem to show, to apply a sweeping generalisation, is that Viking-Age subsistence throughout north-western Europe shows some adaptation to pre-existing economic strategies, though with something of a tendency towards cattle husbandry. The high proportions of cattle at the Irish sites should be seen against the predominance of cattle at Early Christian sites in the same region, and the well-attested importance of cattle in Irish life throughout the first millennium AD (Lucas 1989). In York, the one substantial Middle Saxon assemblage, from Fishergate, included over 60% cattle (*AY* 15/4, 236–7), so the predominance at Coppergate and Micklegate could be seen as a continuation of local practices.

Table 24 Summary of the percent relative abundance of major taxa in 8th- to 11th-century assemblages from north-western Europe. Note that not all sources have quantified bird and fish bones, and that the sample sizes vary considerably. These percentages should only be directly compared with considerable caution. 'OM' is all other mammals; * indicates that the taxon was not included in the published data

	Cattle	Sheep	Pig	OM	Fish	Bird	N frags
Anglo-Scandinavian and Late Saxon							
16–22 Coppergate (*AY* 15/3, 151) All Anglo-Scandinavian	59.0	21.7	12.1	1.8	0.2	4.6	54020
1–9 Micklegate All Anglo-Scandinavian	61.4	12.6	13.4	7.2	1.1	4.3	1184
Flaxengate, Lincoln (O'Connor 1982) All Anglo-Scandinavian	52.7	27.2	10.4	5.7	0.7	0.7	13104
North Elmham Park II (Noddle 1980) Late 9th–early 11th century	26.9	38.6	21.2	6.3	0.1	7.0	3892
Site 1092, Thetford (Jones 1984) 9th–10th century	38.5	26.1	16.5	6.6	2.8	9.6	2386
Portchester Castle (Grant 1976) Late period, 10th–11th century	40.5	24.6	15.1	8.9	0.2	10.5	2542
'Viking Age' or equivalent Scotland and Ireland							
Skaill, Orkney (Noddle 1997) 9th–10th century century	45.7	37.6	11.6	5.2	*	*	6024
Buckquoy, Orkney (Noddle 1978) 9th–10th century	43.1	26.8	14.4	6.6	4.3	4.7	3236
Waterford (McCormick 1997) Late 11th–early 12th century	53.1	19.8	23.7	3.3	*	*	1891
12th century	61.5	17.0	17.2	4.3	*	*	2594
Dublin, Fishamble Street (McCormick 1982) 10th century	74.3	19.5	5.1	0.8	*	*	1927
Middle Saxon England							
Melbourne Street, Southampton (Bourdillon and Coy 1980) 8th–9th century	49.5	30.0	14.4	1.0	2.7	2.5	48258
Brandon (Crabtree 1996) 8th–9th century	26.1	47.8	17.7	2.2	*	6.2	51478
Wicken Bonhunt (Crabtree 1996) 8th–9th century	14.4	10.8	58.5	1.3	*	15.1	35800
Ipswich (Crabtree 1996) Late 7th–9th century	41.4	20.8	30.0	1.8	*	6.3	10426
Peabody site, London (West 1993a) Late 7th–9th century	45.1	22.0	28.9	1.1	0.0	2.8	5077
Maiden Lane, London (West 1993b) Late 7th–9th century	52.3	15.4	27.9	1.6	*	2.8	5537
Mainland north-western Europe							
Deventer (Ijzereef and Laarman 1986) 10th–12th century	61.9	12.7	22.6	2.9	*	*	700
Ribe (Hatting 1991) 8th century	51.1	18.8	25.0	3.7	0.2	1.1	6102
Birka (Ericson et al. 1988) 9th–10th century	38.1	16.0	34.2	0.9	10.8	3.3	11750
(Wigh 2001) Phase 6 AD 860–900	33.7	18.1	41.4	6.8	*	*	4094
Phase 7 900–930/940	39.3	14.5	39.2	7.1	*	*	3486
Phase 8 mid 10th century	36.4	15.5	42.5	5.6	*	*	2949

Table 24 (*contd*)

	Cattle	Sheep	Pig	OM	Fish	Bird	N frags
Hedeby (Reichstein and Thiessen 1974) Late 9th–early 11th century	47.3	14.3	37.1	0.7	*	0.6	29772
Eketorp (Boessneck et al. 1979) 10th–11th century	32.1	49.2	13.5	3.8	0.4	1.0	210548
'Slavic' Eastern Europe							
Cositz (Muller 1985) 8th–10th century	29.3	29.1	31.6	6.5	0.1	3.5	1955
Menzlin (Benecke 1988) 9th–10th century	30.0	9.5	55.4	1.9	*	3.2	29567
Arkona, phase 1 (Muller 1980) 9th–10th century	21.3	33.6	37.3	1.5	1.3	5.1	3200
Oldenburg, horizont 3–5 (Prummel 1991) 10th century	29.8	17.0	46.2	3.0	0.0	4.0	15980
Mecklenburg (Muller 1984) 10th–11th century	22.0	13.7	53.5	4.1	*	6.8	8054
Schonfeld (Teichert 1985) 11th–12th century	50.3	15.9	23.4	8.5	*	1.9	517

Moving eastwards, the continental examples are marked by an increasing relative abundance of pig bones. This is most marked in the 'Slavic' sites, with the exception of the small sample from Schonfeld, but can be seen to a lesser extent at Hedeby and Birka. Eketorp III, with its abundance of sheep, is an exception to the trend, a high-status rural site that stands out in much the same way as Brandon and North Elmham Park. Wigh (2001, 102) cites mostly unpublished data from sites in Sweden to show that a high proportion of pigs is seen in towns such as Birka and Sigtuna, and at several 'aristocratic manor' sites, though not at all rural sites of this date. Pigs are relatively uncommon in the small assemblages from Lingnare A (10th century) and Paviken (9th–10th century). Those exceptions aside, the greater abundance of pigs in more easterly sites is quite a distinct trend, and seems to continue across any nominal eastern boundary of 'Scandinavian' influence into the 'Slavic' region. The comparatively high relative abundance of pigs at Birka and Hedeby may therefore reflect regional trends in husbandry regimes, which in turn were probably a reflection of large-scale environmental zonation.

One means of isolating a distinctively 'Scandinavian' animal husbandry regime might be to examine the regime that was transported to newly colonised lands in the North Atlantic region. Amorosi (1991) provides a summary of data from sites in Iceland. Whether or not Iceland was completely unoccupied at the time of the first Scandinavian settlement, there would not have been an in situ husbandry tradition to which to adapt. Amorosi shows that the earliest settlements, representing the *landnam* period from AD 860 to about 930, have yielded assemblages in which bird bones predominate, indicating highly targeted wildfowling, presumably while the first herds and flocks were established. The domestic mammal bones are mostly cattle, with some caprines (probably mostly sheep) and a few horse bones. These assemblages are most unusual for Iceland. By the Commonwealth period (930 to late 1200s), caprines are overwhelmingly predominant amongst the domestic mammals, with the proportions of birds and fish varying between sites according to local opportunities and needs. Again, there are indications of an initial tendency towards a cattle-based husbandry regime, in this instance rapidly abandoned as the new settlers adapted to conditions in Iceland.

What the regional comparisons appear to show is a capacity to adapt animal husbandry strategies to local traditions and circumstances, and the York data should be seen in that light. A numerical predominance of cattle, mostly kept to adulthood as multi-purpose edible tractors, was in place in the 8th century. That regime continues through the 9th, 10th and 11th centuries, with some changes in the utilisation of pigs, birds and fish, perhaps reflecting changes in social relations within the city.

Conclusions

The Anglo-Scandinavian period is important in the study of the city's zooarchaeology, not so much because of any outstandingly 'Viking' characteristics as because it is the period in which York was re-established as a major trading and service centre. What we have been able to infer about the husbandry and utilisation of livestock in York shows a general similarity to other sites in the zone of Scandinavian influence, with the differences attributable to pre-existing regional differences in animal husbandry. Further investigation of the Scandinavian connections might focus on the importation of animals, for example, by re-examining some of the accumulations of antler from sites such as Clifford Street specifically for the presence of elk or reindeer. Deer as a whole are represented almost exclusively by antler. We might wonder whether the apparent lack of hunting was dictated by a lack of need, lack of time and personnel, or by the statutory restriction of the right to hunt. We are accustomed to think of exclusive hunting 'forests' as a phenomenon of Norman and later England, but recent research indicates that the arrogation of hunting rights by the social elite can be traced to the Late Saxon period (Naomi Sykes, *in litt.*).

The evidence that carcasses were used intensively is interesting. This appears to have been the case in each of the samples of Anglo-Scandinavian York examined to date, and could be tested in any subsequent excavations without needing particularly large samples. It remains unclear whether the butchering of foot-bones for marrow, for example, indicates a real need to extract all possible food value from a carcass, or whether it was simple custom and practice. Certainly there are few other indications of a food supply under severe strain. The cattle skulls from Blake Street give a hint that deposition of primary butchery waste did sometimes occur in Anglo-Scandinavian York. The lack of butchery apparent on those skulls argues that the generally more inten-

sive butchery was driven by custom rather than need, and was not an invariable practice.

The animal bones have given some indications that York's rivers might have been adversely affected during this period. Obviously, this is not a question that can be addressed through bones alone. Data pertaining to river levels, and evidence of water quality, for example from freshwater molluscs, will be necessary to resolve the interpretation of the changes in the freshwater fish seen in 9th- to 11th-century assemblages. Another topic that requires further data is the question of heterogeneity in livestock during this period. Given some larger samples to compare with the assemblage from Coppergate, it might be possible to test for the presence of different demes of livestock, as has been demonstrated for medieval York (*AY* 15/5). At the moment, even given the material from Micklegate, North Street and other sites, the large size of the Coppergate assemblage means that it predominates in any studies of 9th- and 10th-century livestock from the city and its catchment. The analysis of ancient DNA, for example through analysis of mtDNA haplotypes, is a potential line of investigation of genotype, though heterogeneity in husbandry regime might also become apparent given further material.

It might seem inappropriate to be phrasing these conclusions in terms of the further lines of research that merit investigation. However, the point is that there is still much to be investigated about the zooarchaeology of Anglo-Scandinavian York. Some further research can, and should, be based on further studies of the material to hand, particularly the enormous quantity from Coppergate. However, it is clear that some important questions require the targeted recovery and study of further material from new sites around the city. Even small excavations will yield some useful information, such as confirming the generally intensive use of carcasses or the near-absence of deer, but some lines of investigation, such as spatial variation in sources of livestock, will only be feasible given quite substantial assemblages. This overview has shown that a considerable amount of information has been inferred about the livestock, companion animals, vermin and wildlife of Anglo-Scandinavian York, and the intention has been that it should inform and stimulate further research into a topic which is far from fully investigated.

Art in Pre-Conquest York

By Dominic Tweddle

On the eve of the Coppergate excavations in 1976, it was scarcely possible to frame questions about the development of art in York from the Anglian period through into the Viking Age. The gaps in the evidence were simply too large. This is not to suggest that no work had been done. York antiquaries had made formidable and extensive collections of objects from excavations in the city over some 200 years; much of this material was deposited in the Yorkshire Museum. These objects, supplemented by those from more systematic archaeological work in the early 20th century, had been summarised by Dudley Waterman (Waterman 1959). More modern excavations, including those by York Archaeological Trust, had also contributed to the understanding of the material culture and art of the pre-conquest city. This material had been surveyed by Arthur MacGregor (MacGregor 1978). Above all, James Lang, building on the work of W.G. Collingwood (Collingwood 1927) and Ian Pattison (Pattison 1973), had embarked on a masterly analysis of the sculpture of late pre-conquest York and Yorkshire, showing how Viking forms and styles were assimilated into Anglian art to form something recognisably new and equally recognisably focused on York (Lang 1978a). This work has since been consolidated in the *Corpus of Anglo-Saxon Stone Sculpture* (Lang et al. 1991). Apart from Lang's well-founded and documented conclusions drawn from the relatively abundant sculptures, all of this work did little more than demonstrate a few simple facts: that practically nothing was known of art in York in the Anglian period, although individual small objects decorated in recognisable styles such as the Trewhiddle style, could be identified; that there was a handful of objects from the city decorated in recognisable Viking art styles; and that there was the possibility of a substantial continental European stream of influence on the art of Anglian and Viking-Age York.

At the end of the Coppergate excavations in 1981, over 30,000 individual objects had been identified and recorded, supplemented with additional material from the subsequent watching brief (1981–2) and excavations at the adjacent 22 Piccadilly (1987). It cannot be pretended that this material presents the scholar with the artistic riches of say the excavations of Viking-Age Dublin (e.g. Lang 1988), but enough material has emerged and of sufficient diversity for a radical re-appraisal of art in York from the conversion of the Kingdom of Northumbria in the 7th century to the eve of the Norman conquest.

Arguably the earliest decorated post-Roman object from Coppergate, and clearly the most significant, is the late 8th-century helmet from Coppergate (*AY* 17/8). For the first time, this object affords an insight into the lavish metalwork of Anglian York recorded so abundantly in the historical sources, as in Alcuin's *Poem on the Kings, Bishops and Archbishops of York* (Godman 1982; *AY* 1, 141–4), but hitherto absent from the archaeological record. Equally, the helmet tells us something about manuscript art in York, a subject which has tantalised generations of scholars in the absence of any illuminated manuscript which could firmly be assigned to a York *scriptorium*, although there is now emerging evidence that the Durham *Cassiodorus* was in the Library of York Minster (Alexander 1978, *17*, ills.74–7). The inscriptions on the helmet form a clear and tangible link between metalwork and manuscript, and at least allow the general nature of manuscript decoration in the city in this period to be discerned. The decoration of the helmet and of the Durham *Cassiodorus* appear closely related, particularly in their use of paired animals with contoured and textured bodies enmeshed in interlace. All this, of course, assumes that the helmet was made and not just lost in York, a supposition that is reasonable if not certain (see p.352). If so, then the craftsmen of York were capable of creating objects of subtle and ordered beauty within a liturgical or at least literate framework. Of course, the Coppergate helmet is special and may even be royal; what is arguably the earliest service for consecrating Anglo-Saxon kings preserved in the Lanalet pontifical, for example, uses a helmet instead of a crown (Deansley 1962, 81; Tweddle 2001a, 24, 26).

The helmet from Coppergate at least helps to make sense of the other fragments of 8th-century art from York, such as the motif piece from York Castle (*AY* 7/2, *171*, fig.106), a fine bone pin head from York (Waterman 1959), the pin head from St Mary's Abbey

(*AY* 7/2, *59*, fig.71), the reworked sgraffito decorated fragment from Blake Street (Tweddle 1984; *AY* 7/2, *80*, fig.76), and the enamel brooch from Paragon Street (ibid., *76b*, fig.73). All of these, if small or fragmentary, are accomplished and cosmopolitan objects, as fine as anything to be found elsewhere in Anglo-Saxon England.

The helmet from Coppergate stands in date at the edge of a major period of change in Anglo-Saxon art, essentially reflecting new ideas and impulses generated by the Carolingian Empire. Several objects from Coppergate illuminate this change. The first of them is a small blue glass hemispherical stud mounted in false filigree (Fig.105) (*AY* 17/14, *10541*, 2554–5). This can only come from an object such as the Ormside bowl; indeed the stud would fit neatly onto the bowl in place of one of its missing studs. The Ormside bowl has a new and novel repertoire of decoration involving naturalistic animals inhabiting lush and naturalistically drawn plants. The formal arrangement of the decoration on the object continues earlier traditions, but the decoration is new in form and spirit (Garri-

son et al. 2001, 25, *42*). It is arguable that the Ormside bowl is a York product. More importantly, we can now see that the same impulses which shaped the decoration of the bowl were active in York. From the York Minster excavations has come an extraordinarily fine fragmentary cross shaft decorated with similar birds and animals inhabiting a plant scroll (ibid., 14; Lang et al. 1991, Minster 1, pls.1–5). Other similar plants and animals, sometimes in combination with naturalistic human figures, are found at sites across Yorkshire, including the archbishops' estate at Otley (Collingwood 1927, fig.52), Little Ouseburn (Garrison et al., 33, *51*), Easby (Collingwood 1927, fig.53), Rothwell (Collingwood 1915, 236, Rothwell a), Masham (Collingwood 1927, fig.55) and Dewsbury. At Masham and Dewsbury there are shafts of circular section decorated with superimposed ranges of figures, arguably intended as triumphal columns to echo those of Trajan and Marcus Aurelius in Rome. It is highly likely that these new classicising artistic trends focus on and emanate from York (Tweddle 2001b, 16–18).

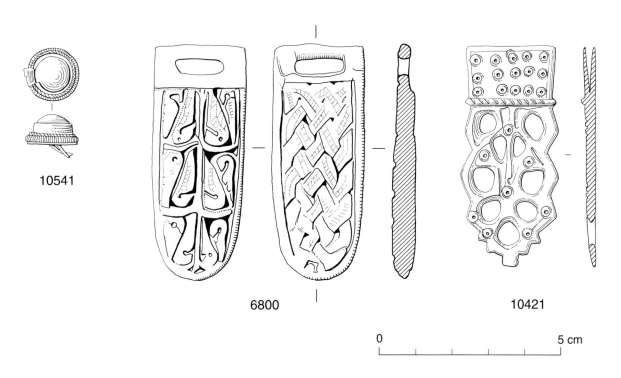

10541

6800

10421

0   5 cm

Fig.105 *Artefacts from 16–22 Coppergate which reflect new ideas generated by the Carolingian Empire: blue glass stud mounted in false filigree,* 10541; *bone strap-end with interlocked leaves,* 6800; *openwork copper alloy strap-end with debased plant decoration,* 10421. *Scale 1:1*

Returning to Coppergate, fragments of a cross shaft (*AY 7/2, 23*, fig.69) are decorated with finely drawn plant ornament in this new naturalistic tradition of the late 8th and early 9th centuries, reflecting the links between the Carolingian Empire and York, a relationship reflected or even mediated by Alcuin (Tweddle 2001b, 17–18). More prosaically, these naturalistic plants are transmuted into formal patterns on everyday objects, such as a bone strap-end with classic 9th-century leaves interlocked (*AY* 17/12, 1942–3, *6800*) and on an openwork copper alloy strap-end where the plant has been made almost unrecognisable (*AY* 17/14, 2569–70, *10421*) (Fig.105). Interestingly, the bone strap-end deploys a 9th-century leaf form, but on an object which on grounds of its form is arguably 10th century. This hints at the re-use of early

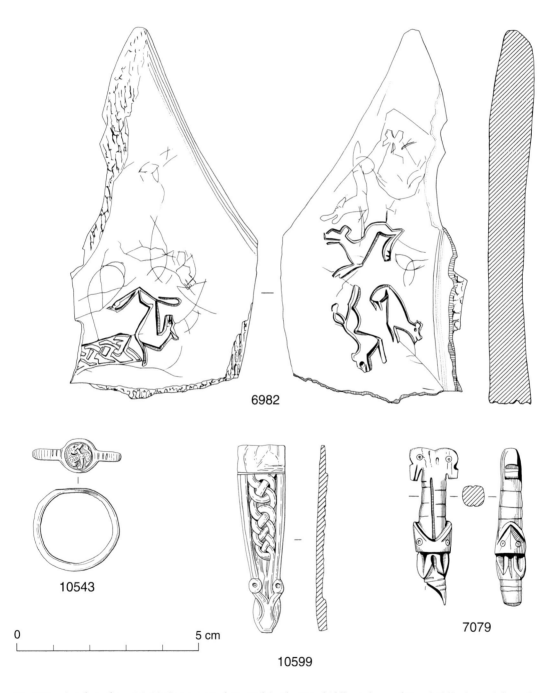

Fig.106 *Artefacts from 16–22 Coppergate decorated in the Trewhiddle style or of Trewhiddle-derived form: bone motif piece, 6982; silver finger-ring, 10543; lead alloy strap-end, 10599; bone tuning peg, 7079. Scale 1:1*

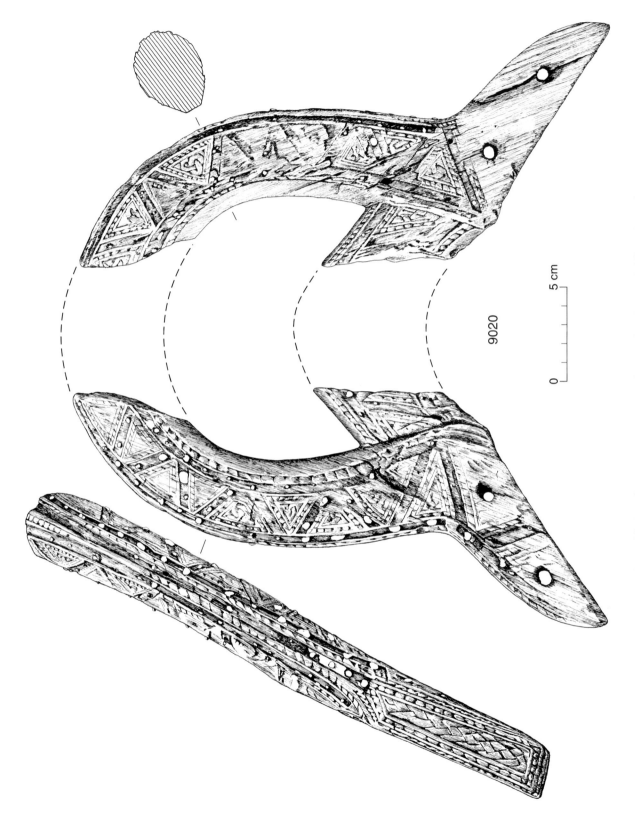

9020

5 cm

0

Fig.107   Wooden saddle bow from 16–22 Coppergate decorated in the Trewhiddle style. Scale 1:2

449

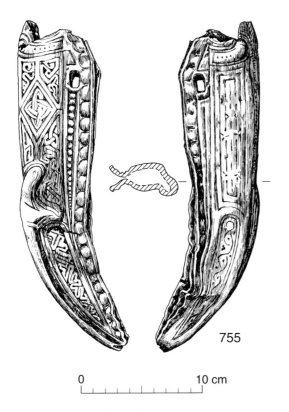

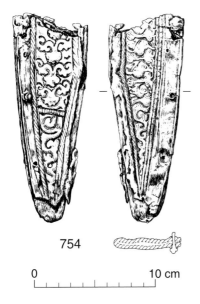

decorative schemes in later contexts, something encountered in York also in the Viking Age and discussed in more detail below.

This new interest in naturalistic animals and plants finds expression in other objects from Coppergate, particularly those decorated in the so-called Trewhiddle style (Wilson and Blunt 1961; Wilson 1964, 21–35). A bone motif piece from the site is decorated on both sides with animals in this style (*AY* 17/12, 1961, *6982*) and a finger-ring is similarly decorated (*AY* 17/14, 2585, *10543*) (Fig.106). A single strap-end also exhibits Trewhiddle-derived form if not decoration (ibid., 2569, *10599*) (Fig.106). This style was ubiquitous in 9th-century England, and equally so in York. There are dozens of small pieces of copper alloy decorated in this style from York (e.g. *AY* 7/2, *175–6*, fig.107; *185–9*, fig.111), and it is reflected also in gold on a ring from Fishergate (ibid., *170*, figs.104–5), in wood on a saddle bow from Coppergate (*AY* 17/13, 2341–5, *9020*) (Fig.107), in leather on a scabbard from Parliament Street (*AY* 17/4, 240–1, *755*) (Fig.108) and in bone on innumerable decorated antler tines (*AY* 7/2, *153–4*, fig.102) and pin heads (ibid., *151–2*, fig.102) from the Clifford Street area, and a tuning peg from Coppergate (*AY* 17/12, 1979–80, *7079*) (Fig.106). Hall has pointed out that the Trewhiddle style objects from Coppergate, which are the best-stratified and most closely datable examples from

Fig.108   *Leather scabbard from Parliament Street decorated in the Trewhiddle style. Scale1:3*

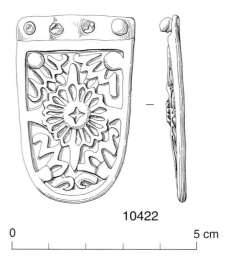

Fig.109   *Artefacts decorated with acanthus in the Winchester style: leather scabbard* 754 *from the Parliament Street sewer trench (scale 1:3) and copper alloy strap-end* 10422 *from 16–22 Coppergate (scale 1:1)*

York, are all from Anglo-Scandinavian contexts. He has suggested that such objects continued to be made and used in York, even after the Viking conquest (R.A. Hall, pers. comm.). Hall's view is substantiated by the late date of some of the contexts from which Trewhiddle style objects have been recovered. The saddle bow for example comes from a context dated c.975–11th century. However, it must be recalled that the Trewhiddle style was long lived, not just a 9th-century phenomenon. For this reason Wilson assigned a broad 9th-/10th-century date to it.

After the Viking conquest of York, the city certainly remained open to artistic influences and impulses from elsewhere in England. A heavily corroded strap-end from 6–8 Pavement is decorated with acanthus in the manner of the Winchester style (*AY* 17/3, 89, *451*, fig.46, pl.IIIb–c). A scabbard from York is also decorated with acanthus-derived foliage (*AY* 17/4, 237–40, *754*) (Fig.109). This type of decoration again is derived from the Carolingian world, and a classic Carolingian acanthus-decorated strap-end has come from Coppergate itself (*AY* 17/14, 2570, *10422*) (Fig.109). That such strap-ends influenced the craftsmen of both Anglo-Saxon and Viking England is demonstrated by the change in form of strap-ends witnessed at the turn of the 9th and 10th centuries, from the more pointed forms of the Trewhiddle style to the more rounded form of the Carolingian type. One object that we know was imported from southern England into York is the York Gospels, still preserved in the library of York Minster (Temple 1976, *61*, pls.181–4). The evangelist portraits and other decoration of this manuscript are in the Winchester style (Fig.110). It is thought that this Gospel book was commissioned from the *scriptorium* of Christ Church Canterbury before 1020 and then brought to York c.1020–30.

Fig.110 *Portrait of St Matthew from the York Gospels (67 MS Add.1, fo.22v; reproduced by courtesy of York Minster Archive, © Dean and Chapter of York)*

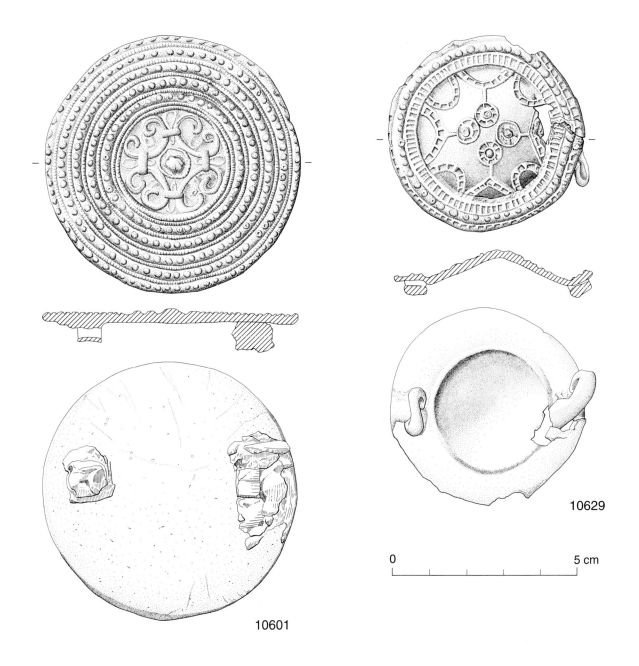

Fig.111 *Disc brooches from 16–22 Coppergate which reflect both southern English fashions and the fashions of Ottonian Germany. Scale 1:1*

Reflecting both southern English fashions and also the fashions of Continental Europe, in this case Ottonian Germany, are the numerous small disc brooches from Coppergate and other sites in York and the area (*AY* 17/14, 2571–4, *10601–2, 10629*; Waterman 1959, fig.10; *AY* 7/2, *103*, fig.88). These usually have a central circular field which is decorated and surrounded by concentric ribbed circles representing false filigree (Fig.111). Examples are known with real filigree cir-

cles held together on the reverse by soldered plates (Hinton 1974, 14, *6*, pl.V), and with skeuomorphic plates on the reverse (*AY* 7/2, *103*, fig.88), the whole brooch actually being cast as a single piece, so the evolution of the type is clear. Such brooches are found widely in southern England (e.g. Wilson 1964), and in Ottonian Germany, and although the decoration varies in detail, the repertoire is usually much the same — crosses, foliage often arranged as a cross, and

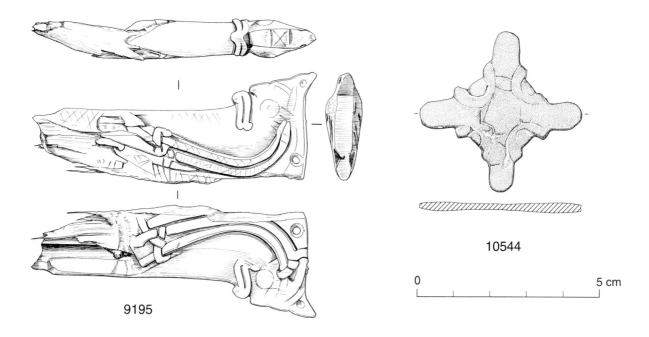

Fig.112   *Artefacts from York decorated in the Ringerike style: wooden knife handle from 22 Piccadilly, 9195; quatrefoil lead matrix from 16–22 Coppergate, 10544. Scale 1:1*

sometimes animals or coin-derived motifs. All of these occur in York.

If York remained open to and in touch with the artistic trends of southern England, it was also opened to new sources of artistic inspiration by the Viking conquest. The Coppergate excavations have been crucial in understanding the extent to which York became Viking, at least in artistic terms. In fact there are very few decorated objects from York which are purely Scandinavian. A Jellinge-style scabbard chape from Coppergate, but not from the recent excavations, is a classic Scandinavian object with parallels from as far away as Russia (Waterman 1959, fig.6, cf. Wilson and Klindt-Jensen 1964). Similarly, a Borre-style pendant matrix in the Yorkshire Museum is part of the manufacturing process of a classic Scandinavian type, seen, for example in the Tolstrup hoard, Denmark (Roesdahl et al. 1981, YMW13). A Borre-style strap-end from St Mary Bishophill Junior (ibid., YD39, 121) employs a classic ring chain, but on a form of object which is derived from the Carolingian world and used widely in Anglo-Saxon England. The Ringerike decorated knife handle from 22 Piccadilly deploys the full stylistic repertoire of the style and would be equally at home anywhere in the

Viking world (*AY* 17/13, 2284, *9195*), while a Ringerike-style quatrefoil from Coppergate deploys one formal element of the style and may be considered as more or less pure in style (*AY* 17/14, 2476, *10544*) (Fig.112). For the rest, the objects retain elements of a given Scandinavian art style, but are so changed as to become something new or different. This raises the question as to how far these Scandinavian styles were actually understood in York. Here it may be helpful to extend Olwyn Owen's classification of the Urnes style to other Viking art styles found in England. She divided Urnes objects into those in the Urnes style, those which are Urnes made in England and those which are English Urnes, reflecting the degree to which they differ from classic Urnes-style objects (Owen 1979). If this is done, then the overwhelming number of Viking-style objects from York are in English versions of the style, preserving only echoes and resonances of the original.

Coppergate has produced a small number of Borre-style objects: a strap-end decorated with a ring chain (*AY* 17/14, 2569, *10423*, fig.1265) and two openwork badges (ibid., 2650, fig.1197, *4277–8*; discussed fully in Tweddle 1991). The strap-end deploys an Anglo-Saxon form, combined elsewhere with Trewhiddle-

Fig.113 (above and below) *Bone motif piece* 6981 *from* 16–22 *Coppergate decorated in the Jellinge style*

Fig.114 *Limestone grave-cover* 10826 *from* 16–22 *Coppergate decorated in the Jellinge style*

derived decoration, with a simplified ring chain or knot. It must be classified as English Borre. Equally the badges deploy openwork coiled animals combined with masks, all typical features of the Borre style. The animal forms are, however, deployed without understanding, and the objects themselves are of a form unknown in Scandinavia. Again a classification as English Borre seems appropriate. Looking elsewhere in the city Borre motifs, usually ring knot or chains, occur, but the whole repertoire of the style is not encountered as, for example, on sculptures from St Mary, Castlegate, adjacent to the Coppergate site (*AY* 8/2), or a wooden spoon from Clifford Street (Roesdahl et al. 1981, YDL11). A trefoil brooch mould from Blake Street preserves a Scandinavian form, with small Borre-related animal masks at the junctions of the arms, but otherwise the decoration of the arms is in the late Anglo-Saxon Winchester style (MacGregor 1978, 42, fig.24; Hall 1994, fig.96).

Jellinge-style objects also occur at Coppergate on a motif piece (*AY* 17/12, 1961–3, *6981*), a small lead alloy brooch (*AY* 17/14, 2571–2, *10604*) and a sculptured slab (ibid., 2601–2, *10826*; Hall 1994, colour pl.5; Lang et al. 1991, Coppergate 2, pls.327, 329–30) (Figs.113–14). Both the slab and the motif piece deploy pairs of ribbon-like animals with head lappets which are interlocked, a classic Jellinge-style arrangement. The slab also uses contouring and has the spiral hips also common in the Jellinge style. The animal bodies are, however, less elongated than those on the motif piece, a feature more common in Anglo-Saxon

art. If the animals on the motif piece were more complete, then they may have exhibited a more classic Jellinge form. Those on the slab are best thought of as either Jellinge made in England or more plausibly English Jellinge. Within York they fit into a context of sculptural production which deploys the same forms and stylistic tricks in various combinations, almost on an industrial scale. The small lead alloy disc brooch, and another closely similar from York (Waterman 1959, fig.10), deploy a classic Jellinge-style animal, encountered widely on pendants in Scandinavia. The animal from the Coppergate brooch again is chunkier and more naturalistic than those in Scandinavia. Equally, the form of the object is not Scandinavian. The animal decorated field is enclosed in concentric circles of false filigree, a form which, as noted above, is commonplace across Anglo-Saxon England and Ottonian Germany, but not in Scandinavia. Again the term English Jellinge seems appropriate.

Of the later Scandinavian art styles, Mammen, Ringerike and Urnes, there is little trace in York. There are no Mammen-style or derived objects from the city. In the Ringerike style, in addition to the knife handle and lead alloy object discussed on p.453, there are two other pieces, a fragmentary copper alloy mount from the College of the Vicars Choral at Bedern (*AY* 17/14, 2555, *10708*) and a hooked tag from Coppergate (ibid., 2576, *10437*) (Fig.115). The mount deploys tendrils with clubbed ends typical of the Ringerike style, but not enough survives for finer

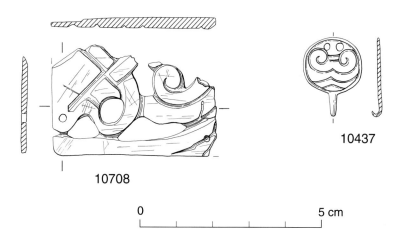

Fig.115 *Artefacts from York decorated in the Ringerike style: copper alloy mount from Bedern, 10708; copper alloy hooked tag from 16–22 Coppergate, 10437. Scale 1:1*

10708

10437

0   5 cm

judgements to be made about its style and affinities. The hooked tag deploys a bifurcating leaf motif typical of the Ringerike style, but which could equally have other stylistic origins. A single sculptured fragment from Holy Trinity Priory, Micklegate, exhibits some features of the Urnes style, but definitively English Urnes (Lang et al. 1991, Holy Trinity Micklegate 1, pl.203; *AY* 8/1, *40*, pl.Ib). It is possible that the decorated knife scabbard from Parliament Street (*AY* 17/4, 237–40, *753*, fig.107) with its interest in writhing ribbon-like bodies enmeshed in finer filliform strands indicates a relationship with the Urnes style, but if so it is a remote one and difficult to document adequately.

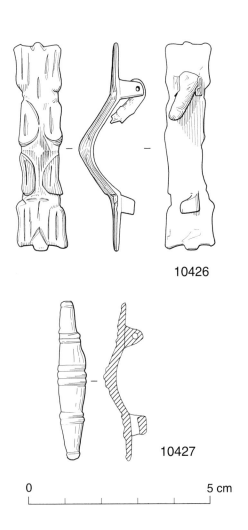

10426

10427

0   5 cm

Fig.116 Ansate brooches from 16–22 Coppergate possibly imported direct from continental Europe. Scale 1:1

Most of the objects from Coppergate having affinities with Viking art are from archaeological contexts later than the commonly suggested dates for the currency of the styles. They may, of course, be residual in later levels, but there is equally the possibility that motifs derived particularly from the Borre and Jellinge styles entered the repertoire of craftsmen in Anglo-Scandinavian York and simply went on being used without understanding long after those styles had fallen out of common currency in the Viking homelands. The two openwork badges noted above exemplify this point. They both come from late contexts, a 12th- or 13th-century context in one case (*4278*) and a 13th-century context in the other (*4277*). Their decoration, however, has very clear and marked parallels with the Borre style, even if debased and misunderstood. The most likely derivation for their decoration is from silver filigree disc brooches found widely in Scandinavia and decorated with gripping beasts in the Borre style. A classic example of the type comes from Finkarby, Taxinge, Södermanland, Sweden (Wilson 1978, 140; Wilson and Klindt-Jensen 1966, pl.XXIXk). On this brooch the four animal masks are placed in the centre with their bodies curving around them, whereas on the York badges the animal masks are placed on the rim of the object, as is the case with some of the pendants from Vårby, Huddinge, Södermanland, Sweden (ibid., pl.XXXIIb). While their decoration appears to be Borre-derived, the parallels for the form of the badges are wholly late, that is, 11th and 12th century. A similar badge from Lurk Lane, Beverley, for example, also comes from a 12th- or early 13th-century context (Tweddle 1991, 156, *708*, fig.117), so this is not simply an issue of residuality. There is the clear possibility that objects using Borre-derived motifs were being made in York after the Norman conquest. On the evidence discovered to date, this is a point which should not be pressed, but it does remind us that the course of assimilation of classic Viking art into the repertoire of York craftsmen is unlikely to have been simple or straightforward.

The material from Coppergate also raises some real issues about the artistic character of York in the late 9th, 10th and 11th centuries. As noted above, there is very little classic Viking art in the city. Instead Viking motifs, ideas and concepts are lifted and transformed, not necessarily with any clear understanding. Equally important are artistic ideas surviving from the Anglian tradition, and indeed deriving

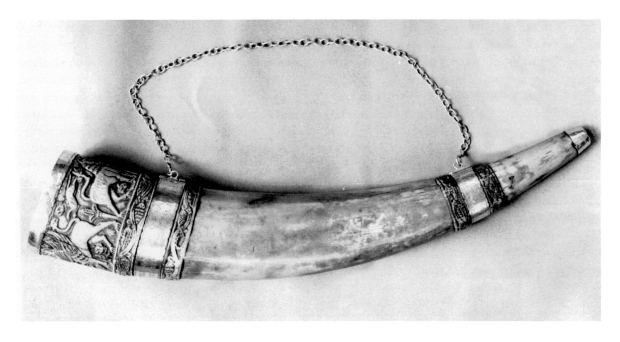

Fig.117 (a) Ivory Horn of Ulf in York Minster, with exotic animals carved around the throat; (b) drawing of decoration around the throat (scale 2:5)

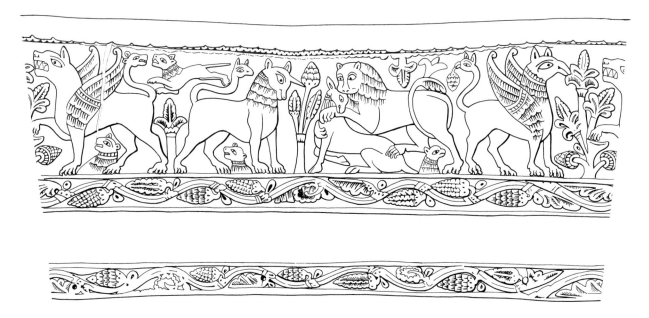

from the most up-to-date works of southern England, where the Winchester style and its varieties and derivatives became dominant. Anglian art and Anglo-Saxon art of the 10th and 11th centuries owed much to new ways of thinking about and viewing the world worked out in the Carolingian Empire and its successor states. These artistic impulses were also brought to bear in York, both through intermediaries and probably directly by the importation of works of art from continental Europe. Ansate brooches from Coppergate and other sites in York (*AY* 17/14, 2571, 10426–7), as well as pottery from continental Europe (*AY* 16/5, 477–84), remind us of these direct links (Fig.116). One object from York whose history it would be informative to discover is the Horn of Ulf in York Minster (MA/TR14). This magnificent ivory horn is an object of extraordinary richness, both in material and decoration. The exotic, orientalising animals

457

carved round its throat (Fig.117) point to an origin in Sicily or even the Near East, and the horn has a history which connects it with York just before the Norman conquest. This single object must now stand for the rich and varied objects which were probably reaching York from all parts of Europe and even beyond, and by a variety of different routes.

Indeed the pattern of artistic development and influences seen at Coppergate is what we might expect from studying the historical sources. Late Anglian York, viewed through the eyes of Alcuin at least, was rich and vibrant, fully in touch with developments at the Carolingian court. In many respects developments at the Northumbrian court may have paralleled those at the heart of the Empire (Tweddle 2001b). With the Viking conquest of York in 866, York and its hinterland were not cut off from Anglo-Saxon England and simply assimilated into Scandinavia. Instead the picture is more complex, with new links both political and commercial formed with Scandinavia, but within the context of continuing relationships with both Europe and the rest of England. What we may be seeing are different distributions of wealth and power reflected in the art as the balance between kings, nobles and the church varied over time. At least such questions can now be articulated, and in some in part answered: a sufficient tribute in itself to the importance both of the Coppergate excavation and the post-excavation marathon.

Craft and Economy in Anglo-Scandinavian York

By Ailsa Mainman and Nicola Rogers

From 866 to 1066 Anglo-Scandinavian York was a growing centre of producers and consumers, and an important focus for regional exchange and international trade. This chapter aims to summarise recent and current work on the range of crafts and industries which operated in the city and to draw some conclusions about the contribution they made to the economy of Viking-Age York.

Using artefacts and pottery evidence to plot the extent of Anglo-Scandinavian York

Several attempts have been made over the last 50 years to plot the extent of the Anglo-Scandinavian town which developed between 866 and 1066. Waterman's map (1959, fig.2) shows the distribution of artefacts of this date clustering around the Coppergate, High Ousegate and Piccadilly area, with only occasional dots elsewhere. Radley's map shows the Ousegate and Pavement area in more detail (Radley 1971, fig.7), and this concentration of discoveries is reflected again in Ramm's map (Ramm 1972, 251) which places this area in the wider York context. Ramm's map paints a very similar picture to Waterman's 1959 map, and this had not changed much by 1978 when Hall's map (Hall 1978, fig.20) showed essentially the same concentration with a few outliers. Even in 1986 the picture had not vastly altered; Moulden and Tweddle (AY 8/1, fig.1) show a denser cluster of dots in the Coppergate area and a scatter in the Roman fortress, the walled town south-west of the River Ouse, Walmgate and suburban districts.

These maps had been based mostly on diagnostic artefacts characteristic of the period, while some included coin hoards, pre-conquest churches and stone sculptures. There was little hope of separating the 200-year span of this period. Hall, however, made an attempt to chart broadly the evolution of the city from 866 to 1066 (Hall 1994, fig.12), suggesting that occupation in 866 might have clustered along the riverbanks and main Roman arteries, and might have been focused around known early ecclesiastical or high-status sites. He suggested a modest expansion by 900 and increasingly intense occupation by 950,

culminating in widespread settlement south-west of the River Ouse, around the fortress, the Walmgate suburb and along roads leading out of the city by 1066. This hypothetical sequence was based on knowledge of the accumulating evidence collected up until this time by York Archaeological Trust.

Of the evidence available, the most easily datable is the pottery. Studies based on the assemblage from 16–22 Coppergate (AY 16/5) have shown there were three main types of pottery current during the period. York wares dominate the market from the mid 9th–early/mid 10th century and were gradually replaced by Torksey-type wares in the course of the 10th century. York ware was probably out of production by c.950, if not earlier, and Torksey-type wares dominate the second half of the 10th century and early 11th century. Stamford wares, present throughout the 10th century, become more prominent in the second half of the 11th century. These three ceramic types can, therefore, operate as broad chronological indicators for the periods c.860–950, 950–1050, 1050–1100.

An attempt has been made here to draw together pottery data from antiquarian sources, from the records created by York Archaeological Trust since 1972 and from data collected by other archaeological units that have excavated in the city, and to use the evidence to chart the extent of the evolving city. Within the scope of this project it has not been possible to examine the assemblages of these 1,000 or more interventions in any detail; a rapid assessment was done to record the presence or absence of these pottery types from as many as possible of these sites (about 90%), using site records, published data and by scanning assemblages collected in the 1970s and early 1980s.

In assessing the value of the exercise several points need to be made. The currency of the various wares overlap so they can only serve as broad rather than exact chronological indicators. Using presence/absence gives no measure of the intensity of occupation across the city; that will have to wait for the more in-depth analysis of the assemblages. Blank areas on the map, most notably in the area around the Minster in the northern quadrant of the old Roman fortress, indicate lack of opportunity to excavate as much as lack of evidence. Equally, current planning policies have meant that excavation at some sites stops well above deposits of Anglo-Scandinavian date, although where these wares are present residually those data have been included. The question of redeposition of material from its original location has also to be considered, but perhaps does not affect the broad picture which the distribution patterns show.

With these limiting factors in mind, the distribution of York ware across the city suggests that between c.860–950 occupation was in the southern part of the old fortress and in the area to the south and south-east of the Roman fortress wall (Fig.118). This latter area had been largely blank on previous maps. The recognised focus around the Coppergate area is still apparent but there is more evidence to the south on the triangle of land between the two rivers. There is a greater density of dots south-west of the Ouse than on Moulden and Tweddle's 1986 map (*AY* 8/1), especially along the river bank. Most striking is the increased evidence for occupation at this early date in the Walmgate area, following the route of the street itself.

The distribution pattern of Torksey-type wares (Fig.119) illustrates an expanding city in the mid/second half of the 10th century. The core in the Coppergate area is still very evident but occupation has spread further to the south-east of the fortress between the old fortress wall and the River Foss. Recent borehole survey in this area has produced substantial quantities of Torksey-type wares and Stamford wares, indicating intensive activity and raising questions about the importance of the River Foss. South-west of the River Ouse, within the former Roman *colonia,* occupation has intensified along the river banks and has spread inland. In the Walmgate area there is evidence for expansion away from the street of Walmgate and along the modern Fulford Road. The distribution of Stamford ware (Fig.120), which takes the period into the later 11th century, shows the same pattern but with increased intensity. There is now evidence of occupation outside the fortress wall to the north, north-east and north-west for the first time (the Clarence Street, Monkgate and Marygate areas).

Bearing in mind the limitations of this approach, these maps give some index of the expanding occu-

pation of the town during the 200 years of the Anglo-Scandinavian period and provide a backdrop against which the other artefactual evidence can be analysed.

Economy and industry

Networks of regional exchange and international trade brought raw materials to the city. Silk cloth came from the east (*AY* 17/5) and amber was imported from the Baltic regions. Ores, ingots and charcoal used in the manufacture of iron, copper and other non-ferrous metal objects were obtained from the local region and other sources throughout the British Isles (*AY* 17/6; *AY* 17/7). Stone suitable for many purposes could be obtained in the local region, while lava quern stones were brought from the Rhineland; soapstone, schist and phyllite were brought from Scotland and southern Scandinavia (*AY* 17/14); hides and different species of wood were utilised for specific purposes (*AY* 17/16; *AY* 17/13), and raw materials for the production of woollen and linen cloth were available within the region (*AY* 17/11). Jet could be obtained from the North Yorkshire moors and coast (*AY* 17/14). Bones of wild and domestic animals were made into a range of everyday objects, while red deer antlers were gathered to make others (*AY* 17/12).

The mechanisms behind the supply of raw materials, and the production and distribution of finished products, can be only partially reconstructed. Far-reaching trade connections brought silks to York; club moss (used in cloth dyeing) and amber arrived as occasional items in long-distance exchange with Scandinavia which might have included fur, hides and other perishables as its main commodities. Other materials, such as deer antler, wool and flax, were available locally, but only seasonally, while other industries such as metal working could rely on a more steady supply of ores and fuel. The supply of raw materials, therefore, must have varied according to the vagaries of long-distance and regional trade, the season and the reliability of middlemen; sometimes, perhaps, local estate owners supplied their own in-town producers direct.

Some industries were fundamentally more important to the city's economy than others. Some required much more investment in infrastructure, technology and skills than others. Some might have been intermittent, as raw materials or peripatetic skilled craftsmen were available, while others were domestic in scale and character. There was, therefore, variety in

○ not located accurately

Fig.118   *Plan of York showing the distribution of York ware*

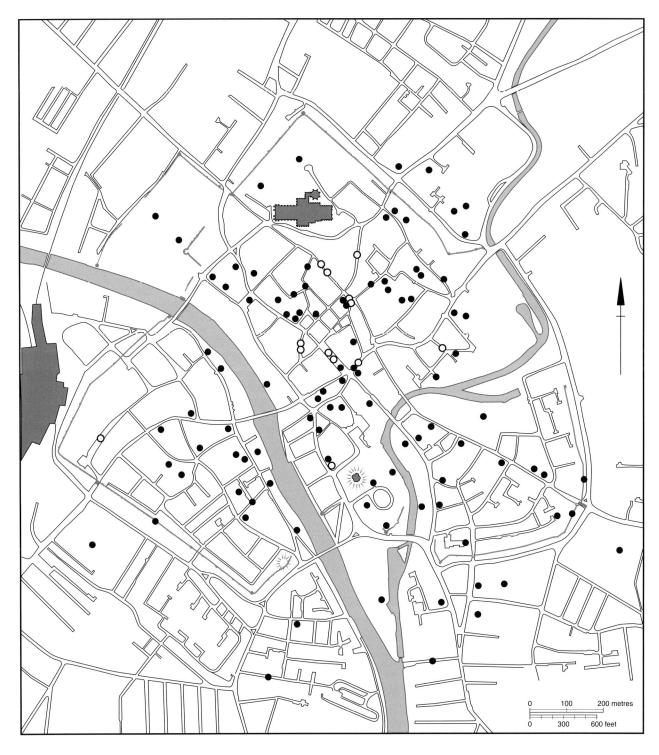

○ not located accurately

Fig.119 *Plan of York showing the distribution of Torksey-type ware*

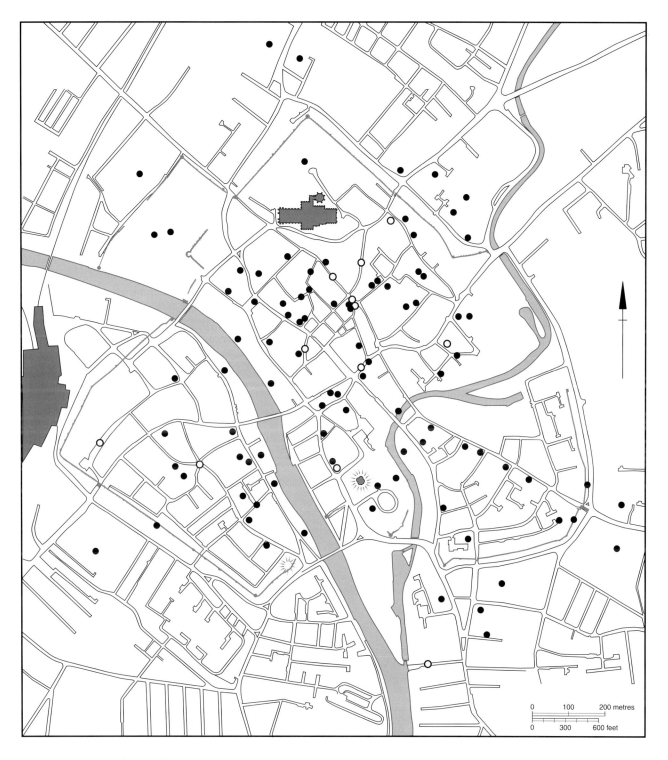

○ not located accurately

Fig.120   *Plan of York showing the distribution of Stamford ware*

the complexity and character of the various crafts and their operation.

The distribution of the evidence of production in the Anglo-Scandinavian city

The process employed

As with the pottery, data relating to Anglo-Scandinavian crafts and industries have been gathered from excavations, evaluations and watching briefs by York Archaeological Trust from 1972 to 2000. Artefacts recorded during excavations, evaluations and watching briefs by other archaeological organisations or groups working in the city, both those pre-dating the existence of YAT and those working alongside YAT, have also been noted, as have records made by antiquaries in the 19th and early 20th century. This evidence is presented as a gazetteer in an Appendix (pp.484–7). From this evidence, a series of tables relating to different manufacturing activities was compiled, and distribution maps based on these tables were produced.

The identification of craft activities

The following craft activities were identified:

1. iron working (from references to slag and/or smelting waste)

2. non-ferrous metal working (from references to crucibles, non-ferrous metal debris, brooch moulds and offcuts)

3. wood working (from references to wood working tools or pieces of worked wood including cores from lathe turning)

4. leather working (from references to leather working tools, and offcuts, scraps and other leather debris)

5. bone and/or antler working (from references to offcuts of bone or antler, and unfinished bone or antler objects). Some simple bone objects, however, would have been manufactured in a domestic context by non-specialists (see *AY* 17/12, 1913)

6. amber working (from references to the recovery of raw amber, amber offcuts and waste, partially worked and unfinished amber objects)

7. glass working (from references to glass bead-making, bead waste and unfinished beads)

8. jet working (from references to raw jet, jet rough-outs and offcuts, and unfinished jet objects)

9. textile working (from references to textile working tools). Textile production is classed as essentially a domestic activity (see pp.474).

Considerations and drawbacks

When considering the information collected, certain caveats in relation to the nature of the evidence must be borne in mind.

1. Chronology: some of the literature, particularly that concerning finds made during the last century, refers to material which cannot now be traced, so its nature and dating cannot be confirmed. Even amongst the material obtained more recently, some types of artefact are more readily and/or more specifically datable than others.

2. The nature of the burial deposits will undoubtedly have affected the chances of survival or non-survival of some types of material, particularly organic materials, so that the apparent absence of a certain type of activity on a particular site may have more to do with destructive soil conditions than with an actual absence.

3. Some materials are significantly less destructible than others, and less appropriate for recycling; a good example is antler, offcuts of which survive frequently and in good condition.

4. Recovery of any evidence is the result of an opportunity to work or observe work; certain parts of the city have not produced any evidence of Anglo-Scandinavian activity, but this may reflect the lack of investigation rather than the lack of evidence. The Coppergate/Clifford Street/Ousegate area has produced many opportunities for antiquarian and archaeological investigation and has long been considered the hub of the Viking-Age city, while there have been fewer opportunities for investigation around York Minster.

The crafts and industries

Iron working (Fig.121)

This activity is evident from iron slag and/or smelting waste. Although slag in particular is found on most sites, in some cases it might represent material dumped from elsewhere. To be confident that slag relates to iron working on site, it must be recovered in quantity and from stratified Anglo-Scandinavian deposits, as at 16–22 Coppergate (*AY* 17/6). The level of analysis applied at 16–22 Coppergate has not been

Fig.121 *Plan of York showing the distribution of evidence for iron working (for key see p.466)*

applied to most sites in this survey, and thus the presence of slag alone has not been taken to indicate iron working, although on some sites it may have resulted from such activity. Iron working is, therefore, almost certainly under-represented on Fig.121.

Apart from Coppergate, the most convincing evidence for iron working of this period comes from the York Minster excavations, where two major groups of 9th- to 11th-century metal working debris were identified, one of which came from contexts which also contained remains of a forge (see pp.493–4) (Phillips and Heywood 1995, 193). Elsewhere, possible contemporary iron working has been indicated at the south corner tower of the Roman fortress on Feasegate in the form of an iron smelting hearth

Key to sites on Figs.121–8

1. 31–37 Gillygate
2. Lord Mayor's Walk
3. Monkgate, County House
4. Monkgate, County Hospital
5. York Minster
6. 1–5 Aldwark
7. Jewbury
8. Goodramgate, Hunter and Smallpage
9. 9 Blake Street
10. St Andrewgate
11. 12–18 Swinegate
12. Little Stonegate/Swinegate
13. 1 King's Square
14. Little Stonegate/Davygate
15. 17–21 Davygate
16. Silver Street
17. 9 St Saviourgate
18. Peasholme Green
19. Haymarket, Peasholme Green
20. Hungate
21. Feasegate, south corner tower
22. Feasegate, British Home Stores
23. 16 Parliament Street
24. 11–13 Parliament Street
25. 24–30 Tanner Row
26. North Street, pumping station
27. 13–17 Coney Street
28. 39–41 Coney Street
29. 44–45 Parliament Street
30. Parliament Street, sewer trench
31. Pavement (Waterman 1959)
32. Parliament Street/Pavement
33. 22 Pavement
34. 6–8 Pavement
35. Parliament Street/High Ousegate (Radley 1971)
36. 1–9 Micklegate
37. 5 Coppergate
38. 20–21 High Ousegate
39. 25–27 High Ousegate

40. High Ousegate (1988.20)
41. Nessgate, Coach and Horses
42. Castlegate/Coppergate (Benson 1906)
43. 2 Clifford Street
44. 16–22 Coppergate
45. Coppergate watching brief
46. 22 Piccadilly
47. 5–13 Clifford Street
48. 23 Clifford Street
49. Clifford Street (Raine 1891)
50. Trinity Lane, Ideal Laundry
51. Trinity Lane, car park
52. Bishophill (Waterman 1959)
53. Skeldergate, NCP car park
54. 37 Bishophill Senior
55. 58–59 Skeldergate
56. Skeldergate, Albion Wharf
57. 38 Piccadilly
58. 41–49 Walmgate
59. 76–82 Walmgate
60. George Street
61. 104–112 Walmgate
62. 118–126 Walmgate
63. York Castle, car park 1
64. York Castle, car park 2
65. 50 Piccadilly
66. York Castle yard/Eye of York (Waterman 1959)
67. York Castle Yard, former female prison
68. York Castle/Eye of York (Grove 1940)
69. 84 Piccadilly
70. 41 Piccadilly
71. Margaret Street, St George's School
72. Leadmill Lane
73. Paragon Street/Kent Street
74. Fawcett Street
75. St George's Field
76. Baile Hill
77. 35–41 Blossom Street

(RCHMY **4**, xxix; Stead 1958), and on Fawcett Street, where slag was recovered from a 10th- to 11th-century pit. An iron mood or knife blank found in the Parliament Street sewer trench (*AY* 17/4) and a lead tank containing various iron tools apparently for recycling found in excavations at 9 St Saviourgate in 1997 may indicate the presence of a smith or smiths in that area in the late 9th–10th century (Spriggs and Vere-Stevens n.d.; Anon. 1998a).

Non-ferrous metal working (Fig.122)

The Coppergate/High Ousegate area has produced the most conclusive evidence of non-ferrous metal working. Benson noted barrow loads of copper alloy sheet offcuts from High Ousegate and the remains of furnaces which may date to the Anglo-Scandinavian period (Benson 1902, 66), while 16–22 Coppergate provided evidence that gold, silver, a range of copper alloys, lead, tin and pewter were all worked on the site from the late 9th century onwards (*AY* 17/7). At York Minster, non-ferrous metal working debris was recovered from contexts which had remains of a forge (see p.465). A Borre-/Winchester-

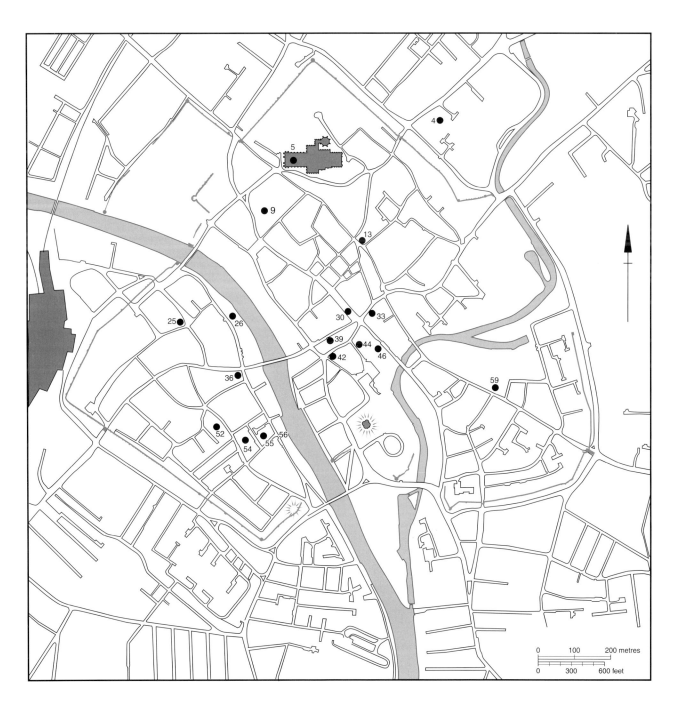

Fig.122 *Plan of York showing the distribution of evidence for non-ferrous metal working (for key see p.466)*

style (late 10th–early 11th century) trefoil brooch mould and a crucible fragment were found at Blake Street (*AY* 3/4, 363). On other sites, the main evidence for Anglo-Scandinavian non-ferrous metal working is in the form of Stamford ware crucibles, although some may have been for glass working rather than metal working. These are not suitable for recycling and are virtually indestructible. Small amounts of such debris have been recovered along the line of North Street/Skeldergate; elsewhere in the city a site on Walmgate produced a crucible and some waste, and an ingot mould was found at 1 King's Square.

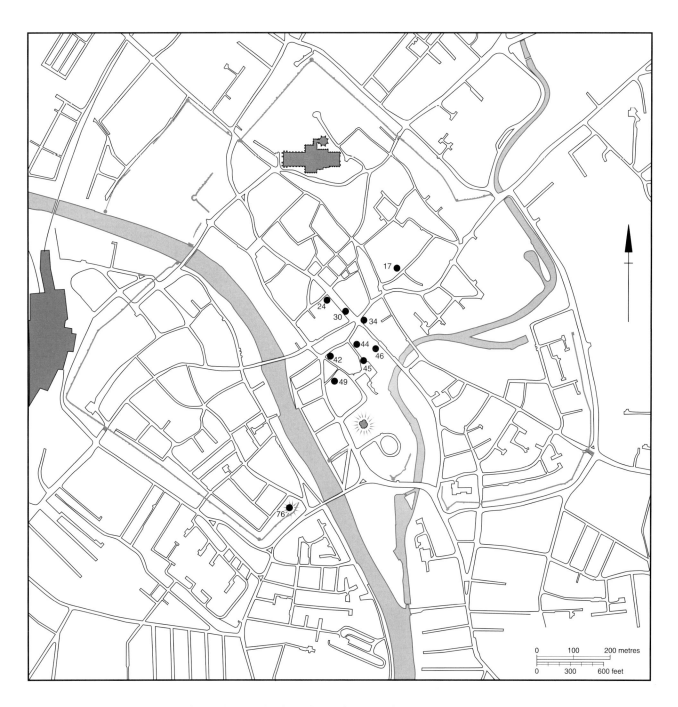

Fig.123 *Plan of York showing the distribution of evidence for wood working (for key see p.466)*

Wood working (Fig.123)

The sites excavated in the 1970s–1980s by YAT at 16–22 Coppergate (including the later watching brief) and 22 Piccadilly produced large quantities of waste, including cores, from the lathe turning of bowls and cups, and also iron tools for felling/splitting (wedges, axes), shaping (axes, slice, paring chisel, hand gouges, mallet), boring holes (bow drills, spoon bits, gimlets), other specialised tools (round shave), and lathe turners' tools (tool-rest). Dr Carole Morris in her study of the wood working evidence from the area was of the opinion that 'in addition to strong street-name evidence' (that the name Coppergate comes from the Old Scandinavian for 'street of the makers of wooden vessels'; see p.364), the waste and tools 'indicate that this entire sector of the Anglo-Scandinavian city of York was an area of intense specialist lathe turning activity, on either a semi-permanent or seasonal basis, for over 200 years in the 9th–11th centuries' (*AY* 17/13, 2391).

No other sites in the city have produced evidence of wood working in the form of significant amounts of wooden waste, but elsewhere in York different types of soil conditions will not have allowed preservation of organic materials in the same way. As Dr Morris also points out, 'most wooden objects would have been re-used or burnt as fuel when they were worn out or broken' (ibid., 2094), as might large quantities of otherwise useless waste; this again may account for the lack of survival of such material elsewhere. The recovery of over 300 wooden cores at 16–22 Coppergate is, therefore, perhaps, out of the ordinary. A hook-ended iron used for lathe turning was found nearby in excavations in 1906 at the corner of Castlegate/Coppergate, a site which also produced other tools including two wooden mallets (Benson 1906).

In the same general area of the city, iron tools associated with wood working have been recovered: axes used for tree felling, hewing and splitting have been found on Coppergate (Waterman 1959, 72, fig.5, *8*) and at Baile Hill (Addyman and Priestley 1977, 139, fig.10, *5*). Wooden wedges used in splitting wood were recovered at 6–8 Pavement (*AY* 17/3, *484–6*), and a T-shaped axe for shaping was found at Parliament Street (Waterman 1959, 72, fig.5, *7*). Nearby on Clifford Street another wooden mallet along with 'pieces of wrought wood' were found (Raine 1891). Axes and mallets may have been used in construction activities rather than the production of wooden

vessels. Every household might have owned an axe, using it to chop firewood. These tools cannot therefore be considered definitely diagnostic of wood working in the way specific lathe turning tools can.

Finally, the lead tank found at 9 St Saviourgate contained various iron tools including an auger, its blade apparently removed for recycling; this appears to be a hoard deposit, however, and may be related to the activities of a smith (see p.466) rather than a wood worker (P.J. Ottaway, pers. comm.).

Leather working (Fig.124)

As with wood, scraps of leather only survive in certain conditions, thus biasing the recovery of this material. Unlike wood, however, there is little use for the discarded pieces after working, so recycling is not an issue in the interpretation of leather working debris.

Leather working comprises different activities which might, as in the medieval period, have been undertaken by different craftsmen; shoe-makers or cordwainers made footwear, while belts, purses, sheaths and other products were made by other craftsmen. Cobblers repaired shoes and bought old shoes to repair and sell on (see *AY* 17/16). The most comprehensive range of evidence, as might be expected, comes from 16–22 Coppergate, where large quantities of leather artefacts and offcuts were recovered, as well as iron tools indicating both the manufacture and cobbling of shoes, and the manufacture of sheaths and scabbards, possibly by different craftsmen (see *AY* 17/16). Elsewhere, 1–9 Micklegate produced a large assemblage of manufacturing debris and shoes, scabbards and sheaths. Offcuts suggesting cobbling were also found at Feasegate, Hungate, King's Square, 6–8 Pavement and St Andrewgate, and a note refers to leather found on Silver Street (Benson 1902, 67), although it is unclear what that leather included. Finally, the St Saviourgate lead tank contained iron leather working tools, including awls and drawknives; awls seem to have had less value as scrap than other tools and it is possible that the owner of the objects, perhaps a smith, also engaged in leather working (P.J. Ottaway, pers. comm.).

Bone and antler working (Fig.125)

Large amounts of debris from the making of combs, pins, skates and other artefacts have been

Fig.124   *Plan of York showing the distribution of evidence for leather working (for key see p.466)*

recovered from the same Coppergate/Castlegate/ Clifford Street/High Ousegate area. Excavations at 16–22 Coppergate produced a considerable amount of both antler and bone waste, although even this was not considered sufficient to indicate a long-term settled workshop. It might indicate itinerant crafts-men skilled in the production of antler combs; decor-ated bone pins or strap-ends might also be part of a specialist's repertoire (*AY* 17/12, 2005). At the same time, the presence of simple bone objects such as plain pins, buzz-bones or femur head spindle whorls may represent a domestic rather than a com-mercial activity, making use of discarded food and other debris.

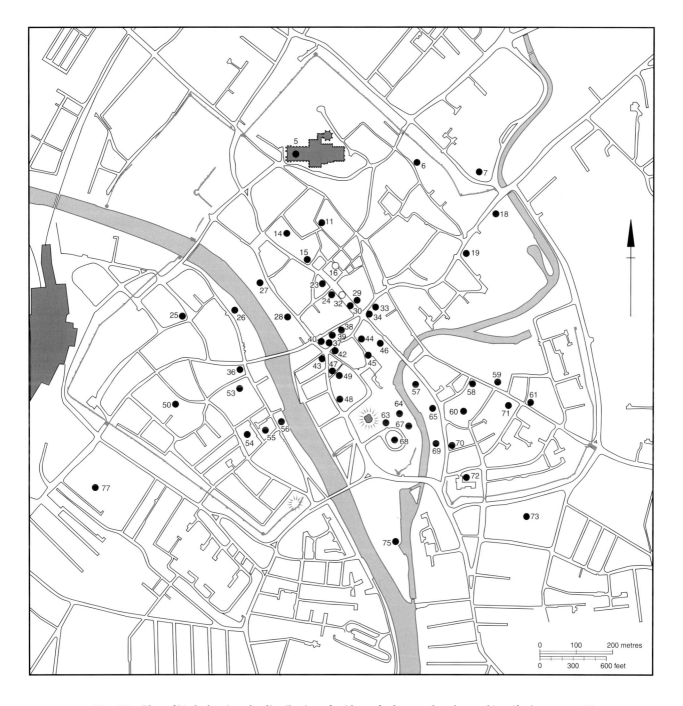

Fig.125 *Plan of York showing the distribution of evidence for bone and antler working (for key see p.466)*

Antiquarian references to large collections of bone and antler recovered at Clifford Street, Coppergate/Castlegate and High Ousegate are supported by finds made during recent excavations, albeit in smaller quantities. Excavations on sites close to the west bank of the River Ouse, in particular on North Street, and at 1–9 Micklegate and Albion Wharf, Skeldergate,

also produced bone and antler working debris. A handful of offcuts of bone (and antler) found in a concentration at the York Minster excavations have been interpreted as evidence of bone working on the site (Phillips and Heywood 1995, 193). Elsewhere in the city, scattered finds have been made, particularly to the south-east in the Walmgate area.

471

Antler debris survives well, was discarded rather than recycled and is fairly easily recognised; its survival on many sites must in part owe something to its relatively indestructible nature, but may also point to antler working activity being fairly ubiquitous. Its widespread use in York during the Anglo-Scandinavian and, to a lesser extent, Anglian periods was rapidly curtailed in the Anglo-Norman period due to strict forest laws (MacGregor 1985, 32), and so its presence is a good indicator of Anglo-Scandinavian activity.

Amber working (Fig.126)

The excavations at 16–22 Coppergate produced an assemblage of amber including waste, roughouts and finished objects which complemented the un-

Fig.126 *Plan of York showing the distribution of evidence for jet and amber working (for key see p.466)*

472

stratified collection found nearby at Clifford Street in 1884 (Waterman 1959; *AY* 17/14, 2504–16). The latter comprised an 11th-century group of material including raw amber, roughouts, and representatives of various stages in the making of beads, finger-rings and pendants, as well as finished objects. Raw amber was also recorded at the corner of Castlegate/Coppergate (Benson 1906), with further evidence in King's Square, Pavement/Piccadilly and one or two fragments on the west bank of the River Ouse.

Jet working (Fig.126)

Although some fine jet objects dating to the Anglo-Scandinavian period have been found in York, including a pendant in the form of a coiled snake

Fig.127 *Plan of York showing the distribution of evidence for glass bead manufacture (for key see p.466)*

(Waterman 1959, 94, fig.21, *3*), there is very little recorded evidence of jet manufacturing debris from the city. 16–22 Coppergate produced four pieces of raw material, a worked fragment and two disc-shaped roughouts, some or all of which could be residual Roman (*AY* 17/14, 2498). A roughout found at 6–8 Pavement may be Anglo-Scandinavian (*AY* 17/3, *392*); another from the Parliament Street sewer trench is possibly medieval (*AY* 17/4, *692*). 'Jet and cannel coal in the shape of rings etc.' was recorded at Clifford Street in 1884; these sound like completed objects and do not suggest production. Two unfinished pieces of worked jet found at York Minster were interpreted as suggesting 'the presence of a jet workshop in the vicinity' (Henig in Phillips and Heywood 1995, 432).

Glass working (Fig.127)

Evidence for glass working comes mainly in the form of beads. At 16–22 Coppergate high-lead glass was being made in the later 10th–11th centuries and some of the high-lead glass objects found on the site, mainly beads, may have derived from this industry (*AY* 17/14, 2528). At the same period at 22 Piccadilly, blue soda glass was being recycled to make beads (ibid.). The late 19th-century assemblage from Clifford Street produced numerous beads and debris, including misshapen and unfinished ones (Raine 1891, 217). Not far away, over 230 beads of Anglo-Scandinavian date were found on Parliament Street/ High Ousegate, although there appears to be no clear evidence of manufacture (Radley 1971, 49–50). Apart from this area, the only other site to have produced evidence of probable glass bead-making is North Street although some crucibles recorded elsewhere as evidence of non-ferrous metal working might have been used for glass working (see p.468).

Textile manufacture (Fig.128)

This industry differs from all the others discussed in that it was a common and frequent domestic activity; analysis of the evidence from 16–22 Coppergate, for example, indicated that during the mid 10th century (Period 4B) wool-combing, spinning, weaving, dyeing and needlework took place indoors, with flax processing and laundering in the backyard (*AY* 17/11, 1824). Iron wool-combs and flax heckles, used in fibre preparation, are both composed of iron spikes of similar shapes to iron nails. These spikes were identified as parts of fibre preparation tools at 16–22 Coppergate, but elsewhere may not have been distin-

guished from nails; this suggests they may be under-represented in the archaeological record. Spindle whorls made of lead, bone, stone or fired clay are very recognisable tools, and are the most common finds referred to in relation to textile manufacture. The site at Clifford Street (Raine 1891, 218) produced whorls and a spindle (presumably wooden). Clay loomweights were used on warp-weighted looms, which were replaced during the 10th century by two-beam vertical looms which did not need loom-weights (*AY* 17/11, 1760). Such loomweights have been found on a number of sites scattered across the city, including Clifford Street, Micklegate, Pavement and Goodramgate (Radley 1971). Weavers' hand tools of bone and antler called pin-beaters have also been recognised from excavated sites and are hinted at in earlier records by the mention of 'bone tools'. Linen smoothers, usually made of glass or stone and used for smoothing linen after laundering, have been noted at Clifford Street and Pavement as well as at unspecified sites in the city. Finally, tools used in cutting and stitching such as shears and needles have been recorded, although some tools described in the past as bone needles might be termed pins today; those made from pig fibula bones in particular are now considered more likely to be pins, on the basis of lack of wear within the perforations and the heads being rather large and rough (MacGregor 1985, 193).

The widely scattered nature of these finds (see Fig.128) suggests that this activity was carried out all over the city, probably in a domestic context by individual households (see below). It is, however, perhaps worth noting those sites where textile production tools of several types were found — 16–22 Coppergate, Castlegate/Coppergate (Benson 1906), Clifford Street (Raine 1891), Goodramgate (ibid.), Micklegate, North Street and Pavement — suggesting, perhaps, that production could be focused in certain households or zones.

Summary

This research confirms, and the maps serve to illustrate, several points about the distribution of Anglo-Scandinavian craft activity. Most striking is the clear concentration of evidence for all crafts in the core Coppergate/Castlegate/Ousegate area. This is partly accounted for by the relatively high level of archaeological activity and good preservation conditions.

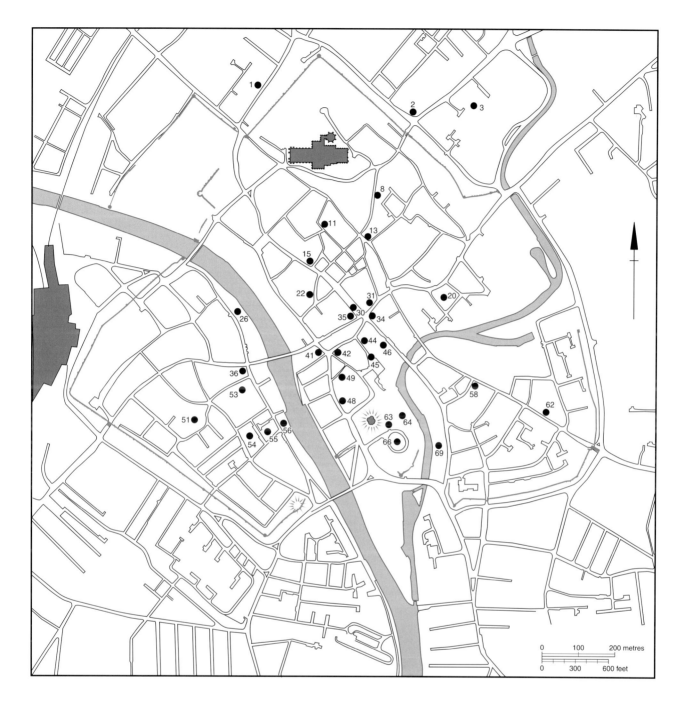

Fig.128 Plan of York showing the distribution of evidence for textile manufacture (for key see p.466)

Outside this core, however, there are indicators of more widespread activity. Antler waste and ceramic crucibles from non-ferrous metal working are valuable indicators of industrial activity which are datable, unlikely to be recycled and less destructible than other materials. The evidence for these two crafts is spread over a wide area, including sites on the south-west bank of the River Ouse and out along Walmgate and modern Piccadilly.

The Walmgate/Piccadilly evidence is of considerable interest as it sheds new light on this area of the city. The investigations which have taken place in this vicinity have usually been small in scale, with the result that only small numbers of objects have been recovered. These assemblages have, however, consistently produced bone and antler working evidence, as well as small and varying amounts of other craft evidence. Before these excavations in the 1980s and 1990s this area had largely been a blank in terms of Anglo-Scandinavian activity but it is now clear that the Viking-Age city had developed away from the main thoroughfare of Walmgate itself; the pottery distribution maps indicate that this had been a gradual process during the course of the 10th century.

The continuing paucity of Anglo-Scandinavian evidence from much of the Roman fortress area remains noteworthy. There have, however, been fewer opportunities to excavate in this area and these have not always reached Anglo-Scandinavian deposits. The excavations in and around York Minster demonstrate that where such opportunities have arisen, Viking-Age evidence is present, although more recent excavations at the Minster Library Extension site produced almost nothing of this period. Glimpses gained during repairs to service trenches and other watching briefs in the St Andrewgate/Bedern/Aldwark areas have demonstrated that waterlogged and organic deposits exist below medieval layers in that area. At Bedern itself, where few trenches went deep enough, there is nonetheless evidence of Anglo-Scandinavian pits and perhaps a contemporary structure (*AY* 10/5, 408).

Across the River Ouse, on its south-west bank, the evidence for Anglo-Scandinavian craft activity is concentrated along the riverside and in the streets immediately behind, reinforcing the evidence for Anglo-Scandinavian occupation as indicated by the pottery. The available evidence suggests that the character of the Anglo-Scandinavian occupation in this area was very like that in the Coppergate area, with a similar range of crafts taking place.

Further back from the river there is patchy evidence of occupation in the form of pits and residual pottery. Excavations just beyond the city walls along Blossom Street (for example, at numbers 14–20, 35–41 and 47) have produced plentiful Roman material but no clear Anglo-Scandinavian evidence, suggesting little occupation of this extra-mural area in this period.

16–22 Coppergate

Invaluable detail of how the crafts and industries identified across the city might have operated comes from the excavations at 16–22 Coppergate. Here four properties (Tenements A–D) were occupied by a sequence of buildings and their associated backyards. No traces of occupation on this site between c. AD 400 and the mid 9th century were identified but there was activity from c.860 onwards. This discussion concentrates on an analysis of the evidence from Period 4B (c.930/935–c.975) and Period 5B (c.975–c.1050) when property divisions were clearly established and each plot had one or more buildings.

Many of the factors relevant to an interpretation of the distribution of material across the city also apply here. Preservation was very good, with the detail of many organic materials surviving in the moist anaerobic soils, but both the dumping of rubbish off-site and recycling will have had a significant but unmeasurable impact. Contemporary pit digging and building activities which redeposited soil will have further confused the picture. It is an assumption that debris from activities in the structures at the front of the site will have been thrown away or deposited in pits in the backyards of the same fenced properties. This may not have been the case; rubbish could have been tipped into a neighbouring plot, particularly if that property was empty; or it could have been used to make up levels or fill soggy ground anywhere on site. The digging of the cellars for the Period 5B buildings must have had significant impact on deposit formation and it is noticeable that the pattern of distribution seen across the site is much more diffuse in Period 5B than in Period 4B (see pp.479–81). Distinguishing between residual Period 4B rubbish and contemporary Period 5B activity is often impossible.

Each one of the crafts and industries described in the section above is represented to a lesser or greater extent on these properties. The evidence has been examined as major research projects by a number of specialists and the results have been published in Volume 17 of *The Archaeology of York*. The principal conclusions are summarised here.

Ottaway, in his study of the ferrous metal working, was struck by the range of manufacturing methods 'from simple welding and hammering to sophisticated steeling and decoration with relief work and non-ferrous plating' (*AY* 17/6, 719). He raises the question of whether the same craftsmen could turn their hand to all the metal working crafts. He notes the distribution of slag which 'combined with the evidence of hammer scale, the smithing tools ... and the bar iron, blanks and scrap ... strongly suggests that Tenements B, C and D were the sites of smithies' during Period 4B (ibid., 479). Plating of iron objects with non-ferrous metals occurs on 171 objects; most of the evidence comes from Period 4B (and 5A) and clusters around the buildings in Tenements C and D. Ottaway suggests that the smithies which operated in these tenements might have included among their products tin-plated dress and other fittings. He notes that the evidence from Period 5B is more diffuse, that there are no obvious smithing areas and that much of the material in Period 5B must be redeposited from earlier activity.

Bayley concluded from her study on the non-ferrous metal working that it 'was widespread through the city at this period and that Coppergate was not the only centre ... though the site must also have been one of the most important metal working areas in the city' (*AY* 17/7, 815). She makes reference to the wide range of metals which were worked and to the different concentrations of the various ferrous and non-ferrous industries at different times in different tenements. She notes how, especially in Tenement C, both types of metal working seem to be taking place at the same time. She alludes to the possibility that metal working was a general skill, widespread throughout the population in the Viking Age, but thinks that this is unlikely in an urban context where specialised skills might be practised. Alternatively, she suggests that since these metal working industries required similar workshop facilities their practitioners might have chosen to work together. She points out that the crafts might have been seasonal or lasted for shorter periods than are separable in the archaeological record (ibid., 816).

The evidence for wood working and wood turning shows a somewhat different pattern. Morris discusses the wood working tools which include axes and wedges for felling and splitting, axes, slices, chisels and gouges for shaping, parts of bow-drills, augers, spoon bits, gimlets and shaves for drilling and smoothing. The main evidence for the presence and location of a lathe turner, however, takes the form of wooden cores and waste. This is the largest collec-

tion of waste cores found on any site in Britain (*AY* 17/13, 2145) and, while there is some evidence for lathe turning in Periods 3 and 4A, there is much more in Period 4B (ibid., 2198). 'The cores are widely distributed, mainly over Tenements B–D, both inside and outside the wattle structures ... It is almost certain that at some time over the 40-year period between 930/5 and 975, lathe-turners worked in and behind the structures on each of the four tenements, but mainly on Tenements B–D, with a marked concentration of different types of waste in Tenement B.' Morris also remarks that 'seasonality may have played a major role in the lathe turning craft' (ibid., 2200), and 'that wood was only cut at certain times of the year' (ibid., 2191). In Period 5B 'there is again a great deal of evidence for lathe turning', widely distributed across all tenements 'but the majority of cores and other waste products are from Tenements C and D. On Tenement C there is a large concentration behind the single structure', making this 'a very firm candidate for being a lathe turner's workshop at some time in Period 5B' (ibid., 2203–4).

The evidence for leather working includes offcuts from the trimming of hides and cutting out of shoes. Several different styles and sizes of shoes were made and repaired as well as sheaths, scabbards, pouches, belts, straps and other objects. The evidence comes in the form of different types of waste (primary, secondary and tertiary), finished and incomplete items, as well as the iron and wooden tools used (*AY* 17/16). Analysis shows that the majority of every category of waste comes from Tenements B and C. In Period 4B the emphasis is on Tenement B, with most of the material coming from the area behind the post and wattle building at the street frontage (ibid., figs.1582–4). In Period 5B there is considerably less waste overall, and predominance changes to Tenement C (ibid., figs.1585–7).

Smaller-scale crafts include antler (and bone) working. While comb-making and the manufacture of other decorative fittings may have been the work of skilled craft workers, other items may have been domestically produced. This may also have been a seasonal craft, as the antler supplies almost exclusively derived from those shed by deer over a two-month period (in the case of red deer, in late winter and early spring) and subsequently collected. In Period 4B the antler working debris is concentrated mainly at the street frontage of Tenements B and C, suggesting that antler working was carried out in and around the post and wattle buildings (*AY* 17/12, fig.881). In the case of Tenements B and C there is also evidence scattered down the length of the backyards. This is more noticeable in Tenement C 'where, in Period 5B, deposits in and around successive structures produced the greatest concentration of working debris' (ibid., 1921). Although there are these concentrations in one or two of the buildings at different periods, 'there is insufficient manufacturing debris to suggest a long-term settled workshop. Itinerant craftsmen may have operated from these tenements, and, as the bulk of the detritus results from comb manufacture, this activity perhaps formed the mainstay of their business' (ibid., 2005).

There is amber working evidence on the site from Period 3 onwards (*AY* 17/14, 2509). In Period 4B it is concentrated in and around structures on Tenement B, but there is also evidence from the structures and backyards on other properties. The pattern is much more diffuse over the whole area in Period 5B. The evidence for jet working at Coppergate is very limited and inconclusive, reflecting the pattern seen across the city. Jet working, it seems, was only a very minor craft at this time.

The evidence for glass working in the Anglo-Scandinavian period is difficult to interpret. Both Roman glass working evidence and Roman vessel sherds appear residually throughout the Anglo-Scandinavian deposits. Sherds of glass from Anglian vessels also appear in the Anglo-Scandinavian layers (*AY* 17/14, 2537–41). There is evidence for high-lead glass working in the Coppergate area during the Anglo-Scandinavian period, which has been summarised by Bayley and Doonan (*AY* 17/14, 2520–5); this appears to be mainly 11th-century in date, and possibly produced beads. The evidence takes the form of crucibles, part made and failed beads, and glass waste, but the working debris is difficult to relate to the products found on site. The quantity of evidence from 16–22 Coppergate, however, suggests that glass working was on a small scale.

Penelope Rogers's research on Anglo-Scandinavian textiles and textile production has provided many new insights into this activity. Her work on the Coppergate material concludes that textile production began early on all four properties and she was able to show that 'all the processes of production,

which take raw flax and wool and make it into finished cloth and garments, were being practised on or near the site in the first 40 or 50 years of the Anglo-Scandinavian occupation (Periods 3 and 4A)' (*AY* 17/11, 1793). In Period 4B fibre processing, as indicated by the distribution of iron spikes, was undertaken widely across the site. Spinning took place in and around the buildings, and the two-beam vertical loom was used in or near buildings on the street frontage. Dyeing may have occurred in and around the buildings and in the backyards, while tools for making and maintaining garments were recovered from Tenements B, C and D. These activities continued in Period 5B when there was a new emphasis on fibre processing, although, as with so much of the evidence from this site, the pattern is much more diffuse (ibid., 1803–6). In summary she concludes that 'textile production was important, but not the most significant activity on the site'. She goes on to say 'The fact that textile tools have been recovered from almost all York sites of Anglo-Scandinavian date confirms that the craft was widely practised. On the other hand the quantity of material from 16–22 Coppergate is considerably more than at other sites, except perhaps Clifford Street ... one explanation of the evidence may be that more cloth was being produced at Coppergate than elsewhere' (ibid., 1824–5).

While textile production may have been a domestic, household activity, the securing of raw materials and the distribution of finished cloth must have involved households in trade both on a regional and an international level. Penelope Rogers suggests of production at Coppergate that 'the general picture seems to be of a broad lower tier of home-made goods, some of which may have been exchanged at local markets; and an upper tier of exotic, specialist and best-quality fabric exchanged over longer distances' (*AY* 17/11, 1827). Standard types of fabric for local markets were the main product, but traders would also have been familiar with foreign goods, perhaps being involved in copying or redistributing them (ibid., 1827).

During these researches on the individual industries attempts were made to look at the spatial distribution patterns of the manufacturing evidence. These are published and discussed in full in the various fascicules in *AY* 17 (*AY* 17/6, figs.177, 179, 191, 195, 218, 242; *AY* 17/7, figs.324, 329, 337, 351, 353–5, 358; *AY* 17/11, figs.839–48; *AY* 17/12, fig.881; *AY* 17/13, figs.1045–7, 1059–61; *AY* 17/14, figs.1204, 1213–16, 1224–6; *AY* 17/16, figs.1582–7). Here an attempt is made to draw out some conclusions from these researches and to paint a broad picture of the scale of the various activities on each tenement.

Period 4B

Tenement A

The successive Period 4B post and wattle buildings at the street frontage were almost completely destroyed by the subsequent Period 5B building, leaving only a small number of undisturbed Period 4B layers. The information retrieved, therefore, is inconclusive. There is a very small amount of evidence, however, that non-ferrous metal working, iron working, leather working, antler working and textile production might have taken place on the property.

Tenement B

Although the successive Period 4B street front buildings on this tenement were also substantially destroyed, more deposits of this period survive along the rest of the plot. These produced evidence for several crafts being carried out here throughout Period 4B.

This tenement produced the most debris associated with lead, lead-tin alloy and tin working from this period and there is also some evidence for gold, silver and copper alloy working. Fifty percent of iron working slag recovered from Period 4B deposits came from this property. Other evidence relating to iron working, including tools, incomplete objects, hones and grindstones, was also present.

The majority of the Period 4B leather working waste came from behind the post and wattle structures on this tenement, although some was incorporated in the surviving floor deposits within the building. The greatest range and quantity of Period 4B wood turning waste and cores is also concentrated in the central part of this property, behind the structures.

Of the crafts which might have operated intermittently or seasonally, this tenement has the greatest quantity of the Period 4B evidence for antler and amber working.

Tenement C

Tenement C presents the best-quality evidence; the structures were well preserved and the entire property was excavated apart from a block of Period 4B deposits in the backyard area. The picture which emerges should, therefore, be the most reliable. It shows that many different activities were taking place around the successive structures throughout the period.

There is substantial evidence for lead, tin, lead alloy, silver and copper alloy working from this tenement, putting the non-ferrous metal working industry almost on a par with the level of activity on Tenement B. The evidence for the production of iron objects in terms of bars, strips and plates which were made into objects including dress fittings, riding equipment, needles and plated objects is greater here than on any other property. In addition, there is further slag, punches, a hammer, an anvil, hones and grindstones.

There are significant quantities of all categories of leather waste from the floors of the structure and from the backyards behind them. The greatest quantity of evidence for the manufacture of sheaths and scabbards comes from this property. The pattern of distribution of wood cores and other waste here is similar to that from Tenement B; the same pattern is repeated in terms of amber working and antler comb-making evidence. Textile production is also evident and this tenement produced silk offcuts.

Tenement D

Again the evidence in Tenement D was well preserved and reasonably complete, except for part of the backyard which was cut by later cellars and part of the tenement which lay outside the area of excavation.

Although there is less evidence for lead, lead-tin alloy and tin working here than in Tenements B and C, there is significantly more evidence of silver and copper alloy working in the form of crucibles with residues. There is also less iron working evidence and less leather waste than on Tenements B and C. Wood turning waste is also less evident than in Tenement C, with a concentration along the fence boundary between Tenements C and D. Amber and antler working debris is also on a diminished scale.

Summary of Period 4B

The best evidence for this period comes from Tenements C and D, and it is clear that during the 40–45 years of occupation (two to three generations) there were four major crafts in operation: iron working, non-ferrous metal working, leather working and wood turning. There were also at least two minor crafts in operation: amber working and antler working. In addition, domestic crafts such as textile manufacture and domestic activities such as food preparation and cooking took place on all the tenements. There are some apparent concentrations of activity, for example, leather working, wood working, lead alloy and tin working in Tenement B, iron working and the manufacture of leather sheaths and scabbards in Tenement C, and silver and copper alloy working in Tenement D.

Period 5A

Period 5A represents the period in each tenement between the two main occupation phases when the post and wattle buildings were replaced by plank-built structures with basements.

Period 5B

Tenement A

In Period 5B two successive structures occupied the front of Tenement A, with the backyard stretching behind. Much of the backyard of this tenement lay outside the excavated area so the data set is small by comparison with the other properties. There is further very limited debris from antler working, lead and silver working, iron working, leather working, fibre processing and spinning, amber working and wood turning.

Tenement B

In Period 5B, all the crafts appear to continue in this tenement but on a smaller scale than in Period 4B. Antler working debris continues to be recovered, though in reduced quantities, and the quantities of leather working waste also diminish. Copper, lead and tin working evidence continues in smaller quantities. The pattern is the same for the iron working. Amber working and wood turning evidence are present at a slightly reduced scale. Fibre processing and spinning are still carried out. The evidence in almost all these classes of material is more diffused down the length of the tenements and not always so

clearly associated with the structures. Residuality is a factor to be considered: the digging of the basements for the plank-built structures of this period, and the continuing pit digging, ensured the redeposition of earlier material from Period 4B, further confusing the picture.

Tenement C

In Period 5B there is continued evidence of antler working. Leather working evidence in the form of waste increases, accounting for 49% of the leather waste recovered for the period. This was found in and around the structures, and was distributed along three-quarters of the length of the property. There is less evidence for the range of non-ferrous metal working and that which there is relates mostly to lead and tin working in and behind the two successive buildings, Structures 5/5 and 5/6. Waste, tools and slag relating to iron working continue to be present throughout the deposits. There appears to be greater emphasis on fibre preparation, though equipment relating to spinning, cutting, smoothing and stitching continues. Amber working continues at a slightly reduced scale, while the number of wood turning cores and other wooden waste rises somewhat, especially in the central portion of the tenement behind the structures.

Tenement D

Here antler working continues. Leather waste increases and this evidence is distributed along the full length of the property. The non-ferrous metal working activities continue on a diminished scale but with a little more gold working evidence. The same pattern of continuing but diminished activity is evident for iron working. Amber working continues on the same scale as before but the quantities of wood turning waste increase slightly. Spinning and fibre processing seem to have increased from Period 4B.

Summary of Period 5B

The distribution plots published in the various specialist reports illustrate that there is generally less intense activity on all the properties in this period. As this period lasts almost twice as long as Period 4B (i.e. 75 years or around four generations) and at least some of the material in Period 5B deposits must derive from Period 4B activities, the overall impression is that the level of craft activity in Period 5B is considerably lower than previously. In some cases it can be demonstrated that there is a change of focus of activities from Tenement B in Period 4B to Tenement C in this period (for example, in the case of the leather working and possibly wood turning).

It is possible that the apparent diminution of some craft activities in Period 5B marks a change in the function of the new buildings with basements at 16–22 Coppergate. This in turn might be linked with the expansion of the city in the later 10th and 11th centuries seen from the pottery data. Manufacturing, which had formerly been focused in the Coppergate/ Ousegate area, might have spread more broadly through the city.

Conclusions

Crafts at Coppergate

The picture of Anglo-Scandinavian craft and economy which emerges from the Coppergate data is a complex one of many crafts operating within and across the tenements. These crafts include those requiring hearths and heat, such as non-ferrous metal working and iron smithing, and also perhaps glass bead-making. The evidence also points to wood working and wood turning, which would require a lathe, as well as leather working, particularly shoe-making, and textile production. Antler and bone working (producing combs and other objects) and amber working (which produced jewellery) appeared to operate less intensively.

Analysis has indicated that all these crafts were undertaken in Tenements B, C and D during the 40–45 years of Period 4B and the 75 years of Period 5B. Analysis of the floor levels attempted to determine the scale of each of these activities within each tenement and within each period. Overall, this analysis confirmed that the same range of crafts was practised throughout the entire Anglo-Scandinavian period, although a change of emphasis from metal working in earlier levels to leather working in later levels was identified in Tenement C in Period 4B.

The sharing of the tenements by the various crafts-people who worked there has been noted by most of the specialists who have studied the working evidence. While noting in her study of wood working that the Coppergate area must have been an area of

'intense specialist lathe turning activity for over 200 years', Morris accepted that the turners 'had to share the tenements ... with many other crafts[men] using a variety of materials' (AY 17/13, 2391). Bayley noted in her study of the non-ferrous metal working that both ferrous and non-ferrous metal working appeared to be carried out at the same period in the same areas; she suggested that one explanation might be that as they required similar workshop facilities, 'a group of craftsmen with different specialities might choose to work together' (AY 17/7, 816).

Spatial studies of working debris from other large urban excavations appear to present a similar picture to that provided by Coppergate. At the Middle Saxon Royal Opera House site in London, a similar but less diverse range of crafts was in evidence, although the paucity of evidence for both wood and leather working compared to that from York is likely to be the result of the absence of waterlogged levels preserving the organic materials rather than a genuine absence of such crafts. Analysis of the debris from the site suggested that more than one craft may have been practised in an individual building, and that several had a 'relationship of interdependence for their products in a situation of close spatial proximity' (Malcolm and Bowsher 2003, 168). There were, for example, indications of bone and antler working being carried out alongside iron working (ibid., 175), and weaving alongside bone working, smithing or non-ferrous metal working (ibid., 169). In one building, a hearth seemed to have been used for both smithing and domestic purposes (ibid.,178). Some iron slag was recovered where non-ferrous metal working was being undertaken, although no non-ferrous debris was recovered from the two smithies which were identified (ibid., 179). Evidence from contemporary *Hamwic* also seems to demonstrate no zoning of particular industries; different industries were pursued in individual, often adjacent, properties or buildings, sometimes contemporaneously. With the possible exception of iron working, a single property did not remain associated with a particular activity over an extended period of time (Andrews 1997, 205).

Similar analysis of Viking-Age sites in Britain appears harder to obtain. At Flaxengate, Lincoln, it has been noted that non-ferrous metal working was carried out in the same buildings in which glass beads were being made (Richards 2000, 112), and that ferrous and non-ferrous metal workers also had a close relationship, sometimes using the same buildings (ibid., 115). Perhaps surprisingly, while excavations in Late Saxon London have produced numerous traces of trades and industries, this evidence has been located in small and dispersed quantities, and certainly does not suggest groups of artisans producing goods for the market, as at Coppergate. It is not until the later 11th century that non-ferrous metal working in London can be identified 'as operating on more than a domestic level' (Vince 1991, 433).

It has not been possible at any of these sites to establish precisely how the different crafts related to each other, to determine if they operated simultaneously in the same plots, or sequentially, or both of these at different times. At Ribe in Denmark, however, where there was evidence of a market place founded in the early 8th century with some 40–50 plots, analysis of the layout of the site and of the craft debris has led to some interesting conclusions about the nature of the craft operations there. It appears that the plots were often subdivided, while the lack of substantial buildings has led to the view that work was probably carried out on a seasonal basis (Jensen 1991, 7). The nature of the craft debris has been interpreted as showing that, in some cases, one particular craft was practised on the same spot for several successive years (ibid., 42). One plot, for example, appeared to have been used by a comb-maker for some years, to be followed by a metal caster who also occupied the plot for several years; could this have been a father handing on his option as seasonal tenant on this particular site to a son? In other cases, plots were subdivided to accommodate several activities concurrently (Jensen 1993, 203).

It seems unlikely that it will ever be possible to determine the permanency or seasonality of craft and industrial activities on the four tenements at Coppergate. Each craftsman could have been working independently in his rented tenement for periods too short to be recognised in the archaeological record before being succeeded by a different craft. Alternatively, several crafts may have been operating concurrently within the same tenement. It is unclear whether the craft workers lived in the buildings on each tenement or if they simply rented the outside working area and others lived in the structures. Some products from Coppergate suggest that some co-operation amongst craftsmen was likely; for example, a considerable number of tinned iron objects were found clustering in the area of the Period 4B smithies in Tenements C and D. Were these the products of an iron smith who also did the tinning? Or did a non-ferrous metal worker plate the iron objects? Even if the iron worker plated the objects, perhaps the non-ferrous metal worker provided the metal required? Similarly, a comb-maker required metal rivets to assemble every comb; these must have been provided by a metal worker. All the crafts undertaken at Coppergate needed iron tools, which would presumably have been made by a smith. The proximity of these crafts to each other, as evident in the debris, may point to a group of mutually supportive artisans, sharing facilities on a permanent or temporary basis. While the hearths and forges required for metal working might argue for permanent or semi-permanent metal workers, other crafts, particularly comb-making, appear more likely to be seasonal; the raw material of preference, antler, was seasonally available, and while some might have been stockpiled for use over the year, the amounts of debris recovered from Coppergate suggested foci of activity at different times, but were insufficient to 'suggest a long-term settled workshop' (AY 17/12, 2005). Seasonality may also have affected the condition of wood suitable for the lathe turners. The supply of raw amber may also have been intermittent, depending as it did on ships' cargoes from Scandinavia. These occupations may not have sustained the Coppergate craftsmen on a permanent long-term basis but were practised steadily enough to leave the patterns of debris found on the various tenements.

Crafts in York

The question remains as to how typical Coppergate was of York as a whole. The surviving street-name, 'the street of the cup-makers', suggests this might have been the focus of wood turners for the entire city, and there is evidence of wood turning from at least three of the four properties. Metal working, both ferrous and non-ferrous, was also carried out there on an intensive level in Period 4B. The supply of raw materials for metal working was not governed by seasonal factors and the amount of debris from at least two properties suggests that metal working was the main occupation for at least the first one or two generations after c.930. There is as yet nothing comparable from elsewhere in the city.

482

The 19th-century collection of amber from Clifford Street, situated near the River Ouse where cargoes would be landed, suggests more intensive amber production there in the 11th century. Amber working did not take place on this scale at Coppergate, where it seems to have been a consistent but small-scale activity. The spread of comb-making evidence along Piccadilly, at Coppergate and elsewhere in the city suggests that this too was a widespread, small-scale activity. How far the level of leather working observed at Coppergate is typical or unusual will always be difficult to judge, given the problems of survival. There is better evidence for glass bead manufacture at 22 Piccadilly in the 11th century than on the adjacent Coppergate, suggesting that small specialist workshops operated spasmodically.

This chapter has attempted to pull together and synthesise the evidence for Anglo-Scandinavian craft activity and to demonstrate the contribution that re-cent work, especially at 16–22 Coppergate, has made to our understanding of the economy of the city. Many questions remain only partly answered. A little light has been cast on the basis on which properties were occupied and how that changed through time. The relationship with the rural manors and farms in the hinterland and the urban economy remains unclear in the absence of excavated contemporary sites in the hinterland. Many raw materials were drawn from these areas and contact must have been regular and frequent. Both urban and rural dwellers must have served as middlemen transporting raw materials and finished products in both directions alongside the essential foodstuffs needed to feed the city. Although the last 50 years has produced substantial new evidence and a greater understanding of the urban hub of this network, much remains to be learned about how the complex strands which led into and out of the hub interlinked and operated in the whole late Anglo-Saxon economy.

Appendix

Gazetteer of sites in York with evidence for Anglo-Scandinavian craft working

The numbers in parentheses in bold italics relate to the numbered sites on distribution plots (Figs.121–8)

(6) **1–5 Aldwark**, 1976–7.15 (unpublished)
Antler working (antler offcuts)

(76) **Baile Hill** (Addyman and Priestley 1977, 139)
Wood working (tools)

(52) **Bishophill** (Waterman 1959, 102, fig.24)
Non-ferrous metal working (crucible)

(54) **37 Bishophill Senior**, 1973.15 (*AY* 7/2)
Non-ferrous metal working (lead alloy debris)

Antler working (antler offcuts)

Textile manufacture (bone textile tool, stone spindle whorls)

(9) **9 Blake Street**, 1975.6 (*AY* 3/4, 363; Roesdahl et al. 1981, 118, YMW14)
Non-ferrous metalworking (mould fragment for a Borre-style trefoil brooch)

(77) **35–41 Blossom Street**, 1989.21 (unpublished)
Antler working (offcuts)

(42) **Castlegate/Coppergate** (Benson 1906, 73)
Textile manufacture (lead spindle whorl, bone needles, fired clay spindle whorls)

Amber working (3 lumps raw amber, amber bead)

Antler and bone working (tines and burr, goat horns)

Non-ferrous metal working (lead lump, possibly working debris)

Wood working (iron axe, iron bit, small mallets, socketed curved hook published in *AY* 17/13, 9162–5)

(49) **Clifford Street** (Raine 1891, 216–18)
Textile manufacture (glass linen smoothers, spindle whorls, spindle, bone needles)

Wood working (pieces of wrought wood, wooden mallet)

Amber working (raw amber, also published in *AY* 17/14, 2504–7)

Antler and bone working (combs in all stages of manufacture, deer horn, antler tines)

Glass working (molten glass and glass beads)

(43) **2 Clifford Street**, 1999.256 (unpublished)
Antler working (offcuts)

(47) **5–13 Clifford Street**, 1990.3 (unpublished)
Antler working (antler offcuts)

(48) **23 Clifford Street,** 1990.8 (unpublished)
Bone and antler working (offcuts)

Textile manufacture (loomweight fragment)

(27) **13–17 Coney Street**, 1991.3 (unpublished)
Bone working (offcuts)

(28) **39–41 Coney Street**, 1974.18 (unpublished)
Bone and antler working (offcuts, comb blanks and trimmings)

(37) **5 Coppergate**, 1974.8 (*AY* 17/3)
Antler and bone working (offcuts)

(44) **16–22 Coppergate**, 1976.7 (*AY* 17/6, 17/7, 17/11, 17/12, 17/13, 17/14, 17/16)
Iron working, non-ferrous metal working, bone and antler working, amber working, jet working, glass working, wood working, leather working (working debris); textile production (tools)

(45) **Coppergate watching brief**, 1982.22 (*AY* 17/6, 17/11, 17/12, 17/13, 17/14, 17/16)
Iron working, bone and antler working, wood working, leather working, amber working (working debris); textile production (tools)

(15) **17–21 Davygate**, 1974.2 (unpublished)
Bone and antler working (offcuts)

Textile manufacture (possible bone textile tool)

(74) **Fawcett Street**, 1998.693 (unpublished)
Iron working (slag)

(22) **Feasegate**, 1998.2 (unpublished)
Textile manufacture (spindle whorl fragment)

(21) **Feasegate, south tower** (RCHMY **4**, xxix; Stead 1958)
Iron working ('iron-smelting hearth' excavated in front of south corner tower)

(21) **Feasegate** (Radley 1971, 51)
Leather working (cobbling waste)

(60) **George Street**, 1990.26 (unpublished)
Bone and antler working (offcuts)
Leather working (offcuts and fragments)

(1) **31–37 Gillygate**, 1972.14 (unpublished)
Textile manufacture (possible bone textile tool)

(8) **Goodramgate, Hunter and Smallpage** (Raine 1891, 219)
Textile manufacture ('Pottery, spindle whorls, implements in iron, bone and stone, found in 1878'). cf. loomweights from Goodramgate (Radley 1971, 52)

(19) **Haymarket, Peasholme Green**, 1986.14 (unpublished)
Antler working (offcuts)

(40) **High Ousegate**, 1988.20 (unpublished)
Antler working (tines)

(38) **20–21 High Ousegate**, 1992.172 (unpublished)
Antler working (antler offcuts)

(39) **25–27 High Ousegate** (Benson 1902, 65, 66)
Bone and antler working ('20 stone of bones and horns were gathered in one day, 12 stones on other days, and with little digging two bags resulted for the day's work. Antlers were numerous, also tips of same; some were ornamented, whilst one was carved into an animal's head')
Non-ferrous metal working ('two barrow loads of thin copper' and 'remains of two furnaces')

(20) **Hungate** (Richardson 1959, 63)
Leather working (cobbling and possible shoe-making waste)
Textile manufacture (loomweight)

(7) **Jewbury**, 1982–3.5 (unpublished)
Antler working (antler offcuts)

(13) **King's Square** (Radley 1971, 52)
Textile manufacture (loomweights)

(13) **1 King's Square**, 1987.30 (unpublished)
Leather working (leather scraps)
Non-ferrous metal working (ingot mould)

(13) **1 King's Square**, 1988.8 (unpublished)
Amber working (raw amber, unfinished beads)
Leather working (scraps, possible cobbling waste)

(72) **Leadmill Lane** (*AY* 17/3)
Bone working (debris from bone comb-making)

(14) **Little Stonegate/Davygate**, 1996–7.102 (unpublished)
Antler working (offcuts, tines and comb fragment)

(12) **Little Stonegate/Swinegate**, 1990.1 (unpublished)
Amber working (amber waste flakes)

(2) **Lord Mayor's Walk**, 1972.17 (unpublished)
Textile manufacture (spindle whorl)

(71) **Margaret Street, St George's School**, ARCUS 1995 (unpublished)
Antler working (offcuts)

(36) **1–9 Micklegate**, 1988.17 (unpublished)
Amber working (amber fragments)
Antler working (antler offcuts)
Non-ferrous metal working (crucibles)
Leather working (manufacturing offcuts)
Textile manufacture (loomweight fragments; fired clay, bone and stone spindle whorls)

(4) **Monkgate, County Hospital**, 1982–3.19 (unpublished)
Non-ferrous metalworking (crucible)

(3) **Monkgate, County House**, 1997.103 (unpublished)
Textile manufacture (spindle whorl)

(41) **Nessgate, Coach and Horses** (Waterman 1959, 81, fig.12.2)
Textile manufacture (possible pin-beater)

(26) **North Street, pumping station**, 1993.1 (unpublished)
Amber working (raw amber fragments)
Antler working (antler offcuts)
Glass working (glass beads/waste)
Non-ferrous metal working (lead alloy offcuts)
Textile manufacture (bone, stone and fired clay spindle whorls, bone tool)

(73) **Paragon Street/Kent Street, Barbican Leisure Centre**, 1987.27 (unpublished)
Bone and antler working (offcuts)

(30) **Parliament Street, sewer trench** (*AY* 17/4)
Antler working (antler offcuts, unfinished comb plates)
Wood working (tool)
Leather working (leather offcuts)
Non-ferrous metal working (crucible, mould fragment, lead alloy run-off)
Iron working (iron mood or knife blank)
Textile manufacture (spindle whorls, fibre processing spikes)

(24) **11–13 Parliament Stree**t, 1971.288 (*AY* 17/4)
Bone and antler working (working debris)

Wood working (axe)   cf. carpenter's T-shaped axe from Parliament Street (Waterman 1959, 72)

(23)   **16 Parliament Street**, 1987.13 (unpublished)
Bone and antler working (unfinished skate, antler offcuts)

(29) **44–45 Parliament Street**, 1994.3210 (unpublished)
Bone and antler working (comb tooth plate blanks, horn cores)

(35) **Parliament Street/High Ousegate** (Radley 1971, 50)
Glass working (manufacture of beads)

Textile manufacture (glass linen smoother)

(32) **Parliament Street/Pavement**, 1987.22 (unpublished)
Antler working (antler offcuts)

(31) **Pavement** (Waterman 1959, 102, fig.25)
Amber working (bead and fragments)

Textile manufacture (iron shears)

(34) **6–8 Pavement** (Radley 1971, 50)
Leather working (evidence of tan pits)

(34) **6–8 Pavement** (*AY* 17/3)
Amber working (unfinished amber ring)

Wood working (tools)

Bone and antler working (unfinished pins, antler tines)

Jet working (jet roughout)

Leather working (offcuts, awls, shoe last)

Textile manufacture (spindle whorl, loomweight, linen smoother)

(33) **22 Pavement**, 1990.31 (unpublished)
Antler working (offcuts)

Non-ferrous metal working (possible crucible)

(18)   **Peasholme Green**, 1990–1.13 (unpublished)
Antler working (offcuts)

(46) **22 Piccadilly** (*AY* 17/12, 17/13, 17/14, 17/16)
Glass working (glass bead-making debris)

Non-ferrous metal working (possible mould fragment, haematite)

Wood working (turning waste)

Leather working (waste from shoe-making and cobbling)

Bone and antler working (offcuts)

Amber working (raw amber)

Textile manufacture (loomweight)

(57) **38 Piccadilly**, 1992.4 (unpublished)
Bone working (offcuts)

(70) **41 Piccadilly**, 1992.18 (unpublished)
Bone and antler working (offcuts)

(65) **50 Piccadilly**, 1992.10 (unpublished)
Bone and antler working (offcuts)

(69) **84 Piccadilly**, 1991.16 (unpublished)
Bone and antler working (offcuts from comb-making)

Textile manufacture (bone spindle whorl)

(16)   **Silver Street** (Benson 1902, 67)
Bone working, leather working ('deposits of bone, horn and leather')

(56) **Skeldergate, Albion Wharf**, 1989.1 (unpublished)
Textile manufacture (bone pin-beater)

Antler working (antler offcuts)

(55) **58–59 Skeldergate**, 1973–5.14 (unpublished)
Bone and antler working (offcuts)

Non-ferrous metal working (lead alloy offcuts, crucibles)

Textile manufacture (bone tool, stone spindle whorls)

(53) **Skeldergate, NCP car park**, 1998–9.844 (unpublished)
Antler working (offcuts)

Textile manufacture (spindle whorl)

(10)   **St Andrewgate**, 1991.2 (unpublished)
Leather working (offcuts)

(75) **St George's Field**, 1986.11 (unpublished)
Antler working (offcuts)

(17)   **9 St Saviourgate**, MAP 1997 (unpublished)
Leather working (4 awls, 2 drawknives)

Wood working (auger)

Iron working (tools)

(11)   **12–18 Swinegate**, 1990.28 (unpublished)
Antler working (offcuts)

Textile manufacture (spindle whorls)

(25)   **24–30 Tanner Row**, 1983–4.32 (unpublished)
Non-ferrous metal working (crucibles)

Antler working (offcuts)

(51) **Trinity Lane, car park**, 1981.18 (unpublished)
Textile manufacture (fired clay spindle whorl)

(50) **Trinity Lane, Ideal Laundry**, 1991.5 (unpublished)

Antler working (offcuts)

(58) **41–49 Walmgate** (Macnab et al. 2003)

Amber working (raw amber fragment)

Antler working (offcuts)

Iron working (slag)

Leather working (offcuts, shoe)

Textile manufacture (spindle whorls, pin-beater)

(59) **76–82 Walmgate**, 1987.33 (unpublished)

Bone and antler working (offcuts)

Non-ferrous metal working (crucible fragments, copper alloy waste)

(61) **104–12 Walmgate**, 1991.21 (unpublished)

Bone and antler working (offcuts)

(62) **118–26 Walmgate**, 1978–9.8 (unpublished)

Textile manufacture (bone tools; stone, fired clay and bone spindle whorls)

(68) **York Castle/Eye of York** (Grove 1940, 285–7)

Bone working (bone motif piece)

(66) **York Castle Yard/Eye of York** (Waterman 1959, 102)

Textile manufacture (loomweights)

(63) **York Castle, car park 1**, 1992.5 (unpublished)

Bone and antler working (antler/bone offcuts)

Textile manufacture (bone spindle whorl)

(64) **York Castle, car park 2**, 1995.58 (unpublished)

Antler working (offcuts)

Textile manufacture (loomweights)

(67) **York Castle Yard, adjacent to former female prison**, 1998.32 (unpublished)

Antler working (offcuts)

(5) **York Minster** (Phillips and Heywood 1995)

Bone and antler working (antler/bone offcuts)

Jet working (worked jet fragments)

Metal working, iron and non-ferrous (smithing slag; also forge with associated ferrous and non-ferrous metal working debris)

The Topography of Anglo-Scandinavian York

By R.A. Hall

Introduction

The area within and immediately beyond the medieval walls of York, the historic core of the 21st-century city, reflects clearly in its layout a series of accretions, alterations and additions that successive generations of York's occupants have imprinted on the settlement they inherited. Working back through time from the plan of 21st-century York, the form and shape of the city as it was c.1600 can be defined with reasonable assurance by cartographically removing well-attested post-medieval and early modern streets and other intrusive features. Additionally, the impact on the townscape of some major Anglo-Norman and later medieval institutions, both secular and ecclesiastical, can be itemised and allowed for, and documentary references to their names testify to the existence of many streets by the later medieval period. Two late 11th-century documents are the earliest records of any York street-names, between them mentioning six streets, and by 1300 just under half of the medieval streets are mentioned in written sources (Palliser 1978, *passim*; cf. Fellows-Jensen, *infra*), although, of course, these sources do not indicate the date at which the streets originated. Nonetheless, it can be demonstrated that the plan of York in the late 11th century was already broadly that of the late medieval city, which can still be seen today in many places.

It is also clear that some important elements in the topographical framework derive from the Roman origins of intensive and large-scale settlement on this site during the first four centuries AD. It is equally clear that other facets of the Roman layout completely disappeared during a period of some seven centuries, c.400–1100, that is largely devoid of documentary evidence for the evolution of the settlement pattern. This is the critical period within which the late Roman layout was transformed into the plan recognisable today. This study considers the archaeological evidence for change over these centuries, outlining new discoveries and reviewing current theories, in the hope of presenting an up-to-date assessment of the topic.

York before the Vikings

Assessment of how York developed in the Anglo-Scandinavian period (c.866–1069) is made possible by advances made over the last three decades in the understanding of Roman (71–400) and Anglian (400–850) York that provide a physical, social and economic context for discussion of the Viking-Age city.

Change during the last century or so of Roman rule affected the internal layout and environmental conditions within both the legionary fortress and the walled civilian town (*colonia*) on the opposite bank of the River Ouse. Within the 50 acre/20 hectare fortress, with its massive stone perimeter walls, the 4th century was certainly a time when individual buildings were altered. This has been seen most clearly at the *principia* and its adjacent barrack blocks (Phillips and Heywood 1995, *passim*), and in the structures excavated at 9 Blake Street in the *praetentura* (*AY* 3/4, 349f.). There are also suggestions, for example in the possibility of a building being erected over a roadway on the Blake Street site, that relatively minor elements in the fortress infrastructure may have been altered. There is no evidence as yet for major changes to the internal plan of the fortress, or for variation to the extent of its defended area.

Across the River Ouse, the *colonia* was also in transition in the 4th century. Beside the Roman bridgehead, a large multi-phase stone building which had stood since the later 2nd century became roofless and derelict in the later 4th century. There are suggestions of 5th-century activity here (Whyman 2001), and demolition of the building continued piecemeal over a long period. The approach road to the bridge was also encroached upon during the 4th century by timber structures which occupied half of its width (Ottaway 1993, 114). At another site close to the waterfront, but some 200m downstream from the Roman bridgehead (1–9 Micklegate), a massive building, tentatively identified as a bath complex, had been erected in the late 3rd century. In the 4th century or later at least part of it was systematically demolished, depositing 1·5m of rubble over its floors. Regularly spaced post-holes cut into the surviving upper surface of one wall suggest the fabrication of a timber building on the Roman alignment, although it is not clear whether the demolition and the construction with post-holes were virtually contemporary or wholly separate episodes. The date of the post-holes is uncertain; nearby pits, apparently cut from the same level as the holes in the wall top, contained pottery of 7th- to 9th-century date.

These intriguing archaeological sequences demonstrate change in the late and post-Roman periods but also highlight the continuing difficulties in establishing a more precise chronology for events on individual sites and thus a general overview of what was happening in York in the period c.400–700. This era has also proved to be archaeologically elusive in and around the city, apart from the characteristic Anglian cremation burials and the incidence of a small number of equally characteristic artefact types. It does seem, however, that the principal legacy of Roman *Eboracum* that survived into the 7th century was the two defended enclosures, with their well-defined entrances. In contrast, most Roman buildings within these defences may have been reduced to rubble, stub walls or dangerous states of dereliction by the 7th century.

There is rather more evidence for York's form and function in the historically documented period of the 7th, 8th and early–mid 9th centuries. On the basis of contemporary documents, Rollason (*AY* 7/2, 133–8) has emphasised a predominant role in 7th- to 9th-century York for the bishopric/archbishopric. The writings of both Bede and Alcuin inevitably dwell on the importance of the cathedral church, its school and, perhaps, an associated monastery. At this time the settlement was called *Eoforwic*; as Fellows-Jensen has noted (*AY* 1, 230), the final element *wic* is attached to the names of a small group of pre-Viking sites including *Hamwic* (Southampton), *Lundenwic* (London) and *Gipeswic* (Ipswich) in England as well as *Quentovic* in the Pas-de-Calais. To judge from these examples, *wic*s were relatively large and densely occupied settlements with a diversity of manufacture and trade, thereby fulfilling a quasi-urban function.

Archaeologically, on the basis of identifying as 'Anglian' a range of objects from sites widely scattered throughout York, a recent study (*AY* 7/2) has proposed a pattern of extensive growth and topo-graphic development during this period. It suggests that many of the medieval streets, including ones which cut through and thereby weakened the south-eastern defences of the Roman fortress, were laid out by as early as 850, and that several of what we know as later medieval parish churches had been established by that time. This interpretation requires the earliest conceivable dates to be assigned to many of the streets and to some of the churches in question; at present, there is no clear-cut evidence to support these speculations. This interpretation also accepts the hypothetical dating to the Anglian period of some supposed secular structures, none of which, however, stands up to stringent scrutiny.

In its interpretation of portable material culture, despite a caveat that Anglian style does not necessarily equate with Anglian (i.e. pre-Viking) date (ibid., 259), the study generally attributes stylistically Anglian objects to the Anglian period, and in particular to the early–mid 9th century. This must also be questioned, as it makes no allowance for the continued use of these styles on objects made after the Viking take-over of York, in the second half of the 9th century or even slightly later. The loss of these objects and their deposition at their findspots may, of course, have occurred later still. If this argument is accepted, it casts doubt on the validity of interpreting the distribution of Anglian artefacts as a reliable guide to the extent of pre-Viking settlement.

In summary, a more critical reading of the evidence leaves virtually no reasonably clear or detailed archaeological data for the nature and extent of occupation and activity within the Roman defended areas, which may not have been occupied by anyone other than the archbishops at their cathedral church complex during the 7th–mid 9th century.

A contrast to these many uncertainties is provided by data recovered in excavations by York Archaeological Trust some 750m south-east of the Roman fortress and outside the limits of dense Roman occupation, at 46–54 Fishergate (*AY* 7/1). There, just beyond the confluence of the Rivers Ouse and Foss, parts of two large plots of land were revealed and investigated. The more fully excavated plot enclosed at least 1200m^2 and contained perhaps three 'hall'-style buildings. It was suggested that this was part of a deliberately planned settlement, initiated c.700 and lasting, with some interruption, until c.850. Subsequent excavations undertaken beyond the southern edge of this site by Field Archaeology Specialists at Blue Bridge Lane have also encountered Anglian occupation (Garner-Lahire, pers. comm.). Provisional interpretation suggests that occupation started there in the early 8th century, and continued to the mid 9th century and beyond. Boundary divisions marked by linear arrangements of rubbish pits, like those identified at 46–54 Fishergate, were seen.

Artefacts from 46–54 Fishergate indicated that a range of craft activities was undertaken on the site. These include iron working, copper alloy working, bone and antler working, fur and skin preparation, leather working, textile working and, possibly, the reworking of glass. The number of each class of object was small, however, and so the scale of these craft activities is uncertain (*AY* 17/9, 1442). Goods imported from Northern France, the Low Countries and the Rhineland point to York being a focus for international traders. The restricted animal bone assemblage suggests that the people living and working at Fishergate were supplied with meat (and possibly other food) by an outside authority through processes of redistribution — in other words, they were not themselves free marketeers but the agents of some higher power (*AY* 15/4, 276–84; O'Connor 2001). When a similar phenomenon was observed at the site of *Hamwic*, it was suggested that this higher power was the king (Bourdillon 1994), but other groups or individuals within the socio-economic elite, both secular and ecclesiastical, might have been responsible.

At the same time, however, the volume and ubiquity of 8th- and 9th-century coinage in York suggests that an incipient market economy was beginning to develop. Single finds of Anglian sceattas and, more particularly, 9th-century stycas, are quite commonly made in excavations, albeit often as residual items in later contexts. If their findspots are taken to be an accurate reflection of their original (i.e. pre-Viking) incidence throughout York, then it seems that coin use in *Eoforwic* was widespread. Coin hoards amplify and extend this picture. Seven coin hoards of 8th- to 9th-century date have been found in York, although details of some of them are sparse since all were recovered in the 18th or 19th century. One hoard was concealed c.800; the other six are all dated c.865, apparently coincident with the first Viking attack on York in 866. Several of these later hoards contained hundreds or even, in a few cases, thousands of these

relatively low-value coins, thereby suggesting that coinage was an accepted medium for transactions. This opens the possibility that the Fishergate properties were independent units, not all controlled directly by one single power (the king or the archbishop) but each belonging to an individual, such as a landowning aristocrat. They might have been used as manufacturing and commercial depots, where surplus raw materials from rural estates were made into saleable items. With the income thus gained, utilitarian necessities might have been purchased from other local or regional suppliers, and luxury goods acquired from foreign merchants or middlemen. When considered in conjunction with the mechanisms that must have been in place to provide the ecclesiastical community with the wide variety of necessities that they required, it seems reasonable to suggest that York was already the focus of an incipient supply network which linked it to an extensive hinterland. Against this backdrop, the economic developments of the late 9th and 10th centuries are not quite so revolutionary as is sometimes suggested, and can be compared with trends in economic activity elsewhere, such as at London (Blackburn 2003, 33–4).

The defended areas: their nature and extent

There is no doubt that late Roman York had two defended areas, fortress and *colonia*, on opposite banks of the River Ouse. The stone walls of the fortress are relatively well known (*AY* 3/3) and their position certain. By remarkable contrast it is assumption and analogy, coupled with limited 19th-century observations, which suggest that the *colonia* was defended by a stone wall. Those observations were confined to a 250m length of the north-west wall, and have been taken to suggest that at least the south-western corner of the medieval walled enclosure lay outside its Roman predecessor (RCHMY 1, 49). No archaeological examination of this defensive circuit south-west of the Ouse has taken place since the 19th century, and there is no evidence for how the supposed Roman defences evolved into the later medieval circuit. It is assumed that the Roman defensive line was refortified as and when necessary during the early medieval period.

A third possible Roman walled area lies immediately beyond the southern half of the north-western fortress defences, where three short but substantial lengths of wall revealed briefly in the 19th and 20th centuries were identified as being Roman in date and defensive in purpose. The boundary of the area enclosed is thought to continue the line of the south-west wall of the fortress beyond the north-west corner ('Multangular') tower, as far as Marygate; from there it is presumed to turn a right-angle and run alongside Marygate to Bootham, the main road approaching the fortress, and thence along Bootham to the Roman gateway. It has not been possible to determine the function of this area in the Roman period. However, the location at its periphery of the church of St Olave (St Olaf), built for and burial place of Earl Siward who died in 1055, suggests that the Roman walls may have enclosed *Earlsburgh*, the site of the earls' residence (cf. p.314).

The Roman fortress defences in the post-Roman period

It has sometimes been suggested that the south-west wall of the Roman fortress continued to be strengthened and to function as a defence into or throughout the Anglo-Scandinavian period. This proposition has been supported by reference to data recorded during an observation of building works at 2 St Helen's Square, approximately mid-way along that façade of the fortress. An undated post-hole recorded there probably forms the basis for a conjectural reconstruction of supposed post-Roman defences, published posthumously and without any explanatory note (Radley 1972, 57, fig.14; cf. Radley 1971, 39 n6); but this is just one of several possible interpretations of this evidence. Equally problematic is the interpretation of a series of post-Roman trenches found in front of remains of the south-west fortress wall at Roman interval tower SW5. The hypothesis that they are 'palisade trenches' and represent an attempt to strengthen surviving Roman defences at some time in the Anglo-Scandinavian or Anglo-Norman period (Addyman 1975, 207) may be countered with the suggestion that they are more likely to represent fence lines or demarcations of property subdivisions. Indeed, while the remains of both the north-west and north-east fortress walls were reinforced and heightened by post-Roman ramparts which eventually enveloped the Roman walls (cf. Radley 1972), traces of such post-Roman ramparts have not been identified at any point along either of the other two fortress walls. Thus, if the Roman defences on these two sides of the fortress continued in active use in the Anglo-Scandinavian period,

present evidence suggests that it would have been the walls themselves rather than post-Roman earthen ramparts which protected the settlement.

The evidence available up to c.1990 for the surviving state of the Roman fortress walls has been summarised elsewhere (*AY* 8/3, 264–77). Since then little additional relevant data has been gathered. The most notable new discoveries were made by York Archaeological Trust in 1997 during further redevelopment of the site of the former Davygate Centre, east of Newgate and south of Davygate. There, small-scale excavations demonstrated that the wall top still stood at least 2m above the Roman ground surface at the time of the Norman conquest, and that even in the 12th century it projected 1m or more above the contemporary ground level in front of it (Evans 1997). This indicates that along this south-west façade of the fortress, as also along the south-east side, the Roman fortress wall remained visible and was a topographic determinant until the end of the Anglo-Scandinavian era.

Two discoveries within the area between the south-east fortress wall and the River Foss have influenced interpretations of how the defences evolved thereabouts in the pre-Norman period. The first is a 'wickerwork hedge' or 'stockade' that was observed in 1902–3 below 5–7 Coppergate (Benson 1902), beyond the south corner tower of the Roman fortress. The other, uncovered in 1950–1 in K.M. Richardson's excavation in Hungate, was what she described as an 'Anglo-Danish embankment' fronting the River Foss. Richardson's published account describes and illustrates 18·30m of an embanked, curving feature averaging 2m in height and at least 14·60m in width (its rear, north-western limit was not reached). It had been thrown up over a 0·6m thick layer of brushwood, perhaps put down to consolidate an underlying sequence of sandy silts (Richardson 1959, 59). Delineated in reconstruction as a relatively simple affair in structural/stratigraphic terms (ibid., fig.5), the excavation record (ibid., fig.4) clearly shows a complex construction, which may have been heightened and extended towards the river at several different periods or at least in several different episodes.

Primary dating evidence comes in the form of a small quantity of pottery (61 pre-conquest sherds). The various pottery types are distributed without significant variation throughout 'the embankment';

with the exception of six possibly intrusive sherds they, and the associated artefacts, can all be dated to the period c.850–1100. The assemblage stratified directly over 'the embankment' produced mainly very abraded sherds of the 13th and 14th centuries; elsewhere on the site, however, stratigraphically equivalent layers produced 'gritty ware' cooking pots (ibid., 92) which are now thought to date to the period c.1075–1250 (*AY* 16/1, 11). These pottery sherds provide a *terminus ante quem* for 'the embankment'. Together, the stratigraphic and chronological evidence could be interpreted as suggesting that the feature may have evolved through several phases of accretion during the Anglo-Scandinavian and/or early Norman period, functioning successively as a waterfront and a flood barrier. Alternatively, it may be a one-period construction, a barrier to flooding thrown up in the late 11th century when the River Foss was dammed. Its absolute heights above Ordnance Datum — 9·15m AOD at its highest point and 7·5m at its base — compare with an Anglo-Scandinavian river level of 5·5–6m AOD, which rose to about 7m in the 12th century (*AY* 10/6, 774f, 857). There is, however, no evidence that this or any other feature defended the western (city centre) side of the River Foss — there was no trace, for example, of any palisade associated with Richardson's 'embankment'.

Richardson (1959, 60–1) related her 'embankment' to Benson's 'stockade' on the basis that both were associated with brushwood layers, that she perceived them to be broadly contemporary, and that Benson had referred to the Coppergate area as swampy and subject to flooding, just as Hungate was. Despite the considerable differences between the archaeological remains on the two sites, the Coppergate and Hungate discoveries subsequently became lynch-pins in the suggestion (RCHMY **2**, 8; Radley 1971, 38–9; Ramm 1972, 248) that there was a defended enclave beyond the south-east side of the Roman fortress. This hypothetical defensive line ran from the east corner of the Roman fortress to Peasholme Green and along the River Foss, via Hungate, to a point where it turned to run north-north-west, via Benson's 'stockade', to the south corner of the fortress. It is now suggested (*AY* 8/3, 239–42) that Benson's 'stockade' was a simple fence of standard Anglo-Scandinavian type, whereas Richardson's 'embankment' is a more substantial feature of entirely different character and function, as discussed above. This hypothetical enclosure should therefore be disregarded, and with it Ramm's

suggestions (1972, 248) that it formed a separate 'Danish enclave', and that the disappearance of the Coppergate 'stockade' could be linked to the report by William of Malmesbury that Athelstan had razed a *castrum* at York (*AY* 1, 165–6). This clears the way for a fresh examination of how the former Roman defensive lines may have been transformed into the medieval defensive circuit.

By the later medieval period the line of the north-eastern defences of the Roman fortress had been extended beyond the east corner tower and on, via a re-entrant, to the site of the medieval Layerthorpe Postern Gate, close to the River Foss. There is no clear-cut evidence for when this extension originated. The suggestion (RCHMY **2**, 8–10) that it was contrived in two distinct episodes — from the east corner of the Roman fortress probably as far as Peasholme Green in the Anglo-Scandinavian period, with the re-entrant down to Layerthorpe Postern added after the Norman conquest — was predicated on the 'Danish enclave' hypothesis that has been dismissed above. It is more likely, though unproven, that the whole of this extension to the north-east side of the fortress, as far as the west bank of the River Foss, was erected in the Anglo-Scandinavian period to protect the important and expanding commercial areas south-east of the fortress. This would also be the time when the north-west approach to the Ouse waterfront and the commercial area was similarly strengthened by adding the short length of rampart that links the south-west wall of the Roman fortress to the river bank, close to the modern Lendal Bridge.

Although the approaches from the north on the western side of the Foss may have been defended in the manner suggested above, there may have been several routes that led across the Foss from the east into the town centre. It is likely that just beyond the extended north-east defences there was a ford leading north-eastwards to the suburb of Layerthorpe, which was first recorded c.1070–88 (Palliser 1978, 12). Downstream of Layerthorpe the medieval crossing point at Foss Bridge (possibly on the line of a Roman predecessor) must, on topographical grounds, have been in existence before the Norman conquest. It has generally been believed that this crossing point was undefended, for excavations by York Archaeological Trust have confirmed the documentary evidence (RCHMY **2**, 11) that the medieval defensive rampart around the Walmgate area was an entirely new creation of the 13th century. It has, however, been suggested (Hall 1991, 91) that the arcing line of the St Denys' parish boundary, which embraces the area within a loop of the River Foss, reflects a former defensive line with its apex some 250m east of the river crossing. Analysis of the street pattern supports this suggestion, for the line of the now relatively insignificant George Street, which represents the northern part of the medieval street Fishergate, the main approach to the city from the south-east, runs up to and along this parish boundary; only where it joins Walmgate, the principal road out to the east, is the arcing line breached. This convergence of Fishergate and Walmgate on the parish boundary may reflect the former presence of a gateway through a defensive line, rather as the junction of Shambles and Colliergate indicates the position of the now-vanished *porta principalis sinistra*, mid-way along the south-eastern façade of the Roman fortress. Defended bridgeheads such as this were well known in 10th-century England: Edward the Elder, for example, erected several — and similar works had also been encountered by Viking raiders in Carolingian Europe. The creation of one at York would not, therefore, be remarkable, and it would have shielded much of the west bank of the Foss from direct attack across the river; as noted above, no evidence has yet been found for any defensive structures in that area.

Having defined so far as is currently possible the defended limits of *Jorvík,* it is possible to make a minimal and approximate estimate of the area available for occupation. This includes the Roman fortress of 20 hectares; the 35 hectares south-west and south-east of the fortress, between the fortress and the rivers Foss and Ouse respectively; and the 27 hectares within the Roman *colonia.* This total of some 82 hectares (200 acres) takes no account of the hypothetical Walmgate bridgehead of 6 hectares, of strip settlements along the approach roads such as Walmgate, of *Earlsburgh,* or of any other extra-mural settlement.

Settlement layout

Within the fortress, opportunities to collect data since 1970 have predominantly been south-east of a central line defined by Stonegate, the *via praetoria.* With only one significant exception (see below) assemblages of manufacturing debris are all found south-east of this line. The extent to which this phenomenon also reflects better chances of surviving modern dis-

turbance in this part of the former fortress is uncertain; it is, however, clear that there is an increasing depth of deposits above a natural ground surface which slopes downwards into the south corner of the fortress and beyond. Within the very slightly more elevated north-western half of the former fortress, the archbishop apparently owned at least one quadrant of the defended area from the late 7th century, if not more (*AY* 1, 140–1). Indeed, Norton (1998, 17f) has suggested that a block of land encompassing the entire northern quadrant of the former fortress and the outer half of the western quadrant, as well as a small salient into the eastern quadrant, was in the hands of the church by the time the Viking army conquered York.

The pre-Norman cathedral stood somewhere here, perhaps either to the south or to the north of its Norman successor, but not below it on the site of the basilican cross-hall of the Roman *principia* (Phillips 1985, 1; Norton 1998). There are opposing views on the longevity of the Roman *basilica* — Phillips and Heywood (1995, 65f.) believe that it stood into the 9th century, while Carver (ibid., 195) offers the interpretation that it had collapsed or been dismantled during the 6th–8th centuries. In either case, there is no evidence for Anglo-Scandinavian occupation or activity within the *basilica* apart from the establishment of a high-status cemetery.

To the west, however, within the shell of the nearby Roman legionary Barrack 2, a freestanding hearth was in use during this epoch, interpreted as a smith's forge, and there is also evidence there of ferrous and non-ferrous metal working (ibid., 193). Carver has floated the idea that the relict Roman townscape determined the form of Anglo-Scandinavian developments hereabouts — that the stub remains of Roman walls 'were contrived into houses', that earth was imported or displaced for allotments, and that industrial activities were practised. He has proposed 'a moderately dense, even urban exploitation of the Minster area in the Anglo-Scandinavian period', while being uncertain whether the specific acts listed above reflected ecclesiastical or secular imperatives (ibid., 194). The enduring influence of the Roman military layout at this time — as opposed to the years after the Norman conquest — is not in doubt, but the transformation of derelict and dilapidated Roman buildings into 'houses' has not been recognised elsewhere in York, or in late Saxon England. The waist-level forge is presently unparalleled in 9th- to 11th-century Britain, and the scale of metal working is impossible to judge; but the possibility that this was for the benefit of the cathedral community, rather than for wholly commercial reasons, cannot be ignored.

Beyond the *principia*/York Minster core, a majority of the streets now existing within the fortress are likely to be of Anglo-Scandinavian origin, apart from well-known additions (e.g. Deangate; Parliament Street; New Street). Not all contemporary streets have survived to the present day, however, particularly within the medieval precinct of York Minster. For example, there is documentary evidence for the existence of a street which ran north-east from Petergate parallel to the south-east side of the Roman *principia* as far as its eastern corner (Norton 1998, 20). From there it perhaps ran due north until it met the *via decumana* (now Chapter House Street). Documentary evidence and topographic inference indicate that this Anglo-Scandinavian street remained in use into the Anglo-Norman period. This does not itself prove that the *porta decumana* also remained in use; the date at which it was closed, and replaced by a gateway in the position now occupied by Monk Bar, is uncertain.

South-east of the fortress, as has been increasingly well recognised since the 1970s (Radley 1971), sites in the Coppergate/Ousegate/Pavement vicinity had their boundaries defined during the Anglo-Scandinavian period, either certainly or probably in the early 10th century (McComish and Macnab forthcoming; *AY* 8/5 in prep.). This layout of relatively long narrow occupation plots, typically about 5.5m (16ft 6in.) wide, seems to have had a formative and enduring influence on the townscape, being reproduced through successive centuries (*AY* 10/6, *passim*). This area, on the northern side of the only crossing point of the Ouse, was clearly the scene of much redevelopment and represents the economic boom that occurred in the generations after the Viking invasion and settlement.

Further to the east, across the River Foss, a series of excavations undertaken in 1990–2000, albeit mostly of a small-scale evaluatory character, have demonstrated something of the extent to which Walmgate was occupied in the Anglo-Scandinavian era and the density of that occupation. The largest scale work, embracing some 250m², was carried out by York Archaeological Trust in 2000–1 at 41–49 Walmgate,

about 200m beyond Foss Bridge, and revealed evidence for structures, occupation and a variety of industrial or craft activities (Macnab et al. 2003). The earliest layers investigated there are dated to the 10th century and included stake and wattlework alignments running back at 90° to the Walmgate street line. A succession of structural elements was identified at the modern street frontage, continuing on past the Norman conquest.

In 1995 a 3m square excavated by ARCUS on Walmgate, near the corner of Margaret Street, some 300m from Foss Bridge, revealed structural remains in the form of clay layers interpreted as floors, alignments of upright timbers parallel to Walmgate interpreted as internal wall lines, and other features. These remains are dated to the Anglo-Scandinavian period; associated artefacts and environmental remains were characterised as 'domestic' (Foster 1995). Further out of the city's centre, evaluation trenches excavated by York Archaeological Trust close to the modern frontage at 104–112 Walmgate, 350m from Foss Bridge, revealed possible structural traces of timber buildings, floors and other evidence for occupation of 10th- to 11th-century date (Evans 1992, *passim*). Slightly nearer to the late medieval defences, at 118–26 Walmgate, York Archaeological Trust excavations in 1978 also revealed traces of Anglo-Scandinavian occupation.

Although the scope of some of these investigations has resulted in the collection of only limited data, the evidence does indicate that the frontages of Walmgate were occupied along most if not all its length by the 10th–11th century. The extent to which the wider area later enclosed within the Walmgate rampart was occupied at this time is unclear. Observations at Leadmill Lane revealed a dump of comb-makers' waste which is probably of Anglo-Scandinavian date (Addyman 1975, 217); this may relate to activity/occupation along the main approach road to York from the south, Fishergate, now renamed George Street in this area. A similar interpretation probably accounts for the small quantities of pre-conquest pottery recovered from slightly further from the urban core, at a handful of sites along or close to ancient Fishergate and at sites beyond Walmgate Bar (see p.460), but the significance of this material requires further elucidation. So too do the traces of pits, possible fence and boundary lines, and structural remains, found just behind Leake Street, in the angle between Foss Islands

Road and Lawrence Street; dated to the 10th–12th centuries, they hint at occupation well behind the frontage of the main road running east towards the Humber.

In contrast, the other main approaches to the city — Blossom Street from the south-west, Bootham from the north-west, and both Monkgate and Layerthorpe from the north-east — have (as yet) produced hardly any evidence of occupation or activity along their margins. Beyond the former Roman fortress, excavations within and alongside the River Foss at Layerthorpe, undertaken by MAP Archaeological Consultancy Ltd when Layerthorpe Bridge was rebuilt, uncovered wattlework alignments and other layers/features of 10th- to 11th-century date. Anglo-Scandinavian deposits contained much bark, suggestive of tanning, and associated soil samples contained abundant remains of flax stems, indicative of flax retting (Anon. 1998b, *passim*). No traces of the Anglo-Scandinavian buildings or properties which made up the Layerthorpe settlement have yet been located, however. Other peripheral settlements may have included a religious foundation at Clementhorpe, 140m southeast of the *colonia* area. Like Layerthorpe, this name is first attested 1070–88, half a century before the foundation of St Clement's nunnery, and it has been suggested that the kernel of the settlement here was a pre-conquest church dedicated to St Clement, as were so many contemporary churches in settlements with Scandinavian connections. There is some structural evidence, stratigraphically sandwiched between Roman and 12th-century deposits, which could be the remains of a pre-conquest church, although further excavation is needed to verify this (*AY* 8/1, 57–61).

The density of settlement within and south of the former fortress, and within the former *colonia*, will have been determined in part by issues of land ownership and usage. Long, narrow property plots such as those identified at Coppergate presumably represent many of the almost 2,000 *mansiones* to which the *Domesday Book* entry for York refers. They may not, however, have been the only or the original form of Anglo-Scandinavian landholding within the city; there is the possibility that larger land units existed, 'urban estates' like the *haga* recorded in documents relating to late 9th-century London (Dyson 1978; 1990) or early 10th-century Worcester (Robert-son 1956, 34–9; Sawyer 1968, 371; Baker and Holt 1996, 134f).

The usage of the former *colonia* area may also have been very variable. Property divisions running perpendicular to the River Ouse, fronting on to Skeldergate, were created in the Anglo-Scandinavian period, but there is no clear archaeological evidence for the economic activities associated with the pre-conquest buildings excavated at 58–9 Skeldergate (*AY* 8/1, 37–52). There is now an imperative to investigate further the records made in York Archaeological Trust's 1988–9 excavations at Wellington Row, a street which is the riverside equivalent of Skeldergate on the northern (upstream) side of Ouse Bridge. Provisional analysis of the excavated data suggests that there was activity or occupation on this site in the Anglo-Scandinavian period but its precise nature, layout and extent are currently unknown.

Data from York Archaeological Trust's rescue excavations carried out in 1988–9 at 1–9 Micklegate have also not yet been analysed in detail, but they contain no obvious indication of a prevalent industry or activity. Those excavations were important, however, for revealing that Anglo-Scandinavian timber structures were laid out to respect the line of Micklegate, the 'great street'. The sweeping curve of Micklegate, which cuts across and is therefore later than the Roman street grid, is the main approach to the medieval and modern Ouse Bridge. It can thus be proved that the street had been created by the 10th century, and that the crossing point had moved by then from its earlier, Roman, site about 160m upstream.

All of these excavations in the former *colonia* have been in the vicinity where Anglo-Scandinavian riverside commercial activities might be anticipated. This is, after all, where pre-Viking overseas trade is best attested by the occurrence of imported pottery vessels (Mainman 1993). Unfortunately, the only opportunity which has yet arisen for an investigation of the Anglo-Scandinavian river frontage itself has been a 5·5m diameter shaft dug by York Archaeological Trust in 1993 at North Street Pumping Station. This is next to *Divelinestaynes* ('Dublinstones'), a lane and quay first recorded in the 13th century (Palliser 1978, 9). Yet again, financial considerations have precluded any detailed analysis of the records to date, but the presence of well-preserved wattlework hurdles lying on the foreshore suggests the repeated stabilisation of a beaching area in the Anglo-Scandinavian era (Finlayson 1993).

Analysis of the records from this suite of sites holds the key to defining more closely the nature of activity hereabouts. Stocker (2000, 203–5) has recently suggested that the unusually large number of 10th-century grave stones from St Mary Bishophill Senior indicates that this was a church patronised by a community of Hiberno-Norse traders; Palliser (1984, 105) has proposed that elements in the street plan of this vicinity can be interpreted as a deliberate act of town planning by late 9th-century archbishops of York. This hypothetical commercial quarter could have fostered an embryonic trading organisation which developed into the Gild Merchant; in the early 12th century this had its headquarters in its *hanshus* south of the Ouse (ibid., 107).

Any traders (or others) resident in Bishophill would have been neighbours to what was, in the 11th century at least, an ecclesiastical institution of first rank importance, Christ Church/Holy Trinity, forerunner of the later medieval Holy Trinity Priory. At the time of *Domesday Book* Christ Church/Holy Trinity was one of a select few churches in northern England — York Minster, Ripon Minster, Beverley Minster and St Cuthbert Durham were the others — with an especially privileged and independent status. It has been suggested that it owed this ultimately to the building campaigns of Archbishop Aelberht in the late 8th century, that it represents his architecturally innovative *Alma Sophia* referred to by Alcuin, and that this was the site of an Anglo-Saxon monastery (Morris 1986).

It has also been suggested that there was an ecclesiastical precinct here which contained other churches, including St Mary Bishophill Senior, St Mary Bishophill Junior and St Gregory. Norton, however, believes that St Mary Bishophill Junior was built in the 1080s as part of a package of measures associated with the founding of Holy Trinity Priory (C. Norton, pers. comm.). Furthermore, if Stocker's suggestion about the patronage of St Mary Bishophill Senior is correct, it would probably not have been under the control of Christ Church/Holy Trinity in the 10th and 11th centuries. The concept of an ecclesiastical precinct here in either the pre-Viking or Anglo-Scandinavian period thus requires corroboration. Nonetheless, the status of Christ Church/Holy Trinity in the 11th century is unimpeachable, and it may have had some precinct around it.

The hypothesis that St Mary Bishophill Senior was a merchants' church — perhaps a guild church — is built on the knowledge that wealthy townsmen sponsored the building of their own private churches. The clearest example of this practice in York is St Mary Castlegate, where a dedication stone records the founding by three individuals (Okasha 1971, 131; *AY* 8/2, 147–65) (see Fig.85, p.353). Elsewhere, the presence of grave stones, which are thought to have marked the burials of founding patrons and their immediate relations, indentifies churches in existence in the Anglo-Scandinavian era. By comparing the list of seven churches named in *Domesday Book* with locations where Viking-Age sculpture has been found, and then collating this evidence with other documentary data, it seems possible to identify twelve churches founded in the pre-Norman period. They include St Mary Bishophill Senior, St Mary Bishophill Junior, St Mary Castlegate, All Saints Pavement, St Cuthbert Peasholme Green, St Crux Pavement, Holy Trinity Micklegate, St Andrew Fishergate, St Martin Micklegate, St Denys Walmgate, St Sampson and St Olave.

Excavated evidence now indicates that further churches may be added to this list. In three cases it is the discovery of a cemetery which has given chronological definition. Within the former fortress, there is documentary evidence for a church of St Benet in Swinegate which was closed in 1263; dendrochronological study of wooden coffins excavated in Swinegate and presumed to come from this church's cemetery has now demonstrated that they were fashioned from timbers cut down c.890–1050. Another cemetery that existed in the Anglo-Scandinavian period is represented by grave markers found when Parliament Street was created in the 1830s; they may be associated with 'rude wooden coffins' found in Parliament Street, probably below numbers 36–7, in 1878 (Raine 1891, 74; Lang et al. 1991, 108). Dowelled wooden coffins, comparable in their description to those found in Swinegate, were also reputedly found in 1840 at a depth of 14ft (4·27m) below the south-west corner of St Saviour's Church, St Saviourgate (Raine 1955, 77). It may be that they represent an early medieval cemetery associated with this church, which is known to have existed by AD 1100; St Saviour's is not, however, included in this list of pre-conquest churches. By coincidence, a similarly dowelled coffin was found nearby in 1839, when excavating foundations for the Salem Chapel that stood in St Saviour's Place, facing the north-east end of St Saviourgate

(Wellbeloved 1875, 135; RCHMY **5**, 54); its context, date and associations are unclear.

In methodological contrast, at William the Conqueror's castle between the Rivers Ouse and Foss, it is the fact that skeletons were found below a layer interpreted as the remains of William's bailey rampart which suggests the existence of an Anglo-Scandinavian church. Together with one of the seven shires of the city, this putative church was *devastata in castellis* — destroyed to make way for the castles. In two other cases the remains of both a church and its cemetery have been excavated by York Archaeological Trust. The 'lost' church of St Helen-on-the-Walls, Aldwark, made redundant and demolished in the 16th century, has been located. It originated as a small, single-cell church of perhaps 10th-century date, measuring 7·5 x 5·8m externally and built on a stone rubble foundation (*AY* 10/1, 16f). The other excavated church was found beside the medieval Gilbertine Priory of St Andrew in Fishergate (*AY* 11/2, 74–6); it is this discovery which suggests that the *Domesday Book* reference to a St Andrew's related to this church rather than to St Andrew's in St Andrewgate. This Fishergate church was a timber structure, so badly disturbed by later activities that its size could not accurately be calculated; it can be dated to c.1000–50.

It is not clear whether the absence of funerary sculpture from several of these ecclesiastical sites reflects the date of their foundation. The majority of large grave covers are dated to the first half of the 10th century, and it could be that churches without these monuments were founded later — although the York Minster cemetery evidence shows that grave covers, albeit re-used ones, were still fashionable as signals of status into the later 10th and 11th centuries.

It may have been the magnates who commissioned the surviving grave covers and who, perhaps, founded the churches in which they were buried, who were also responsible for developing the associated urban estates. The sculpture, which cannot be dated precisely, is bracketed within the period c.900–50, the time when tenement plots at 16–22 Coppergate were defined.

Further expansion of the town's economy could be reflected in a variety of ways, including the subdivision of existing landholdings within the core of the urban area, and the development of previously vacant land at the edge of the built-up area. More intensive use of individual plots was initiated in the 960s–970s at 16–22 Coppergate, where a single rank of earlier buildings on the street frontage had a second rank of buildings added just behind it. At the same time, the long-established single-storey form of buildings constructed in the post and wattle technique was replaced by cellared, two-storey plank-built structures. This not only transformed the appearance of buildings but multiplied the usable space in a manner that seems geared towards new patterns of activity within them.

In conclusion, the changing patterns of land usage and structural development that have been the subject of this chapter have a relevance far beyond their intrinsic interest. They represent some of the most important sources of evidence for the political, social and economic strategies decided by or foisted upon those who controlled *Jorvik*. The implementation of those strategies determined the broad course of York's development, and provided a framework within which — area by area, street by street, property by property — individual landowners pursued their own ambitions and thus contributed to the shaping of the city. At present there is sufficient evidence to assure us that the Anglo-Scandinavian period was fundamental to York's development. With very few exceptions, however, chronological and other detail is lacking, and so the overall picture of urban growth remains somewhat unfocussed. The challenge now is to match the obvious needs — to provide core data on a number of topics (the waterfronts, for example) and to determine more precisely the overall trajectory of urban growth — with the opportunities provided by redevelopment proposals and with other research initiatives.

Afterword

By R.A. Hall

There is a measure of agreement here that the mid 9th-century pre-Viking settlement at York, *Eoforwic*, was different in scale and character from the *Jorvik* that was documented in *Domesday Book* and that has been sampled, albeit spasmodically, in archaeological investigations. *Eoforwic* fulfilled several complementary functions — it contained the cathedral of the Archbishop of the Northumbrians, it attracted foreign traders and their goods, and it was a place of significance to Northumbrian kings. The nature of the coinage suggests (p.325) that these later 8th- and 9th-century rulers were becoming increasingly isolated, politically and economically, although it is also suggested here (p.490) that York may have participated in, perhaps even been the centre of, an incipient Northumbrian market economy (cf. Naylor 2001, *passim*).

Bioarchaeological evidence from excavations, both in and around the Roman walled areas and also approximately 1km downstream of them, at Fishergate, is interpreted as showing that *Eoforwic* was not a thriving town. There is no sign yet of the closely built-up streetscapes which characterise at least parts of the Viking-Age city, nor of the much denser contemporary occupation now known from Southampton, London and Canterbury (p.424). The absence of black rat bones from the Fishergate site and elsewhere in York is likewise taken to be an indication that Anglian York did not have a human population sufficiently numerous to create the conditions that attracted this synanthropic species (pp.440–1; *AY* 15/4, 256–8). A recent survey of the artefactual and archaeological evidence, incorporating a hypothetical overview of topographical development, concurs that York was not a densely settled urban area in the 8th or 9th centuries (*AY* 7/2, 212). It is suggested here that a review of the artefactual and structural evidence challenges even some of the more modest claims made in that study for the extent and nature of occupation and activity in Anglian York (p.489).

Documentary evidence states that *Eoforwic* was captured by the Viking army in 866/7. Two excavated sites indicate that patterns of occupation and land-use in York changed at around the time of this takeover. It is suggested that there was a withdrawal from the Fishergate area east of the River Foss in the late 860s and 870s, and a virtually simultaneous resumption of occupation in the Coppergate area to the west of the Foss (*AY* 7/1, 83–4). A coin of Ethelbert of Wessex (858–66) has been taken as an indicator of the date after which Fishergate was abandoned; this disregards a quarter of a penny minted in York c.895–905, found in a context believed to date to a period of renewed activity on the site c.1000 (*AY* 11/2, 78).

The *Anglo-Saxon Chronicle* records that part of this Viking army settled in the countryside of Northumbria in 876; presumably the Viking warriors took control of pre-existing estates. The disruption of established socio-economic norms caused by this Viking takeover led to transformations of Yorkshire's rural settlement pattern in the 9th–10th century that have been revealed in a handful of key archaeological investigations (Hall 2003, 176f). This Viking settlement, under the leadership of Halfdan, rewarded a successful army with spoils of war from which a long-term benefit could be reaped. It also ensured the continued presence in England of warriors who might still go on to raid or conquer other areas — a variant of Rollason's view of the Viking kings of York as being 'basically leaders of a Viking army based in York' (p.311). Halfdan, however, apparently did not live long enough to enjoy the fruits of his success; he disappears from the historical record in 877 (*AY* 1, 63–4). The strategic goal of Guthfrith, the next secular Viking ruler in Northumbria about whom we have any information, is also unknown. During his reign Northumbrian Vikings raided southwards, but he obviously employed the tactic of accommodation with the Christian church, for in 895 he was buried in York Minster. He did not issue a coinage of any size, however, and therefore seems not to have realised the economic and political advantages that accrue from minting.

Positive archaeological evidence for what happened in York in the second half of the 9th century has been identified with reasonable certainty only at 16–22 Coppergate. The block of land there does not appear to have been subdivided into long, narrow property plots, as it was in the 10th century, and neither are there any readily identifiable traces of buildings on the site at this time. There are, however, incontrovertible signs of activity, including some evidence for craft processes — blacksmithing (*AY* 17/6, 720), copper alloy working (*AY* 17/7, 816), textile-making (*AY* 17/11, 1793–5), bone and antler working (*AY* 17/12, 1919), and amber working (*AY* 17/14, 2509). Quantitatively, these activities were relatively minor in comparison with the central decades of the 10th century, and they could be said to represent a continuation of the scale of craft activities carried out on the pre-Viking Fishergate site. Their modest scale might be taken to support Blackburn's suggestion (p.325) that it was difficult to do business in York in the 870s and 880s because this was a time when no new coins were minted in Northumbria and the stock of pre-Viking coinage was diminished. That debased coinage would have been of little interest to Vikings, for whom silver was the recognised and desirable medium of exchange, and such business as there was might have been conducted using bullion.

From c.895, however, there was a York regal coinage of remarkable volume; Rollason (p.322) attributes its quality to an influx of Viking silver acquired by trade or plunder. What led to the inception of this coinage? More than simply a desire by the Viking kings to emulate and surpass those Viking settlers further south who had earlier begun to strike coins in imitation of Anglo-Saxon issues, it marks a sea change in the attitude of Viking kings of Northumbria to how they should utilise their new conquest. Whatever its varied propaganda impact locally, nationally and internationally, this coinage was presumably struck to facilitate commerce and to open the way for taxation. Its introduction c.895, and the initial reorganisation of the Coppergate site into tenement plots c.900, may both mark a new and deliberate fiscal policy to create an urban economic infrastructure which would raise revenue for York's rulers. Such developments correspond with contemporary strategies in Wessex and English Mercia. From c.875 onwards King Alfred was overseeing the start of a programme to expand the number of mints there (Blackburn 1996, 162–4). Aethelred and Aethelflaed, Lord and Lady of the Mercians, were granting trading rights in their new fortified *burh* at Worcester in c.889–99 (Whitelock (ed.) 1979, 540), and Alfred and Aethelred jointly were granting land in London at the same time for purposes connected with commerce (Dyson 1990, 102–3).

The extent to which this economic evolution was a carefully planned and controlled process may be debatable, but the archaeological evidence for a significantly increased volume of craft production in 10th-century York points to a 'boom town' economy. The new phenomenon of mass production by specialist artisans is attested archaeologically both in their products and in their manufacturing debris (p.464f). There is also the evidence of streets with names of Old Norse form that suggest the presence of craft specialists, such as cup-makers (Coppergate) and shield-makers (Skeldergate). These 'professional' street-names are not recorded until the 12th century or later, so it is archaeology that provides the evidence for the presence and grouping of specialised crafts at an earlier date. Cup-making was certainly in full swing in Coppergate in the 10th century; in contrast, shield-makers have yet to be identified in York's archaeological record (p.365).

The correlation of street-names with Viking-Age economic specialisms can present problems, however. *Domesday Book* has a reference to *ii bancos in macello* ('two stalls in the meat market'), an area equated with the street now called Shambles, which takes this name from the Middle English for butchers' stalls, *flesshammelles*/flesh shambles. Superficially this suggests the presence of a well-established meat market or street of butchers in Anglo-Scandinavian York. Yet archaeological evidence indicates that butchery and meat distribution in the pre-Norman period was carried out at household or neighbourhood level (p.435). Perhaps the Shambles meat market was a recent innovation in 1086; or is there some more fundamental misunderstanding of the onomastic or animal bone evidence?

The burgeoning growth of 10th-century *Jorvik*, identified in the artefactual remains, is also attested by several other strands of evidence. The area occupied by the town seems to have expanded, as the widening distributions of successive pottery types indicate (pp.459–63). Although later soil moving can seriously distort the evidential value of artefact distribution plots, as Atkin and Evans (2002, 236) have discussed in relation to middle-Saxon Ipswich, several positive correlations at York between the incidence of Anglo-Scandinavian pottery and contemporary structural evidence (e.g. in Walmgate; p.494) provide some confirmation of the more extensive patterns which the pottery distributions imply.

One clarification of the timing of this urban growth that is provided by archaeology concerns the apparent development of the Walmgate area. The documentary evidence of the *Rights and Laws* of Archbishop Thomas indicates that at the end of the 11th century the archbishop's shire included Walmgate (p.316). Structural evidence from the mid–late 10th century, one hundred years or more before this earliest documented occupation, has recently been discovered at 41–49 Walmgate (p.494). This is not necessarily the earliest occupation on this site, although pottery from other sites in the vicinity suggests that development hereabouts got underway in the 10th century rather than the 9th (pp.475–6). A biologically based model for the evolution of this 'peripheral' area suggests that at an early stage of urban settlement it might have been crowded with smallholdings, perhaps originally farmyards, that would later be subdivided into tenements (p.408). It remains to be seen if this hypothesis can be substantiated archaeologically through an examination of earlier levels in adjacent sites.

Biological evidence is also contributing to the topographical study of the Anglo-Scandinavian city. The phrase 'old-fashioned farmyard' has been employed in the interpretation of conditions at sites in various parts of *Jorvik*, including the outer end of Walmgate (at Nos.118–26) and St Saviourgate (p.423). At other sites, albeit not extensively studied, such as 4–7 Parliament Street, the keeping of livestock might be one of the reasons for the generally foul conditions (p.421). Extrapolating from these examples, Hall and Kenward provisionally draw a distinction between two areas of *Jorvik*, a central core incorporating land on either side of the River Ouse, and its periphery. They suggest that one reason for the bio-archaeological distinction between these two areas may be a difference in the material typically used in each locale for making the roofs of buildings.

There is a correlation between the core zones which Hall and Kenward define and the area within which cellared or 'sunken' buildings of Anglo-Scandinavian date have been located. These two-storey buildings double the available floor area, and indicate where there was greatest pressure on land. The only precise date available for any of these cellared buildings in York, from the Coppergate excavation, shows that they were erected in the 970s. Thus both the expansion into Walmgate and the intensifying use of Coppergate point to a booming economy in the mid–late 10th-century town. Blackburn (pp.340–1) has commented on the considerable volume of minting in York in the 940s to mid-950s; this urban expansion may be a corollary of that prosperity.

It was at this time, as the millennium approached, that Archbishop Oswald (970/1–992) occupied jointly the sees of York and Worcester. Rollason (p.317) has suggested that this was a time of 'low status and resources' for the archbishopric, even though it seems that York was still enjoying a period of wealth and growth. His reign, for example, coincided with the expansion of occupation at Coppergate. More relevant, however, since a century later it was definitely in the archbishops' hands, is the suggestion that Walmgate's commercial value was developing at this time. If this did not add to Oswald's treasury, then his Thames-side property holding should also have been generating an increased income at a time when London's commerce seems to have been developing rapidly (Dyson 1990, 102–5; Thomas 2002, 3–9). Unquantifiable though these income streams may be, they nonetheless suggest that Oswald and his near contemporaries in the archbishopric may not have been financially bereft.

Other biological evidence also points to a growing 10th- and 11th-century city. O'Connor has noted that fishing supplied an important component in the provisioning of York, and that there was a progressive increase in the range of the fishermen's operations, ultimately taking them out from York into the Humber basin and then into North Sea inshore waters (p.438). Were they forced to expand their fishing grounds simply because a stable population in York was depleting the reaches close to the city, or does this phenomenon represent the needs of a growing population? A population of 6,000 to 10,000 is estimated by Hall and Kenward (p.395) on the basis of what might be described as faecal guesswork. At its upper limit this estimate is in step with figures calculated with reference to other, documentary, evidence (pp.320–1). Yet Hall and Kenward's overall estimation is predicated on a belief that, on average, only two people occupied each of the tenement plots excavated at Coppergate. This is a much lower multiplier than that customarily employed when calculating populations on the basis of numbers of households; perhaps, therefore, the figure should be revised upwards.

However many of them there were, where did these new townsfolk come from? Moneyers' personal names indicate that there was a notable Frankish component among that particular elite group in the period 927–54 (p.342), apparently representing an influx of practitioners experienced in the business of mint management. In the period 971–1016 individuals with Scandinavian names account for 70% of this same group, while *Domesday Book* records that 57% of the named householders had Scandinavian names (p.359). In later 10th-century York, however, the names given to individuals may represent political choices rather than simple custom, and therefore they cannot be taken at face value as a guide to their bearer's origins. And for the overwhelming majority of York's population there is not even this potentially biased form of information about their descent. It seems inherently likely that the majority of York's inhabitants throughout this entire era were drawn from a region corresponding to the county of Yorkshire, but this awaits proof.

If their geographical origins are largely elusive, what clues are there as to how York's mid 9th- to mid 11th-century population defined its 'cultural identity'? One means of addressing this issue is through an analysis of the characteristics of their possessions; but it must be recognised that, as with their personal names, these very artefacts were the means by which identity could be deliberately manipulated or incidentally distorted (Hall 2000, 317f). In terms of decoration, Tweddle points out (p.453) that pure Scandinavian Viking art styles occur infrequently on objects found in York. Instead, elements from some of the earlier of these Viking art styles, the Borre and Jellinge, which were current in the Scandinavian homelands from the mid 9th to mid/later 10th century, were adapted into innovative Anglo-Scandinavian decorative schemes, in which southern English and Continental influences were also blended with northern English traditions.

In questioning the extent to which these Scandinavian styles were understood in York, and in stressing that the process of assimilating them into the local repertoire 'is unlikely to have been simple or straightforward' (p.456), Tweddle prompts a consideration of several key factors. For example, when the rise of mass production brought artisans rather than artists/craftsmen to a position of crucial economic importance, what was the creative impact, and how did that affect the choice of models upon which products were based?

The relatively little evidence for Scandinavian art styles being crucially influential after c.950–75 may be explained by the contemporary political circumstances, in which the last independent Viking king of York, Erik Bloodaxe, was expelled from the city in 954. Yet even in the earlier stages of the Scandinavian settlement of Yorkshire, it appears that pure Scandinavian decorative traditions were not widely adopted. It seems that by the time that mass production took hold, in the years after 900, the inhabitants of York had already coalesced socially and politically into a coherent Anglo-Scandinavian community. They thereby created a climate in which craftsmen with eclectic and cosmopolitan vision could establish a new artistic identity appropriate to the new political circumstances. Lang (1988, 48), on the basis of his analysis of the decorated wooden artefacts recovered there, concluded that a broadly comparable phenomenon occurred in Viking-Age Dublin; further comparative studies, for example of London, would helpfully place these observations within a wider perspective.

Other aspects of life in *Jorvik* that demanded a deliberate choice from the population also demonstrate either continuity or innovative adaptation rather than wholesale adoption of contemporary Scandinavian norms. O'Connor (pp.442–5) has shown how the evidence of animal bones indicates that Anglo-Scandinavian York was supplied by an agricultural subsistence regime generally similar to others across much of north-western Europe, a regime that showed considerable continuity with pre-Viking practices. Continuity was also fostered in terms of the weight standard of the first Viking regal coinage minted at York (p.339), which, in spite of a gap of 30 years or more since the last regional coinage was struck, resumed in this regard as if uninterrupted.

The manipulation of the iconography of the York mint's output indicates both a sophisticated wielding of power and an agenda of social inclusion. Although in times of threat in 919, 939 and c.952 the coinage was used to appeal to 'distinctive Norse sentiments', it was presumably the monied, land-owning classes who were principally being canvassed. Some of these were probably descendants of the land-takers in the 'great heathen army', others were, perhaps, the associates of Ragnald and his Hiberno-Norse dynasty; they were the section of society that potentially had most to lose through regime change. At those chronological removes from the invasion and settlement, however, Norse attributes were primarily important as being among the key ingredients that distinguished the Anglo-Scandinavian Kingdom of York from its advancing southerly neighbour. To emphasise them was to emphasise independence — in other words, it was their current political symbolism rather than their original ethnic affiliation that gave them potency and currency.

In contrast to these and other artefacts of Anglo-Scandinavian life (cf. p.356), the street-names of Viking-Age York are believed to represent a more spontaneously generated attribute of the city's culture — its speech and dialect. It is therefore significant that this attribute was expressed largely in the Danish variant of Old Norse, although there are characteristics in the street-name formations which indicate the presence of Norwegians (p.367). Moreover, as Fellows-Jensen has pointed out, York is exceptional among towns with '-*gate*' street-names for the variety of other Scandinavian generics (ibid.); this she links to York having absorbed more Scandinavian settlers over a longer period than was the case in other English towns.

Fellows-Jensen also draws attention to the fact that several of the Scandinavian personal names of York tenants recorded in *Domesday Book* are of types that became common in Denmark after the year 1000. This leads her to suggest that they are likely to represent fairly recent (i.e. 11th-century) immigrants to York (p.359). This observation casts new light on the strength of links across the North Sea around and beyond the millennium. It may also have a relevance *vis-à-vis* the homelands of the merchants mentioned in a passage in the *Life of St Oswald* written c.995–1005: 'York ... enriched with the treasures of merchants who come from all parts, but above all from the Danish people'. An Anglo-Danish origin has sometimes been canvassed for these merchants (e.g. p.322); if the merchants were importing goods rather than purchasing them from York's suppliers, archaeology may be able to offer evidence on this issue.

In the quarter-century since the publication of this work's predecessor, *Viking Age York and The North* (Hall (ed.) 1978a), there have been advances in many strands of our understanding of Anglo-Scandinavian York. As this volume has clearly demonstrated, a growing body of data, culled from many sources and studied through diverse disciplines, is fuelling more intensive and extensive investigations of York and its development in the two centuries before the Norman conquest. These examinations have shed considerable light on both acute episodes and chronic conditions, and for the first time it has been possible to propose frameworks for several aspects of York's evolution over these crucial centuries in the city's history. Nonetheless, there remain themes in the study of Anglo-Scandinavian York about which there is considerable disagreement, and topics of which we are largely or wholly ignorant. Recognising and confronting these issues, and challenging the ideas and interpretations presented here, should help to formulate the agenda for future research.

Acknowledgements

Richard Hall is grateful to present and former colleagues in all departments of York Archaeological Trust who have facilitated the study of early medieval York in general and this project specifically. Particular thanks to those who have supplied information, stimulated discussion, generated ideas and contributed to the outcome.

The archaeological evidence that underpins many of the chapters in this volume has been retrieved and recorded through the efforts of hundreds of archaeologists — volunteers, students and professionals. Its survival and study has been the work of artefact curators, conservators and researchers, supported by computing experts; the presentation of results relies heavily upon the skills of the illustrator and editor.

York Archaeological Trust thanks in particular the authors from external institutions who have contributed their expertise to this volume. The project has been underwritten by English Heritage, and the Trust is grateful for the encouragement it has received from their staff. The York Museums Trust, in the person of Mrs Elizabeth Hartley, kindly facilitated access to the Cook manuscript. The Dean and Chapter of York, in the person of Mrs Louise Hampson, kindly facilitated access to the Horn of Ulf.

D. Rollason is extremely grateful to Professor Donald Bullough and Professor Simon Keynes for their help in the preparation of the chapter on historical sources.

M. Blackburn is very grateful to Stewart Lyon for commenting on a draft of his chapter on coinage.

A.R. Hall and H.K. Kenward are grateful to English Heritage for support in the preparation of their chapter on plant and animal remains. A.R. Hall thanks Marcus Jecock (English Heritage, Yorkshire Region) for discussion of the Yorkshire alum industry.

Numerous people have been involved in collecting, collating, and presenting the evidence given in T.P. O'Connor's chapter on animal bones. The material from 16–22 Coppergate was recorded by T.P. O'Connor and Sally Scott, with specialist studies of the birds and fish respectively by Enid Allison and Andrew Jones. Bones from 1–9 Micklegate, 9 St Saviourgate and 76–82 Walmgate were recorded by Cluny Johnstone and Deborah Jaques. The collation of data for the synthesis was supervised by Keith Dobney, and the database was constructed by Cluny Johnstone, who also undertook the data sorting and retrieval for this chapter.

A. Mainman and N. Rogers are very grateful to John Kenny and Katherine Bearcock for their help with data collection and entry relating to the distribution of pottery and craft working evidence.

Figures for this fascicule were prepared by Lesley Collett (drawings of artefacts by K. Biggs, P. Chew, S. Howarth and T. Pearson; Fig.117b was drawn by Lesley Collett). Fig.72 was photographed by S.I. Hill and is reproduced by courtesy of York Museums Trust, The Yorkshire Museum (©Yorkshire Museum). Fig.75 was photographed by Robin Hill. Fig.76 is reproduced by courtesy of English Heritage and York Minster Archive (© Crown copyright. NMR). Fig.78 was taken by M. Duffy (© YAT). The coins illustrated in Figs.79–83 are all in the Fitzwilliam Museum, Cambridge, except for the following which are in the British Museum: Fig. 79,1; Fig.81, 2–3; Fig.82, 2–4; Fig.83, 3–4. Fig.84 was photographed by M. Duffy (© YAT). Fig.85 was was photographed by S.I. Hill (© YAT). Fig.86 was photographed by M. Andrews (© YAT). Fig.114 was photographed by S.I. Hill (© YAT). Figs.110 and 117 are reproduced by courtesy of York Minster Archive (© Dean and Chapter of York).

The summary was translated into French by Charlette Sheil-Small and into German by Mrs K. Aberg. This fascicule was edited by Frances Mee, who also prepared the text for publication. The project has been funded and the fascicule published with the assistance of a generous subvention by English Heritage.

Summary

Key aspects of the evidence for Viking-Age or Anglo-Scandinavian York are presented in a series of thematic essays that summarise the present state of knowledge, demonstrate the approaches to the data now being taken, illustrate current scholarly preoccupations and reveal some of the themes that require further attention.

A historiographical introduction provides a context for current perceptions by summarising the main episodes of data gathering and some principal emphases of antiquarian and scholarly enquiry, particularly in the 19th and 20th centuries. Documentary evidence is then examined to determine what it independently indicates about the character and history of the city. The next contribution proffers interpretations of the coinage struck for York's rulers in the period up to the final Anglo-Saxon re-conquest in the mid 10th century — some of the most precisely dated evidence for Anglo-Scandinavian York that exists. The juxtaposition of these two chapters emphasises the range of opinions that can exist about the power structures underlying York's 10th-century urban renaissance.

Essays on long-established fields of study, the inscriptions and the street-names of Viking-Age York, both place their subjects within a national and international framework. These two essays, and that on art produced by or for the 9th- to 11th-century inhabitants, provide insights into the evolution or creation of new cultural norms. More recently established disciplines — the study of animal bones, and of other biological evidence, notably plant and insect remains — are rapidly and continuously being refined. The contributions here not only present exciting new perspectives on a wide range of topics, but also provide an updated commentary on the significance of these data.

A synthesis of recent artefact studies provides both an overview of craft activity in *Jorvik* and a focus upon the range of information revealed in York Archaeological Trust's excavation of four adjacent tenement plots at 16–22 Coppergate. Evidence for the evolving topography of the settlement throughout the two centuries under discussion is presented, and an Afterword notes and briefly comments upon some of the issues raised.

Résumé

Les aspects clés des indices pour York à l'époque des Vikings ou à l'époque anglo-scandinave sont présentés sous la forme d'une série d'essais thématiques qui résument l'état actuel des connaissances, qui décrivent les approches poursuivies à l'heure actuelle à l'égard des données, qui illustrent les préoccupations des chercheurs à l'heure actuelle et qui révèlent certains des thèmes devant être poursuivis.

Une introduction historiographique fournit un contexte pour les perceptions actuelles en résumant les principaux épisodes de collecte des données et certains des points auxquels les recherches antiquaires et universitaires accordent une grande importance, tout particulièrement aux 19ème et 20ème siècles. Ensuite, les indices documentaires sont examinés dans le but de déterminer ce qu'ils indiquent indépendamment concernant le caractère et l'histoire de la ville. L'article suivant avance des interprétations concernant les monnaies frappées pour les dirigeants d'York au cours de la période allant jusqu'à la reconquête anglo-saxonne finale au milieu du 10ème siècle — certains des indices les plus précisément datés existant encore d'York à l'époque anglo-scandinave. La juxtaposition de ces deux chapitres souligne la diversité des opinions qu'il est possible d'avoir concernant la répartition des puissances à la base de la renaissance urbaine d'York au 10ème siècle.

Des essais sur des domaines d'études établis de longue date, les inscriptions et les noms de rues d'York à l'époque des Vikings, situent tous les deux leurs sujets dans un cadre national et international. Ces deux essais, et celui sur l'art produit par ou pour les habitants du 9ème au 11ème siècle, donnent un aperçu de l'évolution ou de la création de nouvelles normes culturelles. Les disciplines établies de plus récente date — l'étude des os d'animaux, et d'autres indices biologiques, notamment les restes de plantes et d'insectes — sont rapidement et continuellement raffinées. Les articles ci-inclus présentent non seulement de nouvelles et passionnantes perspectives sur des sujets très variés mais ils fournissent également un commentaire mis à jour concernant le sens de ces données.

Une synthèse d'études récentes sur les objets fabriqués fournit une vue d'ensemble des activités artisanales à *Jorvík* et, à la fois, met l'accent sur la diversité des informations révélées par les fouilles de quatre terrains construits adjacents réalisées au 16–22 Coppergate par York Archaeological Trust. Les indices de l'évolution de la topographie du peuplement au cours des deux siècles en discussion sont présentés, et une postface note certaines des questions soulevées et fait de brèves remarques à ce propos.

Zusammenfassung

Kernfragen, die sich aus dem Befund in York für die Wikinger- oder anglo-skandinavische Zeit ergeben, werden in einer Reihe von thematisch angelegten Abhandlungen vorgelegt. Diese fassen den gegenwärtigen Stand der Forschung zusammen, zeigen die Wege, die jetzt bei der Auswertung von Data eingeschlagen werden, erläutern die laufenden Schwerpunkte der Forschungsarbeiten und legen einige der Themen vor, die der weiteren Aufmerksamkeit bedürfen.

In einer historiografischen Einführung wird ein Rahmen für den gegenwärtigen Stand der Forschung geschaffen, indem die wichtigsten Episoden in der Zusammenstellung der Data und einige der Schwerpunkte der altertumskundlichen und gelehrten Forschung, besonders im 19. und 20. Jahrhundert behandelt werden. Daran anschließend wird der dokumentarische Befund untersucht, um festzustellen, welche Information er unabhängig für den Charakter und die Geschichte der Stadt liefern kann. Der folgende Beitrag bietet Interpretationen der Münze, die für die Herrscher Yorks in der Zeit bis zur endlichen Rückeroberung durch die Angelsachsen in der Mitte des 10. Jahrhunderts geprägt wurde — dies sind die am exaktesten datierten Befunde, die für die angelsächsische Zeit in York vorhanden sind. Mit der Gegenüberstellung dieser beiden Kapitel wird die Variationsbreite in den Ansichten betont, die im Hinblick auf die Machtgefüge bestehen können, auf denen die städtische Renaissance Yorks im 10. Jahrhundert basierte.

Zwei Abhandlungen über lang etablierte Forschungsfelder — Inschriften und Straßennamen in York in der Wikingerzeit — setzen ihre Sujets in einen nationalen und internationalen Rahmen. Diese beiden Abhandlungen, zusammen mit dem Beitrag, der sich mit Kunstgegenständen befaßt, die für und von Einwohnern im 9. bis 11. Jahrhundert hergestellt wurden, erlauben Einsicht in die Entwicklung oder Begründung neuer kultureller Normen. Jüngere Disziplinen — das Studium der Tierknochen und anderer biologischer Befunde, ins besondere der Pflanzen- und Insektenreste — werden schnell und stetig weiterentwickelt. Die vorliegenden Beiträge bieten nicht nur anregende neue Perspektiven für eine weitgreifende Anzahl von Themen, sondern geben auch einen auf den neuesten Stand gebrachten Kommentar im Bezug auf die Bedeutung dieser Data.

Eine Synthese der jüngsten Untersuchungen an Artefakten liefert einen Überblick der handwerklichen Tätigkeit in Jorvik und einen Einblick in die Vielfalt der Information, die während der Ausgrabungen auf den vier benachbarten Parzellen von 16–22 Coppergate durch den York Archäologischen Trust gewonnen wurde. Befunde für eine sich entwickelnde Siedlungstopographie im Laufe der hier behandelten zwei Jahrhunderte werden vorgelegt, und ein Nachwort erwähnt und nimmt kurz Stellung zu den aufgeworfenen Fragen.

Abbreviations

AML	Ancient Monuments Laboratory
BMC	Keary 1887; Grueber and Keary 1893
CTCE	Blunt, Stewart and Lyon 1989
EAU	Environmental Archaeology Unit, York
EPNS	Publication of the English Place-Name Society
MEC	Grierson and Blackburn 1986
SCBI	Sylloge of Coins of the British Isles
YAT	York Archaeological Trust
YPSAR	*Yorkshire Philosophical Society Annual Report*

Bibliography

Abrams, L., 2001. 'The conversion of the Danelaw' in Graham-Campbell et al. (eds) 2001

Addyman, P.V., 1975. 'Excavations in York 1972–1973. First Interim Report', *Antiq. J.* **54**, 200–31

Addyman, P.V. and Black, V.E., 1984. *Archaeological Papers from York Presented to M.W. Barley* (York)

Addyman, P.V. and Priestley, J., 1977. 'Baile Hill, York', *Yorkshire Archaeol. J.* **134**, 115–156

Alexander, J.J.G., 1978. *Insular Manuscripts 6th to the 9th Century* (London)

Alldritt, D., Carrott, J.B., Hall, A.R., Kenward, H.K. and Richardson, J.E., 1990. 'Environmental evidence from Adams Hydraulics I (YAT/Yorkshire Museum site code 1990.13)', prepared for YAT

Allison, E., Hall, A.R. and Kenward, H.K., 1999a. 'Living conditions and resource exploitation at the Early Christian rath at Deer Park Farms, Co. Antrim, N. Ireland: evidence from plants and invertebrates. Part 1: Text', *Reports from the EAU* **99/8**

Allison, E., Hall, A. and Kenward, H., 1999b. 'Living conditions and resource exploitation at the Early Christian rath at Deer Park Farms, Co. Antrim, N. Ireland: evidence from plants and invertebrates. Part 2: Tables', *Reports from the EAU* **99/10**

Amorosi, T., 1991. 'Icelandic archaeofauna — a preliminary review', *Acta ArchaeolAogica* **61**, 272–84

Amorosi, T., Buckland, P.C., Olafsson, G., Sadler, J.P. and Skidmore, P., 1992. 'Site status and the palaeoecological record: a discussion of the results from Bessastaðir, Iceland' in C.D. Morris and D.J. Rackham (eds), *Norse and Later Settlement and Subsistence in the North Atlantic* (Glasgow)

Anderson, A.O., 1922. *Early Sources of Scottish History, AD 500 to 1286*, 2 vols (Edinburgh), repr. Stamford 1990 with corrections and supplement by M.O. Anderson

Andrews, G., 1984. 'Archaeology in York: an assessment. A survey prepared for the Ancient Monuments Inspectorate of the Department of the Environment' in Addyman and Black (eds) 1984, 173–208

Andrews, P., 1997. *Excavations at Hamwic Volume 2: excavations at Six Dials*, Counc. Brit. Archaeol. Res. Rep. **109**

Anon., 1998a. '9 St Saviourgate, York', *Forum 1998. Annual Newsletter of Counc. for Brit. Archaeol. Yorkshire*, 15–17

Anon., 1998b. (unpublished) *Layerthorpe Bridge York I and II,* MAP Archaeological Consultancy Ltd

Anon., n.d. (unpublished) *Excavations at 9 St Saviourgate, York,* MAP Archaeological Consultancy Ltd

Archibald, M.M., 1980. 'Coins and currency' in J. Graham-Campbell (ed.), *Viking Artefacts* (London), 102–22

—— 1984. 'Anglo-Saxon coinage, Alfred to the Conquest' in J. Backhouse, D.H. Turner and L. Webster (ed.), *The Golden Age of Anglo-Saxon Art 966–1066* (London), 170–91

—— 1986. 'Anglo-Saxon and Norman Lead Objects with Official Coin Types' in A. Vince (ed.), *Aspects of Saxo-Norman London: 2*, London and Middlesex Archaeol. Soc. Special Paper **12** (1991), 326–47

—— 1988. 'A Viking copy of an Alfred London-Monogram penny from Doncaster', *Yorkshire Numis.* **1**, 9–11

—— 1990. 'Pecking and bending: the evidence of British finds' in K. Jonsson and B. Malmer (ed.), *Sigtuna Papers. Proceedings of the Sigtuna Symposium on Viking Coinage* (Stockholm), 11–24

—— 1991. 'Anglo-Saxon and Norman lead objects with official coin types' in A.G. Vince (ed.), *Aspects of Anglo-Saxon and Norman London 2: Finds and Environmental Evidence*, London and Middlesex Archaeol. Soc. Special Paper **12** (London), 326–46

Archibald, M.M., Lang, J.R.S. and Milne, G., 1995. 'Four early medieval coin dies from the London waterfront', *Numis. Chronicle* **155**, 163–200

Armitage, P.L., 1977. *The mammalian remains from the Tudor site of Baynards Castle, London: a biometrical and historical analysis*, PhD thesis, University of London

Arnold, T. (ed.), 1882–5. *Symeonis monachi Opera omnia*, 2 vols (London)

Atkin, M. and Evans, D.H., 2002. *Excavations in Norwich 1971–1978 Part III*, E. Anglian Archaeol. **100**

Auden, G.A., 1907. 'York', *Saga Book of the Viking Club* **5**/1, 55–59

—— 1908. 'York', *Saga Book of the Viking Club* **5**/2, 247–50

—— 1910 'Abstract of a Paper on antiquities Dating from the Danish Occupation of York', *Saga Book of the Viking Club* **6**/2, 169–79

AY. Addyman, P.V. (ed.). *The Archaeology of York* (London)

1 *Sources for York History before 1100*

Rollason, D. with Gore, D. and Fellows-Jensen, G., 1998. *Sources for York History before 1100*

3 *The Legionary Fortress*

4 Hall, R.A., 1997. *Excavations in the* Praetentura: *9 Blake Street*

7 *Anglian York (AD 410–876)*

1 Kemp, R.L., 1996. *Anglian Settlement at 46–54 Fishergate*

2 Tweddle, D., with Moulden, J. and Logan, E., 1999. *Anglian York: A Survey of the Evidence*

8 *Anglo-Scandinavian York (AD 876–1066)*

1 Tweddle, D. and Moulden, J., 1986. *Anglo-Scandinavian Settlement South-west of the Ouse*

2 Wenham, L.P., Hall, R.A., Briden, C.M. and Stocker, D.A., 1987. *St Mary Bishophill Junior and St Mary Castlegate*

3 Addyman, P.V. and Hall, R.A., 1991. *Urban Structures and Defences. Excavations from Lloyds Bank, Pavement, and Other Sites*

5 Hall, R.A., in prep. *Defining York's Townscape: Viking-Age Urbanisation in Coppergate*

10 *The Medieval Walled City north east of the Ouse*

1 Magilton, J.R., 1980. *The Church of St Helen-on-the-Walls, Aldwark*

2 Hall, R.A., MacGregor, H. and Stockwell, M., 1988. *Medieval Tenements in Aldwark, and Other Sites*

3 Richards, J.D., 1993. *The Bedern Foundry*

5 Richards, J.D., 2001. *The Vicars Choral of York Minster: The College at Bedern*

6 Hall, R.A. and Hunter-Mann, K., 2002. *Medieval Urbanism in Coppergate: Refining a Townscape*

11 *The Medieval Defences and Suburbs*

2 Kemp, R.L. with Graves, C.P., 1996. *The Church and Gilbertine Priory of St Andrew, Fishergate*

12 *The Medieval Cemeteries*

2 Stroud, G. and Kemp, R.L., 1993. *Cemeteries of the Church and Priory of St Andrew, Fishergate*

3 Lilley, J.M., 1994. *The Jewish Burial Ground at Jewbury*

14 *The Past Environment of York*

2 Kenward, H.K. and Williams, D., 1979. *Biological Evidence from the Roman Warehouses in Coney Street*

3 Hall, A.R., Kenward, H.K. and Williams, D., 1980. *Environmental Evidence from Roman Deposits in Skeldergate*

4 Hall, A.R., Kenward, H.K., Williams, D. and Greig, J.R.A., 1983. *Environment and Living Conditions at two Anglo-Scandinavian sites*

5 Kenward, H.K., Hall, A.R. and Jones, A.K.G., 1986. *Environmental Evidence from a Roman Well and Anglian Pits in the Legionary Fortress*

6 Hall, A.R. and Kenward, H.K., 1990. *Environmental Evidence from the Colonia: General Accident and Rougier Street*

7 Kenward, H.K. and Hall, A.R., 1995. *Biological Evidence from 16–22 Coppergate*

15 *The Animal Bones*

1 O'Connor, T.P., 1984. *Selected Groups of Animal Bones from Skeldergate and Walmgate*

2 O'Connor, T.P., 1988. *Bones from the General Accident site, Tanner Row*

3 O'Connor, T.P., 1989. *Bones from Anglo-Scandinavian Levels at 16–22 Coppergate*

4 O'Connor, T.P., 1991. *Bones from 46–54 Fishergate*

5 Bond, J.M. and O'Connor, T.P., 1999. *Bones from Medieval Deposits at 16–22 Coppergate and Other Sites in York*

16 *The Pottery*

1 Holdsworth, J.P., 1978. *Selected Pottery Groups AD 650–1780*

5 Mainman, A.J., 1990. *Anglo-Scandinavian Pottery from 16–22 Coppergate*

17 *The Small Finds*

3 MacGregor, A., 1982. *Anglo-Scandinavian Finds from Lloyds Bank, Pavement, and Other Sites*

4 Tweddle, D., 1986. *Finds from Parliament Street and Other Sites in the City Centre*

5 Walton, P., 1989. *Textiles, Cordage and Raw Fibre from 16–22 Coppergate*

6 Ottaway, P., 1992. *Anglo-Scandinavian Ironwork from 16–22 Coppergate*

7 Bayley, J., 1992. *Anglo-Scandinavian Non-Ferrous Metalworking from 16–22Coppergate*

8 Tweddle, D., 1992. *The Anglian Helmet from Coppergate*

9 Rogers, N.S.H., 1993. *Anglian and Other Finds from 46–54 Fishergate*

11 Walton Rogers, P., 1997. *Textile Production at 16–22 Coppergate*

12 MacGregor, A., Mainman, A.J. and Rogers, N.S.H., 1999. *Craft, Industry and Everyday Life: Bone, Antler, Ivory and Horn from Anglo-Scandinavian and Medieval York*

13 Morris, C.A., 2000. *Craft, Industry and Everyday Life: Wood and Woodworking in Anglo-Scandinavian and Medieval York*

14 Mainman, A.J. and Rogers, N.S.H., 2000. *Craft, Industry and Everyday Life: Finds from Anglo-Scandinavian York*

16 Mould, Q., Carlisle, I. and Cameron, E., 2003. *Craft, Industry and Everyday Life: Leather and Leatherworking in Anglo-Scandinavian and Medieval York*

18 *The Coins*

1 Pirie, E.J.E., Archibald, M.M. and Hall, R.A., 1986. *Post-Roman Coins from York Excavations 1971–1981*

19 *Principles and Methods*

2 O'Connor, T.P., 2003. *The Analysis of Urban Archaeological Bone Assemblages: A Handbook for Archaeologists*

Ayers, B. 1987. *English Heritage Book of Norwich* (London)

Baines, H., 1840. *Flora of Yorkshire* (London)

Baker, N. and Holt, R., 1996. 'The City of Worcester in the Tenth Century' in N. Brooks and C. Cubitt (eds), *St Oswald of Worcester: Life and Influence* (Leicester), 129–46

Balachowsky, A., 1949. 'Coléoptères scolytides', *Faune de France* **50** (Paris)

Barclay, C., 1997. 'Coin finds reported to the Yorkshire Museum, 1992–96', *Yorkshire Numis.* **3**, 159–73

Barker, N. (ed.), 1986. *The York Gospels: A Facsimile*, with introductory essays by Jonathan Alexander, Patrick McGurk, Simon Keynes and Bernard Barr (London)

Barlow, F., 1979. *The English Church 1066–1154* (London)

Barlow, F., Biddle, M., Von Feilitzen, O. et al., 1976. *Winchester in the Early Middle Ages: An Edition and Discussion of the Winton Domesday*, Winchester Studies **1** (Oxford)

Barnes, M.P., 1993. 'Towards an edition of the Scandinavian runic inscriptions of the British Isles: some thoughts', in *Twenty-eight Papers Presented to Hans-Bekker Nielsen* (*NOWELE* **21–2**), 21–36

Barnes, M.P. et al., 1997. *The Runic Inscriptions of Viking Age Dublin* (Dublin)

Barrow, J., 1994. 'English Cathedral Communities and Reform in the Late Tenth and Eleventh Centuries' in D. Rollason, M. Harvey and M. Prestwich (eds.), *Anglo-Norman Durham 1093–1193* (Woodbridge), 25–39

Bates, D. (ed.), 1998. *Regesta Regum Anglo-Normannorum: The Acta of William I 1066–1087* (Oxford)

Belshaw, R., 1989. 'A note on the recovery of *Thoracochaeta zosterae* (Haliday) (Diptera: Sphaeroceridae) from archaeological deposits', *Circaea* **6**, 39–41

Benecke, N., 1988. *Archaologische Untersuchungen an Tierknochen aus der fruhmittelalterlichen Siedlung von Menzlin. Schwerin*, Museum fur Ur- und Fruhgeschichte

Benson, G., 1902. 'Notes on excavations at 25, 26, and 27, High Ousegate, York', *YPSAR for 1902*, 64–7

—— 1906. 'Notes on an Excavation at the corner of Castlegate and Coppergate', *YPSAR for 1906*, 72–6

Beresford, M.W., 1967. *New Towns of the Middle Ages* (London)

Biddle, M., 1972. 'Excavations at Winchester, 1970: Ninth Interim Report', *Antiq. J.* **52**, 93–131

—— 1975. '*Felix Urbs Wintonia*: Winchester in the Age of Monastic Reform' in D. Parsons (ed.), *Tenth-Century Studies* (London and Chichester), 123–40

—— (ed.), 1976. *Winchester in the Early Middle Ages*, Winchester Studies **1** (Oxford)

Biddle, M. and Keene, D.J., 1976. 'The early place-names of Winchester' in M. Biddle (ed.) 1976, 231–9

Binns, J.W., Norton, E.C. and Palliser, D.M., 1990. 'The Latin inscription on the Coppergate helmet', *Antiquity* **64**, 134–9

Blackburn, M., 1989a. 'The Ashton hoard and the currency of the Southern Danelaw in the late ninth century', *Brit. Numis. J.* **59**, 13–38

—— 1989b. 'A variety of Cnut's *Short Cross* coinage depicting a banner', in U. Ehrensvärd et al. (eds), *Festskrift till Lars O. Lagerqvist* (Stockholm), 39–43

—— 1990. 'The earliest Anglo-Viking coinage of the Southern Danelaw (late 9th century)', in I.A. Carradice (ed.), *Proc. 10th International Congress of Numismatics* (London), 341–8

—— 1996. 'Mints, burhs and the Grately code, cap. 14.2', *The Defence of Wessex* in D. Hill and A.R. Rumble (eds), *The Burghal Hidage and Anglo-Saxon Fortifications* (Manchester), 160–75

—— 1998. 'The London mint in the reign of Alfred' in M.A.S. Blackburn and D.N. Dumville (ed.), *Kings, Currency and Alliances* (Woodbridge), 105–23

—— 2001a. 'Expansion and control: aspects of Anglo-Scandinavian minting south of the Humber', in Graham-Campbell et al. (eds) 2001, 125–42

—— 2001b. 'A Viking hoard from Thurcaston, Leics.: preliminary report', *Numis. Chronicle* **161**

—— 2003. '"Productive" sites and the pattern of coin loss in England, 600–1100' in T. Pestell and K. Olmschneider (eds), *Markets in Early Medieval Europe* (Macclesfield), 20–36

Blackburn, M. and Bonser, M.J., 1990. 'A Viking-Age silver ingot from near Easingwold, Yorks.', *Medieval Archaeol.* **34**, 149–50

Blackburn, M. and Davies, J., forthcoming. 'An iron coin die' in H. Wallis (ed.), *Excavations at Mill Lane, Thetford, 1995*, E. Anglian Archaeol.

Blackburn, M. and Mann, J., 1995. 'A late Anglo-Saxon coin die from Flaxengate, Lincoln', *Numis. Chronicle* **155**, 201–8

Blackburn, M. and Pagan, H., 1986. 'A revised check-list of coin hoards from the British Isles, c.500–1100', in M.A.S. Blackburn (ed.), *Anglo-Saxon Monetary History* (Leicester), 291–313

—— 2002. 'The St Edmund coinage in the light of a parcel from a hoard of St Edmund pennies', *Brit. Numis. J.* **72**

Blair, J., 1988. 'Introduction: from minster to parish church', in J. Blair (ed.), *Minsters and Parish Churches: the Local Church in Transition 950–1200* (Oxford), 1–19

—— 1995. 'Debate: Ecclesiastical Organization and Pastoral Care in Anglo-Saxon England', *Early Medieval Europe* **4**, 193–212

—— 1996. 'Palaces or Minsters? Northampton and Cheddar Reconsidered', *Anglo-Saxon England* **25**, 97–121

Blair, P.H., 1963. 'Some Observations on the Historia Regum Attributed to Symeon of Durham' in N.K. Chadwick (ed.), *Celt and Saxon: Studies in the Early British Border* (Cambridge University Press), 63–118, reprinted in his *Anglo-Saxon Northumbria*, ed. M. Lapidge and P.H. Blair (London) 1984, no.III

Blunt, C.E., 1974. 'The coinage of Athelstan, 924–939. A survey', *Brit. Numis. J.* **42**, 35–158

—— 1985. 'Northumbrian coins in the name of Alwaldus', *Brit. Numis. J.* **55**, 192–4

Blunt, C.E. and Stewart, B.H.I.H., 1983. 'The Coinage of Regnald I of York and the Bossall Hoard', *Numis. Chronicle* **143,** 146–63

Blunt, C.E., Stewart, B.H.I.H. and Lyon, C.S.S., 1989. *Coinage in Tenth-Century England from Edward the Elder to Edgar's Reform* (Oxford)

Boessneck, J., von den Driesch, A. and Stenberger, L., 1979. *Eketorp, Befestigung und Siedlung auf Oland, Schweden, Die fauna* (Stockholm)

Bond, J.M., 1998. 'Beyond the fringe? Recognising change and adaptation in Pictish and Norse Orkney' in C.M. Mills and G. Coles, *Life on the Edge. Human settlement and marginality,* Oxbow Monogr. **100**, 81–90

Bourdillon, J., 1988. 'Countryside and town: the animal resources of Saxon Southampton' in D. Hooke (ed.), *Anglo-Saxon Settlements* (Oxford), 177–95

—— 1994. 'The animal provisioning of Saxon Southampton' in Rackham (ed.) 1994, 120–5

Bourdillon, J. and Coy, J.P., 1980. 'The animal bones' in P. Holdsworth, *Excavations at Melbourne Street, Southampton 1971–76,* Counc. Brit. Archaeol. Res. Rep. 33 (London), 79–121

Brentano, R.J., 1953. 'Whithorn and York', *Scottish Hist. Review* **32**, 144–6

Briden, C., 1997. 'York as a tidal port', *Yorkshire Archaeol. J.* **69**, 165–71

Brooke, C.N.L. and Keir, G., 1975. *London 800–1216: The Shaping of a City* (London)

Brooke, G.C., 1950. *English Coins from the Seventh Century to the Present Day* 3rd edn. (London)

Brooks, N., 1977. 'The Ecclesiastical Topography of Early Medieval Canterbury' in M.W. Barley (ed.), *European Towns: Their Archaeology and Early History* (Leicester)

—— 1984. 'The Early History of the Church of Canterbury: Christ Church from 597 to 1066' in N. Brooks (ed.), *Studies in the Early History of Britain* (Leicester)

Brooks, N. and Cubitt, C. (eds.), 1996. *St Oswald of Worcester: Life and Influence* (London)

Brothwell, D.R. and Pollard, A.M. (eds), 2001. *Handbook of Archaeological Sciences* (Chichester)

Buchanan, R.H., 1957. 'Thatch and thatching in North-East Ireland', *Gwerin* **1**, 123–42

Buck, F.D., 1954. 'Coleoptera (Lagriidae ... Meloidae)', *Handbooks for the Identification of British Insects* **5**(9) (London)

Buckland, P.C., 1995. 'St George's School, Margaret Street, Walmgate, York. The insect remains. Appendix 5' in P. Foster (ed. J. Symonds), 'An archaeological evaluation at St George's School, Margaret Street, Walmgate, York', *ARCUS Report* **208**

Buckland, P.C., Greig, J.R.A. and Kenward, H.K., 1974. 'York: an early medieval site', *Antiquity* **48**, 25–33

Buckland, P.C., McGovern, T.H., Sadler, J.P. and Skidmore, P., 1994. 'Twig layers, floors and middens. Recent palaeoecological research in the Western Settlement, Greenland' in B. Ambrosiani and H. Clarke (eds.), 'The twelfth Viking Congress: Developments around the Baltic and North Sea in the Viking Age', *Birka Studies* **3** (Stockholm)

Bullough, D.A., 1983. 'Alcuin and the Kingdom of Heaven: Liturgy, Theology, and the Carolingian Age' in U.-R. Blumenthal (ed.), *Carolingian Essays: Andrew W. Mellon Lectures in Early Christian Studies* (Washington, DC), 1–69, repr. D.A. Bullough, *Carolingian Renewal: Sources and Heritage* (Manchester) 1991, 161–240

Bund, K., 1979. *Thronsturz und Herrscherabsetzung im Fruhmittelalter,* Bonner Historische Forschung **44** (Bonn)

Burton, J.E., 1999. *The Monastic Order in Yorkshire, 1069–1215,* Cambridge Studies in Medieval Life and Thought **4th series, 40** (Cambridge)

Cambridge, E. and Morris, R., 1989. 'Beverley Minster before the Early Thirteenth Century', *Medieval Art and Architecture in the East Riding of Yorkshire* (London), 9–32

Cambridge, E. and Rollason, D., 1995. 'The Pastoral Organization of the Anglo-Saxon Church: A Review of the "Minster Hypothesis"', *Early Medieval Europe* **4**, 87–104

Cameron, K., 1959. *The Place-Names of Derbyshire Parts 1–3,* EPNS **27–9** (Cambridge)

—— 1985. *The Place-Names of Lincolnshire Part 1,* EPNS **58** (Nottingham)

Campbell, A. (ed.), 1962. *The Chronicle of Æthelweard* (London)

Campbell, J., 1975. 'Norwich' in M.D. Lobel and W.H. Johns (eds.), *Historic Towns Atlas: Volume 2: Bristol, Cambridge, Coventry, Norwich* (London), 1–25

Cardon, D. and du Chatenet, G., 1990. *Guide des teintures naturelles* (Lausanne)

Carrott, J.B. and Kenward, H.K., 2001. 'Species associations among insect remains from urban archaeological deposits and their significance in reconstructing the past human environment', *J. Archaeol. Sci.* **28**, 887–905

Carrott, J.B., Hall, A.R. and Kenward, H.K., 1991. 'Assessment of biological remains from excavations at Carmelite Street, York (YAT/Yorkshire Museum site code 1991.9)' unpublished report prepared for YAT **1991/15**

Carrott, J.B., Dobney, K.M., Hall, A.R. and Kenward, H.K., 1992a. 'An evaluation of biological remains from excavations at 104–112 Walmgate, York (YAT site code 1991.21)', unpublished report prepared for YAT

Carrott, J.B., Dobney, K.M., Hall, A.R., Kenward, H.K. and Milles, A., 1992b. 'An evaluation of environmental evidence from excavations at 38 Piccadilly, York (YAT/Yorkshire Museum site code 1992.4)', unpublished report prepared for YAT

Carrott, J.B., Hall, A.R., Issitt, M., Kenward, H.K. and Lancaster, S., 1993a. 'Assessment of biological remains from Roman to medieval riverside deposits at North Street, York (YAT/Yorkshire Museum code 1993.1)', unpublished report prepared for YAT **1993/14**

Carrott, J.B, Dobney, K., Hall, A.H., Jaques, D., Kenward, H.K., Large, F. and Milles, A., 1993b. 'An evaluation of biological remains from excavations on land to the rear of Gowthorpe, Finkle Street and Micklegate in Selby town centre (site code Selby 1993)', *Reports from the EAU* **1993/8**

Carrott, J.B., Dobney, K., Hall, A.R., Irving, B., Issitt, M., Jaques, D., Kenward, H.K, Large, F. and Milles, A., 1994a. 'Assessment of biological remains from excavations at 148 Lawrence Street, York (site code 1993.11)', *Reports from the EAU* **1994/25**

Carrott, J., Dobney, K., Hall, A.R., Jaques, D., Kenward, H.K., Lancaster, S. and Milles, A., 1994b. 'Assessment of biological remains from excavations at 12–18 Swinegate, 8 Grape Lane, and 14, 18, 20 and 22 Back Swinegate/Little Stonegate, York (YAT/Yorkshire Museum site codes 1989–90.28 and 1990.1)', *Reports from the EAU* **1994/13**

Carrott, J., Dobney, K., Hall, A.R., Issitt, M., Jaques, D., Kenward, H.K., Large, F., Milles, A. and Shaw, T., 1995. 'Assessment of biological remains from excavations at 22 Piccadilly (ABC Cinema), York (YAT/Yorkshire Museum sitecode 1987.21)', *Reports from the EAU* **1995/53**

Carrott, J.B., Hughes, P., Jaques, D., Kenward, H.K., Large, F. and Worthy, D., 1997. 'An evaluation of biological remains from excavations at British Gas, Davygate, York (site code 1997.102)', *Reports from the EAU* **1997/51**

Carrott, J.B., Hall, A.R., Hughes, P., Jaques, D., Johnstone, C., Kenward, H.K. and Worthy, D., 1998a. 'An assessment of biological remains from excavations at St Saviourgate, York (site code 1995.434)', *Reports from the EAU* **1998/14**

Carrott, J.B., Hall, A.R., Hughes, P., Jaques, D., Johnstone, C., Kenward, H.K. and Worthy, D., 1998b. 'An assessment of biological remains from excavations at St Saviourgate, York (site code 1995.434)', EAU archive report

Carrott, J.B., Hall, A.R., Jaques, D., Johnstone, C., Kenward, H.K. and Rowland, S., 2001. 'Plant and animal remains from excavations in Blanket Row, Kingston-upon-Hull (site codes BWH97-00)', *Reports from the EAU* **2001/12**

Coates, R., 1995. 'A breath of fresh air through Finkle Street', *Nomina* **18**, 7–36

Collingwood, W.G., 1908. 'Anglian and Anglo-Danish Sculpture at York', *Yorkshire Archaeol. J.* **20**, 149–213

—— 1915. 'Anglian and Anglo-Danish Sculpture in the West Riding', *Yorkshire Archaeol. J.* **23**, 129–299

—— 1927. *Northumbrian Crosses of the Pre-Norman Age* (London)

Cooper, J., 1968. 'The Dates of the Bishops of Durham in the First Half of the Eleventh Century', *Durham Univ. J.* new series, **29**, 131–7

—— 1970. *The Last Four Anglo-Saxon Archbishops of York*, Borthwick Paper **38** (York)

Coupland, S., 1998. 'From poachers to gamekeepers: Scandinavian warlords and Carolingian kings', *Early Medieval Europe* **7:1**, 85–114

Cox, B., 1998. *The Place-Names of Leicestershire Part 1*, EPNS **75** (Nottingham)

Coxe, H. (ed.), 1841–2. *Rogeri de Wendover, Chronica sive flores historiarium*, English Hist. Soc., 4 vols (London)

Crabtree, P., 1990. 'Zooarchaeology and complex societies' in M.B. Schiffer (ed.), *Archaeological Method and Theory 2* (Arizona), 155–204

—— 1996. 'Production and consumption in an early complex society: animal use in Middle Saxon East Anglia', *World Archaeol.* **28**, 58–75

Cramp, R., 1967. *Anglian and Viking York*, Borthwick Paper **33** (York)

Cubbin, G.P. (ed.), 1996. 'MS D' in D.N. Dumville and S. Keynes (eds), *The Anglo-Saxon Chronicle: A Collaborative Edition* **6** (Cambridge)

Daniels, R.E. and Eddy, A., 1990. *Handbook of European Sphagna* (London)

Darby, H.C., 1987. 'Domesday Book and the Geographer' in Holt (ed.) 1987, 101–19

Darby, H.C. and Maxwell, I.S., 1962. *The Domesday Geography of Northern England* (Cambridge)

Dark, P., 2000. *The Environment of Britain in the First Millennium A.D.* (London)

Darlington, R.R., McGurk, P. and Bray, J. (eds.), 1995. *The Chronicle of John of Worcester, Volume II, The Annals from 450 to 1066*, Oxford Medieval Texts (Oxford)

Davis, S.J.M., 1996. 'Measurements of a group of adult female Shetland sheep skeletons from a single flock: a baseline for zooarchaeologists', *J. Archaeol. Sci.* **23**, 593–612

Deansley, M., 1962. *Sidelights on the Anglo-Saxon Church* (London)

Dickens, A.G., 1961. 'Anglo-Scandinavian Antiquities' in P.M. Tillott (ed.), *The Victoria County History of Yorkshire: The City of York* (London), 332–6

Dobney, K.M. and Jaques, D., 1993. 'Assessment of animal bones from Roman to medieval riverside deposits at North Street, York (YAT/Yorkshire Museum code 1993.1)', archive report prepared for YAT

Dobney, K. and Hall, A.R., 1992. 'An evaluation of biological remains from excavations at 41 Piccadilly, York (YAT/Yorkshire Museum site code 1992.18)', unpublished report prepared for YAT **1992/20**

Dobney, K., Hall, A.R., Kenward, H.K. and O'Connor, T., 1993. 'Assessment of samples for biological analysis and of bone from excavations at the Queen's Hotel site, York (site code 1988–9.17)', unpublished report prepared for YAT **1993/22**

Dobney, K., Kenward, H.K. and Roskams, S., 1997. 'All mixed up but somewhere to go? Confronting residuality in bioarchaeology' in G. De Boe and F. Verhaeghe (eds.), *Method and theory in historical archaeology,* Papers of the 'Medieval Europe Brugge 1997' Conference **10**

Dobney, K., Kenward, H.K., Ottaway, P. and Donel, L., 1998. 'Down, but not out: biological evidence for complex economic organisation in Lincoln in the late fourth century', *Antiquity* **72**, 417–24

Dobney, K., Hall, A.R. and Hill, M., 2000. 'Why did the chicken dig a hole? Some observations on the excavation of dust baths by domestic fowl and their implications for archaeology' in J.P. Huntley and S. Stallibrass (eds.), 'Taphonomy and interpretation', *Symposia of the Association for Environmental Archaeol.* **14** (Oxford)

Dodgson, J. McN., 1981. *The Place-Names of Cheshire Part 5/ 1,* EPNS **48** (Nottingham)

Dolley, R.H.M., 1957–8. 'The post-Brunanburh Viking coinage of York', *Nordisk Numismatisk Årsskrift,* 13–88

—— 1965. *Viking Coins of the Danelaw and of Dublin* (London)

—— 1978. 'The Anglo-Danish and Anglo-Norse coinages of York', in R.A. Hall (ed.) 1978a, 26–31

—— 1982. 'Dateringen af de seneste St. Petersmønter fra York', *Nordisk Numismatisk Unions Medlemsblad,* 82–92

Drake, F., 1736. *Eboracum; or the History and Antiquities of the City of York* (London)

Duffy, E.A.J., 1953. *A monograph of the immature stages of British and imported timber beetles (Cerambycidae)* (London)

Dumas-Dubourg, F., 1971. *Le trésor de Fécamp et le monnayage en France occidentale pendant la seconde moitié du Xe siècle* (Paris)

Dumville, D.N., 1987. 'Textual archaeology and Northumbrian history subsequent to Bede', in Metcalf 1987a, 43–55

—— 1992. 'Ecclesiastical lands and the defence of Wessex' in D.N. Dumville, *Wessex and England from Alfred to Edgar* (Woodbridge), 29–54

Dyson, T., 1978. 'Two Saxon Land Grants for Queenhithe', *Collectanea Londiniensia. Studies Presented to Ralph Merrifield,* London and Middlesex Archaeol. Soc. Special Paper **2**, 200–15

—— 1990. 'King Alfred and the Restoration of London', *London J.* **15**(2), 99–110

Edlin, H.L., 1951. *British Plants and their Uses* (London)

Ekwall, E., 1930. 'How long did the Scandinavian language survive in England?' in *A Grammatical Miscellany Offered to Otto Jespersen* (Copenhagen and London), 17–30

—— 1954. *Street-Names of the City of London* (Oxford)

—— 1959. *Etymological Notes on English Place-Names,* Lund Studies in English **27** (Lund)

Ericson, P.G.P., Iregren, E. and Vretemark, M., 1988. 'Animal exploitation at Birka — a preliminary report', *Forvännen* **83**, 81–8

Esty, W.E., 1986. 'Estimation of the size of a coinage: a survey and comparison of methods', *Numis. Chronicle* **146**, 185–215

Evans, D.T., 1992. (unpublished) *Report on an Archaeological Evaluation at 104–112 Walmgate, York,* YAT site investigations 1991/21

—— 1997. (unpublished) *Former Davygate Centre, Davygate, York. Report on an Archaeological Excavation and Watching Brief,* YAT Field Rep. 1997/28

Evans, E.E., 1974. 'Folk housing in the British Isles in materials other than timber', *Geoscience and Man* **5**, 53–64

Everson, P. and Stocker, D.A., 1999. *Lincolnshire. British Academy Corpus of Anglo-Saxon Sculpture* vol.??

EYC **1**. Farrer, W. (ed.), 1914. *Early Yorkshire Charters* **1** (Edinburgh)

EYC **6**. Clay, C.T. (ed.), 1939. *Early Yorkshire Charters* **6**: *The Paynel Fee* (Wakefield)

Feilitzen, O. von, 1937. *The Pre-Conquest Personal Names of Domesday Book* (Uppsala)

Fell, C.E., 1994. 'Anglo-Saxon England: a three-script community?' in J. Knirk (ed.), *Proceedings of the Third International Symposium on Runes and Runic Inscriptions* (Uppsala), 119–37

Fell, V., 2000. 'The nit combs' in K. Buxton and C. Howard-Davis, *Bremetanacum. Excavations at Roman Ribchester 1980, 1989–1990,* Lancaster Imprints Series **9** (Lancaster)

Fellows-Jensen, G., 1968. *Scandinavian Personal names in Lincolnshire and Yorkshire* (Copenhagen)

—— 1972. *Scandinavian Settlement Names in Yorkshire* (Copenhagen)

—— 1979a. 'The name Coppergate', *Interim. Bulletin of the York Archaeolological Trust* **6**/2, 7–8

—— 1979b. 'Hungate. Some observations on a common street-name', *Ortnamnssällskapets i Uppsala Årsskrift,* 44–51

—— 1985. *Scandinavian Settlement Names in the North-West* (Copenhagen)

—— 1997. 'Byer i vikingetidens England. Dansk indflydelse på deres udformning' in V. Dalberg and B. Jørgensen (eds), *Byens navne. Stednavne i urbaniserede områder.* NORNA-rapporter **64**, 77–89

—— 1998. *The Vikings and their Victims: the Verdict of the Names,* The Dorothea Coke Memorial Lecture in Northern Studies delivered at University College London 21 February 1994. Corrected reprint 1998

Fenton, A., 1978. *The Northern Isles: Orkney and Shetland* (Edinburgh) (reprinted 1997, East Linton)

Finlayson, R., 1993. (unpublished) *North Street 1993.1 archive report,* YAT site investigations

Foster, P., 1995. (unpublished) *An Archaeological Evaluation at St George's School, Margaret Street, Walmgate, York,* ARCUS **208**

Foulds, T. (ed.), 1994. *The Thurgarton Cartulary* (Stamford)

Garrison, M., Nelson, J. and Tweddle, D., 2001. *Alcuin and Charlemagne. The Golden Age of York* (York)

GDB Greater Domesday Book. Section references are to M.L. Faull and M. Stinson (eds.), the Phillimore edition of *Domesday Book* **30**, *Yorkshire* 1–2, 1986

Gearey, B. and Lillie, M., 1999. 'Aspects of Holocene vegetational change in the Vale of York: palaeoenvironmental investigations at Askham Bog' in R. van de Noort and S. Ellis (eds), *Wetland Heritage of the Vale of York* (Hull)

Geddes, A., 1955. *The Isle of Lewis and Harris: a study in British community* (Edinburgh)

Godman, P., 1982. *Alcuin, The Bishops, Kings and Saints of York* (Oxford)

Godwin, H. and Bachem, K., 1959. 'Appendix III. Plant remains' in Richardson 1959

Gover, J.E.B., Mawer, A. and Stenton, F.M., 1940. *The Place-Names of Nottinghamshire,* EPNS **17** (Cambridge)

Graham-Campbell, J. (ed.), 1992. *Viking Treasure from the North-West. The Cuerdale Hoard in its Context,* National Museums and Galleries on Merseyside Occas. Papers, Liverpool Museum **5** (Liverpool)

—— 1993. 'A "vital" Yorkshire Viking hoard revisited' in M. Carver (ed.), *In Search of Cult: Archaeological Investigations in Honour of Philip Rhatz* (Woodbridge), 79–84

Graham-Campbell, J. et al. (eds), 2001. *Vikings and the Danelaw. Select Papers from the Proceedings of the Thirteenth Viking Congress, Nottingham and York, 21–30 August 1997* (Oxford)

Grant, A., 1976. 'The animal bones' in B.W. Cunliffe (ed.), *Excavations at Portchester Castle II, Saxon: The Outer Bailey and its Defences*, Soc. Antiq. Res. Rep. **33** (London), 262–87

Green, B.H., 1968. 'Factors affecting the spatial and temporal distribution of *Sphagnum imbricatum* Hornsch. ex Russ. in the British Isles', *J. Ecology* **56**, 47–58

Greig, J.R.A., 1983. 'Pollen samples from York', *AML Report Old Series* **3921**

Grierson, P. and Blackburn, M., 1986. *Medieval European Coinage with a Catalogue of the Coins in the Fitzwilliam Museum, Cambridge, 1, The Early Middle Ages (5th–10th Centuries)* (Cambridge)

Grove, L.R.A., 1940. 'A Viking bone trial piece from York Castle', *Antiq. J.* **20**, 285–7

Grueber, H.A. and Keary, C.F., 1893. *A Catalogue of English Coins in the British Museum. Anglo-Saxon Series* **2** (London)

Hadley, D.M., 1996. '"And they proceeded to plough and to support themselves": the Scandinavian settlement of England' in C. Harper-Bill (ed.), *Anglo-Norman Studies XIX: Proceedings of the Battle Conference 1996* (Woodbridge), 69–96

Haigh, D.H., 1876. 'The coins of the Danish kings of Northumberland', *Archaeologia Æliana* 2nd ser. **7**, 21–77

Hajnalova, M. and Charles, M., 1995. 'St George's School, Margaret Street, Walmgate, York. The charred plant remains. Appendix 7' in P. Foster (ed. J. Symonds), 'An archaeological evaluation at St George's School, Margaret Street, Walmgate, York', *ARCUS Report* **208**

Hall, A.R., 1988. 'Medieval and post-medieval plant remains from a site adjacent to 1–5 Aldwark, York (YAT site code 1976–7.15)', unpublished report deposited at EAU and AML **1988/5**

—— 1998. 'Adding colour to the story: recognising remains of dyeplants in medieval archaeological deposits' in M. Dewilde, A. Ervynck and A. Wielmans (eds), 'Ypres and the medieval cloth industry in Flanders', *Archeologie in Vlaanderen Monografie* **2** (Zellik)

—— 2003. 'Recognition and characterisation of turves in archaeological occupation deposits by means of macrofossil plant remains', *Centre for Archaeol. Rep.* **1916/2003**

Hall, A.R. and Kenward, H.K. (eds), 1994. *Urban-rural connexions: perspectives from environmental archaeology,* Oxbow Monogr. **47** (Oxford)

—— 1998. 'Disentangling dung: pathways to stable manure', *Environmental Archaeology* **1**, 123–6

—— 2000a. 'Plant and invertebrate remains from Anglo-Scandinavian deposits at 4–7 Parliament Street (Littlewoods Store), York (site code 1999.946)', *Reports from the EAU* **2000/22**

—— 2000b. 'Plant and invertebrate remains from Anglo-Scandinavian deposits at 2 Clifford Street, York (site code 1999.256)', *Reports from the EAU* **2000/17**

—— 2003. 'Can we identify biological indicator groups for craft, industry and other activities?' in P.E.J. Wiltshire and P.L. Murphy (eds), *The Environmental Archaeology of Industry*

Hall, A.R., Jones, A.K.G. and Kenward, H.K., 1983b. 'Cereal bran and human faecal remains from archaeological deposits — some preliminary observations' in B. Proudfoot (ed.), 'Site, environment and economy', Symposia of the Association for Environmental Archaeology 3, *Brit. Archaeol. Rep. Internat. Series* **173**

Hall, A.R., Carrott, J., Kenward, H.K. and Nicholson, R.A., 1991. 'Biological analyses of samples from 20–4 Swinegate (YAT/Yorkshire Museum sitecode 1990.25)', prepared for YAT **1991/23**

Hall, A.R., Kenward, H.K. and Carrott, J.B., 1998. 'Plant and invertebrate remains from excavations associated with renovations at All Saints Church, Pavement, York (site code 1995.47, *Reports from the EAU* **1998/30**

Hall, A.R., Carrott, J., Jaques, D., Johnstone, C., Kenward, H.K., Large, F. and Usai, R., 2000a. 'Studies on biological remains and sediments from Periods 1 and 2 at the Magistrates' Courts site, Kingston-upon-Hull (site codes HMC 94 and MCH99). Part 1: Text', *Reports from the EAU* **2000/25**

Hall, A.R, Kenward, H.K., Jaques, D. and Carrott, J., 2000b. 'Environment and industry at Layerthorpe Bridge, York (site code YORYM 1996.345)', *Reports from the EAU* **2000/64**

Hall, A.R., Rowland, S., Kenward, H.K., Jaques, D. and Carrott, J.B., 2000c. 'Evaluation of biological remains from excavations on land to the rear of 7–15 Spurriergate, York (site code: 2000.584), *Reports from the EAU* **2000/80**

Hall, R.A., 1976. *The Viking Kingdom of York*

—— (ed.), 1978a. *Viking Age York and the North,* Counc. Brit. Arachaeol. Res. Rep. **27** (London)

—— 1978b. 'The topography of Viking York' in R.A. Hall (ed.) 1978a, 31–6

—— 1984 *The Viking Dig* (London)

—— 1988. 'The Making of Domesday York' in D. Hooke (ed.), *Anglo-Saxon Settlements* (Oxford), 233–47

—— 1989. 'The Five Boroughs and the Danelaw: a review of present knowledge', *Anglo-Saxon England* **18**, 149–206

—— 1991. 'Sources for Pre-Conquest York' in I. Wood and N. Lund (eds), *People and Places in Northern Europe 500–1600* (Woodbridge), 83–94

—— 1994. *Viking Age York* (London)

—— 1996. *English Heritage Book of York* (London)

—— 2000. 'Anglo-Scandinavian Attitudes: archaeological ambiguities in late ninth- to mid-eleventh-century York' in D.M. Hadley and J.D. Richards (eds), *Cultures in Contact: Scandinavian Settlement in England in the Ninth and Tenth Centuries*

—— 2003. 'Yorkshire 700–1066' in T.G. Manby, S. Moorhouse and P.J. Ottaway (eds), *The Archaeology of Yorkshire. An assessment at the beginning of the 21st century,* Yorkshire Archaeol. Soc. Occas. Paper **3**, 171–80

Hamilton, N.E.S.A. (ed.), 1870. *Willelmi Malmesbiriensis monachi, De gestis pontificum Anglorum libri quinque,* Rolls Series **52** (London)

Hamlin, A. and Lynn, C., 1988. *Pieces of the Past* (Belfast)

Hammond, P.M., 1971. 'Notes on British Staphylinidae 2. On the British species of *Platystethus* Mannerheim, with one species new to Britain', *Entomologist's Monthly Magazine* **107**, 93–111

Harcourt, R.A., 1974. 'The dog in prehistoric and early historic Britain', *J. Archaeol. Sci.* **1**, 151–75

Hatting, T., 1991. 'The archaeozoology' in M. Bencard, C.B. Jorgensen and H.B. Madsen (eds), *Ribe Excavations 1970–76* (Esbjerg), 43–57

Hayhurst, H., 1940. *Insect Pests in Stored Products* (London)

Hickin, N.E., 1975. *The Insect Factor in Wood Decay*, 3rd edn revised by R. Edwards (London)

Higham, N.J., 1992. 'Northumbria, Mercia and the Irish Sea Norse, 893–926', in Graham-Campbell 1992, 21–30

Hill, D., 1981. *An Atlas of Anglo-Saxon England* (Oxford)

Hill, M.J., 1993. (unpublished) *Insect death assemblages and the interpretation of woodland history: evidence from the Vale of York*, DPhil thesis, University of York

—— 1994. 'Insect assemblages as evidence for past woodland around York' in Hall and Kenward (eds) 1994, 45–54

Hill, R.M.T. and Brooke, C.N.L., 1977. 'From 627 until the Early Thirteenth Century' in G.E. Aylmer and R. Cant (eds.), *A History of York Minster* (Oxford), 1–41

Hines, J., 1991. 'Scandinavian English: a creole in context' in P. Sture Ureland and G. Broderick (eds), *Language Contact in the British Isles* (Tübingen), 403–27

Hinton, D.A., 1974. *Catalogue of Anglo-Saxon Ornamental Metalwork in the Department of Antiquities, Ashmolean Museum* (Oxford)

Hinton, H.E., 1945. *A monograph of the beetles associated with stored products* **1** (London)

Hoffmann, A., 1958. 'Coléoptères curculionides', *Faune de France* **62** (Paris)

Holman, K., 1996. *Scandinavian Runic Inscriptions in the British Isles: their Historical Context* (Trondheim)

Holt, J.C. (ed.), 1987. *Domesday Studies: Papers read to the Novocentenary Conference of the Royal Historical Society and the Institute of British Geographers, Winchester, 1986* (Woodbridge)

Hudson-Edwards, K., Macklin, M.G., Finlayson, R. and Passmore, D.G., 1999. 'Medieval lead pollution in the river Ouse at York, England', *J. Archaeol. Sci.* **26**, 809–19

Hutchinson, G.E. and Wollack, A., 1943. 'Biological accumulators of aluminium', *Trans. Connecticut Academy of Arts and Sciences* **35**, 73–127

Ijzereef, G.F. and Laarman, F., 1986. 'The animal remains from Deventer (8th–19th centuries AD)', *Berichten ROB* (Amersfoort), 405–33

Insley, J., 1979. 'Regional variation in Scandinavian personal nomenclature in England', *Nomina* **3**, 52–60

—— forthcoming. 'The Scandinavian Personal Names in the Later Part of the Durham *Liber Vitae*' in D. Rollason, A.J. Piper, M. Harvey and L. Rollason (eds), *The Durham Liber Vitae and Its Context* (Woodbridge)

Jensen, S., 1991. *The Vikings of Ribe* (Ribe)

—— 1993. 'Early Towns' in S. Hvass and B. Storgaard (eds), *Digging into the Past. 25 Years of Archaeology in Denmark* (Copenhagen), 202–5

Johnstone, C., Carrott, J., Hall, A.R., Kenward, H.K and Worthy, D., 2000. 'Assessment of biological remains from 41–49 Walmgate, York (site code 1999.941)', *Reports from the EAU* **2000/04**

Jones, A.K.G., 1984. 'Some effects of the mammalian digestive system on fish bones' in N. Desse-Berset (ed.), '2nd Fish Osteoarchaeology Meeting, C.N.R.S. Centre de Recherches Archeologiques', *Notes et Monographies Techniques* **16**

—— 1986. 'Fish bone survival in the digestive systems of the pig, dog and man: some experiments' in D.C. Brinkhuizen and A.T. Clason (eds.), 'Fish and archaeology', *Brit. Archaeol. Rep. Internat. Series* **294**

Jones, G., 1984. 'Animal bones' in A. Rogerson and C. Dallas, *Excavations in Thetford 1948–59 and 1973–80,* E. Anglian Archaeol. Rep. **22**, 187–92

Jones, G.R.J., 1967. 'To the Building of Kirkstall Abbey' in M.W. Beresford and G.R.J. Jones (eds), *Leeds and its Region* (Leeds), 119–30

Jørgensen, B., 1999. *Storbyens Stednavne* (Copenhagen)

Kapelle, W.E., 1979. *The Norman Conquest of the North: The Region and its Transformation 1000–1135* (London)

Keary, C.F., 1887. *A Catalogue of English Coins in the British Museum. Anglo-Saxon Series* **1** (London)

Keats-Rohan, K.S.B. and Thornton, D.E. (eds.), 1997. *Domesday Names: An Index of Latin Personal and Place Names in Domesday Book* (Woodbridge)

Kenward, H.K., 1985. 'Outdoors — indoors? The outdoor component of archaeological insect assemblages' in N.R.J. Fieller, D.D. Gilbertson and N. Ralph (eds.), *Palaeobiological investigations. Research design, methods and data analysis*, Symposia Assoc. Environ. Archaeol. 5B, Brit. Archaeol. Rep. Internat. Series **226**, 97–104

—— 1986. 'Insect remains from post-Roman deposits at 1–5 Aldwark, York', unpublished report deposited at YAT, EAU and AML **1986/16**

—— 1997. 'Synanthropic decomposer insects and the size, remoteness and longevity of archaeological occupation sites: applying concepts from biogeography to past "islands" of human occupation', in A.C. Ashworth, P.C Buckland and J.T. Sadler (eds.), 'Studies in Quaternary Entomology: an inordinate fondness for insects', *Quaternary Proceedings* **5**

—— 1999a. 'Pubic lice (*Pthirus pubis* (L.)) were present in Roman and Medieval Britain', *Antiquity* **73**, 911–15

—— 1999b. 'Insect remains as indicators of zonation of land use and activity in Roman Carlisle, England', *Reports from the EAU* **1999/43**

—— 2002. 'Assessment of insect and other invertebrate remains from Viborg Søndersø, Denmark', *Reports from the EAU* **2002/14**

—— in press. 'Honeybees (*Apis mellifera* Linnaeus) from archaeological deposits in Britain', Papers from AEA meeting in celebration of Susan Limbrey

—— in press. 'Did insects from archaeological occupation sites track late Holocene climate in Northern England?', *Environmental Archaeology*

Kenward, H.K. and Allison, E.P., 1994a. 'Rural origins of the urban insect fauna' in Hall and Kenward (eds.) 1994

—— 1994b. 'A preliminary view of the insect assemblages from the early Christian rath site at Deer Park Farms, Northern Ireland' in D.J. Rackham (ed.), *Environment and Economy in Anglo-Saxon England,* Counc. Brit. Archaeol. Res. Rep. **89**

Kenward, H.K and Hall, A.R., 1997. 'Enhancing bioarchaeological interpretation using indicator groups: stable manure as a paradigm', *J. Archaeol. Sci.* **24**, 663–73

—— 2000a. 'Plant and invertebrate remains from Anglo-Scandinavian deposits at the Queen's Hotel site, 1–9 Micklegate, York (site code 1988–9.17)', *Reports from the EAU* **2000/14**

—— 2000b. 'Plant and invertebrate remains from Anglo-Scandinavian deposits at 118–26 Walmgate, York (site code 1978–9.8)', *Reports from the EAU* **2000/20**

—— 2000c. 'Decay of delicate organic remains in shallow urban deposits: are we at a watershed?', *Antiquity* **74**, 519–25

Kenward, H.K. and Hall, A.R. forthcoming. 'Actively decaying or just poorly preserved? Can we tell when plant and invertebrate remains in urban archaeological deposits decayed?', *Proc. PARIS II Conference*

Kenward, H.K. and Large, F., 1998a. 'Recording the preservational condition of archaeological insect fossils', *Environmental Archaeol.* **2**, 49–60

—— 1998b. 'Insects in urban waste pits in Viking York: another kind of seasonality', *Environmental Archaeol.* **3**, 35–53

Kenward, H.K. and Robertson, A., 1988. 'A supplement to the survey of insect remains from post-Roman deposits at 1–5 Aldwark, York', unpublished archive deposited at EAU, YAT and AML **1988/20**

Kenward, H.K., Williams, D., Spencer, P.J., Greig, J.R.A., Rackham, D.J. and Brinklow, D., 1978. 'The Environment of Anglo-Scandinavian York' in R.A. Hall (ed.) 1978a

Kenward, H.K., Dainton, M., Kemenes, I.K. and Carrott, J.B., 1992. 'Evidence from insect remains and parasite eggs from the Old Grapes Lane B site, The Lanes, Carlisle', *AML Report* **1992/76**

Kenward, H.K, Hall, A.R. and Carrott, J., 2000. 'Environment, activity and living conditions at Deer Park Farms: evidence from plant and invertebrate remains', *Reports from the EAU* **2000/57**

Ker, N.R. (ed.), 1964. *Medieval Libraries of Great Britain: A List of Surviving Books*, Royal Hist. Soc. Guides and Handbooks **3** (London)

—— 1969–92. *Medieval Manuscripts in British Libraries* (Oxford)

Keynes, S.D., 1999. 'Rulers of the English, c.450–1066' in Lapidge et al. (eds) 1999, 500–16

Keynes, S. and Lapidge, M. (eds.), 1983. *Alfred the Great: Asser's Life of King Alfred and Other Contemporary Sources* (Harmondsworth)

Knowles, D., 1963. *The Monastic Order in England: A History of its Development from the Times of St Dunstan to the Fourth Lateran Council, 940–1216* 2nd edn (Cambridge)

Krzywinski, K. and Kaland, P.E., 1984. 'Bergen — from farm to town' in A.E. Herteig (ed.), *Bryggen Papers Suppl. Ser.* **1** (Bergen)

Lang, J.T., 1978a. 'Anglo-Scandinavian Sculpture in Yorkshire' in R.A. Hall (ed.) 1978a, 11–20

—— (ed.) 1978b. *Anglo-Saxon and Viking Age Sculpture in England and its Context,* Brit. Archaeol. Rep. Brit. Ser. **49** (Oxford)

—— 1988. *Viking-Age decorated Wood. A Study of its Ornament and Style. Medieval Dublin Excavations 1962–81.* Series B, volume **1** (Dublin)

—— 1995. 'Pre-conquest Sculpture' in Phillips and Heywood 1995, 433–67

Lang, J.T. with Higgitt, J. et al., 1991. *York and Eastern Yorkshire, British Academy Corpus of Anglo-Saxon Stone Sculpture in England* **3** (Oxford)

Lapidge, M., 1983. 'Ealdred of York and the MS Cotton Vitellius E.xii', *Yorkshire Archaeol. J.* **55**, 11–25, repr. M. Lapidge, *Anglo-Latin Literature 900–1066* (London and Ronceverte) 1993, 453–67

Lapidge, M., Blair, J., Keynes, S. and Scragg, D. (eds.), 1998. *The Blackwell Encyclopaedia of Anglo-Saxon England* (Oxford)

Latouche, R. (ed.), 1930–7. *Richer, Histoire de France (888–995)*, Les Classiques de l'Histoire de France au Moyen Age, 2 vols (Paris)

Lee, F., 1995. 'Palaeopathological report on selected skeletons from the pre-Norman cemetery' in Phillips and Heywood 1995, 559–73

Letts, J. B. 1999. *Smoke Blackened Thatch* (London)

Levillain, L. (ed.), 1964. *Loup de Ferrières: Correspondance*, Les Classiques de l'Histoire de France au Moyen Age, 2 vols (Paris)

Liebermann, F., 1903–16. *Die Gesetze der Angelsachsen*, 3 vols (Halle)

Liestøl, A., 1971. 'The literate Vikings' in P. Foote and D. Strömbäck (eds), *Proc. Sixth Viking Congress* (Uppsala), 69–77

Lindgren, E., Tälleklint, L. and Polfeldt, T., 2000. 'Impact of climatic change on the northern latitude limit and population density of the disease-transmitting European tick *Ixodes ricinus*, *Environmental Health Perspectives* **108**, 119–23

Lindkvist, H., 1926. 'A study on early medieval York', *Anglia* **50**, 345–94

Lobel, M.D., 1935. *The Borough of Bury St Edmund's: A Study in the Government and Development of a Monastic Town* (Oxford)

Long, A.J., Innes, J.B., Kirby, J.R., Lloyd, J.M., Rutherford, M.M., Shennan, I. and Tooley, M.J., 1998. 'Holocene sea-level change and coastal evolution in the Humber estuary, eastern England: an assessment of rapid coastal change', *The Holocene* **8**, 229–47

Lucas, A.T., 1989. *Cattle in Ancient Ireland* (Kilkenny)

Luff, R.M. and Moreno Garcia, M., 1995. 'Killing cats in the medieval period. An unusual episode in the history of Cambridge, England', *Archaeofauna* **4**, 93–114

Lyon, C.S.S., 1970. 'Historical problems of Anglo-Saxon coinage (4). The Viking Age', *Brit. Numis. J.* **39**, 193–204

—— 1987. 'Ninth-century Northumbrian chronology', in Metcalf 1987a, 27–41

Lyon, C.S.S., and Stewart, B.H.I.H., 1961. 'The Northumbrian Viking coinage in the Cuerdale hoard', in R.H.M. Dolley (ed.), *Anglo-Saxon Coins* (London), 96–121

Mac Airt, S. and Mac Niocaill, G. (eds.), 1983. *The Annals of Ulster (to A.D. 1131): Part I: Text and Translation* (Dublin)

McComish, J. and Macnab, N., forthcoming. *Excavations at 28–9 High Ousegate, York*, AY Web Series

McCormick, F., 1982. *Man and Domesticated Animals in Early Christian Ireland*, MA thesis, University College, Cork

—— 1988. 'The domesticated cat in Early Christian and medieval Ireland' in G. Mac Niocaill and P.F. Wallace (eds), *Keimelia. Studies in Medieval History and Archaeology in Honour of Tom Delaney* (Galway), 218–28

—— 1997. 'The animal bones' in M.F. Hurley, O.M.B. Scully and S.W.J. McCutcheon, *Late Viking Age and Medieval Waterford. Excavations 1986–1992* (Waterford), 819–53

MacGregor, A., 1978. 'Industry and Commerce in Anglo-Scandinavian York' in R.A. Hall (ed.) 1978a, 37–57

—— 1985. *Bone, Antler, Ivory and Horn: The Technology of Skeletal Materials since the Roman Period* (London)

McKenna, W.J.B., Hutchinson, A.R. and Jones, A.K.G., 1988. 'Parasitological investigations on samples of sediment from excavations at 7–9 Aldwark, York', *AML Report New Series* **37/88**

McMillan, R.A., 1984. 'The Yorkshire teazle-growing trade', *Yorkshire Archaeol. J.* **56**, 155–65

Macnab, N. et al., 2003. *Anglo-Scandinavian, Medieval and Post-Medieval Urban Occupation at 41–49 Walmgate, York*, AY Web Series **1**

Mainman, A.J., 1993. 'Imported Wares in York AD 700–1000' in D. Piton (ed.), *Travaux du Groupe de Recherches et d'Études sur la Céramique dans le Nord-Pas-de-Calais*, Actes du Colloque d'Outreas (10–12 Avril 1992), La Céramique du Vème au Xème Siècle dan l'Europe du Nord-Ouest

Malcolm, G. and Bowsher, D. with Cowie, R., 2003. *Middle Saxon London. Excavations at the Royal Opera House 1989–99*, MoLAS Monogr. **15** (London)

Maltby, J.M., 1979. *The Animal Bones from Exeter 1971–1975*, Exeter Archaeol. Rep. **2** (Sheffield)

Markell, E.K. and Voge, M., 1976. *Medical Parasitology* 4th edn (Philadelphia)

Martin, G.H., 1985. 'Domesday Book and the Boroughs' in P.H. Sawyer (ed.), *Domesday Book: A Reassessment* (London), 143–63

Mawer, A., 1923. 'The Redemption of the Five Boroughs', *English Hist. Review* **38**, 551–7

Metcalf, D.M., 1958. 'Eighteenth-century finds of medieval coins from the records of the Society of Antiquaries', *Numis. Chronicle* 6th ser. **18**, 73–96

—— 1981. 'Continuity and change in English monetary history c.973–1086. Part 2', *Brit. Numis. J.* **51**, 52–90

—— (ed.), 1987a. *Coinage in Ninth-Century Northumbria*, Brit. Archaeol. Rep. Brit. Ser. **180** (Oxford)

—— 1987b. 'Hexham and Cuerdale: two notes on metrology' in Metcalf 1987a, 383–96

—— 1987c. 'The Taxation of Moneyers under Edward the Confessor and in 1086' in Holt (ed.) 1987, 279–93

—— 1993–4. *Thrymsas and Sceattas in the Ashmolean Museum Oxford*, 3 vols (London)

—— 1998. *An Atlas of Anglo-Saxon and Norman Coin Finds 973–1086* (London)

Metcalf, D.M., and Northover, J. P., 1987. 'The Northumbrian royal coinage in the time of Æthelred II and Osberht' in Metcalf 1987a, 187–233

Morris, C.J., 1992. *Marriage and Murder in Eleventh-Century Northumbria: A Study of 'De Obsessione Dunelmi'*, Borthwick Paper **82** (York)

Morris, R.K., 1986. 'Alcuin, York, and the *Alma Sophia*' in L.A.S. Butler and R.K. Morris (eds.), *The Anglo-Saxon Church: Papers on History, Architecture, and Archaeology in Honour of Dr H.M. Taylor*, Res. Rep. **60** (London), 80–9

Mossop, H.R., 1970. *The Lincoln Mint c.890–1279* (Newcastle upon Tyne)

Muller, H-.H., 1980. 'Tieropfer in der slawischen Tempelburg von Arkona auf Rugen', *Rapports du IIIe Congres International d'Archeologie Slave, vol 2* (Bratislava), 307–11

—— 1984. 'Die Tierreste aus der Mecklenburg, Kr. Wismar' in P. Donat, *Die Mecklenburg — eine Hauptburg der Odobriten*, Schriften zur ur- und fruhgeschichte **37** (Berlin), 161–82

—— 1985. 'Die Tierknochenfunde aus der slawischen Burganlage von Cositz, Kr. Kothen', *Zeitschrift fur Archaologie* **19**, 83–114

Mynors, R.A.B., Thomson, R.M. and Winterbottom, M. (eds.), 1998. *William of Malmesbury, rGesta Regum Anglorum*, The History of the English Kings **1**, Oxford Medieval Texts (Oxford)

Naylor, J., 2002. 'York and Its Region in the Eighth and Ninth Centuries AD: An Archaeological Study', *Oxford J. Archaeol.* **20** (1), 79–105

Nicholson, R.A., 1993. 'An investigation into the effects on fish bone of passage through the human gut: some experiments and comparisons with archaeological material', *Circaea* **10**, 38–51

Noddle, B.A., 1978. 'The animal bones from Buckquoy, Orkney', *Proc. Soc. Antiq. Scotland* **108**, 201–14

—— 1979. 'A brief history of domestic animals in the Orkney Islands, Scotland, from the 4th millennium BC to the 18th century' in M. Kubasiewicz (ed.), *Archaeozoology* (Sczeczin) 286–303

—— 1980. 'Identification and interpretation of the mammal bones' in P. Wade-Martins, *Excavations in North Elmham Park*, E. Anglian Archaeol. Rep. **9**, 377–409

—— 1997. 'Animal bone' in S. Buteux, *Settlements at Skail, Deerness, Orkney*, Brit. Archaeol. Rep. Brit. Series **267**, 234–75

Nordal, S. (ed.), 1933. *Egils Saga Skalla-Grímssonar* **1**, Islenzk Fornrit **2** (Reykjavík)

North, J.J., 1994. *English Hammered Coinage, Volume I, Early Anglo-Saxon to Henry III, c.600–1272* 3rd edn (London)

Norton, C., 1998. 'The Anglo-Saxon Cathedral at York and the Topography of the Anglian City', *J. Brit. Archaeol. Assoc.* **151**, 1–42

O'Connor, T.P., 1982. *Animal Bones from Flaxengate, Lincoln, c.870–1500, Archaeology of Lincoln* **18**/1 (London)

—— 1984. 'Hand-collected molluscs from 16–22 Coppergate, York', *AML Report* **1984/20**

—— 1985. 'Terrestrial and freshwater mollusca from Anglo-Scandinavian levels at 16–22 Coppergate, York (1976-81.7)', *AML Report* **4735**

—— 1986a. 'Osseous artefacts from 16–22 Coppergate, York', *AML Report* **1986/20**

—— 1986b. 'Animal Bones from Blake Street', *AML Report*

—— 1990. 'An assessment of residues of bulk-sieved samples from the Queen's Hotel site (1988-9.17)', prepared for YAT **1990/21**

—— 1992. 'Pets and pests in Roman and medieval Britain', *Mammal Review* **22**, 107–13

—— 1994. '8th–11th century environment and economy in York' in Rackham (ed.) 1994, 136–47

—— 2000a. *The Archaeology of Animal Bones* (Stroud)

—— 2000b. 'Human refuse as a major ecological factor in medieval urban vertebrate communities' in G. Bailey, R. Charles and N. Winder (eds), *Human Ecodynamics* (Oxford), 15–20

—— 2001a. 'Collecting, sieving, and zooarchaeological quantification' in H. Buitenhuis and W. Prummel (eds), *Animals and Man in the Past* (Groningen), 7–16

—— 2001b. 'On the interpretation of animal bone assemblages from *wics*' in D. Hill and R. Cowie (eds), *Wics: The Early Medieval Trading Centres of Northern Europe* (Sheffield), 54–60

Okasha, E., 1971. *Hand-List of Anglo-Saxon Non-runic Inscriptions* (Cambridge)

—— 1983. 'A supplement to *Hand-List of Anglo-Saxon Non-runic Inscriptions*', *Anglo-Saxon England* **11**, 83–118

—— 1992. 'A second supplement to *Hand-List of Anglo-Saxon Non-runic Inscriptions*', Anglo-Saxon England **21**, 37–85

Osborne, P.J., 1971. 'An insect fauna from the Roman site at Alcester, Warwickshire', *Britannia* **2**, 156–65

Ottaway, P., 1993. *Roman York* (London)

Owen, D.M., 1984. *The Making of King's Lynn. A Documentary Survey* (London)

Owen, O.A., 1979. (unpublished) *A Catalogue and Re-evaluation of the Urnes Style in England*, MA thesis, University of Durham

Pagan, H.E., 1969. 'Northumbrian Numismatic Chronology in the Ninth Century', *Brit. Numis. J.* **38**, 1–15

Page, R.I., 1969. 'Runes and non-runes' in D.A. Pearsall and R.A. Waldron (eds), *Medieval Literature and Civilization* (London), 28–54; reprinted in Page 1995, 161–78, and cited from the reprint

—— 1971. 'How long did the Scandinavian language survive in England? The epigraphical evidence' in P. Clemoes and K. Hughes (eds), *England Before the Conquest* (Cambridge), 165–81; reprinted in Page 1995, 181–95, and cited from the reprint

—— 1995. *Runes and Runic Inscriptions: Collected Essays on Anglo-Saxon and Viking Runes* (Woodbridge)

——1999. *An Introduction to English Runes*, 2nd edition (Woodbridge)

Palliser, D.M., 1978. 'The Medieval Street-Names of York', *York Historian* **2**, 2–16

—— 1984. 'York's West Bank: Medieval Suburb or Urban Nucleus?', in Addyman and Black (eds) 1984, 101–8

—— 1990. *Domesday York*, Borthwick Papers **78** (York)

—— 1996. 'The "Minster Hypothesis": A Case Study', *Early Medieval Europe* **5**, 207–14

Palm, R., 1992. *Runor och regionalitet: studier av variation i de nordiska minnesinskrifterna* (Uppsala)

Pálsson, H. and Edwards, P. (eds.), 1976. *Egil's Saga*, Penguin Classics (London)

Pattison, I.R., 1973. 'The Nunburnholme cross and Anglo-Danish Sculpture in York', *Archaeologia* **104**, 209–34

Pegler, D.N., Laessøe, T. and Spooner, B.M., 1995. *British Puffballs, Earthstars and Stinkhorns* (Kew)

Perrott, M., 1979. (unpublished) *The Place-Names of the Kesteven Division of Lincolnshire*, MPhil thesis, University of Nottingham

Pheifer, J.D., 1974. *Old English Glosses in the Épinal-Erfurt Glossary* (Oxford)

Phillips, D., 1985. *Excavations at York Minster, Volume 2: The Cathedral of Archbishop Thomas of Bayeux* (HMSO, London)

Phillips, D. and Heywood, B., 1995. *Excavations at York Minster, Volume 1: From Roman Fortress to Norman Cathedral* (HMSO, London)

Pickles, R., 2002. 'Historical overview' in I. Miller (ed.), *Steeped in History: the Alum Industry of North-East Yorkshire*

Piper, P.J. and O'Connor, T.P., 2001. 'Urban small vertebrate taphonomy: a case study from Anglo-Scandinavian York', *Internat. J. Osteoarch.* **11**, 336–44

Pirie, E.J.E., 1975. *Coins in Yorkshire Collections*, Sylloge of Coins of the British Isles **21** (London)

Platnauer, H.M., 1906 'York during the Anglo-Danish Period' in G.A. Auden (ed.), *A Handbook to York and District*, 28–41

Plummer, C. (ed.), 1892–9. *Two of the Saxon Chronicles Parallel with Supplementary Extracts from the Others*, 2 vols (Oxford), a revised text on the basis of an edition by J. Earle, revised in 1952 with a bibliographical note by D. Whitelock

Prummel, W., 1991. 'Haus und Wildtiere' in M. Muller-Wille, *Starigrad/Oldenburg*, Karl Wachholtz Verlag, 299–306

Rackham, D.J. (ed.), 1994. *Environment and Economy in Anglo-Saxon England*, Counc. Brit. Archaeol. Res. Rep. **89**

Rackham, O., 1976. *Trees and Woodland in the British Landscape* (London)

—— 1989. *The Last Forest: the Story of Hatfield Forest* (London)

Radley, J.D., 1971. 'Economic aspects of Anglo-Danish York', *Medieval Archaeol.* **15**, 37–57

—— 1972. 'Excavations in the defences of the city of York: an early medieval stone tower and the successive earthen ramparts', *Yorkshire Archaeol. J.* **44**, 38–64

Raine, A., 1955. *Mediaeval York: A Topographical Survey based on Original Sources* (London)

Raine, J. (ed.), 1879–94. *The Historians of the Church of York and its Archbishops*, Rolls Series **71**, 3 vols (London)

c

Ramm, H.G., 1971. 'The end of Roman York' in R.M. Butler, *Soldier and Civilian in Roman Yorkshire* (Leicester)

—— 1972. 'The growth and development of the City to the Norman Conquest' in A. Stacpoole (ed.), *The Noble City of York*, 225–54

—— 1976. 'The Church of St Mary, Bishophill Senior, York: Excavations 1964', *Yorkshire Archaeol. J.* **48**, 35–68

Rashleigh, J., 1869. 'Remarks on the coins of the Anglo-Saxon and Danish kings of Northumberland', *Numis. Chronicle* 2nd ser. **9**, 54–105

RCHMY Royal Commission on Historical Monuments, England. *An Inventory of the Historical Monuments in the City of York*. **1**: *Eburacum, Roman York* (1962); **2**: *The Defences* (1972); **3**: *South-West of the Ouse* (1972); **4**: *Outside the City walls East of the Ouse* (1975); **5**: *The Central Area* (1981) (HMSO, London)

Rees Jones, S. R., 1987. (unpublished) *Property, Tenure and Rents: Some Aspects of the Topography and Economy of Medieval York*, 2 vols, PhD thesis, University of York

Reeves, W., 1864. *The Culdees of the British Isles* (Dublin), repr. Lampeter 1994

Reichstein, H. and Tiessen, M. 1974. *Berichte uber die Ausgrabungen in Haithabu, Bericht 7*, Karl Wachholz, Neumunster

Reynolds, S., 1977. *An Introduction to the History of English Medieval Towns* (Oxford)

—— 1987. 'Towns in Domesday Book' in Holt (ed.) 1987

Rheingans, A. and Reichstein, H. 1991. 'Untersuchungen an Tierknochen aus mittelalterlichen bis neuzeitlichen Siedlungsablagerungen in Lübeck (Ausgrabung Alfstrasse 36/38)', *Lübecker Schriften zur Archaeologie und Kulturgeschichte* **21**, 143–81

Richards, J.D., 2000. *Viking Age England*

Richardson, K.M., 1959. 'Excavations in Hungate, York', *Archaeol. J.* **116**, 51–114

Robertson, A.J. (ed.), 1956. *Anglo-Saxon Charters* 2nd edn. (Cambridge)

Robinson, J.A., 1919. *St Oswald and the Church of Worcester*, Brit. Acad. Supp. Paper **5** (London)

Robinson, M.A., 1981. 'Waterlogged plant and invertebrate evidence' in N. Palmer, 'A Beaker burial and medieval tenements in the Hamel, Oxford', *Oxoniensia* **45**, 124–225

Roesdahl, E., Graham-Campbell, J., Connor, P. and Pearson, K. (eds), 1981. *The Vikings in England* (London)

Rollason, D., 2000. *Symeon of Durham, On the Origins and Progress of this the Church of Durham*, Oxford Medieval Texts (Oxford)

—— forthcoming. *Northumbria: The Making and Destruction of an Early Medieval Kingdom* (Cambridge)

Rowell, T.A., 1986. 'Sedge (*Cladium mariscus*) in Cambridgeshire: its use and productivity since the seventeenth century', *Agricultural Hist. Review* **34**, 140–8

Sandred, K.I. and Lindström, B., 1989. *The Place-Names of Norfolk Part 1*, EPNS **61** (Nottingham)

Sawyer, P.H., 1968. *Anglo-Saxon Charters: An Annotated List and Bibliography*, Royal Hist. Soc. Guides and Handbooks 8 (London)

—— 1995. 'The Last Scandinavian Kings of York', *Northern History* **31**, 39–44

—— 1998. *Anglo-Saxon Lincolnshire* (Lincoln)

Schelvis, J., 1991. 'Lice and nits (*Pediculus humanus*) from medieval combs excavated in the Netherlands', *Proceedings of the section Experimental and Applied Entomology of the Netherlands Entomological Society Amsterdam* **2**, 14–15

—— 1992. 'Luizen, neten en vlooien' in P.H. Broekhuizen, H. Gangelen, K. Helfrich, G.L.G.A. Kortekaas, R.H. Alma and H.T. Waterbolk (eds.), *Van boerenerf tot bibliotheek. Historisch, bouwhistorisch en archeologisch onderzoek van het voormalig Wolters-Noordhoff-Complex te Groningen* (Groningen)

—— 1998. 'Remains of sheep ectoparasites as indicators of wool processing in the past' in M. Dewilde, A. Ervynck and A. Wielemans (eds), 'Ypres and the medieval cloth industry in Flanders', *Archeologie in Vlaanderen Monografie* **2** (Asse-Zellik, Belgium)

Scott, S. 1984. *Report on a survey of Anglo-Scandinavian bones from 16–22 Coppergate*, Archive report, Environmental Archaeology Unit, University of York

Seaby, P., 1992. 'Some recent coin finds from Yorkshire and North Humberside', *Yorks. Numis.* **2**, 105–27

Seaward, M.R.D., 1976. 'Observations on the bracken component of the pre-Hadrianic deposits at Vindolanda, Northumberland' in F.H. Perring and B.G. Gardiner (eds.), 'The biology of bracken', *Botanical J. Linnaean Society* **73** (1–3)

Seaward, M.R.D. and Williams, D., 1976. 'An interpretation of mosses found in recent archaeological excavations', *J. Archaeol. Sci.* **3**, 173–7

Seim, K.F., 1988. 'A review of the runic material' in *The Bryggen Papers: Supp. Series* **2** (Norwegian University Press), 10–23

Singer, C., 1948. *The Earliest Chemical Industry* (London)

Skaare, K., 1976. *Coins and Coinage in Viking-Age Norway* (Oslo)

Smart, V., 1973. 'Cnut's York Moneyers' in F. Sandgren (ed.), *Otium et Negotium* (Stockholm), 221–31

—— 1985. 'The moneyers of St Edmund', *Hikuin* **11**, 83–90

—— 1986. 'Scandinavians, Celts, and Germans in Anglo-Saxon England: the Evidence of Moneyers' Names' in M.A.S. Blackburn (ed.), *Anglo-Saxon Monetary History* (Leicester), 171–84

Smith, A.H., 1928. *The Place-Names of the North Riding of Yorkshire*, EPNS **5** (Cambridge)

—— 1937. *The Place-Names of the East Riding of Yorkshire and York*, EPNS **14** (Cambridge)

—— 1956. *English Place-Name Elements Parts 1 and 2*, EPNS **25–6** (Cambridge)

Smith, D.N., 1996. 'Thatch, turves and floor deposits: a survey of Coleoptera in material from abandoned Hebridean blackhouses and the implications for their visibility in the archaeological record', *J. Archaeol. Sci.* **23**, 161–74

Smith, D., Letts, J. and Cox, A., 1999. 'Coleoptera from late medieval smoke-blackened thatch (SBT): their archaeological implications', *Environmental Archaeol.* **4**, 9–17

Smith, J., 1882. *A Dictionary of Popular Names of the Plants which furnish the Natural and Acquired Wants of Man, in all matters of Domestic and General Economy* (London)

Smyth, A.P., 1975–9. *Scandinavian York and Dublin: The History and Archaeology of Two Related Viking Kingdoms*, 2 vols (Dublin)

—— 1977. *Scandinavian Kings in the British Isles 850–880* (Oxford)

—— 1978. 'The Chronology of Northumbrian History in the Ninth and Tenth Centuries' in R.A. Hall (ed.) 1978a, 8–10

Solloway, J., 1910. *The Alien Benedictines of York, being a Complete History of Holy Trinity Priory, York* (Leeds)

Spahn, N. 1986. *Untersuchungen an Skelettresten von Hunden und Katzen aus dem mittelalterlichen Schleswig Ausgrabung Schild 1971–1975*, Ausgrabungen in Schleswig Berichte und Studien **5**, Karl Wachholz Verlag

Spriggs, J.A. and Vere-Stevens, L., n.d. (unpublished) 'Material from the Wattle-Lined Pit (Context 3109)' in Anon. n.d.

Stead, I.M., 1958. 'Excavations at the south corner tower of the Roman fortress at York, 1956', *Yorkshire Archaeol. J.* **39**, 515–37

—— 1968. 'An excavation at King's Square, York, 1957', *Yorkshire Archaeol. J.* **42**, 151–64

Stenton, F.M., 1927. 'York in the Eleventh Century' in A.H. Thompson (ed.), *York Minster Historical Tracts 627–1927* (London) (unpaginated)

—— 1947 *Anglo-Saxon England,* 1st edn

—— 1971. *Anglo-Saxon England,* 3rd edn (Oxford)

Stevenson, W.H. (ed.), 1959. *Asser's Life of King Alfred together with the Annals of Saint Neot's erroneously ascribed to Asser* (Oxford), new impression with article on recent work on Asser's Life of Alfred by D. Whitelock

Stewart, I., 1982a. 'The anonymous Anglo-Viking issue with sword and hammer types and the coinage of Sihtric I', *Brit. Numis. J.* **52**, 108–16

—— 1982b. 'The Nelson collection at Liverpool and some York questions', *Brit. Numis. J.* **52**, 247–51

—— 1987. 'CVNNETTI reconsidered' in Metcalf 1987a, 345–54

Stewart, I. and Lyon, S., 1992. 'Chronology of the St Peter coinage', *Yorkshire Numis.* **2**, 45–73

Stocker, D.A., 2000. 'Monuments and Merchants: Irregularities in the Distribution of Stone Sculpture in Lincolnshire and Yorkshire in the Tenth Century' in D.M. Hadley and J.D. Richards (eds*)*, *Cultures in Contact: Scandinavian Settlement in England in the Ninth and Tenth Centuries*, 179–212

Summerson, H., 1993. *Medieval Carlisle: the City and the Borders from the Late Eleventh to the Mid-Sixteenth Century*, Cumberland and Westmorland Antiq. and Archaeol. Soc., extra series **25**, 2 vols (Kendal)

Swift, S.M., Racey, P.A. and Avery, M.I., 1985. 'Feeding ecology of *Pipistrellus pipistrellus* (Chiroptera: Vespertillionidae) during pregnancy and lactation. II. Diet', *J. Animal Ecology* **54**, 217–25

Tait, J., 1936. *The Medieval English Borough: Studies on its Origins and Constitutional History* (Manchester)

Taylor, E.L., 1955. 'Parasitic helminths in medieval remains', *Veterinary Record* **67**, 216

Teichert, L., 1985. 'Die Tierknochenfunde von Schonfeld und Seese, Kr. Calau', *Veroffentlichungen des Museums fur Ur- und Fruhgeschichtliche Potsdam* **19**, 187–98

Tellenbach, G., 1993. *The Church in Western Europe from the Tenth to the Early Twelfth Century* (Cambridge)

Temple, E., 1976. *Anglo-Saxon Manuscripts 900–1066* (London)

Thomas, C., 2002. *The Archaeology of Medieval London* (Stroud)

Thompson, A.H. (ed.), 1923. *Liber vitae ecclesiae Dunelmensis: A Collotype Facsimile of the Original Manuscript: vol.1: Facsimile and General Introduction*, Surtees Society **136** (Durham)

Tomlinson, P.R., 1989a. 'Plant remains from excavations at 58–9 Skeldergate (Bishophill I), York', *AML Report New Series* **61/89**

—— 1989b. 'Plant remains from 118–26 Walmgate, York', *AML Report New Series* **1989/60**

—— 1989c. 'Plant remains from 36 Aldwark (Police Garage), York', *AML Report New Series* **1989/59**

—— 1989d. 'Plant remains from 7-9 Aldwark, York', *AML Report New Series* **1989/58**

Tooley, M.J., 1990. 'Sea-level and coastline changes during the last 5000 years' in S. McGrail (ed.), *Maritime Celts, Frisians and Saxons*, Counc. Brit. Archaeol. Res. Rep. **71** (London)

Tsuda, K., Kikkawa, Y., Yonekawa, H. and Tanabe, Y., 1997. 'Extensive interbreeding occurred among multiple matriarchical ancestors during the domestication of dogs: evidence from inter- and intraspecies polymorphisms in the D-loop region of mitochondrial DNA between dogs and wolves', *Genes and Genetic Systems* **72**, 229–38

Tweddle, D., 1984. 'A Fragment of Anglian Metalwork from Blake Street' in Addyman and Black (eds) 1984, 58–62

—— 1991. 'Brooches' in P. Armstrong et al., *Excavations at Lurk Lane, Beverley 1979–82, Sheffield Excavation Reports* **1** (Sheffield), 155–6

—— 2001a. 'The Catalogue' in Garrison et al. 2001, 24–32

—— 2001b. 'The Glory that was York', *Brit. Archaeol.* **59**, 14–19

Urry, W., 1967. *Canterbury under the Angevin Kings* (London)

VCH Yorkshire **2**. Page, W. (ed.), 1912. *The Victoria History of the County of Yorkshire* **2** (London)

Venkatrao, S., Krishnamurthy, K., Narasimhan, K.S., Daniel, V.A., Majumder, S.K. and Swaminathan, M., 1960. 'Assessment of insect infestation and acceptability of market samples of food grains, Part 1: Studies on wheat flour', *Food Science* **9**, 8–10

Vince, A. (ed.), 1991. *Aspects of Saxo-Norman London: 2 Finds and Environmental Evidence*, London and Middlesex Archaeol. Soc. Special Paper **12** (London)

—— 2001. 'Lincoln in the Viking Age' in J. Graham-Campbell et al. (eds) 2001

Wallace, P.F., 1992. *The Viking Age Buildings of Dublin,* Medieval Dublin Excavations 1962–81. Series A, vol.1, Parts 1 and 2 (Dublin)

Waterman, D.M., 1959. 'Late Saxon, Viking and Early Medieval Finds from York', *Archaeologia* **97**, 59–105

Webb, S.C., Hedges, R.E.M. and Robinson, M., 1998. 'The seaweed fly *Thoracochaeta zosterae* (Hal.) in inland archaeological contexts: $d^{13}C$ and $d^{15}N$ solves the problem', *J. Archaeol. Sci.* **25**, 1253–7

Wellbeloved, C. (ed.), 1875. *Handbook to the Antiquities in the Grounds and Museum of the Yorkshire Philosophical Society, 6th edn* (York)

Wenham, L.P., 1961. 'Excavations and discoveries adjoining the south-west wall of the Roman legionary fortress in Feasegate, York, 1955–1957', *Yorkshire Archaeol. J.* **40**, 329–50

—— 1962. 'Excavations and discoveries within the legionary fortress in Davygate, York, 1955–8', *Yorkshire Archaeol. J.* **40**, 507–87

—— 1968. 'Discoveries in King's Square, York, 1963', *Yorkshire Archaeol. J.* **42**, 165–8

—— 1972. 'Excavations in Low Petergate, York, 1957–58', *Yorkshire Archaeol. J.* **44**, 65–113

West, B. 1993a. 'Birds and mammals from the Peabody site' in R.L. Whytehead and R. Cowie, 'Excavations at the Peabody site, Chandos Place, and the National Gallery', *Trans. London and Middlesex Archaeol. Soc.* **40**, 150–68

—— 1993b. 'Birds and mammals in R. Cowie and R.L. Whytehead, 'Two Middle Saxon occupation sites: excavations at Jubilee Hall and 21–22 Maiden Lane', *Trans. London and Middlesex Archaeol. Soc.* **39**, 150–4

Whitelock, D., 1959. 'The Dealings of the Kings of England with Northumbria in the Tenth and Eleventh Centuries' in P. Clemoes (ed.), *The Anglo-Saxons: Studies Presented to Bruce Dickins* (Cambridge), 70–88, repr. in Whitelock1981, no.III

—— 1965. 'Wulfstan at York' in J.B. Bessinger and R.P. Creed (eds.), *Franciplegius: Medieval and Linguistics Studies in Honor of Francis Peabody Magoun, Jr* (New York), 214–31, repr. in Whitelock 1981, no.XV

—— 1968. 'Archbishop Wulfstan, Homilist and Statesman' in R.W. Southern (ed.), *Essays in Medieval History* (London), 42–60, repr. in Whitelock 1981, no.XI

—— (ed.), 1976. *Sermo Lupi ad Anglos,* 3rd (rev.) edn (Exeter)

—— (ed.), 1979. *English Historical Documents, I, c.500–1042* (London)

—— 1981. *History, Law and Literature in Tenth–Eleventh Century England* (London)

Whyman, M., 2001. (unpublished) *Late Roman Britain in Transition, AD 300–500: A Ceramic Perspective from East Yorkshire*, DPhil thesis, University of York

Wigh, B., 2001. *Animal husbandry in the Viking Age town of Birka and its hinterland*, Riksantikvieambetet (Stockholm)

Williams, G., 1999. 'Anglo-Saxon and Viking coin weights', *Brit. Numis. J.* **69**, 19–36

Wilson, B. and Mee, F., 1998. *The Medieval Parish Churches of York: The Pictorial Evidence* (York)

Wilson, D.M., 1964. *Anglo-Saxon Ornamental Metalwork 700–1100* (London)

—— 1978. 'The Dating of Viking Art in England' in Lang (ed.) 1978b, 135–43

Wilson, D.M. and Blunt. C.E., 1961. 'The Trewhiddle Hoard', *Archaeologia* **98**, 75–122

Wilson, D.M. and Klindt-Jensen, O., 1966. *Viking Art* (London)

Woolf, A., 1999. 'Erik Bloodaxe Revisited', *Northern History* **34**, 189–93

Yvinec, J.-H. 1997. 'Etude archeozoologique du site de la Place des Hallettes à Compiègne (Oise) du Haut Moyen Age au XIIe siècle', *Revue Archeologique de Picardie* **13**, 171–206

Index

By Sue Vaughan

Illustrations are denoted by page numbers in *italics*. Places are in York unless otherwise stated.

The Archaeology of York

General Editor P.V. Addyman

Reports on the work of the York Archaeological Trust for Excavation and Research are published as separate parts or fascicules making up a series of twenty volumes entitled **The Archaeology of York**:

For further information on all York Archaeological Trust publications please see
http://www.yorkarchaeology.co.uk/pubs.htm